CRIMINAL LITIGATION

CRIMINAL LITIGATION

John Holtam, LLB (Southampton), LLM (Edinburgh), Solicitor

Published by

College of Law Publishing,
Braboeuf Manor, Portsmouth Road, St Catherines, Guildford, GU3 1HA

British Library Cataloguing-in-Publication Data

A catalogue record for this book is available from the British Library.

ISBN 0 905835 71 9

Typeset by Style Photosetting Ltd, Mayfield, East Sussex

Printed in Great Britain by Antony Rowe Ltd, Chippenham

Preface

This book has been written primarily for use by students on the Legal Practice Course. The content and depth of subject covered are determined by the requirements of the course. The aim of the book is to provide the framework upon which the criminal litigation course is built. Because students are expected to carry out their own research in some aspects of the course and will receive further tuition in others, the book is not intended as a standard textbook on the subject.

Each chapter contains suggestions on further reading. These are intended as examples of primary and secondary sources to which the reader should refer to follow up a subject.

Although I am responsible for this edition of *Criminal Litigation*, I remain indebted to John Clegg (now District Judge Clegg) for his valuable contributions in previous years.

I have endeavoured to state the law as at 31 May 2004. This has enabled me to include some of the changes introduced by the Criminal Justice Act 2003, namely CPS responsibility for charging, conditional cautions, the revised exceptions to bail and the new provisions concerning memory refreshing documents.

JOHN HOLTAM
Guildford

Contents

PREFACE   v

TABLE OF CASES   xi

TABLE OF STATUTES   xv

TABLE OF STATUTORY INSTRUMENTS, CIRCULARS AND GUIDANCE   xix

TABLE OF INTERNATIONAL LEGISLATION   xxiii

TABLE OF ABBREVIATIONS   xxv

Chapter 1	INTRODUCTION TO CRIMINAL PROCEDURE	1
	1.1 The solicitor's role	1
	1.2 Classification of criminal offences	1
	1.3 The courts and court personnel	2
	1.4 The prosecution and the defence	3
	1.5 An overview of criminal procedure	5
	1.6 Substantive criminal law	6
	1.7 Professional ethics	12
	1.8 European Convention on Human Rights	13
	1.9 Further reading	16

Chapter 2	THE SUSPECT IN THE POLICE STATION	17
	2.1 Introduction	17
	2.2 The serious arrestable offence (PACE 1984, s 116 and Sch 5)	17
	2.3 Police powers of detention	18
	2.4 The right to legal advice	21
	2.5 Interviewing the suspect	22
	2.6 Methods of interview	23
	2.7 The right to have a solicitor present at interviews	25
	2.8 Safeguards for the suspect	25
	2.9 Tactical considerations	27
	2.10 Identification	37
	2.11 Evidential considerations	40
	2.12 Samples	41
	2.13 Alternatives to prosecution	41
	2.14 Further reading	43

Chapter 3	COMMENCEMENT OF CRIMINAL PROCEEDINGS	45
	3.1 Preliminary considerations	45
	3.2 Commencing the prosecution	46
	3.3 Financing the defence – Criminal Defence Service	47
	3.4 Adjournments, remands and bail	52
	3.5 Bail and the Human Rights Act 1998	62
	3.6 Further reading	62

Chapter 4	THE PROSECUTION OF AN OFFENCE TRIABLE EITHER WAY	63
	4.1 Introduction	63
	4.2 Advance disclosure of the prosecution case	63
	4.3 The plea before venue procedure	63
	4.4 The mode of trial procedure	64
	4.5 Practical points on mode of trial procedure	65

| | 4.6 | Advising the client | 66 |
| | 4.7 | Further reading | 68 |

Chapter 5		DISCLOSURE	69
	5.1	Introduction	69
	5.2	Duty to provide advance information	69
	5.3	Duty to disclose 'unused material'	70
	5.4	Primary disclosure by the prosecution (CPIA 1996, s 3)	70
	5.5	Defence disclosure (CPIA 1996, ss 5 and 6)	72
	5.6	Secondary disclosure by the prosecution (CPIA 1996, s 7)	73
	5.7	Public interest immunity	74
	5.8	Application to court for disclosure (CPIA 1996, s 8)	74
	5.9	The prosecution's continuing duty of disclosure (CPIA 1996, s 9)	74
	5.10	Consequences of failure to comply with disclosure requirements (CPIA 1996, ss 10 and 11)	74
	5.11	Further reading	75

Chapter 6		COMMITTAL PROCEEDINGS AND SENDING FOR TRIAL	77
	6.1	Introduction	77
	6.2	Types of committal proceedings	77
	6.3	Preliminary points	77
	6.4	Committal without consideration of the evidence (Magistrates' Courts Act 1980, s 6(2))	79
	6.5	Committal with consideration of the evidence (Magistrates' Courts Act 1980, s 6(1))	80
	6.6	Deciding on the type of committal proceedings	81
	6.7	Sending for trial procedure (Crime and Disorder Act 1998, ss 51, 52 and Sch 3)	82
	6.8	Linked summary offences	84
	6.9	Further reading	86

Chapter 7		PREPARATIONS FOR TRIAL ON INDICTMENT	87
	7.1	Introduction	87
	7.2	The indictment	87
	7.3	Cases committed to the Crown Court for trial	87
	7.4	Cases sent to the Crown Court for trial	88
	7.5	Disclosure	92
	7.6	Notices of further evidence	92
	7.7	Preparing for the plea and directions hearing	93
	7.8	Plea and directions hearing	93
	7.9	Pre-trial hearings	94
	7.10	Preparatory hearings	94
	7.11	Briefing counsel	95
	7.12	Trial on indictment	95
	7.13	Further reading	96

Chapter 8		SUMMARY TRIAL	97
	8.1	Introduction	97
	8.2	Disclosure	97
	8.3	Preparing the case for trial	98
	8.4	Procedure on a not guilty plea	100
	8.5	Further reading	103

Chapter 9		CRIMINAL EVIDENCE	105
	9.1	Introduction	105
	9.2	Preliminary points of evidence	107
	9.3	Methods of proof	111
	9.4	Corroboration and identification evidence	116

9.5   Particular rules of admissibility of evidence   119
9.6   Hearsay evidence   123
9.7   The defendant   134
9.8   Further reading   142

Chapter 10   SENTENCING   143
10.1   Introduction   143
10.2   The powers of the court   143
10.3   Sentencing procedure   160
10.4   The plea in mitigation   162
10.5   Sentencing guidelines   165
10.6   Further reading   166

Chapter 11   THE YOUTH COURT   167
11.1   General   167
11.2   Sentencing   167
11.3   Further reading   169

Chapter 12   APPEALS   171
12.1   Appeals from the magistrates' court and youth court   171
12.2   Appeals from the Crown Court   172
12.3   Further reading   172

APPENDICES   173

Appendix 1   PROCEDURAL CHARTS AND DIAGRAMS   175

Appendix 2   DOCUMENTS   199

Appendix 3   MAGISTRATES' ASSOCIATION SENTENCING GUIDELINES   263

Appendix 4   POLICE STATION ADVICE: ADVISING ON SILENCE   297
The legal position   297
Advising the client   300

Appendix 5   LAW COMMISSION GUIDANCE FOR BAIL DECISION-MAKERS AND
THEIR ADVISERS   307

Appendix 6   PACE CODES   313
Police and Criminal Evidence Act 1984 Code C   313
Police and Criminal Evidence Act 1984 Code D   359

INDEX   393

Table of Cases

C

Chief Constable of Norfolk v Clayton (Terence Edward); Chief Constable of Norfolk v Clayton
(Eileen Annie); In re Clayton [1983] 2 AC 473   100
Condron and Another v United Kingdom [2000] Crim LR 679   29

D

Director of Public Prosecutions v P (A Father) [1991] 3 All ER 337   137
Director of Public Prosecutions v Smith [1961] AC 290   11

H

Halawa v Federation Against Copyright Theft [1995] 1 Cr App R 21   127

J

Jones v Director of Public Prosecutions; R v Jones [1962] AC 635   136

K

Khan v United Kingdom [2000] Crim LR 684   110
Kuruma v The Queen [1955] AC 197   109

M

Miller v Ministry of Pensions [1947] 2 All ER 372   107
Murdoch v Taylor [1965] AC 574   141
Murray v United Kingdom (Right to Silence) (1996) 22 EHRR 29   32

N

Neill v North Antrim Magistrates' Court and Others [1992] 1 WLR 1221   131

P

Practice Direction (Costs in Criminal Proceedings) (No 2) [2000] 1 Cr App R 60   156
Practice Direction (Crime: Costs) [1991] 1 WLR 498   156
Practice Direction (Criminal Proceedings: Consolidation) [2002] 3 All ER 904   65, 88, 93, 135, 141, 160
Practice Direction (Section 51 of the Crime and Disorder Act 1998 – Guidance on listing
of preliminary hearings) (22 December 1998)   89
Practice Direction (Submission of No Case) [1962] 1 WLR 227   102

R

R v Acton Justices, ex p McCullen; R v Tower Bridge Magistrates Court, ex p Lawlor
(1991) 92 Cr App R 98   129
R v Ali and Others [2001] EWCA Crim 863, [2001] All ER (D) 16 (Apr)   34
R v Alladice (Colin Carlton) (1988) 87 Cr App R 380   126
R v Argent (Brian) [1997] 2 Cr App R 27   28, 32
R v Bailey [1989] Crim LR 723   141
R v Baskerville [1916] 2 KB 658   116
R v Beckles and Montague [1999] Crim LR 148   29
R v Betts and Hall [2001] EWCA Crim 244, [2001] 2 Cr App R 257   29, 32
R v Birmingham Justices, ex p Hodgson and Another [1985] 2 All ER 193   66
R v Bowden (Brian Thomas) (1999) 2 Cr App R 176   33
R v Calder Justices, ex p Kennedy [1992] Crim LR 496   61
R v Cameron (John McDougal) (1993) 14 Cr App R (S) 801   151
R v Canale (Ramon Michael) [1990] 2 All ER 187   126
R v Colchester Justices, ex p North East Essex Building Co Ltd [1977] 1 WLR 1109   64

R v Cole [1990] 1 WLR 866   131
R v Condron (Karen); R v Condron (William) [1997] 1 Cr App R 185   33
R v Cowan (Donald); R v Gayle (Ricky); R v Ricciardi (Carmine) [1995] 4 All ER 939   135
R v Crossan [1939] NI 106   154
R v Daniel (Anthony Junior) [1998] 2 Cr App R 373   29
R v Davison [1988] Crim LR 442   125
R v Derodra [2000] 1 Cr App R 49, CA   130
R v Director of Public Prosecutions, ex p Lee [1999] 2 All ER 737   79
R v Dragic [1996] 2 Cr App R 232   131
R v Fairfax [1995] Crim LR 949   131
R v Fairfax; R v Batt and Batt [1995] Crim LR 240   131
R v French (Julie Ann) (1994) 15 Cr App R (S) 194   151
R v Fulling [1987] 2 WLR 923   125
R v Galbraith (George Charles) [1981] 2 All ER 1060   81, 96
R v Gall (1990) 90 Cr App R 64   111
R v Gaynor [1988] Crim LR 242   111
R v Grafton [1995] Crim LR 61   131
R v Grannell (Robert James Lawson) (1990) 90 Cr App R 149   111
R v Harris [2003] EWCA Crim 174   38
R v Harvey [1988] Crim LR 241   126
R v Howell [2003] Crim LR 405   32
R v Howells and Others [1999] 1 Cr App R (S) 335   149
R v Ipswich Justices, ex p Callaghan (1995) 159 JP 748   65
R v Iqbal [1990] 1 WLR 756   131
R v Khan (Ashraf Ullah) (1994) 15 Cr App R (S) 320   151
R v Lambert [2001] 3 WLR 206   9
R v Liverpool Juvenile Court, ex p R [1988] QB 1   127
R v Lucas (Ruth) [1981] QB 720   116
R v Lunt (1987) 85 Cr App R 241   137
R v Makanjuola; R v E [1995] 1 WLR 1348   117
R v Mason [1988] 1 WLR 139   127
R v Mattey (Jimmy Cyril); R v Queeley (Juanita Amelia) [1995] 2 Cr App R 409   129
R v McGarry [1999] 1 Cr App R 377   29
R v McGowan [1990] Crim LR 399   9
R v McGuiness (Cyril) [1999] Crim LR 318   29
R v McLeod [1995] 1 Cr App R 591, CA   140
R v Miller (1952) 36 Cr App R 169   136
R v Mitford [2001] Crim LR 330   29
R v Nagah (Jasant Singh) (1991) 92 Cr App R 334   111
R v Neale (1977) 65 Cr App R 304   136
R v Newton (Robert John) (1983) 77 Cr App R 13   161
R v Okinikan (1993) 14 Cr App R (S) 453   151
R v Patel (1993) 97 Cr App R 294   130
R v Pearce (David Anthony) (1979) 69 Cr App R 365   121
R v Radak; R v Adjei; R v Butler-Rees; R v Meghjee [1999] 1 Cr App R 187   131
R v Rafferty [1999] 1 Cr App R 235   160
R v Randall [1998] 6 Archbold News 1   29
R v Randall [2004] 1 All ER 467, HL   140
R v Rankine [1986] 2 All ER 566   122
R v Richardson (1967) 51 Cr App R 381   134
R v Roberts [1942] 1 All ER 187   121
R v Roble (Ali Hersi) [1997] Crim LR 449   32, 33
R v Sang [1980] AC 402   109
R v Savage; R v Parmenter [1991] 4 All ER 698   11
R v Sharp (Colin) (1988) 86 Cr App R 274   125
R v Slater (Robert David) [1995] 1 Cr App R 584   118
R v Smith (1915) 11 Cr App R 229   137
R v Spencer (Alan Widdison); R v Smails (George Glenville) [1986] 3 WLR 348   117
R v Stratford Justices, ex p Imbert [1999] 2 Cr App R 276   69
R v Taylor (Nicholas Jones); R v Goodman (Donald Walter) [1999] Crim LR 407   139
R v Taylor [1999] Crim LR 75   29
R v Thompson; R v Sinclair; R v Maver [1995] 2 Cr App R 589   136
R v Thornton [1995] 1 Cr App R 598   118

R v Trussler (Barry) [1988] Crim LR 446   126
R v Turnbull [1977] QB 224   117
R v Varley [1982] 2 All ER 519   140
R v W [1997] Crim LR 678   131
R v Warley Magistrates' Court, ex p DPP; R v Staines Magistrates' Court, ex p DPP;
    R v North East Suffolk Magistrates' Court, ex p DPP; R v Lowestoft Justices, ex p DPP
    [1998] 2 Cr App R 307   158
R v Weston (Arnold) [1996] 1 Cr App R (S) 297   151
R v Wickins (1958) 42 Cr App R 236   154
R v Wilmot (Alan) (1989) 89 Cr App R 341   33
R v Woodward [1944] KB 118   4
Ratten (Leith McDonald) v The Queen [1972] AC 378   121

S

Selvey v DPP [1970] AC 304   140
Subramaniam v Public Prosecutor [1956] 1 WLR 965   123

T

Trivedi v United Kingdom [1997] EHRLR 521   132

W

Walters (Henry) v The Queen [1969] 2 AC 26   107
Whittall v Kirby [1946] 2 All ER 552   154
Woolmington v Director of Public Prosecutions [1935] AC 462   107

Table of Statutes

Access to Justice Act 1999 235, 236
  ss 12–18 4
  s13 47
  s14 48
  s17 156
  s21 234, 251
  Sch3 4, 49
    para2(2) 61
    para5(1) 48
    para5(2) 48
    para5(2)(a)–(e) 48
Accessories and Abettors Act 1861
  s8 11
Anti-Terrorism, Crime and Security Act 2001 276, 277, 278

Bail Act 1976 307
  Part I 307
  s3 58
  s3(1) 54
  s3(6) 58
  s3A 20
  s4 55
  s5 60
  s5B 62
  s6 54
  s7 60, 309
  s7(1)–(2) 54
  s7(3) 309, 343
  s7(5) 309, 310
  s8(2) 58
  s8(4)–(5) 59
  Sch1 55
    Part I 55
      para2 56
      para2(a) 307
      para2(b) 308
      para2(c) 307
      para2A 55, 56, 237, 307, 308
      para2A(1)–(2) 55
      para3 308
      para5 308
      para6 55, 56, 307, 309
      para6(1)–(3) 56
      para7 307
      para9 56
    Part II 57
      para2 307
      para5 309
    Part IIA 60, 311
      paras2–3 61
Bail (Amendment) Act 1993
  s1(1) 61

Children Act 1989 313
Courts and Legal Services Act 1990
  s119(1) 58

Crime and Disorder Act 1998 41, 77, 295, 346, 368, 375
  s3 156
  s28(1) 144
  s28(4)–(5) 144
  s29 144, 276, 277, 278
  ss30–32 144
  s50 46
  s51 50, 82, 83, 87, 92, 235
  s51(1) 82
  s51(3) 82
  s51(5)–(6) 83
  s51(7) 88, 89
  s51(9) 83
  s51(11)–(12) 82
  s52 82
  s52(5) 83
  s65 370
  s80 165
  Sch3 82
    para1 84, 89
    para2 89
    para4 89
    para6 91
    para6(7) 91
    paras7–12 90
    para13 91
Crime (Sentences) Act 1997
  Sch1 344
Criminal Appeals Act 1995
  s1 172
Criminal Evidence Act 1898
  s1(1) 135, 138
  s1(2) 138
  s1(3) 138, 139, 140
  s1(3)(i) 138
  s1(3)(ii) 127, 138, 139, 140, 257
  s1(3)(iii) 138, 140, 141
  s1(e) 123
Criminal Justice Act 1967 253
  s9 93, 99, 101, 115, 124, 134
  s9(1)–(2) 134
  s10 108
  s10(2)(b) 253
Criminal Justice Act 1972
  s36 195
Criminal Justice Act 1982
  s60 61
Criminal Justice Act 1988 128, 336
  Part VI 349, 350
  s4A 122
  s23 79, 100, 101, 115, 124, 128, 129, 130, 131, 132, 183
  s23(1)–(3) 128
  s24 79, 100, 101, 115, 124, 129, 130, 131, 132, 184
  s24(1)–(2) 129
  s24(4) 130

Criminal Justice Act 1988 – *continued*
  s25 129, 130, 183, 184
  s25(1) 131
  s25(2) 132
  s25(2)(d) 131
  s26 129, 130, 131, 183, 184
  s27 116
  s30 115, 124
  s30(1)–(2) 122
  ss35–36 195
  s39 10, 270, 277
  s40 84, 85, 91
  s40(1) 84
  s41 85
  s41(1) 84-5
Criminal Justice Act 1991 263, 264
  Sch2 267
Criminal Justice Act 2003 Preface
  s3 20
  ss23–27 42
  s139(1) 114
  Sch2 20
Criminal Justice and Court Services Act 2000
  ss43–44 146, 168
Criminal Justice and Public Order Act 1994 17, 28-37, 297
  Part III 335
  s25 54, 309
  s34 28, 29, 30, 31, 32, 33, 34, 35, 117, 297, 298, 334, 351
  s34(1) 28, 32
  s34(1)(a) 28, 298, 304
  s34(1)(b) 304
  s34(4) 28
  s35 135
  s35(1)–(3) 135
  s36 29, 30, 31, 32, 33, 34, 117, 297, 298, 299, 303, 304, 333, 334, 351
  s36(1) 29-30
  s36(4) 30
  s37 30, 31, 32, 33, 34, 117, 297, 298, 299, 303, 304, 333, 334, 351
  s37(1) 30-1
  s38 297
  s38(3) 31, 117
  s136(2) 314, 361
  s137(2) 314, 361
Criminal Law Act 1967
  s3 261
Criminal Law Act 1977
  s1(1) 10
  s1(4) 10
Criminal Procedure Act 1865
  s3 114
  ss4–6 115
Criminal Procedure and Investigations Act 1996 70, 71, 79, 97, 240, 256, 368, 373, 375
  Part III 94
  s3 70
  s5 72
  s5(8) 72
  s6 72
  s7 73

Criminal Procedure and Investigations Act 1996 – *continued*
  ss8–11 74
  s11 240
  ss12–13 71, 73
  s20 122
  s23 70
  s31 94, 95
  s40 94
  s68 87, 115, 124, 132, 188, 189, 243
  Sch1
    paras25–26 81
  Sch2
    para1 87, 115, 124, 132
    para1(1)–(4) 133
    para1(3)(c) 243
    para2 87, 115, 124, 132
    para2(1)–(3) 133
    para2(3)(c) 243
    para2(4) 134

Drug Trafficking Act 1994 336

Human Rights Act 1998 13, 14, 15, 16, 62, 285
  s2 14
  s3 308
  s3(1) 14
  s4(4)(b) 14
  s4(6)(a)–(b) 14
  s6 308
  s6(3) 14
  s7 14
  s8 14
  s8(1) 14
  s10 14

Immigration Act 1971 314
  s2(1)(b) 390
  Sch2
    para16 361, 371
    para17 371
    para18 361
    para18(2) 371
Immigration and Asylum Act 1999
  s10 371
  s141 361
  s141(7)(a)–(f) 371
  s142(3) 314, 361, 371
  s143(5) 390
  s144 361
Imprisonment (Temporary Provisions) Act 1980 314
  s6 344
Indictments Act 1915 87

Magistrates' Courts Act 1980 45
  s5A 133
  s5B 78, 79, 80, 133, 188, 189
  s5C 78, 79, 80, 133
  ss5D–5E 78, 79, 80
  s6(1) 77, 80, 82, 189
  s6(2) 77, 79, 81, 82, 188, 256
  s8 78
  s10(3) 53

Magistrates' Courts Act 1980 – *continued*
s19(3) 64
s24 167
s25(2)–(3) 66
s31 150
s38 153
s38A 153
s97(1)–(2B) 99
s97A 78, 89, 133
s108 171
s111 172
s120(1A) 58
s123 100
s127 45
s128 53, 344
s128(3A) 53
s128A 53
s133(2) 150
Sch1
    para28(c) 65
Malicious Communications Act 1988
s1 372
Mental Health Act 1983 308, 319, 330, 331, 355
s135 321
s136 319, 321, 330, 331, 355
Misuse of Drugs Act 1971 9
s4 272, 274
s4(1) 9
s4(3) 9
s5 9, 271, 273
s5(1)–(2) 8
s5(3) 10
s5(4) 8
s27 156
s28 9
s28(1)–(3) 8
s28(4) 9

Offences Against the Person Act 1861
s20 11, 278, 281
s47 10, 161, 261, 266, 276

Police and Criminal Evidence Act 1984 2, 17, 178,
339, 341, 346, 349, 359, 371, 377, 390
s24 6, 7, 9, 10, 11
s25 334
s27 370, 376
s27(4) 372
ss29–30 18
s34 21
s37(1) 18
s37(2) 19, 180
s37(3) 19
s38 346
s38(1) 20
s38(6) 346
s40 180, 341, 342, 343
s40A 342, 343, 344
s41 180, 341, 350
ss42–43 19, 180, 261, 343, 344
s44 341, 343, 344
s45A 342
s46 346

Police and Criminal Evidence Act 1984 – *continued*
s46(2) 46
s46A 21
s47(3A) 46
s54(1) 322
s54A 373, 374
s54A(1) 372
s54A(1)(a)–(b) 373
s56(1) 21
s58 21
s58(6) 21
s58(8) 22, 297
s61 369-70
s62 41, 117, 377
s62(1) 377
s62(1A) 377
s63 41
s63(3) 377
s63(3A) 377
s63(3B) 378
s63A 378
s64A 368, 373
s73 115
s76 126, 127, 257
s76(1) 124
s76(2) 81
s76(2)(a) 125
s76(2)(b) 125, 126
s76(4)–(6) 128
s76(8)–(9) 125
s78 81, 110, 111, 126, 127, 136, 140, 257
s78(1) 110
s79 102, 135
s80 136
s80(5) 136
s82(1) 124
s107 360
s116 17
s118(2) 349
Sch5 17
Police Reform Act 2002 362
Part 4 315
Powers of Criminal Courts (Sentencing) Act 2000
143, 163, 192
ss1–2 157
s3 156, 158, 159, 187
s4 156, 159, 187
ss12–15 145
ss16–28 169
ss29–32 169, 282
ss33–36 145
s37 147, 168
s38 147
s39 147, 148
s40 147
ss41–42 146, 168
s43 146, 148, 168
ss44–47 146, 168
s48 146, 148, 168
ss49–50 146, 168
s51 146, 148, 168
ss52–55 147, 168
s56 147, 148, 168

Powers of Criminal Courts (Sentencing) Act 2000 –
  continued
  ss57–59 147, 168
  ss60–62 148, 168
  ss63–72 168
  ss73–75 169
  s79 149
  s80 150
  s81(4) 150
  s91 91, 167
  s100 167
  s101 167
  s101(2) 167
  ss102–107 167
  ss111–115 7
  s118 150
  s119 150, 151
  ss120–121 150
  s122 150, 151
  ss123–125 150
  s126 145, 287
  s127 145
  s128 145, 286
  s128(1)–(4) 145
  s129 145
  s130 156, 290
  ss131–134 156
  ss135–136 145
  s137 145, 169
  ss138–142 145
  ss143–145 156
  s146 152
  s147 153, 154
  s151 264
  s151(1)–(2) 144
  s152 165, 252, 283
  s153 144, 264, 282
  s162 284
  Sch1 169
  Sch2 146, 168
  Sch3 146, 147, 168
    paras3–6 148
    paras10–14 148
  Sch5 148, 168
  Sch7 168
  Sch8 169
Proceeds of Crime Act 2002 156
Prosecution of Offences Act 1985
  s16 156
  s18 156
  s22(1) 53
Public Order Act 1986
  s4 85, 92

Rehabilitation of Offenders Act 1974 141
Road Traffic Act 1988 321, 333
  s2 228
  s3 260
  ss4–6 361
  s7 334, 361
  ss8–11 361

Road Traffic Act 1988 – *continued*
  s25 372
  s101(4) 227
Road Traffic Act 1991 45
Road Traffic (New Drivers) Act 1995 154
Road Traffic Offenders Act 1988 45
  Part II 153
  s1 346
  s1(1) 45
  s2 45
  s2(1) 45
  ss15–16 361
  s26 152, 154
  s28(4) 152
  s34 152
  s34(2) 154
  s35(4) 155
  s44 152
  s47(1) 155, 156

Street Offences Act 1959
  s1 372
Supreme Court Act 1981
  s81 61

Telecommunications Act 1984
  s43 372
Terrorism Act 2000 329, 342, 343, 350
  s23 350
  s41 322, 350, 351, 361
  Sch7 314, 322, 332, 350, 351, 361
  Sch8 361
    Part II 342, 344
    Part III 342
    para8 297
    para10 379
  Sch14
    para6 314, 332, 361
Theft Act 1968 290
  s1 6, 256, 279, 280
  s1(1) 226, 259
  s8 262
  s8(1) 7
  s9 268, 269
  s9(1)–(2) 7
  ss12–12A 61
  s15 275
  s15(1) 7
  s15(4) 7
Transport and Works Act 1992 321
  ss26–38 361
  s31 334

Youth Justice and Criminal Evidence Act 1999
  ss16–33 112
  ss34–39 115
  s54 111
  ss55–57 112
  s58 32, 351
  s59 297

Table of Statutory Instruments, Circulars and Guidance

Attorney-General's Guidelines on Disclosure of Information in Criminal Proceedings (29 November 2000)
para43 69-70

Bar Council's Guidance on Drafting Defence Statements 73, 92

Code for Crown Prosecutors 3, 42
CPIA Code of Practice 70
para3.4 337
para6.12 74
para7.3 71
Crime and Disorder Act 1998 (Dismissal of Charges Sent) Rules 1998 (SI 1998/3048) 89, 90
Crime and Disorder Act 1998 (Service of Prosecution Evidence) Regulations 1998 (SI 1998/3115) 89
Criminal Defence Service (General) (No 2) Regulations 2001 (SI 2001/1437) 4, 48
regs5-6 47
regs8-9 50
Criminal Defence Service (Recovery of Defence Costs Orders) Regulations 2001 (SI 2001/856) 156
Criminal Defence Service (Representation Order Appeals) Regulations 2001 (SI 2001/1168) 51
Criminal Procedure and Investigations Act 1996 (Defence Disclosure Time Limits) Regulations 1997 (SI 1997/684)
reg2 73
reg3(2)–(3) 73
reg4(2)–(3) 73
Crown Court (Advance Notice of Expert Evidence) Rules 1987 (SI 1997/716) 122
Crown Court (Modification) Rules 1998 89
Crown Court Rules 1982 (SI 1982/1109)
r22 88
r27 89

Guidance to Courts from the Lord Chancellor's Department – Interests of Justice Tests 49
Guide to the Professional Conduct of Solicitors 1999
Annex 21F 13

Home Office Circular 18/1994 41
Home Office Circular 11/1997 71

Indictment Rules 1971 (SI 1971/1253) 87
r5 87
Indictments (Procedure) (Modification) Rules 1998 (SI 1998/3045) 87

Law Commission Guidance for Bail Decision-makers and their Advisers 62, 307-11

Magistrates' Association Sentencing Guidelines 49, 162, 163, 166, 263-196
para2 163
Magistrates' Courts (Advance Information) Rules 1985 (SI 1985/601) 6, 63, 70, 71, 97
Magistrates' Courts (Advance Notice of Expert Evidence) Rules 1997 (SI 1997/705) 122
Magistrates' Courts (Modification) Rules 1998 (SI 1998/3046) 88
Magistrates' Courts Rules 1981 (SI 1981/552)
r4B 243
Magistrates' Courts (Amendment) Rules 1997 243
Misuse of Drugs Regulations 2001 (SI 2001/3998)
Schs1–5 330

National Police Records (Recordable Offences) Regulations 2000 372

PACE Codes of Practice 17, 40, 202, 315, 317, 362
Code A 314, 373
Code C 17, 36, 126, 127, 207, 297, 302, 303, 313-58, 360
paras1.1–1.3 313
paras1.4–1.5 26, 313, 360
para1.6 313, 360
para1.7 26, 208, 313-14, 360
paras1.8–1.9A 314
paras1.10–1.11 314
para1.12 314-15
paras1.13–1.17 315
Note 1A 21, 315
Note 1B 315
Note 1C 315-16
Notes 1D–1E 316
Note 1F 208, 316
Notes 1G–1I 316
paras2.1–2.3 316
para2.4 19, 27, 316
para2.4A 316
paras2.5–2.7 317
Note 2A 317
paras3.1–3.3 317
para3.4 317-18
paras3.5–3.10 318
paras3.11–3.14 319
para3.15 319, 360
para3.16 319
para3.17 208, 319-20
paras3.18–3.20 320
para3.21 320, 377
paras3.22–3.24 320
Note 3A 320
Notes 3B–3E 321

PACE Codes of Practice – *continued*
paras4.1–4.3 321
para4.4 321-2
para4.5 322
Notes 4A–4C 322
paras5.1–5.3 322
para5.4 207, 322
para5.5 322
para5.6 207, 322
para5.7 322-3
para5.8 323
Notes 5A–5E 323
para6.1 21, 323
paras6.2–6.3 323
para6.4 25, 323
para6.5 323, 377
para6.6 25, 323-4
para6.7 324
paras6.8–6.9 325
para6.10 36, 325
para6.11 325
para6.12 325, 360
paras6.13–6.14 325
para6.15 22, 326
paras6.16–6.17 326
Notes 6A–6C 326
Note 6D 27, 36, 326
Notes 6E–6F 326
Note 6G 326-7
Notes 6H–6K 327
para7.1 208, 327
para7.2 327
para7.3 208, 327
para7.4 327
para7.5 328
Note 7A 328
paras8.1–8.7 207, 328
paras8.8–8.11 328
Notes 8A–8B 329
paras9.1–9.5 329
paras9.6–9.7 330
paras9.8–9.12 207, 330
para9.13 330
para9.14 330-1
paras9.15–9.17 331
Notes 9A–9D 331
Notes 9E–9H 332
para10.1 22, 26, 298, 332
paras10.2–10.4 332
para10.5 26
   332-3 382
para10.6 333, 382
paras10.7–10.10 333
para10.11 30, 31, 298, 333-4
para10.12 208, 334
para10.13 334
Notes 10A–10G 334
para11.1 22, 335
para11.1A 22, 334
paras11.2–11.4 335
para11.4A 24, 335
para11.5 125, 335
para11.6 335-6

PACE Codes of Practice – *continued*
para11.7 336
para11.7(a) 23
para11.7(c) 24
para11.8 24, 336
paras11.9–11.10 336
para11.11 24, 336
para11.12 208, 336
para11.13 336
para11.14 24, 336
para11.15 336
para11.16 337
para11.17 26, 337
paras11.18–11.20 337
Notes 11A–11C 337
Notes 11D–11E 338
para12.1 338
para12.2 26, 208, 338
para12.3 26, 338
para12.4 26, 208, 338
para12.5 304, 339
para12.6 26, 208, 339
para12.7 208, 339
para12.8 26, 339
paras12.9–12.14 339
Notes 12A–12B 340
paras13.1–13.7 340
paras13.8–13.11 341
paras14.1–14.2 341
Note 14A 341
paras15.1–15.2 341
para15.3 207, 208, 341-2
para15.3A 342
para15.3B 207, 342
paras15.4–15.9 342
para15.10 342-3
paras15.11–15.16 343
Note 15A 343
Note 15B 343-4
Notes 15C–15F 344
para16.1 19, 208, 344
para16.2 298, 345
para16.3 345
paras16.4–6.5 23, 345
para16.6 23, 345
para16.7 345-6
paras16.8–16.10 346
Notes 16A–16D 346
Annex A 346-9
   para5 208
   para11 373
Annex B 304, 349-51
   parasA3-A4 22
Annex C 297, 351-3
Annex D 353-4
Annex E 354-6
Annex F 357
Annex G 26, 357-8
Annex H 358
Code D 17, 37, 111, 207, 359-91
   paras1.1–1.7 359
   para2.1 359
   paras2.2–2.11 360

PACE Codes of Practice – *continued*
  paras2.12–2.13 208, 360
  para2.14 208, 360-1
  paras2.15–2.17 361
  paras2.18–2.22 362
  Note 2A 362
  Notes 2B–2D 363
  para3.1 40, 363
  para3.2 37, 363-4
  para3.3 37, 364
  paras3.4–3.10 364
  para3.11 37, 364-5
  paras3.12–3.13 38, 365
  paras3.14–3.16 365
  para3.17 366
  para3.18 39, 366
  para3.19 366-7
  para3.20 367
  paras3.21–3.22 38, 367
  para3.23 38, 39, 367
  para3.24 38, 367
  paras3.25–3.27 367
  para3.28 367-8
  paras3.29–3.33 368
  Notes 3A–3B 368
  Notes 3C–3F 369
  paras4.1–4.2 369
  para4.3 369-70
  paras4.4–4.7 370
  paras4.8–4.12 371
  paras4.13–4.15 372
  Notes 4A–4B 372
  para5.1 372-3
  paras5.2–5.11 373
  para5.12 373-4
  paras5.13–5.20 374
  paras5.21–5.24 375
  Note 5A 375
  Note 5B 375-6
  Notes 5C–5E 376

PACE Codes of Practice – *continued*
  para6.1 376-7
  paras6.2–6.5 377
  para6.6 377-8
  paras6.7–6.12 378
  Note 6A 378
  Note 6B 378-9
  Notes 6C–6E 379
  Annex A 379-81
    paras2–3 38
    para7 40
    para11 38
  Annex B 381-4
    para9 38
    para12 40
    para15 38
  Annex C 384-7
    para2 39
  Annex D 387-8
    para4 39
  Annex E 37, 388-9
  Annex F 389-91
  Code E 17, 336, 340, 341, 346
    paras2.1–2.2 23
  Code F 336, 340, 341, 346
Prosecution of Offences (Custody Time Limits)
  Regulations 1987 (SI 1987/2299) 53
  reg4(2) 53
  reg4(4) 53
  reg5(3)(a) 54
  reg5(6B) 54
Prosecution of Offences (Custody Time Limits)
  (Modification) Regulations 1998 (SI 1998/3037)
  54

Solicitors' Professional Conduct Rules
  rule 20.4 51

Terrorism Act 2000 Code of Practice 314, 332

Table of International Legislation

European Convention on Human Rights 1950 13,
 14, 15, 16, 307, 308, 309, 310, 311
 art3 15, 371
 art5 308
 art5(1)–(2) 15
 art5(3) 15, 307, 308
 art5(4) 15, 310
 art5(5) 15

European Convention on Human Rights – *continued*
 art6 9, 16, 29, 32, 110, 131, 132, 172, 297, 299
 art6(1) 15, 110
 art6(2) 15
 art6(3) 4, 16
 art7(1)–(2) 16
 art8 110, 310
 arts9–11 310

Table of Abbreviations

CPIA	Criminal Procedure and Investigations Act 1996
CPO	community punishment order
CPS	Crown Prosecution Service
DVLA	Driver and Vehicle Licensing Authority
EAH	early administrative hearing
EFH	early first hearing
MCA 1980	Magistrates' Courts Act 1980
PACE	Police and Criminal Evidence Act 1984
PCC(S)A 2000	Powers of Criminal Courts (Sentencing) Act 2000
PDH	plea and directions hearing
PH	preparatory hearing
PTR	pre-trial review
RDCO	recovery of defence costs order
TIC	(offences) taken into consideration

Chapter 1

Introduction to Criminal Procedure

1.1	The solicitor's role	1
1.2	Classification of criminal offences	1
1.3	The courts and court personnel	2
1.4	The prosecution and the defence	3
1.5	An overview of criminal procedure	5
1.6	Substantive criminal law	6
1.7	Professional ethics	12
1.8	European Convention on Human Rights	13
1.9	Further reading	16

1.1 The solicitor's role

Solicitors are involved at every stage of the prosecution of a criminal offence, from police investigation to trial. Solicitors (and their unqualified representatives) are frequently called upon to advise suspects being held in the police station before they are charged. Difficult decisions have to be made with the client. Should police questions be answered? Should the client agree to stand on an identification parade?

Following the commencement of criminal proceedings, a solicitor may be involved in applying for a representation order for a client and in trying to secure his release from custody on bail. Criminal proceedings in a magistrates' court will usually be prosecuted and defended by solicitors, although barristers sometimes appear. If a case is to be dealt with in the Crown Court, most solicitors have limited rights of audience. Their major role is in preparing the case for trial and briefing a barrister (counsel) to represent the client.

Finally, where necessary, a solicitor will advise a client on rights of appeal, will prepare the appeal and, usually, will brief a barrister to represent the client at the appeal hearing.

This chapter provides an introduction to the criminal justice system and covers the basic information required to understand the progress of a criminal case from investigation to trial.

1.2 Classification of criminal offences

Criminal offences are divided into three categories:

(a) summary offences;

(b offences triable either way;

(c) offences triable only on indictment.

Summary offences may be tried only in a magistrates' court.

Offences triable either way may be tried in a magistrates' court or in the Crown Court before a judge and jury. The place of trial will be determined at a mode of trial hearing in a magistrates' court.

Offences triable only on indictment must be tried in the Crown Court.

1.3 The courts and court personnel

1.3.1 Magistrates' courts

Business

The prosecution of all criminal offences starts in the magistrates' court even if the case will ultimately be tried in the Crown Court. The functions of a magistrates' court include:

(a)   to issue search and arrest warrants;

(b)   to issue warrants of further detention under the Police and Criminal Evidence Act 1984;

(c)   to issue summonses to defendants to appear before the court to answer a criminal charge;

(d)   to try summary offences and some either way offences;

(e)   to hold committal proceedings in respect of either way offences (not related to indictable only offences) which are to be tried in the Crown Court;

(f)   to send indictable only offences (and related either way and summary offences) to the Crown Court for trial;

(g)   to deal with applications for a representation order;

(h)   to deal with applications for bail.

Personnel

Most magistrates are not legally qualified. Between two and four magistrates will usually sit in court. The magistrates are advised on points of law, practice and procedure by the clerk to the justices. The clerk should not advise magistrates on questions of fact. In some courts, a legally qualified magistrate known as a district judge (magistrates' court) (formerly known as a stipendiary magistrate) will sit alone.

1.3.2 Youth courts

Youth courts are courts set up to deal with defendants who are under 18 years of age. Lay magistrates and district judges (magistrates' court) sit in youth courts. (See **Chapter 11**.)

1.3.3 The Crown Court

Business

The functions of the Crown Court include:

(a)   to try and to sentence offences triable only on indictment and either way offences committed for trial by a magistrates' court;

(b)   to determine questions of bail and representation;

(c)   to hear appeals against conviction and/or sentence from a magistrates' court and youth court.

Personnel

The judges of the Crown Court are recorders, circuit judges and High Court judges. The judge sits with a jury on not guilty pleas and with magistrates when dealing with appeals from a magistrates' court.

1.3.4 High Court (Queen's Bench Division)

Business

The Queen's Bench Division of the High Court hears appeals on points of law from magistrates' courts and youth courts and appeals on law from re-hearings in the Crown Court (appeals by way of case stated). It also has power to quash a decision by making a quashing order, to order the court to try a case by making a mandatory order, or to stop a court hearing a case by making a prohibiting order.

Personnel

The judges are judges of the Queen's Bench Division of the High Court chosen on an ad hoc basis.

1.3.5 The Court of Appeal

Business

The Court of Appeal (Criminal Division) hears appeals against conviction and/or sentence from the Crown Court.

Personnel

The judges in the Court of Appeal will be drawn from the Lord Chief Justice, Lords Justices of Appeal and High Court judges.

1.3.6 The House of Lords

Business

The House of Lords is the final appeal court. It hears appeals from the Court of Appeal and High Court but only where a point of law of general public importance is involved.

Personnel

The judges in the House of Lords are five Lords of Appeal.

1.4 The prosecution and the defence

1.4.1 The prosecution

Once the police have instituted proceedings, full responsibility for the prosecution will pass to the Crown Prosecution Service (CPS). The CPS will review the evidence and surrounding circumstances of each case and decide whether and how the prosecution should proceed. In appropriate cases the CPS can discontinue proceedings. There is a Code for Crown Prosecutors which gives guidelines on discontinuance and other matters.

Joint charging standards have been drawn up by the police and the CPS. The purpose of joint charging standards is to make sure that the most appropriate charge is selected, in the light of the evidence which can be proved, at the earliest possible opportunity. To date, three joint charging standards have been published: Offences Against the Person (26 April 1996), Public Order Offences (26 April 1996) and Driving Offences (March 1996).

1.4.2 The defence

A defendant has the right to conduct his own defence (*R v Woodward* [1944] KB 118; see also the European Convention for the Protection of Human Rights and Fundamental Freedoms 1950, art 6(3), and **1.8**). There are restrictions on cross-examination by defendants in person (see **9.3.2**). A defendant may, however, be represented by a solicitor whom he will pay privately, or who will be paid under a representation order. If the services of a barrister (counsel) are needed, the solicitor instructs a barrister. The defendant cannot instruct a barrister direct.

A solicitor has a right of audience in a magistrates' court. For most solicitors, rights of audience in the Crown Court are limited to:

(a)   applications in chambers, for example, bail applications;

(b)   appeals against conviction and/or sentence from a magistrates' court, provided a member of the solicitor's firm conducted the proceedings in the magistrates' court;

(c)   on committal by a magistrates' court to the Crown Court for sentence, provided a member of the solicitor's firm conducted the hearing in the magistrates' court;

(d)   preliminary hearings in the Crown Court where the defendant has been sent for trial for an indictable defence.

Thus, solicitors cannot normally conduct a trial by jury in the Crown Court. However, in certain Crown Courts, solicitors enjoy extended rights of audience, including the right to conduct some jury trials. A number of solicitors have now been granted full rights of audience in the Crown Court and higher appeal courts.

1.4.3 Criminal Defence Service

The Criminal Defence Service was created by the Access to Justice Act 1999 (ss 12–18 and Sch 3). The purpose of the Criminal Defence Service is to 'secure the provision of advice, assistance and representation, according to the interests of justice, to people suspected of a criminal offence, or facing criminal proceedings' (*Legal Services Commission Manual* (Sweet & Maxwell, 1D-004)).

The Legal Services Commission funds the Criminal Defence Service and secures the provision of advice, assistance and representation under a General Criminal Contract with solicitors in private practice, or by providing them through salaried public defenders. All contractors are expected to meet quality assurance standards and provide the full range of services from arrest until the case is completed. Only those solicitors with a General Criminal Contract with the Legal Services Commission are able to undertake publicly funded defence work.

The following advice and assistance may be granted without reference to the financial resources of the individual:

(1)   advice and assistance (including advocacy assistance) provided by a solicitor acting as a court duty solicitor;

(2)   police station advice and assistance to a client who is arrested and held at a police station or who is a volunteer;

(3)   advocacy assistance on an application for a warrant of further detention or for an extension to such a warrant (Criminal Defence Service (General) (No 2) Regulations 2001 (SI 2001/1437)).

Where a representation order is requested an applicant will need to satisfy the interests of justice test set out in Access to Justice Act 1999, Sch 3 (see **3.3.2**).

1.5   An overview of criminal procedure

See **Appendix 1(A)** for a flowchart giving an overview of criminal procedure.

1.5.1   Police investigations

Police investigation includes arrest, search and the detention and questioning of a suspect (see **Chapter 2**).

1.5.2   Commencement of criminal proceedings

The commencement of criminal proceedings will be by way of charge or summons. A charge is normally used when a suspect has been arrested and taken to the police station. A summons is normally used for relatively minor offences that may not involve arrest at all (eg, motoring offences). The summons will be served by post and will notify the defendant of the date, time and place of the hearing (see **Chapter 3**).

1.5.3   Magistrates' courts

All cases begin in a magistrates' court. At the initial hearing, questions of adjournments, representation and bail are likely to arise (see **Chapter 3**).

If the offence before the court is a summary offence, it must be dealt with by a magistrates' court. The defendant will plead guilty or not guilty and on conviction will be sentenced (see **Chapter 8**).

If the offence is an either way offence (which is not related to an indictable only offence), the prosecution begins with the plea before venue hearing before the magistrates. If the defendant refuses to indicate a plea, or indicates a not guilty plea, the magistrates will proceed to mode of trial, to determine whether the case should be dealt with by a magistrates' court or by the Crown Court (see **Chapter 4**). If the offence proceeds in the magistrates' court and the defendant is convicted, then the magistrates may commit him to the Crown Court for sentencing in certain circumstances (see **Chapter 10**). If the case is to proceed to the Crown Court, there will be committal proceedings in the magistrates' court. At committal, the defence can require the prosecution to show that there is a case to answer. Alternatively, the defence may not dispute that there is a case to answer. If so, the committal may be a formality (see **Chapter 6**). Following committal, the defendant will be tried by judge and jury. Following conviction, the defendant is sentenced by a judge.

If the offence is an indictable only offence, the magistrates must send the defendant to the Crown Court to be tried. The magistrates must also send related summary only and either way offences to the Crown Court (see **Chapter 6**).

1.5.4   Disclosure of prosecution evidence

In all cases, the defendant has a statutory right to receive a copy of certain documents such as his custody record and the record of an identification parade.

If the defendant is charged with a summary offence, the defendant has no statutory right to see the prosecution evidence before it is presented at the trial. However, the prosecution is usually prepared to disclose its evidence on a voluntary basis.

If the defendant is charged with an either way offence, then prior to the mode of trial decision, he has a right to receive either a summary or a copy of the prosecution witness statements, under the Magistrates' Courts (Advance Information) Rules 1985 (SI 1985/601).

If the defendant's case is to be committed to the Crown Court, the prosecution must serve copies of its evidence on the defence before the case is committed from the magistrates' court to the Crown Court.

If the defendant's case is sent to the Crown Court for trial, the prosecution must serve copies of its evidence on the defence at the Crown Court.

These rules are dealt with in more detail at **5.2**.

1.5.5 Appeal

There are rights of appeal against conviction and/or sentence from the magistrates' court and the Crown Court (see **Chapter 12**).

1.6 Substantive criminal law

This book has been designed as a constituent part of the Legal Practice Course. As such, it will not generally address questions of substantive criminal law. However, an outline knowledge of the offences which have been used to illustrate points of practice, procedure and evidence is necessary. It is also necessary to know how each offence is classified for trial purposes and the maximum penalties that can be imposed on conviction. The offences which are illustrated in this book are summarised below.

1.6.1 Theft

(a) Classification – triable either way.

(b) Theft is an arrestable offence within the meaning of the Police and Criminal Evidence Act 1984, s 24.

(c) Maximum penalties – Crown Court: 7 years' imprisonment and/or unlimited fine. Magistrates' court: 6 months' imprisonment and/or £5,000 fine. If theft of a motor vehicle: discretionary disqualification from driving.

(d) Definition – Theft Act 1968, s 1:

Dishonest appropriation of property belonging to another with the intention of permanently depriving the other of it.

1.6.2 Burglary

(a) Classification – triable either way if involving theft or intention to steal, unless burglary of a dwelling and any person in the dwelling is subjected to violence or the threat of it, in which case triable only on indictment.

(b) Burglary is an arrestable offence within the meaning of the Police and Criminal Evidence Act 1984, s 24.

(c) Maximum penalties – Crown Court: 14 years' imprisonment and/or unlimited fine (maximum 10 years if not of a dwelling). Magistrates' court: 6 months' imprisonment and/or £5,000 fine.

(d) There is a minimum sentence of 3 years' imprisonment for the third conviction of burglary of a dwelling. The court need not impose the minimum term if it is of the opinion that there are particular circumstances which:

(i) relate to any of the offences or the offender; and

     (ii)   would make the prescribed minimum sentence unjust in all the circumstances (Powers of Criminal Courts (Sentencing) Act 2000 (PCC(S)A 2000), ss 111–115).

(e)   Definition – Theft Act 1968, s 9:

    (1)   A person is guilty of burglary if—

        (a)   he enters any building or part of a building as a trespasser and with intent to commit any such offence as is mentioned in subsection (2) below; or

        (b)   having entered any building or part of a building as a trespasser he steals or attempts to steal anything in the building or that part of it or inflicts or attempts to inflict on any person therein any grievous bodily harm.

    (2)   The offences referred to in subsection (1)(a) above are offences of stealing anything in the building or part of a building in question, of inflicting on any person therein any grievous bodily harm, and of doing unlawful damage to the building or anything therein.'

1.6.3 Robbery

(a)   Classification – triable only on indictment.

(b)   Robbery is an arrestable offence within the meaning of the Police and Criminal Evidence Act 1984, s 24.

(c)   Maximum penalties – life imprisonment and/or unlimited fine.

(d)   Definition – Theft Act 1968, s 8(1):

    A person is guilty of robbery if he steals and immediately before or at the time of doing so, and in order to do so, he uses force on any person or puts or seeks to put any person in fear of being then and there subjected to force.

1.6.4 Obtaining property by deception

(a)   Classification – either way.

(b)   The offence is an arrestable offence within the meaning of the Police and Criminal Evidence Act 1984, s 24.

(c)   Maximum penalties – Crown Court: 10 years' imprisonment and/or unlimited fine; Magistrates' court: 6 months' imprisonment and/or £5000 fine.

(d)   Definition – Theft Act 1968, s 15:

    (1)   A person who by any deception dishonestly obtains property belonging to another, with the intention of permanently depriving the other of it ...

    (4)   For the purposes of this section 'deception' means any deception (whether deliberate or reckless) by words or conduct as to fact or as to law, including a deception as to the present intentions of the person using the deception or any other person.

1.6.5 Possession of a controlled drug

(a)   Classification – either way in respect of any class of drug.

    Class A drugs include inter alia cocaine, heroin, LSD and ecstasy (MDA, MDMA and MDEA).

    Class B drugs include inter alia amphetamines and codeine.

    Class C drugs include inter alia cannabis and cannabis resin.

(b)   The offence is an arrestable offence within the meaning of the Police and Criminal Evidence Act 1984, s 24.

(c)   Maximum penalties

    Crown Court:

Class A – 7 years' imprisonment and/or unlimited fine.

Class B – 5 years' imprisonment and/or unlimited fine.

Class C – 2 years' imprisonment and/or unlimited fine.

Magistrates' court:

Class A – 6 months' imprisonment and/or £5000 fine.

Class B – 3 months' imprisonment and/or £2500 fine.

Class C – 3 months' imprisonment and/or £1000 fine.

(d)   Definition – Misuse of Drugs Act 1971, s 5:

(1)   ... it shall not be lawful for a person to have a controlled drug in his possession.

(2)   Subject to section 28 of this Act and to subsection (4) below, it is an offence for a person to have a controlled drug in his possession in contravention of subsection (1) above.

(4)   In any proceedings for an offence under subsection (2) above in which it is proved that the accused had a controlled drug in his possession, it shall be a defence for him to prove—

(a)   that, knowing or suspecting it to be a controlled drug, he took possession of it for the purpose of preventing another from committing or continuing to commit an offence in connection with that drug and that as soon as possible after taking possession of it he took all such steps as were reasonably open to him to destroy the drug or to deliver it into the custody of a person lawfully entitled to take custody of it; or

(b)   that, knowing or suspecting it to be a controlled drug, he took possession of it for the purpose of delivering it into the custody of a person lawfully entitled to take custody of it and that as soon as possible after taking possession of it he took all such steps as were reasonably open to him to deliver it into the custody of such a person.

(e)   Defence under s 28

(1)   This section applies to offences under any of the following provisions of this Act, that is to say section 4(2) and (3), section 5(2) and (3), section 6(2) and section 9.

(2)   Subject to subsection (3) below, in any proceedings for an offence to which this section applies it shall be a defence for the accused to prove that he neither knew of nor suspected nor had reason to suspect the existence of some fact alleged by the prosecution which it is necessary for the prosecution to prove if he is to be convicted of the offence charged.

(3)   Where in any proceedings for an offence to which this section applies it is necessary, if the accused is to be convicted of the offence charged, for the prosecution to prove that some substance or product involved in the alleged offence was the controlled drug which the prosecution alleges it to have been, and it is proved that the substance or product in question was that controlled drug, the accused—

(a)   shall not be acquitted of the offence charged by reason only of proving that he neither knew nor suspected nor had reason to suspect that the substance or product in question was the particular controlled drug alleged; but

(b)   shall be acquitted thereof—

(i)   if he proves that he neither believed nor suspected nor had reason to suspect that the substance or product in question was a controlled drug; or

(ii)   if he proves that he believed the substance or product in question to be a controlled drug, or a controlled drug of a description, such that, if it had in fact been that controlled drug or a controlled drug of that description, he would not at the material time have been committing any offence to which this section applies.

(4)   Nothing in this section shall prejudice any defence which it is open to a person charged with an offence to which this section applies to raise apart from this section.

The House of Lords in *R v Lambert* [2001] 3 WLR 206 decided that the placing of a legal burden on the defence was contrary to the ECHR, art 6. As a result, s 28 imposes an evidential burden only on the defence.

Section 28 does not apply to conspiracies as they are not offences under the Misuse of Drugs Act 1971 (*R v McGowan* [1990] Crim LR 399).

1.6.6   Production or supply of a controlled drug

(a)   Classification — either way in respect of any class of drug.

(b)   The offence is an arrestable offence within the meaning of the Police and Criminal Evidence Act 1984, s 24.

(c)   Maximum penalties

Crown Court:

Class A – life imprisonment and/or unlimited fine.

Class B – 14 years' imprisonment and/or unlimited fine.

Class C – 14 years' imprisonment and/or unlimited fine.

Magistrates' court:

Class A – 6 months' imprisonment and/or £5000 fine.

Class B – 6 months' imprisonment and/or £5000 fine.

Class C – 3 months' imprisonment and/or £2500 fine.

(d)   Definition – Misuse of Drugs Act 1971, s 4:

(1)   It shall not be lawful for a person—

(a)   to produce a controlled drug; or

(b)   to supply or offer to supply a controlled drug to another.

(3)   Subject to section 28 of this Act, it is an offence for a person—

(a)   to supply or offer to supply, a controlled drug to another in contravention of subsection 1 above; or

(b)   to be concerned in the supplying of such a drug to another in contravention of that subsection; or

(c)   to be concerned in the making to another in contravention of that subsection of an offer to supply such a drug.

1.6.7   Possession of a controlled drug with intent to supply

(a)   Classification – either way in respect of any class of drug.

(b)   The offence is an arrestable offence within the meaning of the Police and Criminal Evidence Act 1984, s 24.

(c)   Maximum penalties

Crown Court:

Class A – life imprisonment and/or unlimited fine.

Class B – 14 years' imprisonment and/or unlimited fine.

Class C – 14 years' imprisonment and/or unlimited fine.

Magistrates' court:

Class A – 6 months' imprisonment and/or £5000 fine.

Class B – 6 months' imprisonment and/or £5000 fine.

Class C – 3 months' imprisonment and/or £2500 fine.

(d)   Definition – Misuse of Drugs Act 1971, s 5

(3)   Subject to section 28 of this Act, it is an offence for a person to have a controlled drug in his possession, whether lawfully or not, with intent to supply it to another in contravention of section 4(1) of this Act.

1.6.8 Conspiracy

(a)   Classification – indictable only.

(b)   The offence is an arrestable offence within the meaning of the Police and Criminal Evidence Act 1984, s 24.

(c)   Maximum penalties – the maximum is the same as the maximum provided for the completed offence.

(d)   Definition – Criminal Law Act 1977, s 1:

(1)   ... if a person agrees with any other person or persons that a course of conduct will be pursued which, if the agreement is carried out in accordance with their intentions, either—

(a)   will necessarily amount to or involve the commission of any offence or offences by one or more of the parties to the agreement; or

(b)   would do so but for the existence of facts which render the commission of the offence or any of the offences impossible, he is guilty of conspiracy to commit the offence or offences in question.

(4)   In this part of this Act 'offence' means an offence triable in England and Wales.

1.6.9 Common assault

(a)   Classification – summary only.

(b)   The offence is not an arrestable offence within the meaning of the Police and Criminal Evidence Act 1984, s 24.

(c)   Maximum penalties – 6 months' imprisonment and/or £5000 fine.

(d)   Definition:

There are two ways of committing a common assault; a simple assault or a physical assault (sometimes referred to as a battery). A simple assault is committed when the defendant, intentionally or recklessly, causes the victim to apprehend immediate and unlawful personal violence. A physical assault consists of the infliction of unlawful personal violence, either intentionally or recklessly, by the defendant upon the victim.

All common assaults are offences contrary to the Criminal Justice Act 1988, s 39 and the wording of the charge should make clear whether the prosecution is alleging a simple assault ('assault') or a physical assault ('assault by beating').

1.6.10 Assault occasioning actual bodily harm

(a)   Classification – either way.

(b)   The offence is an arrestable offence within the meaning of the Police and Criminal Evidence Act 1984, s 24.

(c)   Maximum penalties – Crown Court: 5 years' imprisonment and/or unlimited fine. Magistrates' court: 6 months' imprisonment and/or £5,000 fine.

(d)   Definition – Offences Against the Person Act 1861, s 47:

... assault occasioning actual bodily harm.

Any injury can be classified as actual bodily harm. However, the Crown Prosecution Service *Charging Standards* document (issued in April 1996) makes it clear that a s 47 charge is not appropriate if the injuries amount to no more than 'grazes, scratches, abrasions, minor bruising, superficial cuts or a black eye'. For such minor injuries, the appropriate charge is common assault. A verdict of assault occasioning actual bodily harm may be returned on proof of an assault together with proof that actual bodily harm was occasioned by the assault. The prosecution do not have to prove that the defendant intended to cause some actual bodily harm or was reckless as to whether such harm would be caused (*R v Savage*; *R v Parmenter* [1991] 4 All ER 698).

1.6.11 Wounding or inflicting grievous bodily harm

(a)   Classification – either way.

(b)   The offence is an arrestable offence within the Police and Criminal Evidence Act 1984, s 24.

(c)   Maximum penalties

Crown Court: 5 years' imprisonment and/or unlimited fine.

Magistrates' court: 6 months' imprisonment and/or £5000 fine.

(d)   Definition – Offences Against the Person Act 1861, s 20:

> Whosoever shall unlawfully and maliciously wound or inflict grievous bodily harm upon any other person, either with or without any weapon or instrument, shall be guilty of [an offence], and being convicted thereof shall be liable to [imprisonment for not more than five years].

A wound requires the breaking of two layers of skin. In theory, even trivial wounds may qualify, but the Charging Standards urge that minor wounds should not, in practice, be charged under s 20. Grievous bodily harm means really serious harm (*Director of Public Prosecutions v Smith* [1961] AC 290). The Charging Standards list examples of injuries which should normally be prosecuted under s 20, for example, injury resulting in permanent disability or permanent loss of sensory function; injury which results in more than minor permanent, visible disfigurement; broken or displaced limbs or bones, including fractured skull; compound fractures, broken cheek bone, jaw, ribs, etc; injuries which cause substantial loss of blood, usually necessitating a transfusion; and injuries resulting in lengthy treatment or incapacity.

The prosecution must prove that either the defendant intended, or actually foresaw, that the act would cause some harm. It is not necessary to prove that the defendant intended or foresaw that the unlawful act might cause the physical harm described in s 20. It is enough that the defendant foresaw that some physical harm to some person, albeit of a minor character, might result (*R v Savage*; *R v Parmenter*).

1.6.12 Secondary participation

A person who aids, abets, counsels or procures the commission of an offence is a secondary party. Basically, aiding is giving assistance, abetting is giving encouragement at the time of the commission of the offence, counselling is giving encouragement earlier, and procuring is bringing about the offence.

An accomplice will often be jointly charged with a principal offender.

Example

John Smith steals goods while Alan Jones keeps a lookout.

Alan Jones' charge may read:

'Jointly with John Smith stole ...' etc.

The charge reads as though Alan Jones is a principal offender. This is permissible by virtue of the Accessories and Abettors Act 1861, s 8.

1.7 Professional ethics

A solicitor involved in criminal litigation faces many ethical problems. Should a prosecutor reveal information to the defence which will assist the defence case? Can you act for a client who tells you that he is guilty but who wishes to plead not guilty? How should you react to a major change of story by your client? This section seeks to identify the major ethical problems which are likely to arise in a criminal case and suggests solutions to them.

1.7.1 Duty not to mislead the court

The general principle for a solicitor involved in criminal proceedings is that, while he owes a duty to his client to do his best for him, a solicitor must not mislead or deceive the court.

1.7.2 The prosecution

Prosecuting advocates are under a duty to ensure that all material evidence supporting the prosecution case is put before the court in a dispassionate and fair manner. In particular:

(a) all relevant facts known to the prosecution should be put before the court including, after conviction, facts relevant to mitigation;

(b) if a prosecution witness gives evidence in court which is inconsistent with any earlier statement made, there is a duty to disclose this fact to the defence.

When arguing a point of law, all relevant legal authorities should be cited, including those which are against the prosecution.

1.7.3 The defence

A number of ethical problems can arise when conducting a criminal defence. Always bear in mind the duty not to mislead the court (see **1.7.1**). In addition, the following guidelines may be of assistance.

(a) The client who admits his guilt. This may happen before or during the course of proceedings. If the client insists on giving evidence in the witness box denying his guilt, then a solicitor should decline to act. It is, however, proper to act on a not guilty plea if the defence merely intends to put the prosecution to proof of its case without calling defence evidence.

(b) Occasionally, a client will wish to plead guilty notwithstanding that his instructions indicate that he has a defence. Such a client should be advised of the defence available. If he insists on pleading guilty, the solicitor may continue to act but should advise the client that in mitigation it will not be possible to rely on facts that may constitute a defence.

(c) The client who gives inconsistent instructions. The mere fact that a client makes inconsistent statements to his solicitor does not make it improper for the solicitor to continue to act. If it becomes clear that the client is changing his instructions with a view to putting forward false evidence to the court, the solicitor should refuse to act.

(d) Disclosure of the defence case. A solicitor should not, without the express consent of his client, disclose details of his client's case to any other party. Requests for disclosure sometimes come, for example, from the solicitors acting for a co-defendant. Such requests should be treated with caution and the client's instructions taken.

(e)   Arguing a point of law. All relevant authorities should be cited, including those which are against the advocate. This is a positive duty to assist the court in contrast to matters of fact where the duty is a negative one – not to mislead the court.

(f)   The client who gives a false name to the court. A solicitor should not act for a client who, to the knowledge of the solicitor, gives a false name, address or date of birth to the court. If faced with this problem the solicitor should try to persuade the client to change his mind. If the client refuses to do so then the solicitor should cease to act.

(g)   Knowledge of previous convictions. On occasion, the list of previous convictions of a defendant produced to the court by the prosecution will be inaccurate. If asked to confirm the accuracy of the list, a solicitor should decline to comment. To confirm the list as accurate would amount to a positive deception of the court. A solicitor should not mislead the court. On the other hand, disclosing previous convictions without the client's express consent is a breach of the duty of confidentiality to the client. The solicitor should, wherever possible, obtain a list of previous convictions from the police or CPS sufficiently in advance of going to court so that he can discuss any problems with the client. The client should be warned of the dangers of misleading the court. If the client insists that, if asked, he will pretend the list is accurate, the solicitor must cease to act (see the *Guide to the Professional Conduct of Solicitors* (The Law Society, 1999), Annex 21F).

(h)   Conflicts of interest. A solicitor must not continue to act for two or more defendants where a conflict of interest arises between them. Within the context of criminal proceedings, a conflict can arise, for example, where one defendant decides to blame the other and changes his plea to not guilty. Even where pleas are consistent it may not be possible to act for the defendants if one is seeking to implicate the other or to allege that one played a larger role in the offence than the other. If a conflict arises while a solicitor is acting for both defendants then he should consider withdrawing from the case altogether. This would be appropriate where the solicitor has information in his possession about one defendant which could be used to assist the other defendant in the case.

(i)   Interviewing prosecution witnesses. Although there is no property in a witness, defence solicitors should proceed with caution when intending to interview a prosecution witness. The best course of action is to notify the prosecution of the fact that a witness is to be interviewed and to invite a representative to attend as an observer. This will avoid suspicion of an attempt to pervert the course of justice and allegations that a witness has been pressured in some way to change his evidence.

(j)   If circumstances arise which require a solicitor to withdraw from a case (for example, see (f) and (g) above), the reason for withdrawal should not normally be given to the court. The solicitor should simply explain that a matter has arisen which makes it impossible for him to continue to act in the case.

1.8   European Convention on Human Rights

The Human Rights Act 1998, which came into force on 2 October 2000, is intended to give effect in domestic law to the rights and freedoms guaranteed by the European Convention for the Protection of Human Rights and Fundamental Freedoms (the Convention), to which the UK is a party.

(a) All legislation must, if possible, be interpreted so as to be compatible with the Convention (s 3(1)). Domestic courts must strive to find a construction consistent with the intentions of Parliament and the wording of legislation which is nearest to Convention rights. Courts should proceed on the basis that Parliament is deemed to have intended its statutes to be compatible with the Convention. The only basis for the courts concluding that Parliament has failed to carry that intention into effect is where it is impossible to construe a statute so as to be compatible with the Convention (Lord Chancellor, 18 November 1997, House of Lords Committee Stage, *Hansard,* col 535).

(b) Where it is not possible to interpret primary legislation so as to be compatible with the Convention, the courts will have no power to strike it down. However, the House of Lords, the Judicial Committee of the Privy Council, the Court of Appeal and the High Court will have power to make a 'declaration of incompatibility' which (in theory) should prompt government action. Such a declaration does not affect the validity, continuing operation or enforcement of the provision in respect of which it is made (s 4(6)(a)). Nor does it bind the parties to the proceedings in which it is made (s 4(6)(b)). It is intended to operate as a clear signal to Parliament that an incompatibility has been found.

The government envisages that a declaration of incompatibility will 'almost certainly' prompt legislative change (White Paper, 'Rights Brought Home: The Human Rights Bill' (Cm 3782), para 2.9). The Act provides a 'fast track' procedure for amending the law so as to bring it into conformity with the Convention (s 10).

(c) Where it simply is not possible to interpret subordinate legislation so as to be compatible with the Convention, the courts have power to disapply it. The only exception is where primary legislation prevents the removal of any incompatibility (s 4(4)(b)).

(d) All public authorities, including all courts and tribunals, must, if possible, act in a way which is compatible with the Convention. Public authorities include (but are not limited to) courts, tribunals and 'any person certain of whose functions are functions of a public nature' (s 6(3)). The definition is in wide terms and is intended to cover the police.

(e) Individuals who believe that their Convention rights have been infringed by a public authority can rely on their rights as a defence in civil and criminal proceedings or as the basis of an appeal, alternatively seek judicial review, or bring civil proceedings for damages (s 7 and s 8).

(f) Section 8(1) of the Act provides that:

In relation to any act (or proposed act) of a public authority which the court finds is (or would be) unlawful, it may grant such relief or remedy, or make such order, within its powers as it considers just and appropriate.

As a result, criminal courts will have the power to stay proceedings as an abuse of process, quash an indictment or charge, rule evidence inadmissible, quash convictions and even recognise new defences where Convention rights have been violated.

(g) In resolving Convention issues, all courts and tribunals must take into account the case-law of the European Court of Human Rights, Commission of Human Rights and the Committee of Ministers established under the Convention (s 2).

Since the Act came into force, practitioners have been able to rely on the Convention in criminal proceedings. Practitioners can test domestic law and practice for compliance with the Convention, particularly:

Article 3

Prohibition of torture

No one shall be subjected to torture or to inhuman or degrading treatment or punishment. ...

Article 5

Right to liberty and security

1. Everyone has the right to liberty and security of person. No one shall be deprived of his liberty save in the following cases and in accordance with a procedure prescribed by law:

    (a)   the lawful detention of a person after conviction by a competent court;

    (b)   the lawful arrest or detention of a person for non-compliance with the lawful order of a court or in order to secure the fulfilment of any obligation prescribed by law;

    (c)   the lawful arrest or detention of a person effected for the purpose of bringing him before the competent legal authority on reasonable suspicion of having committed an offence or when it is reasonably considered necessary to prevent his committing an offence or fleeing after having done so;

    (d)   the detention of a minor by lawful order for the purpose of educational supervision or his lawful detention for the purpose of bringing him before the competent legal authority;

    (e)   the lawful detention of persons for the prevention of the spreading of infectious diseases, of persons of unsound mind, alcoholics or drug addicts or vagrants;

    (f)   the lawful arrest or detention of a person to prevent his effecting an unauthorised entry into the country or of a person against whom action is being taken with a view to deportation or extradition.

2. Everyone who is arrested shall be informed promptly, in a language which he understands, of the reasons for his arrest and of any charge against him.

3. Everyone arrested or detained in accordance with the provisions of paragraph 1(c) of this Article shall be brought promptly before a judge or other officer authorised by law to exercise judicial power and shall be entitled to trial within a reasonable time or to release pending trial. Release may be conditioned by guarantees to appear for trial.

4. Everyone who is deprived of his liberty by arrest or detention shall be entitled to take proceedings by which the lawfulness of his detention shall be decided speedily by a court and his release ordered if the detention is not lawful.

5. Everyone who has been the victim of arrest or detention in contravention of the provisions of this Article shall have an enforceable right to compensation.

Article 6

Right to a fair trial

1. In the determination of his civil rights and obligations or of any criminal charge against him, everyone is entitled to a fair and public hearing within a reasonable time by an independent and impartial tribunal established by law. Judgment shall be pronounced publicly but the press and public may be excluded from all or part of the trial in the interest of morals, public order or national security in a democratic society, where the interests of juveniles or the protection of the private life of the parties so require, or to the extent strictly necessary in the opinion of the court in special circumstances where publicity would prejudice the interests of justice.

2. Everyone charged with a criminal offence shall be presumed innocent until proved guilty according to the law.

3.   Everyone charged with a criminal offence has the following minimum rights:

(a)   to be informed promptly, in a language which he understands and in detail, of the nature and cause of the accusation against him;

(b)   to have adequate time and facilities for the preparation of his defence;

(c)   to defend himself in person or through legal assistance of his own choosing or, if he has not sufficient means to pay for legal assistance, to be given it free when the interests of justice so require;

(d)   to examine or have examined witnesses against him and to obtain the attendance and examination of witnesses on his behalf under the same conditions as witnesses against him;

(e)   to have the free assistance of an interpreter if he cannot understand or speak the language used in court.

Article 7

No punishment without law

1.   No one shall be held guilty of any criminal offence on account of any act or omission which did not constitute a criminal offence under national or international law at the time when it was committed. Nor shall a heavier penalty be imposed than the one that was applicable at the time the criminal offence was committed.

2.   This Article shall not prejudice the trial and punishment of any person for any act or omission which, at the time when it was committed, was criminal according to the general principles of law recognised by civilised nations.

There is no rule under the Act requiring a Convention point to be taken at any given stage in criminal proceedings. Convention points can be taken before the trial (eg, by challenging the charge or indictment), at trial (by seeking to exclude evidence obtained in breach of the Convention or limiting the basis upon which adverse inferences can be drawn), or on appeal (eg, by quashing a conviction on the basis that it was obtained in breach of the Convention). It is possible that courts may also examine Convention issues of their own volition since they are 'public authorities' under s 6 and, accordingly, are obliged to act in accordance with the Convention.

1.9   Further reading

See, for example:

Archbold: Criminal Pleading, Evidence and Practice (Sweet & Maxwell, 2004)

Blackstone's Criminal Practice (Oxford University Press, 2004)

Pervasive and Core Topics

The Guide to the Professional Conduct of Solicitors (The Law Society, 1999)

J Wadham and H Mountfield, *Blackstone's Guide to the Human Rights Act 1998*, 3rd edn (Oxford University Press, 2003)

Chapter 2

The Suspect in the Police Station

2.1	Introduction	17
2.2	The serious arrestable offence (PACE 1984, s 116 and Sch 5)	17
2.3	Police powers of detention	18
2.4	The right to legal advice	21
2.5	Interviewing the suspect	22
2.6	Methods of interview	23
2.7	The right to have a solicitor present at interviews	25
2.8	Safeguards for the suspect	25
2.9	Tactical considerations	27
2.10	Identification	37
2.11	Evidential considerations	40
2.12	Samples	41
2.13	Alternatives to prosecution	41
2.14	Further reading	43

2.1 Introduction

The police have wide powers to arrest and detain a person, without charge, if that person is suspected of having committed a criminal offence. A suspect who is detained in a police station has the right to legal advice. A solicitor's role in the police station involves advising a suspect of his rights, 'sitting in' on police interviews with a suspect, ensuring 'fair play' in the police station and attending identification parades. This chapter examines the law governing the detention, treatment and questioning of a suspect and considers the role of a solicitor in the police station. The law is contained primarily in the Police and Criminal Evidence Act 1984 (PACE 1984), the Codes of Practice issued under that Act and the Criminal Justice and Public Order Act 1994. References to section numbers in this chapter are, unless otherwise stated, to the Police and Criminal Evidence Act 1984. References to 'Code C' are to the Code of Practice on the Detention, Treatment and Questioning of Suspects (see **Appendix 6**), references to 'Code D' are to the Code of Practice on Identification Procedures (see **Appendix 6**) and references to 'Code E' are to the Code of Practice on Tape Recording of Interviews with Suspects. A diagram showing some of the ranks in the police appears at **Appendix 1(B)**.

2.2 The serious arrestable offence (PACE 1984, s 116 and Sch 5)

An important concept running through the Police and Criminal Evidence Act 1984 is the serious arrestable offence. It is relevant to the powers of the police to detain a suspect for more than 36 hours and to delay access to legal advice.

Of the offences covered in this book, the following are arrestable offences:

Theft

Burglary

Robbery

Assault occasioning actual bodily harm

Wounding or inflicting grievous bodily harm.

Obtaining property by deception

Possession of a controlled drug

Production or supply of a controlled drug

Possession of a controlled drug with intent to supply

Conspiracy

An offence listed above will be a serious arrestable offence if:

(a)   it has led, inter alia, to the death of any person, serious injury of any person, substantial financial gain to any person, or serious financial loss to any person; or

(b)   it is intended or is likely to lead to any of the consequences in (a) above.

Serious financial loss is assessed subjectively. Thus, theft of a relatively small amount of money from a poor person can legitimately be treated as a serious arrestable offence. Substantial financial gain is assessed objectively.

The initial decision as to whether an offence under investigation is a serious arrestable offence will be taken by a superintendent at the police station where a suspect is being held. If necessary, the defence can challenge the decision in court. This may be done, for example, as part of an argument that a confession should not be admitted in evidence (see **Chapter 9**).

In practice, the detailed provisions of the Act must be consulted if there is doubt as to whether an offence is a serious arrestable offence.

2.3   Police powers of detention

A flowchart showing procedure at the police station is included at **Appendix 1(C)**.

2.3.1   Volunteers

A person sometimes attends a police station on a voluntary basis to assist the police with their enquiries. Section 29 of the Act provides that:

Where for the purposes of assisting with an investigation a person attends voluntarily at a police station ... without having been arrested:

(a)   he shall be entitled to leave at will unless he is placed under arrest;

(b)   he shall be informed at once that he is under arrest if a decision is taken by a constable to prevent him from leaving at will.

The status of a suspect is likely to change from volunteer to arrested suspect if answers given to police questions give rise to a reasonable suspicion that the detainee may have committed an offence.

2.3.2   Persons under arrest

Where a suspect is arrested at any place other than a police station, he must be taken to a police station by a police officer as soon as practicable after the arrest (s 30).

A person who is arrested and taken to a police station is taken before the custody officer. The custody officer is a police officer of at least the rank of sergeant. The custody officer:

shall determine whether he has before him sufficient evidence to charge that person with the offence for which he was arrested and may detain him at the police station for such period as is necessary to enable him to do so (s 37(1)).

To enable the custody officer to determine whether there is sufficient evidence to charge the arrested person, he will usually speak to the arresting officer. The test to be applied in determining whether there is sufficient evidence to charge is whether there is sufficient evidence to provide a realistic prospect of a conviction (Code C, para 16.1).

In all but the most trivial of offences there is unlikely to be sufficient evidence to charge the suspect at this stage.

> If the custody officer determines that he does not have such evidence before him the person arrested shall be released either on bail or without bail unless the custody officer has reasonable grounds for believing that his detention without being charged is necessary to secure or preserve evidence relating to an offence for which he is under arrest or to obtain such evidence by questioning him (s 37(2)).
>
> If the custody officer has reasonable grounds for so believing he may authorise the person arrested to be kept in police detention (s 37(3)).

A suspect can, therefore, be detained for samples to be taken or while premises are searched. The most common ground for detention without charge is to question the suspect.

The custody officer is required to open and maintain a custody record for each suspect taken to the police station. The grounds for detention without charge must be recorded in the custody record and a chronological record of events occurring during the suspect's period of detention must be kept. An example of a custody record appears at **Appendix 2(A)**.

A legal representative attending the police station to advise a suspect is entitled to inspect the custody record (Code C, para 2.4). A copy of the custody record must be given to the suspect or his legal representative on request when the suspect is taken before a court or upon the suspect's release from police detention.

2.3.3 Periods of detention without charge

The basic detention process can conveniently be illustrated in chart form (see **Appendix 1(D)**).

The following points in particular should be noted.

(a) The basic maximum period of detention without charge is 24 hours. Normally, this runs from the time the arrested person arrives at the police station. If the person went to the police station on a voluntary basis, then time runs from when he is arrested at the police station.

(b) If the offence under investigation is an arrestable offence further detention up to 36 hours on the detention clock can be authorised by a superintendent on certain specified grounds (s 42).

(c) Detention beyond 36 hours can only be authorised by a magistrates' court on the granting of a warrant of further detention. A warrant of further detention is only available if the offence is a serious arrestable offence (s 43). A warrant may initially be granted for a period not exceeding 36 hours but can be extended for further periods until 96 hours have expired on the detention clock. This is the absolute maximum period of detention without charge.

(d) A review of detention must be carried out by an inspector within 6 hours of detention being first authorised and thereafter at 9-hourly intervals. This is to ensure that the initial grounds for detention still exist. Details of the reviews must be recorded in the custody record.

2.3.4   The decision to charge

Traditionally the decision to charge has been in the hands of the police. Increasingly the CPS is being consulted by the police on whether a suspect should be charged and, if so, with what offence. When the Criminal Justice Act 2003, s 3 and Sch 2 is in force nationwide, the CPS will become responsible for determining the charge in all but the most routine cases. The police will still charge minor or routine cases without reference to the CPS. The Director of Public Prosecutions will issue guidance on what can be charged without reference to the CPS and what must be referred pre-charge to the CPS.

2.3.5   Bail following charge

When a person has been charged with an offence, the custody officer must decide whether to keep that person in custody until his court appearance. Section 38(1) provides that:

> Where a person arrested for an offence ... is charged with an offence, the custody officer shall ... order his release from police detention, either on bail or without bail, unless—
>
> (a)   ...
>
> (i)   his name or address cannot be ascertained or the custody officer has reasonable grounds for doubting whether a name or address furnished by him as his name or address is his real name or address;
>
> (ii)   the custody officer has reasonable grounds for believing that the person arrested will fail to appear in court to answer to bail;
>
> (iii)   in the case of a person arrested for an imprisonable offence, the custody officer has reasonable grounds for believing that the detention of the person arrested is necessary to prevent him from committing an offence;
>
> (iv)   in the case of a person arrested for an offence which is not an imprisonable offence, the custody officer has reasonable grounds for believing that the detention of the person arrested is necessary to prevent him from causing physical injury to any other person or from causing loss of or damage to property;
>
> (v)   the custody officer has reasonable grounds for believing that the detention of the person arrested is necessary to prevent him from interfering with the administration of justice or with the investigation of offences or of a particular offence; or
>
> (vi)   the custody officer has reasonable grounds for believing that the detention of the person arrested is necessary for his own protection.'

The custody officer, in deciding whether grounds (ii)–(v) apply, must have regard to the same factors as a court is required to consider when taking a bail decision (see **3.4.3**).

The custody officer has power, when granting bail, to impose the same conditions as a court (with the exception of residence at a bail hostel) (Bail Act 1976, s 3A). A full discussion of conditions of bail and when they may be appropriate can be found at **3.4.3**.

2.3.6   Release without charge on bail

The police may decide that there is insufficient evidence to charge a person with an offence but require him to return to the police station at a later date. This may happen for example, if the police have further enquires to make or where they are waiting for the results of forensic tests or they need to refer the matter to the CPS for a decision on whether or not to charge. In such a case, the person is released on bail. Where a person has been released on bail to return to the police station on a specified date, he may be arrested without a warrant if he fails to attend at the appointed time (Police and Criminal Evidence Act 1984, s 46A).

Section 34 of the Police and Criminal Evidence Act 1984 provides that where a person returns to the police station to answer bail (or is arrested for failing to do so) he is to be regarded as having been arrested for the original offence at that moment. Therefore, the person is in the same position as a person who is being detained without charge and so the rules governing detention without charge set out in **2.3.3** apply.

2.4 The right to legal advice

2.4.1 Volunteers

A person who is attending a police station on a voluntary basis and who is not under arrest has an absolute right to legal advice in private or to communicate with anyone outside the police station at any time (Code C, note 1A). These rights are confirmed in a written notice given to the suspect (see **Appendix 2(B)**).

2.4.2 Persons under arrest

Where a person has been arrested and is being held in custody in a police station, or other premises, he shall be entitled, if he requests, to have one friend or relative or other person who is known to him or is likely to take an interest in his welfare told, as soon as practicable ... , that he has been arrested and is being detained there. (s 56(1))

A person arrested and held in custody in a police station or other premises shall be entitled, if he so requests, to consult a solicitor privately at any time. (s 58)

On arrival at the police station, the suspect will be informed by the custody officer of the right to legal advice and that it is free of charge, the right to have someone informed of his arrest and the right to consult the Codes of Practice. These rights are confirmed in a written notice given to the suspect (see **Appendix 2(C)** and **(D)**). The suspect is then asked to sign the custody record to indicate whether or not he wishes to exercise his rights (see the custody record referred to at **2.3.2**). Even if the suspect indicates that he does not want to exercise his rights, he is entitled to change his mind at any time while he is in police detention.

The suspect is entitled to advice in person, in writing or by telephone (Code C, para 6.1) from his own solicitor, if available, or the duty solicitor. Duty solicitor schemes operate throughout most of the country to ensure that a solicitor is available on a 24-hour basis to attend police stations to advise suspects who are being detained. The advice and assistance given is free of charge, irrespective of the suspect's means, and the solicitor attending the police station is paid under contract on a fixed hourly rate by the Legal Services Commission.

2.4.3 Delaying access to legal advice

The right of access to legal advice can be delayed for a period not exceeding 36 hours from the time of the suspect's arrival at the police station if:

(a)   ... a person is in police detention ... for a serious arrestable offence; and

(b)   if an officer of at least the rank of superintendent authorises it. (s 58(6))

A superintendent can authorise the delaying of access to legal advice only if he has reasonable grounds for believing that the exercise of the right:

(a)   will lead to interference with or harm to evidence connected with a serious arrestable offence or interference with or physical injury to other persons; or

(b)   will lead to the alerting of other persons suspected of having committed such an offence but not yet arrested for it; or

(c)   will hinder the recovery of any property obtained as a result of such an offence. (s 58(8))

In effect, a superintendent may lawfully authorise delaying access to legal advice only if he has reasonable grounds to believe that the specific solicitor seeking access will, inadvertently or otherwise, pass on a message from the suspect which will lead to any of the consequences listed above coming about. Even if the superintendent has such grounds, he is required to offer the suspect access to a different solicitor (see Code C, Annex B, para A3).

- Access to legal advice cannot be delayed on grounds that:

(a)   the solicitor might advise the suspect not to answer questions (Code C, Annex B, para A4); or

(b)   the solicitor was initially instructed by a third party, provided the suspect wishes to see the solicitor. The suspect must be told that the solicitor has come to the police station and must be asked to sign the custody record to signify whether or not he wishes to see the solicitor (Code C, para 6.15 and Code C, Annex B, para A4).

The statutory right for a suspect to have a friend or relative notified of his arrest can be delayed on similar grounds to those for delayed access to legal advice.

2.5   Interviewing the suspect

2.5.1   What is an interview?

An interview is the questioning of a person regarding his involvement or suspected involvement in a criminal offence or offences which, under paragraph 10.1 must be carried out under caution (Code C, para 11.1A).

Example

A police officer notices a young man standing on a street corner with a large bag. He asks the man what he is doing. The replies are evasive. This will not be an interview. The officer then notices a broken window in the shop on the corner and that the man has fragments of glass on his clothing. Any further questioning will constitute an interview. The significance of this is that the rules on the conduct of interviews must be followed (see 2.5.2–2.8).

Questioning solely to establish identity or ownership of a vehicle, or 'in furtherance of the proper and effective conduct of a search' is not an interview (Code C, para 10.1).

2.5.2   Interview following arrest

Following a decision to arrest a suspect, that suspect must not be interviewed about the relevant offence except at a police station (or other authorised place of detention) unless the consequent delay would be likely to:

(a)   lead to interference with, or harm to, evidence connected with an offence or interference with, or physical harm to, other people; or serious loss of, or damage to, property; or

(b)   lead to the alerting of other persons suspected of having committed such an offence but not yet arrested for it; or

(c)   hinder the recovery of property obtained in consequence of the commission of such an offence (Code C, para 11.1).

2.5.3   Interview after charge

Following charge, no further questions relating to the offence charged may be put unless further questioning is necessary to:

(a)   prevent or minimise harm or loss to some other person or to the public; or

(b)   clear up an ambiguity in a previous answer or statement; or

(c)   give the suspect an opportunity to comment on information concerning the offence which has come to light since he was charged (Code C, para 16.5).

If any statement or interview record involving another person is to be put to the suspect, no reply or comment should be invited (Code C, para 16.4).

2.6   Methods of interview

2.6.1   Tape recording

All interviews at the police station except those concerning purely summary offences should be tape recorded. The purpose of the tape-recording procedures is to provide an impartial and accurate record of police interviews with suspects in the police station (Code E, para 2.1).

Two tapes are used at an interview. When an interview comes to an end, the master tape should be sealed and signed by the suspect or by an interviewing officer. The other tape is the working copy from which a summary of the tape-recorded interview will be prepared by the police (Code E, para 2.2).

A summary of the tape-recorded interview will be sent to the defence. The defence has a right of access to a working copy of the tape and the defence solicitor will often listen to the tape to check the accuracy of the summary prepared by the prosecution.

If the defence agrees that the summary served by the prosecution is acceptable then it will be admissible in evidence at the trial (subject to any argument over the admissibility of any confession that may have been made (see **9.6.3**)). See the example of a record of a tape-recorded interview at **Appendix 2(E)**.

If the defence does not agree with the summary then the tape can be transcribed in full for use at the trial. If necessary, the tape can be played at the trial. The tape to be played in court will be the master copy and the seal will be broken in court. It may be necessary to play the tape in court where the manner in which something has been said is relevant; for example, if the admissibility of a confession is being challenged because of the conduct of the police during the interview, the way in which questions have been put may be relevant.

2.6.2   Non-taped interviews

Not all interviews will be tape recorded. A suspect may, on occasions, be interviewed somewhere other than a police station. An interview concerning a purely summary offence may be conducted at a police station off-tape. Any conversation between a police officer and suspect which falls within the definition of an interview and which is not tape recorded is subject to the following rules.

(a)   An accurate record must be made of each interview whether or not the interview takes place at the police station (Code C, para 11.7(a)).

(b)   The record must be made during the course of the interview, unless in the investigating officer's view this would not be practicable or would interfere with the conduct of the interview, and must constitute either a verbatim record of what has been said, or failing this, an account of the interview which adequately and accurately summarises it (Code C, para 11.7(c)). Compiling such a record will usually involve writing down each question and answer during the interview.

(c)   If an interview record is not made during the course of the interview, it must be made as soon as practicable after completion of the interview (Code C, para 11.8).

(d)   Unless it is impracticable, the person interviewed must be given the opportunity to read the interview record and to sign it as correct, or to indicate the respects in which he considers it inaccurate (Code C, para 11.11).

(e)   A record of an interview which has not been taped will be served on the defence. If the interview record has been signed by the defendant or his solicitor then it will be admissible in evidence (subject to the admissibility of any confession that may have been made being challenged (see **9.6.3**)). If the record is not signed by the defence then it is not admissible in evidence. Instead, the interviewing officer will give oral evidence of what happened at the interview, using any contemporaneous notes made to refresh his memory (see **9.3.2**).

(f)   Rather than be interviewed, a suspect may offer to make a 'written statement under caution'. This is simply a prepared statement setting out the suspect's version of events or a confession. See the example of a statement at **Appendix 2(F)**. Note the caution at the top of the page. There is nothing to prevent the police from asking further questions on the written statement made by the suspect.

2.6.3 Comments outside interview

A written record should also be made of any comments made by a suspected person, including unsolicited comments, which are outside the context of an interview but which might be relevant to the offence. Any such record must be timed and signed by the maker. Where practicable, the person shall be given the opportunity to read that record and to sign it as correct or to indicate the respects in which he considers it inaccurate. Any refusal to sign should be recorded (Code C, para 11.14).

Example

A police officer arrests a suspect on suspicion of an assault occasioning actual bodily harm. On the way to the police station, the suspect says, 'I hit him but I was provoked'. The suspect volunteered this information; it was not in response to any question put by the police officer. Such a statement by the suspect does not constitute an interview. The police officer, on arrival at the police station, should make a record of what the suspect said and the time he said it. He should then sign the record and give the suspect the opportunity to read it and to sign it as correct or to indicate the respects in which he considers it inaccurate.

At the beginning of an interview carried out in a police station, the interviewing officer, after cautioning the suspect, should put to the suspect any significant statement or significant silence which has occurred before the suspect's arrival at the police station. The interviewing officer should ask the suspect whether he confirms or denies that earlier statement or silence, and whether he wishes to add anything. A 'significant' statement or silence is one which appears capable of being used against a suspect (Code C, para 11.4A).

2.7   The right to have a solicitor present at interviews

A detainee who has asked for legal advice may not be interviewed or continue to be interviewed until he has received such legal advice (Code C, para 6.6).

Exceptions to this rule are where:

(a)   the right to legal advice can lawfully be delayed (see **2.4.3**); or

(b)   a superintendent has reasonable grounds to believe that:

   (i)   delay will involve immediate risk of harm to persons or serious loss of, or damage to, property; or

   (ii)   a solicitor has agreed to attend but waiting for his arrival would cause unreasonable delay to the process of investigation; or

(c)   a nominated solicitor cannot or will not attend and the suspect has declined the duty solicitor or the duty solicitor is unavailable and an inspector has authorised the interview; or

(d)   the suspect has changed his mind and agrees in writing or on tape to the commencement of the interview and an inspector has authorised the interview.

In addition, no police officer shall at any time do or say anything with the intention of dissuading a detainee in detention from obtaining legal advice (Code C, para 6.4).

2.8   Safeguards for the suspect

2.8.1   Reminders of the right to legal advice

A suspect must be reminded of the right to free legal advice:

(a)   immediately prior to the commencement or recommencement of any interview at a police station;

(b)   before a review of detention takes place;

(c)   after charge, if a police officer wishes to draw the attention of the suspect to any written or oral statement made by another person;

(d)   after charge, if further questions are to be put to a suspect about the offence (see **2.5.3** as to when this is possible);

(e)   before an identification parade, group identification or video identification takes place;

(f)   before an intimate body sample is requested.

If, on being informed or reminded of the right to legal advice, the suspect declines to speak to a solicitor in person, the suspect should be informed of the right to communicate with a solicitor by telephone.

If a suspect continues to waive his right to legal advice, he should be asked his reasons for doing so. Any reasons should be recorded on the custody record or interview record, as appropriate.

2.8.2   The caution

A caution must be given by a police officer to a suspect in the following terms:

> You do not have to say anything. But it may harm your defence if you do not mention when questioned something which you later rely on in court. Anything you do say may be given in evidence.

A caution is required:

(a)   on or immediately before arrest;

(b)   before an interview;

(c)   following a break in questioning (if there is any doubt as to whether the suspect appreciates that he is still under caution) (Code C, paras 10.1 and 10.5).

2.8.3   Detention conditions

In any period of 24 hours, a detained person must be allowed a continuous period of at least 8 hours' rest. This period should normally be at night (Code C, para 12.2).

No person who is unfit through drink or drugs, to the extent that he is unable to appreciate the significance both of questions put to him and his answers, may be questioned about an alleged offence unless a superintendent considers that delay will involve an immediate risk of harm to persons or serious loss of or serious damage to property (Code C, para 12.3 and Code C, Annex G).

Interview rooms should be adequately heated, lit and ventilated (Code C, para 12.4).

Persons being questioned or making statements must not be required to stand (Code C, para 12.6).

Breaks in interviewing should be made at recognised meal times (Code C, para 12.8).

Short breaks for refreshments shall be provided at intervals of approximately 2 hours (Code C, para 12.8).

2.8.4   Suspects at risk

2.8.4.1   Juveniles (under 17) (Code C, paras 1.5 and 1.7)

An 'appropriate adult' must be informed that the juvenile has been arrested and should be asked to attend the police station.

An 'appropriate adult' should be the parent or guardian of the juvenile. If the parent or guardian is unsuitable (eg, because he or she is also involved in the offence), a social worker should be called. If a social worker is unavailable, another responsible adult aged 18 or over (who is not a police officer or employed by the police) should be called. A solicitor who is present at the police station in his professional capacity may not act as 'appropriate adult'.

The purpose of the 'appropriate adult' attending is to ensure the presence of an impartial adult to safeguard the rights of the juvenile. The appropriate adult's role, according to Code C, para 11.17, is not merely to act as an observer, but also to advise the juvenile and, if necessary, to 'facilitate communication with him'.

2.8.4.2   Mentally disordered/handicapped suspects (Code C, paras 1.4 and 1.7)

If an officer has any suspicion, or is told in good faith, that a person of any age may be mentally disordered or otherwise mentally vulnerable, in the absence of clear evidence to dispel that suspicion, the person should be treated as such for the purposes of this Code.

An 'appropriate adult' must be informed that the suspect has been arrested and should be asked to attend the police station.

An 'appropriate adult' should be a relative, guardian or other person responsible for the custody of the suspect. Failing this, a specialist social worker should be called. If a social worker is unavailable, another responsible adult aged 18 or over (who is not a police officer or employed by the police) should be called. A solicitor who is present at the police station in his professional capacity may not act as an 'appropriate adult'.

The purpose of the 'appropriate adult' is as for juveniles.

2.9 Tactical considerations

2.9.1 Purpose of solicitor's attendance

The solicitor's only role in the police station is to protect and advance the legal rights of their client (Code C, note 6D).

2.9.2 Record of attendance

A solicitor's presence in the police station makes him a potential witness in the case. It is essential, therefore, that the solicitor makes a contemporaneous record of everything that happens at the police station. This record should include details of initial contact with the custody officer, information given by the investigating officer, advice given to the client and any other matter that seems to be of significance. (See sample form at **Appendix 2(G)**.)

2.9.3 Custody record   See p19 *1.

On arrival at the police station, a solicitor should speak to the custody officer and ask to inspect the custody record. A solicitor has a right to inspect the custody record as soon as practicable after arrival at the police station (Code C, para 2.4). Matters such as reasons for detention, periods of detention, review periods and details of any interviews should be noted by the solicitor from the custody record.

2.9.4 The investigating officer

After speaking to the custody officer, a solicitor should, wherever possible, speak to the investigating officer about the offence. The investigating officer should be asked what evidence the police have against the suspect. A careful record should be made of information given. If the investigating officer is not forthcoming about the evidence available this is something that should be borne in mind when formulating advice to the client (see **2.9.5**).

2.9.5 Advising the suspect

A suspect held in the police station may be frightened, disorientated and suspicious of anyone who comes to see him. The solicitor should explain to the suspect the role of the solicitor who has been called to see him and, as far as possible, attempt to put him at ease.

The solicitor should take instructions from the suspect (see sample form at **Appendix 2(G)**. The solicitor should then consider the information given to him by the police and his instructions from his client and formulate advice to the client.

2.9.6   Criminal Justice and Public Order Act 1994 – the right to remain silent

Section 34 – failure to mention facts when questioned or charged

(1)   Where in any proceedings against a person for an offence, evidence is given that the accused—

(a)   at any time before he was charged with the offence, on being questioned under caution by a constable trying to discover whether or by whom the offence had been committed, failed to mention any fact relied on in his defence in those proceedings; or

(b)   on being charged with the offence or officially informed that he might be prosecuted for it, failed to mention any such fact,

being a fact which in the circumstances existing at the time the accused could reasonably have been expected to mention when so questioned, charged or informed, as the case may be ...

the court or jury ... may draw such inferences from the failure as appear proper.'

Example 1

Joe is being questioned about a suspected assault. He refuses to answer the questions put by the police. At his trial, Joe raises self-defence. Under s 34, a court may draw inferences from Joe's failure to mention self-defence when being interviewed or when charged.

Example 2

Joanne is being questioned about a suspected theft. She does not answer questions put by the police at interview. At her trial, Joanne raises an alibi defence: she was at home at the time of the theft. Under s 34, a court may draw inferences from Joanne's failure to mention the alibi when being interviewed or when charged.

The following points should be noted about s 34.

(a)   The section does not take away the right of a suspect to remain silent. It simply enables a court to draw inferences from silence if facts are raised in court in the defence of the suspect. If a suspect remains silent and does not raise facts in his defence then s 34 has no effect.

(b)   The section states that a court may draw inferences from silence. Such inferences are not mandatory and may only be drawn if the magistrates or jury are satisfied that in the circumstances existing at the time of the interview it would have been reasonable to expect the suspect to mention the relevant facts (see 'Advising the client' below for examples of when a court may decide not to draw adverse inferences).

(c)   In *R v Argent (Brian)* [1997] 2 Cr App R 27, the Court of Appeal said that before a jury could draw such inferences as appear proper under s 34(1)(a), the following six formal conditions had to be met.

(i)   There had to be proceedings against a person for an offence.

(ii)   The alleged failure had to occur before a defendant was charged.

(iii) The alleged failure had to occur during questioning under caution by a constable or other person authorised under s 34(4).

(iv)   The questioning had to be directed to trying to discover whether or by whom the alleged offence had been committed.

(v)   The alleged failure by the defendant had to be to mention any fact relied on in his defence in those proceedings.

(vi)   The fact which the defendant failed to mention was a fact which, in the circumstances existing at the time, he could reasonably have been expected to mention when so questioned.

(d)   It was generally thought that the inference which the prosecution seeks to draw from failure to mention facts in interview is that they have been subsequently fabricated. In *R v Randall* [1998] 6 *Archbold News* 1, the Court of Appeal held that s 34 could apply where a defendant had an account to give but did not want it subject to scrutiny. A similar approach was taken in *R v Daniel (Anthony Junior)* [1998] 2 Cr App R 373, where the court held that s 34 was not confined to cases of recent fabrication but was apt to cover 'a reluctance to be subject to questioning and further enquiry' (at 383). The same approach was followed by the Court of Appeal in *R v Beckles and Montague* [1999] Crim LR 148, *R v McGuiness (Cyril)* [1999] Crim LR 318, *R v Taylor* [1999] Crim LR 75 and *R v Mitford* [2001] Crim LR 330.

(e)   In those cases where the judge has ruled that there is no evidence on which a jury could properly conclude that the defendant had failed to mention any fact relied on in his defence, and that therefore no question arises of leaving the possibility of drawing inferences to the jury, the judge should specifically direct the jury that they should not draw any adverse inference from the defendant's silence (*R v McGarry* [1999] 1 Cr App R 377).

(f)   In *Condron and Another v United Kingdom* [2000] Crim LR 679, the European Court of Human Rights held that a trial judge had not properly directed the jury on the issue of the defendants' silence during police interview. As a consequence, the applicants had not received a fair trial within the meaning of art 6 of the European Convention on Human Rights. In the court's opinion, as a matter of fairness, the jury should have been directed that if it was satisfied that the applicants' silence at the police interview could not sensibly be attributed to their having no answer to the police's allegations or none that could stand up to cross-examination, it should not draw an inference. The court considered that a direction to that effect was more than merely 'desirable' as found by the Court of Appeal.

The court noted that the responsibility for deciding whether or not to draw an inference rested with the jury. It was impossible to ascertain what weight, if any, was given to the applicants' silence since a jury did not provide reasons for its decisions.

The court did not accept the government's submission that the fairness of the applicants' trial was secured by the appeal process. The Court of Appeal had no means of ascertaining whether or not the defendants' silence played a significant role in the jury's decision to convict. The Court of Appeal was concerned with the safety of the defendants' conviction, not whether they had received a fair trial. Since the jury was not properly directed, the imperfection in the direction could not be remedied on appeal.

(g)   In *R v Betts and Hall* [2001] EWCA Crim 244, [2001] 2 Cr App R 257, a bare admission at trial of part of the prosecution case was held incapable of constituting a fact for the purposes of s 34. Consequently, the jury was not entitled to draw an adverse inference from the defendant's failure to mention it in interview. The Court of Appeal also confirmed that if a defendant remains silent during the first interview, yet answers questions during the second interview, the jury can still draw inferences from the defendant's failure to answer questions during the first interview.

Section 36 – failure to account for objects, substances or marks

(1)   Where:

(a)   a person is arrested by a constable, and there is:

(i)   on his person; or

(ii)   in or on his clothing or footwear; or

(iii)   otherwise in his possession; or

(iv)   in any place in which he is at the time of his arrest, any object, substance or mark, or there is any mark on any such object; and

(b)   that or another constable investigating the case reasonably believes that the presence of the object, substance or mark may be attributable to the participation of the person arrested in the commission of an offence specified by the constable; and

(c)   the constable informs the person arrested that he so believes, and requests him to account for the presence of the object, substance or mark; and

(d)   the person fails or refuses to do so,

then ... the court or jury ... may draw such inferences from the failure or refusal as appear proper.

Example

Fred is arrested on suspicion of assaulting John. On being interviewed, he is asked to account for the fact that on arrest his shirt was covered in blood and he had cut knuckles. Fred does not reply. Under s 36, a court may draw inferences from Fred's failure to account for the bloodstains and cuts.

The following points should be noted about s 36:

(a)   There is a degree of overlap between ss 34 and 36. However, whilst s 34 can only apply if a suspect later raises facts in his defence, s 36 will operate irrespective of any defence put forward. It can apply even if no defence is raised at the trial.

Example

Following a street fight, Joe is arrested nearby. His shirt is badly torn. The police inform Joe that he is suspected of assault at the street fight and ask him to account for his torn shirt. Joe refuses to answer any questions.

If Joe gives evidence at his trial that he was walking home from a night club and tripped up, tearing his shirt, s 34 will apply. Joe did not mention the facts at the interview.

As Joe failed to account for his torn shirt, s 36 will apply irrespective of any defence put forward by Joe.

(b)   As with s 34, the court may draw inferences but there is no obligation to do so (see **2.9.6.2**).

(c)   The section can apply only if the accused has been told, in ordinary language, by the officer requesting the explanation, the effect of failure to comply with the request (s 36(4)). The following points must be brought to the attention of the suspect ('the special warning'):

(i)   what offence is under investigation;

(ii)   what fact the suspect is being asked to account for;

(iii)   that the officer believes this fact may be due to the suspect's taking part in the commission of the offence in question;

(iv)   that a court may draw an inference from failure to comply with the request;

(v)   that a record is being made of the interview and that it may be given in evidence if the suspect is brought to trial (Code C, para 10.11).

Section 37 – failure to account for presence at a particular place

(1)   Where—

(a) a person arrested by a constable was found by him at a place at or about the time the offence for which he was arrested is alleged to have been committed; and

(b) that or another constable investigating the offence reasonably believes that the presence of the person at that place and at that time may be attributed to his participation in the commission of the offence; and

(c) the constable informs the person that he so believes, and requests him to account for that presence; and

(d) the person fails or refuses to do so,

then ... the court or jury ... may draw such inferences from the failure or refusal as appear proper.

Example

Denis is arrested on suspicion of theft. He is found by a police officer standing close to a shop which has a window broken. Goods are missing from the shop. When questioned about the alleged offence, Denis is asked to account for his presence by the shop window. Denis does not reply. A court may draw inferences from Denis's refusal to account for his presence outside the shop.

The following points should be noted about s 37.

(a) There is a degree of overlap between ss 34 and 37. However, while s 34 can apply only if a suspect later raises facts in his defence, s 37 will operate irrespective of any defence put forward. It can apply even if no defence is raised at the trial.

Example

Following a burglary, Joan is arrested walking down a passageway close to the scene of the crime. Joan is interviewed by the police who tell her that she is suspected of committing the burglary. Joan is asked to account for her presence in the passageway. She remains silent at the interview.

If, at her trial, Joan explains that she was in the passageway as she was taking a short cut home, s 34 will apply. Joan did not mention the facts at the interview.

As Joan failed to account for her presence in the passageway, s 37 will apply irrespective of any defence put forward by Joan.

(b) As with s 34, the court may draw inferences but there is no obligation to do so (see **2.9.6.2**).

(c) As with s 36, this section can apply only if the accused has been told in ordinary language by the officer requesting the explanation, the effect of failure to comply with the request ('the special warning' – see further Code C, para 10.11 above).

2.9.6.1 Points common to ss 34, 36 and 37

The following points apply to ss 34, 36 and 37.

(a) The sections will normally apply only to interviews at a police station (it is important to remember the general prohibition on interviewing outside a police station (see **2.5.1**)). The suspect will have been cautioned and given the opportunity of taking legal advice.

(b) By s 38(3), 'a person shall not have the proceedings against him committed to the Crown Court for trial, have a case to answer or be convicted of any offence solely on an inference' drawn under s 34, s 36 or s 37. In other words, the prosecution must always have some other evidence. A defendant cannot be convicted solely because he refused to answer questions.

(c)   No inferences can be drawn from silence when a suspect is questioned at a police station while denied access to legal advice (Youth Justice and Criminal Evidence Act 1999, s 58).

This provision brings the law into compliance with the judgment of the European Court of Human Rights in the case of *Murray v United Kingdom (Right to Silence)* (1996) 22 EHRR 29. In this case, the court held that there was a breach of art 6 of the European Convention on Human Rights as a result of denying the applicant access to legal advice in circumstances where inferences could be drawn from his silence during police questioning.

(d)   The Judicial Studies Board (JSB) specimen directions on ss 34, 36 and 37 are available on the JSB website (www.jsboard.co.uk).

2.9.6.2   Advising the client

In formulating advice to a client on whether to remain silent, a legal adviser must balance the potential effects of the law against good reasons for not answering questions. If a court finds that there were good reasons for remaining silent then inferences should not be drawn from the exercise of that right. In *R v Roble (Ali Hersi)* [1997] Crim LR 449, the Court of Appeal indicated that good reasons for advising silence might be that the interviewing officer had disclosed little or nothing of the nature of the case against the defendant, so that the legal adviser cannot usefully advise his client, or where the nature of the offence, or the material in the hands of the police is so complex, or relates to matters so long ago, that no immediate response is feasible. In *R v Argent (Brian)* [1997] 2 Cr App R 27, the Court of Appeal stated that a court should not interpret the expression 'in the circumstances' in s 34(1) restrictively. Matters such as the time of day, the suspect's age, experience, mental capacity, state of health, sobriety, tiredness, personality and legal advice were all relevant circumstances.

In particular, a legal adviser at the police station should consider:

(a)   The extent of the evidence disclosed by the police. If there is little or no evidence then silence is likely to remain the best advice. All that the suspect is likely to achieve by answering questions is to incriminate himself.

If the police refuse to disclose the evidence available then, normally, a suspect should be advised to remain silent. This is because it is not possible to assess the strength of the case against the suspect and provide proper advice.

(b)   The ability of the suspect to deal with an interview. If a suspect is highly emotional, inarticulate or otherwise unfit to deal with an interview then silence is likely to be the best course of action.

(c)   Whether there is any other good explanation for remaining silent. For example, a suspect may be afraid of associates or may wish to protect another person.

In *R v Betts and Hall* [2001] EWCA Crim 244, [2001] 2 Cr App R 257 the Court of Appeal emphasised that the adequacy of the explanation advanced for silence may well be relevant as to whether or not the advice was the true reason for not mentioning the facts. Adverse inferences could be drawn if the jury is satisfied that the defendant had no answer to the allegations that were being put or none that would stand up to questioning or investigation and the advice of a solicitor was no more than a convenient shield behind which to hide. It was not the quality of the decision to remain silent that matters but the genuineness of the decision. However in *R v Howell* [2003] Crim LR 405, the Court of Appeal took a contrary view. Genuine reliance is not enough. All the circumstances must be taken into account in deciding whether it was reasonable for the suspect to mention the facts in question.

If a suspect decides to remain silent on legal advice, then:

(a)   The legal adviser should explain the potential effect of ss 34, 36 and 37 but state that there appears to be a good reason for a court not drawing inferences should the matter proceed to trial. The client should be warned that the final decision on inferences will be one to be taken by the court.

(b)   The legal adviser, with permission from the suspect, should make it clear to the police the reasons for remaining silent. This is best done on tape at the start of the interview. It is possible that the legal adviser will be called to give evidence at the trial to confirm the reasons for the advice given.

2.9.6.3   Legal professional privilege

Communications between a defendant and his solicitor prior to interview by the police are subject to legal professional privilege. The privilege can be waived by the defendant, though not by the solicitor.

The prosecution may allege that the defendant's failure to mention facts in interview is because they have been subsequently fabricated. There is no waiver of professional privilege where a solicitor gives evidence that the defendant informed him of the material facts at the time of the police interview (*R v Wilmot (Alan)* (1989) 89 Cr App R 341).

If a defendant at trial gives as a reason for not answering police questions that he has been advised by his solicitor not to do so, that advice does not amount to a waiver of privilege. But that bare assertion is unlikely by itself to be regarded as a sufficient reason for not mentioning matters relevant to the defence. So, it will be necessary, if the defendant wishes to invite the court not to draw an inference under s 34, to go further and state the basis or reason for the advice. This may amount to a waiver of privilege, so that the defendant, or, if his solicitor is also called to give evidence, his solicitor, can be asked whether there were any other reasons for the advice, and the nature of the advice given, so as to explore whether the advice may also have been given for tactical reasons. (*R v Condron (Karen)*; *R v Condron (William)* [1997] 1 Cr App R 185; see also *R v Roble (Ali Hersi)* [1997] Crim LR 449 and *R v Bowden (Brian Thomas)* (1999) 2 Cr App R 176.)

2.9.6.4   Selective silence

This is not a good idea. The suspect is answering some questions and not others. Apart from the possibility of ss 34, 36 and 37 applying, such an interview will not impress a jury or magistrates. Clients should be advised to make a decision either to remain silent or to answer questions and to stick by that decision.

2.9.6.5   Answering questions (explanations or denials)

Reasons for advising a suspect to answer questions in order to put forward explanations or denials include:

(a)   to avoid inferences under ss 34, 36 and 37 where there does not appear to be any good reason for remaining silent;

(b)   where a client has a convincing story, an early explanation may avoid charge, particularly where there is little or no evidence against him.

Always remember that suspects are often under immense pressure at a police station and may be inclined to say anything in an attempt to get out as quickly as possible. Before advising a suspect to answer questions, it is important to go through his story carefully and to warn him that if he tells lies now it could damage his defence at trial.

2.9.6.6   Making a written statement

It may be advisable for a suspect to make a written statement rather than answer police questions. A written statement will enable the suspect to refer to relevant facts without the pressure of police questioning. The suspect should sign and date the written statement and also insert the time when the written statement was made. The written statement should be as full as possible and anticipate whether the suspect is likely to be asked questions under s 36 or s 37.

The legal adviser will have to consider carefully whether to hand the written statement to the police. If the written statement is handed in to the police it may be produced as part of the prosecution case.

2.9.6.7   Not handing in the written statement

Not handing the written statement to the police may be an appropriate strategy where the legal adviser has doubts about the instructions received or about information that has been disclosed by the police. Such a strategy may prevent an inference that the defence had been fabricated but it will not prevent other inferences being drawn. These could include an inference that the defendant has made up his defence prior to interview but was not sufficiently confident to expose it to police questioning, or that he had not thought up all the details of the defence at the time of the police interview.

2.9.6.8   Handing in the written statement during interview

Handing in the written statement during interview is a strategy designed to prevent inferences being drawn. In *R v Ali and Others* [2001] EWCA Crim 863, [2001] All ER (D) 16 (Apr), the defendant declined to answer questions in interview but gave the interviewing officers a written statement. At his trial he did not rely on any fact not mentioned in the written statement. The judge directed the jury that they might draw an inference adverse to the defendant on the basis that the information in the written statement was not, in the words of s 34 of the Criminal Justice and Public Order Act 1994, mentioned 'on being questioned'. The inference the prosecution sought, and the judge permitted, was not one of recent fabrication but that the account given by the defendant would not stand up to cross-examination. The Court of Appeal held, quashing the conviction, that this was not a permissible construction of s 34.

It appears that a written statement containing all the facts relied on by the defendant at trial satisfies the reference in s 34 to mentioning facts when questioned. *R v Ali* may prove to be a significant decision. Written statements are often used where pre-interview disclosure is incomplete, but more often may be likely where the suspect has an account that will not withstand cross-examination.

2.9.6.9   Handing in the statement on charge

Alternatively, the written statement may be handed in on charge. Handing in the written statement on charge may be useful if the legal adviser believes that the police will not have enough evidence to charge. A written statement given to the police during the interview may give the police sufficient evidence to charge. Thus, the legal adviser may consider advising a no comment interview and submitting the written statement only if the police decide to charge the suspect. Assuming that the defence put forward at trial is consistent with the written statement, no inferences could be drawn under s 34.

2.9.6.10 Making a confession

If the police evidence appears to be strong and the suspect admits his guilt then there may be advantages in making a confession at the police interview. This can be good mitigation when the suspect is being sentenced, particularly if he implicates others or gives information that leads to the recovery of stolen property.

The Criminal Law Committee of The Law Society has issued guidance to help solicitors decide whether it is in the best interests of their client to answer police questions (see **Appendix 4**).

Whatever advice is given to a client, the final decision as to whether or not to answer police questions is that of the client.

2.9.7 Preparing the suspect for the interview

It is important to explain to a suspect the procedure to be followed at a tape-recorded interview and to warn him about likely police tactics. The following points should be covered:

(a) That the interview will be tape recorded and all parties will be asked to identify themselves on tape.

(b) That the interview can be stopped at any time if the suspect wants further advice.

(c) If the suspect is to remain silent he should be advised to use a stock phrase such as 'No comment'. Most suspects find this easier than remaining in total silence.

(d) Police tactics – a suspect who wishes to remain silent should be warned:

   (i) that the police may try to get him to talk by asking apparently innocuous questions;

   (ii) that the police may try to alienate him from his solicitor by suggesting that poor advice has been given;

   (iii) that the police may make threats such as of arresting members of his family unless he speaks.

   The suspect should be advised to ignore any of these tactics and remain silent.

(e) That the legal adviser is present to protect the suspect's interests and will intervene in the interview as and when necessary.

2.9.8 The solicitor's role at an interview

It is important to understand that a solicitor is not at an interview simply as an observer. It may be necessary for the solicitor to intervene to object to improper questioning or to give the client further advice in private. The following points should be noted.

(a) At the start of a tape-recorded interview, a legal adviser should make an opening statement explaining the role he intends to play in the interview. This will leave the police in no doubt about the reason for the adviser's presence. It also gives an opportunity to state the advice given to the client and the reasons for that advice. A suggested form of statement is:

I am ... a solicitor/authorised representative with [firm name]. I am now required to explain my role. My role is to protect my client's rights. I shall continue to advise my client throughout the interview.

I shall intervene in the interview if:

* my client asks for, or needs legal advice; or

* your questioning is inappropriate; or

* you raise matters which are not based on matters that have been made known to me.

After receiving legal advice my client has decided:

[either]

* to exercise the right to silence [if you consider it appropriate to give a reason] because [reason]. Please respect that decision.

[or]

* to answer questions which you may raise which are relevant to my client's arrest/voluntary attendance.

(Shepherd, *Police Station Skills for Legal Advisers; a Pocket Reference* (The Law Society, 1997))

(b)   A client may need further advice if, for example, matters that the legal adviser was not aware of are raised in the interview. It may also be necessary to give further advice if a client is becoming agitated or uncertain about the conduct of the interview.

(c)   Examples of improper questioning include:

(i)   where questions are put in a confusing manner, for example, two or three questions rolled into one;

(ii)   where questions are put in an aggressive or bullying fashion;

(iii)   where questions are put which are not based on evidence of which the solicitor is aware. Advice given to the client will have been on the basis of the evidence disclosed to the solicitor. If evidence has been held back it may be necessary to take further instructions.

(d)   The police sometimes threaten to exclude legal advisers who have intervened in an interview. It is therefore important to be familiar with the provisions of the Code of Practice in this area:

The solicitor may intervene in order to seek clarification or to challenge an improper question to their client or the manner in which it is put, advise their client not to reply to particular questions, or if they wish to give their client further legal advice. (Code C, note 6D)

The Code further provides that an adviser may be excluded only:

... if the solicitor's approach or conduct prevents or unreasonably obstructs proper questions being put to the suspect or the suspect's response being recorded. Examples of unacceptable conduct include answering questions on a suspect's behalf or providing written replies for the suspect to quote. (Code C, note 6D)

An investigating officer has no power to exclude a legal adviser from an interview. The investigating officer must:

... stop the interview and consult an officer not below the rank of superintendent. ... After speaking to the solicitor, the officer consulted will decide if the interview should continue in the presence of that solicitor.' (Code C, para 6.10)

(e)   If a suspect, against advice, breaks his silence during the interview and begins to answer questions, it is permissible for a legal adviser to remind the suspect of his earlier advice to remain silent. It is also possible to stop the interview to remind the client of the earlier advice. However, continuous interruptions for this purpose would constitute misconduct which could lead to the adviser being excluded from the interview.

(f)   The police may seek to dictate the seating positions of parties at an interview:

The solicitor should be positioned in such a way that there can be no natural eye contact between him and the suspect, nor should he be in a position where he can easily catch the eye of the main interviewer. This makes it much more difficult for him to support the suspect non-verbally and, because he cannot have eye contact with the main interviewer, it is more difficult for him to interject and interrupt the interview verbally.

(John Walkley, *Police Interrogation* (Police Review Publishing Co Ltd, 1987))

Needless to say, any attempt to do this should be resisted. It is important for a legal adviser to be seated in a position whereby he has eye contact with his client and is properly able to advise him.

2.10 Identification

2.10.1 Finding a suspect

Where a witness has seen an offence being committed, that witness may be able to give a description of the culprit to the police. The Code of Practice on Identification Procedures (Code D) prescribes two possible courses of action:

(a)   A police officer may take a witness to a particular neighbourhood or place to see whether he can identify the person whom he said he saw on the relevant occasion (Code D, para 3.2).

(b)   A witness may be shown photographs, photofit, identikit or similar pictures (Code D, para 3.3 and Annex E). Any identification from photographs will not normally be admissible in evidence. One of the reasons for this is that it indicates that the defendant has a criminal record.

2.10.2 Cases where the suspect is known

In a case that involves disputed identification evidence the following identification procedures may be used:

(1)   video identification;

(2)   identification parade;

(3)   group identification;

(4)   confrontation.

All four identification methods must be organised by an officer of at least inspector rank (the identification officer). No officer involved with the investigation of the case may take part (Code D, para 3.11).

The purpose of any method of identification is to test the reliability of an eye-witness who saw someone committing an offence and to obtain admissible evidence of identification for use in court.

2.10.3 Circumstances on which an identification procedure must be held

Whenever a suspect disputes an identification made or purported to be made by a witness, an identification procedure shall be held if practicable. Such a procedure may also be held if the officer in charge of the investigation considers that it would be useful (Code D, para 3.13).

An identification procedure need not be held if, in all the circumstances, it would serve no useful purpose in proving or disproving whether the suspect committed the offence. For example, where the suspect is already known to the witness who saw the suspect commit the crime (see *R v Harris* [2003] EWCA Crim 174) or where there is no reasonable possibility that the witness would be able to make an identification (Code D, para 3.12).

2.10.4 Selecting an identification procedure

The officer in charge of the case has a free choice between a video identification or an identification parade.

A group identification may be offered initially if the officer in the case considers that it would be more satisfactory than a video identification or identification parade and the identification officer considers it practicable to arrange. Otherwise it should only be offered if a video identification or identification parade are refused or considered impracticable.

If none of these methods are practicable then the identification officer has discretion to make arrangements for a covert video identification or covert group identification to take place. A confrontation is the last resort (Code D, paras 3.21–3.24).

2.10.5 Video identification

A video identification is where the witness is shown images of the suspect together with images of other people who resemble the suspect.

The suspect should be asked for his consent to a video identification. However, where such consent is refused, the identification officer has a discretion to proceed with a covert video identification.

If a video identification is to be used, a video should be made of the suspect and at least eight other persons of similar age, height, general appearance and position in life (Code D, Annex A, para 2).

The participants should all be filmed in the same positions and carrying out the same activity under identical conditions (Code D, Annex A, para 3).

Only one witness may see the film at a time. The film may be frozen and there is no limit on the number of times that a witness may see the film (Code D, Annex A, para 11).

2.10.6 Identification parade

An identification parade is where the witness sees the suspect in a line of other people who resemble the suspect.

The parade must consist of at least eight persons in addition to the suspect who so far as possible, resemble the suspect in age, height, general appearance and position in life (Code D, Annex B, para 9).

Witnesses must be properly segregated both before and after the parade and the person conducting a witness to a parade must not discuss with him the composition of the parade and, in particular, must not disclose whether a previous witness has made any identification (Code D, Annex B, para 15).

2.10.7   Group identification

A group identification is where the witness sees the suspect in an informal group of people.

The suspect should be asked for his consent to a group identification. However, where consent is refused, the identification officer has a discretion to proceed with a covert group identification if it is practicable to do so (Code D, Annex C, para 2).

There is no set format for a group identification. A group identification may be arranged, for example, in a room of people, a railway station, a bus station, or a shopping parade. The suspect may be asked to stand anywhere in a group or to walk through a busy shopping area. The witness will be asked whether or not he saw the person he thinks committed the offence.

2.10.8   Confrontation

If no group identification, identification parade or video identification procedure is possible the witness may confront the suspect. The consent of the suspect is not required.

A confrontation involves taking the witness to the suspect and asking whether the suspect is the person in question.

Confrontation must take place in the presence of the suspect's solicitor or friend unless this would cause unreasonable delay (Code D, Annex D, para 4).

A confrontation is only to take place if none of the other procedures are practicable. It should be a last resort (Code D, para 3.23).

2.10.9   Notice to suspect

Before a video identification, identification parade or group identification, the identification officer must explain a number of things to the suspect, including:

(a)   that he is entitled to free legal advice and is entitled to have a solicitor or friend present;

(b)   that he does not have to take part but his refusal may be given in evidence and the police may proceed covertly without his consent or arrange a confrontation identification;

(c)   that he or his solicitor will be provided with details of the description as first given by any witnesses that are to take part in an identification procedure;

(d)   whether the witnesses have been shown photographs or other pictures.

This information must also be contained in a written notice that must be handed to the suspect (Code D, para 3.18).

2.10.10   Identification record

The identification officer must make a record of the video identification, identification parade, group identification or confrontation on forms provided. An example of an identification parade record appears at **Appendix 2(H)**.

2.10.11   Tactical considerations

A suspect may wish to be advised as to whether or not it is in his best interests to agree to take part in a video identification or an identification parade. It will normally be in his best interests to do so. A refusal can lead to one of the other methods of identification being used. If the police decide that a video identification or an identification parade or group identification is not practicable then a confrontation may take place. A confrontation is the least satisfactory method of identification as it involves a witness being asked whether the suspect is the person who was seen at the relevant time. Refusal to take part in an identification procedure may be given in evidence at any subsequent trial.

A solicitor attending the police station is entitled to be given details of the description of a suspect as first given by a potential witness. The police are obliged to keep a record of this description (Code D, para 3.1).

A solicitor attending a video identification must be given a reasonable opportunity to see the complete set of images before it is shown to any witness. A solicitor can object to any of the images or any of the participants (Code D, Annex A, para 7). Similarly a solicitor attending an identification parade can object to the composition of the parade (Code D, Annex B, para 12). Relevant considerations will include whether the participants satisfy the requirements as to age, height, appearance and position in life. Bear in mind that too many objections may force the police into using an alternative method of identification.

All relevant matters should be recorded and the solicitor and suspect will be given an opportunity to comment on any relevant matter that occurred during the course of the parade. The identification officer will record any comments made.

2.11 Evidential considerations

2.11.1 Challenging inferences from silence

In the Crown Court, any arguments over the admissibility of the defendant's silence when being interviewed will take place in the absence of the jury.

The defence may seek to argue that evidence of the defendant's silence should not go before the jury because of a breach of the Codes of Practice such as a failure to caution the defendant. Such a breach will not automatically render the evidence inadmissible but will be a relevant factor for the court to consider.

If a judge rules that evidence of the silence is inadmissible the jury will not hear the evidence. If the evidence is ruled admissible then the judge will direct the jury on the inferences that they are entitled to draw. It will be for the jury to decide whether or not actually to draw the inferences.

In a magistrates' court, it will be for the magistrates to rule on the admissibility of a defendant's silence and to decide whether or not to draw inferences.

2.11.2 Confessions and identification evidence

Evidence of a confession and the outcome of an identification parade, group identification, video identification or confrontation will usually be admissible in evidence.

A breach of the Codes of Practice will not automatically render any evidence obtained inadmissible. However, a breach may be relevant to a challenge by the defence at the trial to the admissibility of evidence such as an identification parade or a confession (see **9.2.5** and **9.6.3**).

2.12 Samples

2.12.1 Intimate samples (s 62)

Intimate body samples are samples of blood, semen or any tissue, fluid, urine or pubic hair, a dental impression, or a swab taken from a person's body orifice other than the mouth.

An intimate sample may be taken:

(a) if the suspect consents; and

(b) if a superintendent authorises the taking of the sample on the basis that the offence under investigation is a recordable offence and that samples will tend to confirm or disprove the suspect's involvement in the offence.

A recordable offence includes an offence punishable by imprisonment.

If a suspect refuses to consent to the taking of an intimate sample then inferences can be drawn from that refusal. A refusal of consent is also capable of amounting to corroboration of any evidence against the person in relation to which the refusal is material.

Example

John is being questioned about a rape. He denies having intercourse with the victim and refuses to give a sample of semen. This refusal is capable of corroborating the evidence of the victim that intercourse took place.

2.12.2 Non-intimate samples (s 63)

Non-intimate body samples include samples of hair, saliva and samples taken from fingernails or toenails.

The consent of a suspect is not required provided a superintendent's authority is given (the grounds are the same as for intimate samples).

A non-intimate sample can also be taken from a person without consent if he has been convicted of a recordable offence.

2.13 Alternatives to prosecution

2.13.1 Formal cautioning

Instead of prosecuting, the police or the CPS may decide to issue a formal caution. A caution can only be used for adults as there is a system of reprimands and warnings introduced for juveniles under the Crime and Disorder Act 1998. A caution is usually administered in the police station by an officer of the rank of inspector or above. Although a caution does not constitute a conviction, records are kept of them for at least five years and they may be cited in court as evidence of the defendant's character should he subsequently be convicted of an offence. Cautioning practice is governed by a Home Office Circular 18/1994 which incorporates revised National Standards for Cautioning.

The major conditions for issuing a caution are that the evidence is strong enough to justify a prosecution and the offender must admit the offence. Where these conditions are satisfied, consideration should then be given as to whether a caution is in the public interest. In deciding whether a caution is in the public interest the following factors should be considered:

(a) The public interest principles in the Code for Crown Prosecutors should be taken into account.

(b) Cautions should not be used for indictable only offences, other than in the most exceptional circumstances.

(c) Other offences may be too serious for a caution. In deciding this, the harm resulting from the offence, whether it was racially motivated, whether it involved a breach of trust and whether it was carried out in an organised way are all relevant factors.

(d) The victim's view of the offence and whether a caution is appropriate should be sought but is not conclusive.

(e) Only where the subsequent offence is trivial or where there has been a sufficient lapse of time since the first caution to suggest that it had some affect should an offender be cautioned for a second time.

(f) There should be a presumption in favour of cautioning rather than prosecuting certain categories of offender, for example, the elderly and those who suffer from mental illness or impairment or a severe physical illness.

(g) The offender's attitude to the offence must be considered.

(h) If the offence was carried out by a group, each offender must be separately considered.

2.13.2 Conditional cautioning

The Criminal Justice Act 2003 (ss 23–27) gives the CPS the power to impose a conditional caution. Under a conditional caution, conditions may be attached to the caution for facilitating rehabilitation or reparation for the offence. A conditional caution may be given to an offender who is 18 or over provided each of the five requirements in s 23 of the Act are satisfied:

(a) there is evidence that the offender has committed the offence;

(b) there is sufficient evidence to charge the offender with the offence, however, it is decided that a conditional caution should be given instead;

(c) the offender admits the offence;

(d) the effect of the conditional caution is explained to the offender and the offender is warned that failure to comply with any of the conditions attached to the caution may result in prosecution for the offence;

(e) the offender signs a document containing;

    (i) details of the offence;

    (ii) an admission that he committed the offence;

    (iii) his consent to the conditional caution;

    (iv) the conditions attached to the caution.

If the offender fails, without reasonable excuse, to comply with any of the conditions attached to the conditional caution then criminal proceedings may be instituted against the offender for the offence in question.

A Code of Practice will be introduced governing the detailed operation of the scheme.

2.13.3 Oral warning

The police may in some cases issue an oral warning (sometimes referred to as 'an informal caution'). Such a warning has no official status and may not be cited in subsequent court proceedings.

2.14 Further reading

See, for example:

Ed Cape with Jawaid Luqmani, *Defending Suspects at Police Stations* (Legal Action Group, 2003)

Andrew Keogh, *CLSA Duty Solicitors' Handbook* (The Law Society, 2002)

Chapter 3

Commencement of Criminal Proceedings

3.1	Preliminary considerations	45
3.2	Commencing the prosecution	46
3.3	Financing the defence – Criminal Defence Service	47
3.4	Adjournments, remands and bail	52
3.5	Bail and the Human Rights Act 1998	62
3.6	Further reading	62

3.1 Preliminary considerations

3.1.1 Time-limits

In this chapter, section numbers refer to the Magistrates' Courts Act 1980 unless otherwise indicated.

If the offence to be prosecuted is a summary offence, a magistrates' court cannot deal with the prosecution if the information is laid more than six months after the alleged offence was committed (s 127). An information is laid when it is received at the court office by an authorised officer (see **3.2.2**).

For most indictable offences (including offences triable either way) there are no statutory time-limits for commencing criminal proceedings. It should be noted, however, that a defendant has a common law right to be protected from undue delay. Courts have a discretion to dismiss proceedings which constitute an abuse of process of the court. The defendant would have to show either substantial delay in bringing the prosecution which cannot be justified, or bad faith on the part of the prosecution. In practice, both are very difficult to establish.

3.1.2 The Road Traffic Offenders Act 1988 (as amended by the Road Traffic Act 1991)

Subject to section 2 of this Act a person shall not be convicted of an offence to which this section applies unless—

(a) he was warned at the time the offence was committed that the question of prosecuting him for some one or other of the offences to which this section applies would be taken into consideration, or

(b) within 14 days of the commission of the offence a summons for the offence was served on him, or

(c) within 14 days of the commission of the offence a notice of the intended prosecution specifying the nature of the alleged offence and time and place where it is alleged to have been committed was ...

served on him or on the person, if any, registered as the keeper of the vehicle at the time of the commission of the offence. (s 1(1))

The requirement of section 1(a) of this Act does not apply in relation to an offence if, at the time of the offence or immediately after it, an accident occurs owing to the presence on a road of the vehicle in respect of which the offence was committed. (2(1))

The offences to which these sections apply include dangerous driving and careless driving.

3.2 Commencing the prosecution

The prosecution usually begins in one of two ways: by charge or by summons. A flowchart summarising the two ways in which criminal proceedings may be commenced is included at **Appendix 1(E)**.

3.2.1 Charge

Having been arrested, the defendant will be taken to a police station, charged and either released on bail to appear before the next available magistrates' court sitting (Police and Criminal Evidence Act 1984, s 47(3A)) or kept in police custody and taken before a magistrates' court 'as soon as practicable' (Police and Criminal Evidence Act 1984, s 46(2)). An example of a charge sheet appears at **Appendix 2(I)**.

Following charge, the CPS lawyer in the police station will review the police file and determine which of the following hearings will be necessary.

3.2.1.1 Defendant charged with a summary offence or an offence triable either way

Bailed to attend court

Early first hearing (EFH)

This hearing is where the defendant is likely to enter a 'simple guilty plea'. A 'simple guilty plea' is where the defendant admits all the elements of the offence, or the offence is witnessed by the police and there is no indication that the defendant intends to deny it. In addition, the offence must involve no complex issues, meaning that there must be no more that two defendants or three key witnesses.

The CPS lawyer will prepare an abbreviated file which will be disclosed to the solicitor representing the defendant at court. The file must contain the charge sheet and key witness statements.

If the court is informed that a case is likely to be a 'simple guilty plea' it will list it before a full bench so that the defendant can be sentenced that day or the case can be adjourned for the court to obtain a pre-sentence report. The prosecution will usually be represented by a designated case worker, a non-legally qualified CPS representative.

Early administrative hearing (EAH)

If the case is not likely to be a 'simple guilty plea' the defendant's first appearance before a magistrates' court may take the form of an early administrative hearing (EAH) (Crime and Disorder Act 1998, s 50). An EAH may occur when the plea is not known, a not guilty plea is expected, or guilty pleas are expected but the case is not one that can be classified as a 'simple guilty plea'. The prosecution will usually be represented by a CPS lawyer.

The main purpose of the EAH is to enable arrangements to be made for the defendant to obtain representation and to consult a solicitor. Sometimes it may be possible at the EAH for the pleas to be entered and if the defendant enters a not guilty plea a date will be set for a pre-trial review (PTR) (see **8.4.2**).

At the EAH, the case will be adjourned. A single justice may remand the defendant on bail or in custody. A justices' clerk cannot remand the defendant in custody.

Detained to attend court

The defendant will be kept in custody and taken before a magistrates' court 'as soon as practicable'. The magistrates will decide how the case is to proceed.

3.2.1.2 Defendant charged with an indictable only offence

The first hearing for an indictable only offence will take the form of a preliminary hearing (see **6.7.2**).

3.2.2 Summons

For less serious offences (which may not involve an arrest at all, for example, careless driving), the prosecution will lay an information. This involves informing a magistrate or magistrates' clerk of the alleged offence with a request for a summons to be issued. Normally an information will be in writing and must specify one offence only. An information which alleges more than one offence is bad for duplicity. An example would be an information alleging that D assaulted A on 15 October and B on 15 October. Assuming that the assaults were two separate acts, two informations are required. This is an important rule as once the trial has commenced there is no power to amend the information to cure the defect. In practice, arguments over duplicity on informations are often complex and the detail involved is beyond the scope of this book.

Following the laying of an information, the magistrate or the magistrates' clerk will issue a summons. A single summons may cover more than one information. The summons will usually be served by posting it to the defendant's last-known or usual address. An example of a summons and certificate of service appears at **Appendix 2(J)**.

3.3 Financing the defence – Criminal Defence Service

Only firms who have a contract with the Legal Services Commission (or public defenders) are able to undertake Criminal Defence Service work funded by the Legal Services Commission.

Criminal Defence Service work falls into two categories:

(a)   advice and assistance; and

(b)   representation orders.

3.3.1 Advice and assistance

The law relating to advice and assistance is to be found in the Access to Justice Act 1999, s 13 and the Criminal Defence Service (General) (No 2) Regulations 2001, regs 5 and 6.

A solicitor will claim under this part of the contract with the Legal Services Commission if he is advising a suspect at the police station, appearing as a duty solicitor at court or representing a suspect in an application for a warrant of further detention or for an extension of such a warrant. Such advice and assistance (including advocacy assistance) is non-means tested.

Solicitors are remunerated for advice and assistance by a fixed hourly rate paid by the Legal Services Commission. There is an upper financial limit on the amount that can be claimed. The upper financial limit can be extended on application to the Legal Services Commission. In general authority to extend the upper limit may only be granted where the work carried out to date and the further work proposed is reasonable. If an extension is refused there is a right of review to the Funding Review Committee of the Legal Services Commission Regional Office.

A claim for payment should be made on the prescribed form and submitted to the Legal Services Commission Regional Office.

3.3.2 Representation orders

Representation in court in a criminal case is normally financed by a representation order.

The law relating to representation orders is largely to be found in the Access to Justice Act 1999, s 14 and the Criminal Defence Service (General) (No 2) Regulations 2001 (SI 2001/1437).

A representation order is available to cover representation in a magistrates' court, the Crown Court, the High Court, the Court of Appeal and the House of Lords.

> Any question as to whether a right to representation should be granted shall be determined according to the interests of justice. (Access to Justice Act 1999, Sch 3, para 5(1))

There is no means test.

3.3.2.1 The interests of justice test

The factors to be taken into account in determining whether it is in the interests of justice for representation to be granted are contained in the Access to Justice Act 1999, Sch 3, para 5(2). They are:

> Whether the individual would, if any matter arising in the proceedings is decided against him, be likely to lose his liberty or livelihood or suffer serious damage to his reputation, (para 5(2)(a)

Loss of liberty may, for example, be apparent from the nature and seriousness of the offence. Loss of livelihood will be relevant, for example, where on conviction the applicant will lose his job. Serious damage to reputation will include a person of previous good character who is charged with a criminal offence involving something like dishonesty or violence.

> Whether the determination of any matter in the proceedings may involve consideration of a substantial question of law, para 5(2)(b)

A substantial question of law will include difficult points of substantive criminal law connected with the offence charged. It may also include points of evidence such as the admissibility of a confession or consideration of the rules relating to cases involving disputed identification evidence.

> whether the individual may be unable to understand the proceedings or to state his own case, (para 5(2)(c)
>
> whether the proceedings may involve the tracing, interviewing or expert cross-examination of witnesses on behalf of the individual, para 5(2)(d).

Expert cross-examination of a prosecution witness will include cross-examination of identification witnesses, cross-examination of police officers as to what happened at a police station and generally any cross-examination that requires an element of legal knowledge.

> Whether it is in the interests of another person that the individual be represented (para 5(2)(e))

A defendant is prohibited from personally cross-examining certain witnesses (see **9.3.2**). In such cases, it is likely that the court will determine that it is in the interests of justice for representation to be granted.

3.3.2.2 Guidelines

In 2001 the Lord Chancellor's Department issued guidelines (Guidance to Courts from the Lord Chancellor's Department – Interests of Justice Test) with the intention of effecting greater consistency of approach when considering the interests of justice test. The guidelines do not replace the statutory criteria set out above but should be used as an aid to their application.

The guidelines include the following.

The Schedule 3 criteria

The Sch 3 criteria are not exhaustive. For example, the fact that a community punishment order is a possibility may be a relevant factor.

Deprivation of liberty

(a) Reference should be made to the Magistrates' Association Sentencing Guidelines (see **Appendix 3**) which provide examples of aggravating factors and mitigating factors for various types of offence. These will assist in deciding whether there is a real and practical risk of loss of liberty.

(b) Conviction should be assumed.

(c) Representation should normally be granted upon a committal to the Crown Court for sentence.

Loss of livelihood

(a) This should be a direct consequence of the conviction or sentence.

(b) This will normally refer to current livelihood.

(c) 'Assertions that disqualification from driving will result in a loss of livelihood should be examined critically ... Though a grant could be justified in exceptional circumstances (eg, if the applicant could show that the disqualification would result in a real risk of dismissal), representation would not usually be justified where the accused sought to avoid a "totting up" disqualification, having acquired twelve or more penalty points.'

Serious damage to reputation

(a) 'This would relate to those cases in which the offence, or the offender's circumstances, are such that the disgrace of conviction, or consequent damage to the applicant's standing, would greatly exceed the direct effect of the penalty which might be imposed.'

(b) 'Reputation, for these purposes, is a question of good character, including honesty and trustworthiness.'

(c) 'The loss of reputation on a conviction for dishonesty is absolute and not relevant to the amount.'

(d) 'Consideration should be given to whether an accused who is undertaking vocational or professional training might suffer damage to reputation so serious that there is a risk that future livelihood might be lost.'

Substantial question of law

'Representation should only be granted under this criterion if a question of law is raised which the applicant cannot be expected to deal with unaided and is a substantial question and is relevant to the applicant's case.'

Tracing and interviewing witnesses

'Details of the witnesses and why there is a necessity for representation to trace and/or interview them, should be included in the application. If details of witnesses are not included, consideration of the application for representation should be deferred until the applicant has provided the court with sufficient information to make a determination.'

Expert cross-examination of a prosecution witness

(a) This 'refers to expert cross-examination of a witness and not only to cross-examination of an expert witness'.

(b) 'Representation should be granted ... when there is a need for professional cross-examination of a witness. This may very likely be the case where the evidence is provided by an expert since an accused person would rarely be capable, for example, of cross-examining a medical or handwriting expert. It may also apply in other cases, such as those where shades of emphasis in the evidence can make an action appear more sinister than it was in fact.'

3.3.2.3 Where to apply for representation

If a case is before a magistrates' court, any application for a representation order should be made to that court.

A magistrates' court which sends a person to the Crown Court for trial or commits a person to the Crown Court for trial or sentence or from which a person appeals to the Crown Court against his conviction or sentence may grant a representation order for the proceedings before the Crown Court (Criminal Defence Service (General) (No 2) Regulations 2001, reg 9).

The Crown Court may grant a representation order for any case that has been sent for trial or has been committed or appealed to it.

3.3.2.4 'Through representation orders'

If the case is going to be sent to the Crown Court for trial under s 51 of the Crime and Disorder Act 1998 (see **6.7**), a solicitor should apply for a 'through representation order' which will enable the solicitor to claim for work done that is relevant to proceedings before a magistrates' court and the Crown Court.

3.3.2.5 How to apply for representation

An application for a representation order in respect of proceedings in a magistrates' court may be made orally or in writing to the justices' clerk (Criminal Defence Service (General) (No 2) Regulations 2001, reg 8).

The more common method of application is in writing using Form A (**Appendix 2(K)**). Particular care should be taken in completing the section of the application form dealing with the 'interests of justice test'. As much information as possible should be given to convince the court that a representation order should be granted to the applicant.

3.3.2.6   The scope of a representation order

If a representation order is granted, a certificate will be issued to the solicitor. An example of a representation order appears at **Appendix 2(L)**.

The following points should be noted in relation to the scope of the certificate.

(a)   Representation orders covering proceedings in a magistrates' court or the Crown Court extend not merely to preparation and representation but also to advice on, and assistance in, preparing a notice of appeal. A separate representation order is necessary, however, for the conduct of the appeal itself.

(b)   A representation order in the magistrates' court will normally consist of representation by solicitor only. Where there is more than one defendant, the same solicitor will act for all defendants unless there is a conflict of interest. If there is a conflict, separate representation is permitted.

(c)   In a magistrates' court, representation by both solicitor and advocate (barrister or solicitor with higher rights of audience) is permitted if the offence is an indictable offence which is unusually grave or difficult and, in the opinion of the court it is desirable to have representation by solicitor and advocate.

(d)   In a magistrates' court, where the order does not provide for representation by an advocate, the solicitor can still instruct an advocate to conduct the proceedings in court. However, the solicitor will not be paid for dictating and delivering the brief to an advocate and no payment will be made for accompanying an advocate in court.

(e)   Representation in the Crown Court normally consists of representation by a solicitor and advocate. For guidance on when an advocate need be attended by a solicitor's representative at the Crown Court, see Solicitor's Professional Conduct Rule 20.04. The principles contained in Rule 20.04 match the provisions restricting the circumstances in which remuneration can be paid for attendance at the Crown Court.

(f)   Representation orders are not generally retrospective. However, pre-order work may be claimed under a representation order (once granted) provided certain conditions are met.

3.3.2.7   Refusal of representation

An applicant who is refused representation can always make another application to the court (Criminal Defence Service (Representation Order Appeals) Regulations 2001 (SI 2001/1168)).

Where an application for a representation order is made and is refused, a claim for payment can still be made by the solicitor under the advice and assistance part of the contract with the Legal Services Commission. However, such a claim is restricted to a maximum of one hour's work. This work could include, for example, advising on whether an application for a representation order is likely to be successful, completing an application for a representation order and, if necessary, advocacy at an early hearing.

3.3.2.8   Payment of fees under a representation order

Work carried out in a magistrates' court under a representation order is remunerated by a standard fee in most cases. At the conclusion of the case, a claim for payment should be made on the prescribed form and submitted to the Legal Services Commission Regional Office.

Certain complex cases are outside the standard fee scheme and are remunerated at fixed hourly rates on a 'work done basis'.

Work done in the Crown Court is in some cases remunerated by the payment of standard fees. In other cases, payment is on a 'work done basis' although fixed hourly rates are prescribed. A claim for payment should be made to the Crown Court Taxing Office.

3.3.3   Court duty solicitors

The court duty solicitor scheme aims to provide an emergency service to those appearing in a magistrates' court who would otherwise be unrepresented. Representation is available on that day only, is free of charge and is restricted to advising those who are in custody and those who are charged with imprisonable offences. A duty solicitor will apply for adjournments, make bail applications and present pleas in mitigation. The regulations do not permit a duty solicitor to conduct the trial of a not guilty plea or committal proceedings.

The court duty solicitor scheme is staffed by contracted solicitors on a rota basis. Remuneration is provided from the Legal Services Commission at fixed hourly rates for advice and assistance (including advocacy assistance). Subject to checking that the client does not want any other solicitor to handle the case and explaining that the client may choose any solicitor to act or a public defender, it is permissible, and indeed usual, for the duty solicitor to agree to take over the conduct of cases that will proceed further. Further work must be financed privately or under a representation order.

3.3.4   Further reading

The *Legal Services Commission Manual* (Sweet & Maxwell) is the standard reference work for publicly funded criminal work. See also Ede and Edwards, *Criminal Defence* (The Law Society, 2002).

3.4   Adjournments, remands and bail

3.4.1   Adjournments

Magistrates may adjourn a case at any time.

Common reasons for adjournments include:

(a)   to enable the prosecution or defence to prepare their case. Examples include enabling the prosecution to receive a full file from the police or for the defence to be provided with advance disclosure of the prosecution case;

(b)   to fix a date for committal proceedings or trial;

(c)   to obtain reports to assist the court in sentencing.

3.4.2   Remands

When a court adjourns a case, it will also consider whether or not to remand the defendant. If the case is adjourned without a remand, the court has not taken any steps to ensure that the defendant attends the next hearing. A remand is an adjournment upon which the court decides to attempt to ensure the defendant's attendance at the next hearing.

A remand may be in custody until the adjourned hearing date or on bail. Magistrates may remand the defendant in any case. Unless the offence is very trivial (eg, careless driving), the defendant is likely to be remanded on an adjournment.

3.4.2.1 Individual duration of remands

Before conviction or committal for trial

The general rule is that a defendant may not be remanded in custody for more than eight clear days at a time. Where the defendant is remanded on bail, subject to his consent, there is no time-limit (Magistrates' Courts Act 1980, s 128).

Where there are successive remands in custody, a defendant need only be brought before the court on every fourth remand, provided he has consented (and such consent has not been withdrawn) and has a solicitor acting for him (whether present in court or not) (Magistrates' Courts Act 1980, s 128(3A)).

Further, a court has power under s 128A to remand a defendant in custody for up to 28 days if it has previously remanded him in custody for the same offence, he is before the court, and it can set a date to remand him to on which it expects the next stage of the proceedings to take place (this may be within the 28-day remand period).

After conviction

After conviction by magistrates, adjournments may be for successive periods of four weeks unless the defendant is remanded in custody, in which case the maximum period is three weeks (s 10(3)).

Following committal to the Crown Court

If a defendant is committed to the Crown Court for trial or sentence, he is remanded on bail or in custody until the case is due to be heard.

3.4.2.2 Time-limits

Under the Prosecution of Offences Act 1985, s 22(1), the Home Secretary has the power to make regulations which lay down time-limits for the prosecution to complete any stage in criminal proceedings and the maximum overall period that a defendant may be remanded in custody.

The Prosecution of Offences (Custody Time Limits) Regulations 1987 (SI 1987/ 2299) lay down maximum overall periods for which a defendant can be remanded in custody awaiting completion of a particular stage in the proceedings.

The maximum overall periods of remand in custody at the magistrates' court are:

(a) 70 days before summary trial (56 days for a summary offence) unless the decision for summary trial is taken within 56 days, in which case the limit is reduced to 56 days;

(b) 70 days before committal proceedings (regs 4(2) and 4(4)).

When the time-limits have expired, the defendant must be released on bail unless the court considers it reasonable to extend the period.

Example 1

Sarah appears before the magistrates for the first time charged with a complicated theft. She is remanded in custody for 7 days. At the next hearing, Sarah is remanded in custody for a further 28 days, after which plea before venue and mode of trial are to take place. Twenty-eight days later, Sarah is back before the court. She indicates a not guilty plea, the magistrates accept jurisdiction and Sarah enters a not guilty plea. The case is adjourned for 7 days for a pre-trial review and Sarah is remanded in custody. At the pre-trial review, a not guilty hearing date is set for 14 days' time and Sarah is remanded in custody. By the time of the next hearing, Sarah will have been in custody for 56 days (7 + 28 + 7 + 14). If the prosecution is not ready to proceed with the not guilty hearing on that date, Sarah must be released on bail unless the magistrates agree that it is reasonable to extend the custody time-limit.

Example 2

Joe appears before the magistrates, for the first time, on a charge of assault occasioning actual bodily harm. He is remanded in custody for 7 days. At the next hearing, Joe is remanded in custody for a further 28 days, after which committal proceedings are to take place. Twenty-eight days later, Joe is back before the court. The prosecution asks for a further 28-day remand as it is not ready to proceed to committal. The magistrates agree, on the basis that the committal will take place at the next hearing. By the time of the next hearing, Joe will have been in custody for 63 days (7 + 28 + 28). If the prosecution is not ready to proceed with committal on that date, then Joe can only be remanded in custody for a further 7 days (and then must be released on bail) unless the magistrates agree that it is reasonable to extend the custody time-limit.

The maximum overall periods for remands in custody at the Crown Court (for indictable only or either way offences) are:

(a)   182 days from sending the case for trial and the start of the trial less any period (or the aggregate of any periods) during which the defendant has been in the custody of the magistrates' court since that first appearance for the offence (reg 5(6B), as amended by the Prosecution of Offences (Custody Time Limits) (Modification) Regulations 1998 (SI 1998/3037));

(b)   112 days from committing the case for trial and the start of the trial (reg 5(3)(a)).

3.4.3   Bail

3.4.3.1   The nature of bail

Whenever magistrates adjourn a case and decide to remand the defendant, they must also decide whether the remand should be in custody or on bail.

A defendant who is granted bail is under a duty to surrender to custody at the time and place appointed (Bail Act 1976, s 3(1)).

A defendant who fails, without reasonable cause, to surrender to custody is guilty of the offence of absconding. The burden of proving reasonable cause lies on the defendant (Bail Act 1976, s 6).

The offence of absconding is punishable on summary conviction in a magistrates' court with up to 3 months' imprisonment and/or a £5000 fine. In the Crown Court, the matter is dealt with as a criminal contempt and is punishable with up to 12 months' imprisonment and/or an unlimited fine.

If a defendant fails to surrender to bail, the court may issue a warrant for his arrest (Bail Act 1976, s 7(1), (2)).

3.4.3.2   Limitations on bail (Criminal Justice and Public Order Act 1994, s 25)

A court may, only in exceptional circumstances, grant bail to a person charged with:

(a)   murder;

(b)   attempted murder;

(c)   manslaughter;

(d)   rape; or

(e)   attempted rape

if that person has been previously convicted of any one of these offences. There is no requirement that the previous conviction be for the same offence as the current charge before the court.

3.4.3.3   The right to bail (Bail Act 1976, s 4)

A court has an obligation to grant bail (except in the 'limited bail' cases above, and as provided in Sch 1 (see below)):

(a)   prior to conviction, to all defendants;

(b)   after conviction, to a defendant whose case is then adjourned for reports or enquiries;

(c)   to offenders brought before a magistrates' court for breach of a community rehabilitation order or community punishment order.

The basic right to bail does not apply:

(a)   where magistrates having convicted a defendant commit him to the Crown Court for sentence (see **10.2.16**);

(b)   when a person is appealing against conviction or sentence.

3.4.3.4   Exceptions to the right to bail for a defendant charged with an imprisonable offence (Bail Act 1976, Sch 1, Part I)

A defendant need not be granted bail if:

(2)   ... the court is satisfied that there are substantial grounds for believing that the defendant, if released on bail ... would:

    (a)   fail to surrender to custody, or

    (b)   commit an offence while on bail, or

    (c)   interfere with witnesses or otherwise obstruct the course of justice, whether in relation to himself or any other person,

(3)   ... the court is satisfied that the defendant should be kept in custody for his own protection or, if he is a child or young person, for his own welfare.

(4)   the defendant is ... in custody in pursuance of the sentence of a court ...

(5)   ... the court is satisfied that it has not been practicable to obtain sufficient information for the purpose of taking the decisions required ... for want of time since the institution of the proceedings against him.

(7)   ... the case is adjourned for inquiries or a report, ... if it appears to the court that it would be impracticable to complete the inquiries or make the report without keeping the defendant in custody.

Paragraph 2A and paragraph 6 provide further exceptions to the defendant's right to bail:

2A(1)   If the defendant falls within this paragraph, he may not be granted bail unless the court is satisfied that there is no significant risk of his committing an offence while on bail (whether subject to bail conditions or not).

(2)   The defendant falls within this paragraph if—

    (a)   he is aged over 18 or over, and

    (b)   it appears to the court that he was on bail in criminal proceedings at the date of the offence.

6(1)   If the defendant falls within this paragraph, he may not be granted bail unless the court is satisfied that there is no significant risk that, if released on bail (whether subject to conditions or not), he would fail to surrender to custody.

(2)   Subject to subparagraph (3) below, the defendant falls within this paragraph if—

(a)   he is aged 18 or over, and

(b)   it appears to the court that, having been released on bail in or in connection with the proceedings for the offence, he failed to surrender to custody.

(3)   Where it appears to the court that the defendant had reasonable cause for his failure to surrender to custody, he does not fall within this paragraph unless it also appears to the court that he failed to surrender to custody at the appointed place as soon as reasonably practicable after the appointed time."

3.4.3.5   Factors

In considering whether the para 2, para 2A or para 6 grounds set out above apply, a court should take into account the following factors:

(a)   the nature and seriousness of the offence or default (and the probable method of dealing with the defendant for it),

(b)   the character, antecedents, associations and community ties of the defendant,

(c)   the defendant's record as respects the fulfilment of his obligations under previous grants of bail in criminal proceedings,

(d)   except in the case of a defendant whose case is adjourned for inquiries or a report, the strength of the evidence of his having committed the offence or having defaulted. (Bail Act 1976, Sch 1, Pt I, para 9)

These factors are not exceptions to the defendant's right to bail. They are factors that the court takes into account when deciding whether to grant bail. Such factors can be used by the prosecution to explain why a particular exception to the defendant's right to bail applies or by the defence in support of the defendant's bail application.

These factors are considered below.

The nature and seriousness of the offence and the probable method of dealing with it

This factor is particularly relevant to an argument that, if released on bail, the defendant will fail to surrender to custody. If the offence is a serious one the prosecution may say that a custodial sentence is likely to follow conviction and if released on bail the defendant will not wish to face that possibility. The defence will sometimes argue that the very fact that an offence is serious will mean that the defendant is likely to answer bail as he will not wish to make matters any worse for himself than they are already. Furthermore, the defence may acknowledge that the offence is serious, state that the defendant is pleading not guilty and is anxious to attend court to clear his name.

The defendant's character and antecedents

The defendant's criminal record is admissible on an application for bail. A history of offending may be relevant to an argument that the defendant would commit an offence while on bail. If he has a history of committing the particular type of offence with which he is charged then, if released on bail, he may offend again. A defendant's previous good character will also be relevant.

The defendant's associations

This factor may be relevant to arguments that the defendant will commit an offence while on bail or interfere with witnesses. If it is alleged that the defendant associates with known criminals or is perhaps a member of an organised gang this could indicate that he will commit further offences. If a prosecution witness is known to the defendant or is perhaps a relative then an argument may be put forward that he will attempt to interfere with that witness by persuading him to change his evidence.

The defendant's community ties

This is likely to be relevant in relation to an argument that the defendant will fail to surrender to custody. If the defendant is of no fixed abode, has no relatives in the area, or has no job then it can be argued that if released on bail there is little to keep him in the area. Conversely, if he has a fixed residence, family ties or secure employment this may indicate that he will stay in the area and surrender to custody.

The defendant's record in relation to previous grants of bail

Any history of failing to surrender to custody or committing offences while on bail will be relevant. Conversely, a defendant with a criminal record who has no history of failure to surrender or of committing offences while on bail is entitled to have this taken into account when a court decides whether there are substantial grounds for believing that he would fail to surrender to custody or would commit an offence while on bail.

Strength of evidence

Except where the case has been adjourned for enquiries or report, the strength of the evidence against the defendant will be a consideration.

If the prosecution alleges that the evidence against the defendant is strong, this will support an argument of probable failure to surrender to custody. This factor is unlikely to be used in isolation but, if combined with a serious offence which indicates a custodial sentence on conviction, it can be very persuasive. Equally, the defence can argue that the evidence against the defendant is not strong (eg, it may consist of disputed identification evidence) and that as a result the defendant is anxious to attend the trial to clear his name.

The arguments cited above are illustrative only and the factors can be used in any way by the prosecution or defence to support or oppose an application for a remand in custody.

3.4.3.6 Exceptions to the right to bail for a defendant charged with a non-imprisonable offence (Bail Act 1976, Sch 1, Part II)

If the defendant is charged with a non-imprisonable offence, the prosecution will not normally oppose bail. Grounds for refusing bail are:

(a) it appears to the court that, having been previously granted bail in criminal proceedings, the defendant has failed to surrender to custody in accordance with his obligations under the grant of bail and the court believes, in view of that failure, that the defendant, if released on bail (whether subject to conditions or not), would fail to surrender to custody;

(b) the defendant ought to be kept in custody for his own protection or, if he is a child or young person, for his own welfare;

(c)   the defendant is in custody in pursuance of the sentence of a court;

(d)   the defendant, having been released on bail in the proceedings, has been arrested for absconding or breaking conditions of bail.

These grounds are largely self-explanatory.

3.4.3.7 Conditions of bail (Bail Act 1976, s 3)

A defendant may be required by a court:

> ... to comply, before release on bail or later, with such requirements as appear to the court to be necessary to secure that—
> (a)   he surrenders to custody,
> (b)   he does not commit an offence while on bail,
> (c)   he does not interfere with witnesses or otherwise obstruct the course of justice whether in relation to himself or any other person,
> (d)   he makes himself available for the purpose of enabling enquiries or a report to be made to assist the court in dealing with him for the offence,
> (e)   before the time appointed for him to surrender to custody, he attends an interview with an authorised advocate or authorised litigator, as defined by s 119(1) of the Courts and Legal Services Act 1990. (s 3(6))

'Authorised advocate' includes a barrister or solicitor and 'authorised litigator' includes a solicitor.

Conditions may be suggested by the defence when attempting to persuade a court to grant bail or they may be imposed by the court of its own volition. Such conditions include sureties, security, reporting regularly to a police station, a curfew and a condition of non-communication with named prosecution witnesses. This list is not exhaustive, and any condition may be imposed which appears to be realistic.

Sureties

A surety is a person who enters into a recognisance of money (eg, X stands surety for Y in the sum of £10,000) and is under an obligation to use every reasonable effort to ensure the defendant's appearance at court. The surety is not required to pay over any money at this stage.

If the defendant fails to appear, the court is required to declare the immediate and automatic forfeiture of the recognisance (Magistrates' Courts Act 1980, s 120(1A)). After declaring the recognisance forfeited, the court must issue a summons to the surety to appear before the court to explain why he should not pay the sum. The court will then decide whether all, part or none of the sum should be paid.

In considering the suitability of a proposed surety the Bail Act 1976, s 8(2) states that:

> ... regard may be had (amongst other things) to—
> (a)   the surety's financial resources;
> (b)   his character and any previous convictions of his; and
> (c)   his proximity (whether in point of kinship, place of residence or otherwise) to the person for whom he is to be surety.

Thus a person without any assets or with a substantial criminal record or who lives a long way from the defendant is unlikely to be acceptable. As a matter of professional conduct, a solicitor should not stand surety for his client.

A court may indicate that it is prepared to grant bail subject to a suitable surety being found. In such a case, the amount of the recognisance should be fixed by the court and the suitability of any surety who is found can be determined by a magistrate, a magistrates' clerk or an inspector at a police station. If a surety is rejected in these circumstances, it is possible to apply to the court for a final decision (see Bail Act 1976, s 8(4), (5)).

Sureties may be put forward to overcome a prosecution objection that the defendant will fail to surrender to custody.

Security

The defendant may be required to give security for his surrender in the form of money or chattels.

This condition is again relevant to a prosecution objection to bail on the basis that the defendant will fail to surrender to custody. Deposit of a sum of money is an example of security.

Reporting to a police station

This condition can again be used to overcome a prosecution objection that the defendant will fail to surrender to custody. Reporting to a police station can be daily or even twice daily, where appropriate.

Curfew

An example of the imposition of a curfew is that the defendant shall not leave his place of residence between the hours of 6 pm and 7 am. The condition is frequently used to overcome an objection to bail that the defendant will commit further offences while on bail. It may be particularly relevant where the defendant is charged with or has a history of night-time offending.

Non-communication with prosecution witnesses

This condition can be used to overcome a prosecution objection to bail that the defendant will interfere with witnesses. If the named witness is a relative with whom the defendant resides it will, of course, be necessary to find the defendant alternative accommodation.

Residence

A condition of residence, frequently expressed as a condition to live and sleep at a specified address, can be used to overcome a prosecution objection to bail that the defendant will fail to surrender to custody. It can be used where the defendant has a known address or where he is allegedly of no fixed abode. If the defendant is of no fixed abode, it may be possible to find a place for him at a bail hostel. These are institutions (often run by the Probation Service) which can provide accommodation for people who would otherwise be refused bail on the basis of no fixed abode. Strict conditions, for example as to hours kept, have to be complied with.

3.4.3.8 Variation and breach of conditions

The court may vary conditions or, subsequent to the granting of bail, impose them on application by either party.

The police have power to arrest without warrant for breach of bail conditions (Bail Act 1976, s 7). Breach of condition is not, of itself, an offence but will create a ground for a court to refuse bail in the present proceedings.

3.4.3.9   Bail procedure

If the prosecution is objecting to bail, the following procedure will apply.

(a)   The prosecutor will make an application for a remand in custody and will hand in to the court a list of the defendant's previous convictions. The prosecutor will state the statutory objections to bail being granted and will cite relevant facts of the case in support.

(b)   The defence advocate will make an application for bail. A good application for bail will deal with each of the prosecution objections in turn, offering conditions of bail where appropriate.

(c)   Evidence may be called at a bail hearing. The court may wish to hear from a prospective employer or someone who is prepared to offer a home to the defendant. However, the usual rules of evidence do not apply and the court may accept hearsay from witnesses and mere assertions of fact from the advocates.

(d)   The court decides whether to remand in custody or on bail. If bail is granted subject to a surety, the court will hear evidence on oath from the surety in order to be satisfied as to the suitability of the surety.

A court which grants or withholds bail or which imposes or varies conditions must make a record of the decision in the prescribed form. A copy will then be given to the defendant.

Further, a magistrates' court or Crown Court must give reasons (and include a note of them in the record) for withholding bail or for imposing or varying conditions and it must normally give the defendant a copy of the note.

If bail is opposed by the prosecutor and a magistrates' court or a Crown Court grants bail, reasons for granting bail must be given (and a note of them included in the record of decision). A copy of the record must be given to the prosecutor if he so requests (Bail Act 1976, s 5).

An example of the prescribed form appears at **Appendix 2(M)**. A chart summarising the above procedure is included at **Appendix 1(F)**.

In preparing for a bail application, it is useful for the defence solicitor to discuss the grounds for objection with the prosecutor and to see whether or not the objections can be overcome by the imposition of suitable conditions.

3.4.3.10   Further applications when bail is refused

To the magistrates' court

If a court refuses bail, it is under a duty at each subsequent hearing to consider the question of bail, provided that:

(a)   the defendant is still in custody; and

(b)   the right to bail still applies.

This does not necessarily mean that the court must hear another full bail application. Part IIA of Sch 1 to the Bail Act 1976 provides:

2. At the first hearing after that at which the court decided not to grant the defendant bail he may support an application for bail with any argument as to fact or law that he desires (whether or not he has advanced that argument previously).

3. At subsequent hearings the court need not hear arguments as to fact or law which it has heard previously.

Example

Daniel is remanded in custody for 7 days on 7 June following a bail application by his solicitor. The solicitor may make a further application on 14 June using the same arguments. If Daniel is remanded in custody again, new arguments will be necessary before the court will hear a further application. New arguments could include matters such as the availability of a job or a surety.

In applying this rule, the court should ignore a hearing at which bail was refused on the basis that it has not been practicable to obtain sufficient information about the defendant (*R v Calder Justices, ex p Kennedy* [1992] Crim LR 496). In the example above, if Daniel was remanded in custody on 7 June on the insufficient information ground, he would still be entitled to bail applications at his next two hearings.

If a magistrates' court remands a person in custody after a fully argued bail application, it must issue a certificate confirming that it has heard full argument. An example of a full argument certificate appears at **Appendix 2(M)**.

To the Crown Court (Supreme Court Act 1981, s 81, as amended by the Criminal Justice Act 1982, s 60)

A defendant who has been remanded in custody by a magistrates' court may apply to the Crown Court for bail provided that the magistrates have issued a full argument certificate on the bail application which has been refused.

A defendant who has been committed in custody to the Crown Court for trial or sentence or who has appealed to the Crown Court can apply to the Crown Court for bail. No full argument certificate is required as the magistrates no longer have jurisdiction to hear applications in the case.

The rights to apply to the Crown Court above are entirely separate. The test is whether or not the case has yet been sent to the Crown Court for trial, sentence or appeal. If it has not, then a full argument certificate is required. If it has been sent to the Crown Court, a full argument certificate is not required.

Representation

A grant of representation in criminal proceedings will cover representation in related bail proceedings (Access to Justice Act 1999, Sch 3, para 2(2)). This means that representation in Crown Court bail proceedings falls within the scope of the original grant of representation in the magistrates' court.

3.4.3.11   Challenging grants of bail

By s 1(1) of the Bail (Amendment) Act 1993:

Where a magistrates' court grants bail to a person who is charged with or convicted of—

(a)   an offence punishable by a term of imprisonment of five years or more; or

(b)   an offence under section 12 (taking a conveyance without authority) or s 12A (aggravated vehicle taking) of the Theft Act 1968,

the prosecution may appeal to a judge of the Crown Court against the granting of bail.

Such an appeal can be made only if the prosecution objected to the magistrates granting bail to the defendant.

3.4.3.12 Prosecution request for reconsideration of bail (Bail Act 1976, s 5B)

If a defendant is charged with an indictable or either way offence and a magistrates' court has granted him bail, the prosecution can ask the magistrates to reconsider their decision. This power can be exercised only if information has come to light which was not available to the court when the decision to grant bail was taken.

A magistrates' court which reconsiders a bail decision may:

(a)   vary conditions of bail;

(b)   impose new conditions of bail; or

(c)   withhold bail.

3.5 Bail and the Human Rights Act 1998

In June 2001 the Law Commission published *Bail and the Human Rights Act 1998* (Paper No 269) accompanied by the Guidance. The Guidance has been disseminated to the judiciary and justice's clerks and is reproduced in **Appendix 5**.

3.6 Further reading

Further details on the law of bail can be found in numerous publications including:

Archbold: Criminal Pleading, Evidence and Practice (Sweet & Maxwell, 2004)

Blackstone's Criminal Practice (Oxford University Press, 2004)

John Sprack, *Emmins on Criminal Procedure* (Oxford University Press, 2002)

Practical guidance can be found in:

Ede and Edwards, *Criminal Defence* (The Law Society, 2002)

Chapter 4

The Prosecution of an Offence Triable Either Way

4.1	Introduction	63
4.2	Advance disclosure of the prosecution case	63
4.3	The plea before venue procedure	63
4.4	The mode of trial procedure	64
4.5	Practical points on mode of trial procedure	65
4.6	Advising the client	66
4.7	Further reading	68

4.1 Introduction

An offence triable either way can be tried either in a magistrates' court or in the Crown Court before a judge and jury. The first substantive step in the prosecution will be plea before venue. If the defendant indicates a not guilty plea or refuses to indicate a plea, the mode of trial enquiry will take place. The purpose of this procedure is to determine whether the case will be dealt with by a magistrates' court or by the Crown Court.

4.2 Advance disclosure of the prosecution case

Under the Magistrates' Court (Advance Information) Rules 1985, SI 1985/601, a defendant charged with an either way offence is entitled to advance disclosure of the prosecution case. Before a decision is made as to plea before venue and mode of trial, the defence should usually request advance disclosure from the prosecution. Advance disclosure will usually include copies of written statements of prosecution witnesses.

4.3 The plea before venue procedure

The procedure is as follows. (This is summarised in chart form at **Appendix 1(K)**.)

(a) The charge is read out by the clerk to the justices.

(b) The clerk to the justices will ensure that the defendant is aware of his right to advance disclosure of the prosecution case. If necessary, the hearing will be adjourned to a future date to enable advance disclosure to take place.

(c) (i) The clerk to the justices will explain to the defendant that he may indicate how he would plead if the matter were to proceed to trial.

(ii) The clerk will tell the defendant that if he indicates that he intends to plead guilty he will be treated as having pleaded guilty before the magistrates who may then sentence him. However, the magistrates could still commit him to the Crown Court to be sentenced if they feel that their powers of sentencing are inadequate.

(iii) The clerk will then ask the defendant for his plea.

(iv) If the defendant indicates a guilty plea, the court will proceed as though he had just pleaded guilty at summary trial (see **10.3.2**).

(v) If the defendant refuses to indicate a plea or indicates that he intends to plead not guilty, the procedure in 4.4 below will be followed.

4.4 The mode of trial procedure

The procedure is as follows. (This is summarised in chart form at **Appendix 1(K)**.)

(a)   The prosecutor will address the court. He will outline the nature of the charge and will indicate in which court the prosecution feels that the case should be tried.

(b)   The defence advocate may then address the court. He may indicate where the defence feels the case should be tried.

(c)   The magistrates then announce whether they are prepared to deal with the case or whether they feel that the case is suitable only for trial in the Crown Court. The Magistrates' Courts Act 1980, s 19(3) states that the magistrates, in reaching their decision, must take into account:

   (i)   the nature of the offence;

   (ii)   whether the circumstances make the offence one of serious character;

   (iii) whether the punishment which a magistrates' court would have power to inflict for it would be adequate; and

   (iv)   any other circumstances which appear to the court to make it more suitable for the offence to be tried in one way rather than the other.

   The defendant's previous convictions are irrelevant for the purpose of deciding mode of trial (*R v Colchester Justices, ex p North East Essex Building Co Ltd* [1977] 1 WLR 1109).

(d)   If the magistrates decide that the case is not suitable for summary trial then the defendant has no choice. The case will be adjourned to a future date for committal proceedings to take place.

(e)   If the magistrates are prepared to deal with the case then:

   (i)   the clerk to the justices will explain to the defendant that he has the right to elect for trial in the Crown Court;

   (ii)   the clerk will inform the defendant that if he consents to be tried by the magistrates and is convicted, the magistrates may commit him to the Crown Court to be sentenced if they feel that their powers of sentencing are inadequate. (Magistrates cannot imprison a defendant for more than 6 months or, if two or more either way offences are committed, for more than a total of 12 months.) Such a decision may be taken, for example, if facts emerge after mode of trial has been determined (ie, usually at a trial of a not guilty plea or a sentencing hearing):

   –   that show that the offence is so serious that only a custodial sentence would be justified; and

   –   that the powers of the magistrates to pass a custodial sentence are inadequate.

   Otherwise, if the magistrates feel at the mode of trial hearing that their powers of sentence are likely to be inadequate they will commit to the Crown Court for trial;

   (iii) the defendant makes his decision. If he consents to magistrates' court trial and pleads guilty (having earlier indicated no plea or now having changed his plea), his case may be dealt with immediately. If he consents to magistrates' court trial and pleads not guilty, the case will be adjourned to a pre-trial review (PTR). At the PTR, the magistrates will set a date for trial (see **8.4.2**). If the defendant asks for Crown Court trial, he will not be asked to plead. The case will be adjourned to a future date for committal proceedings to take place.

4.5 Practical points on mode of trial procedure

4.5.1 Guidelines

In reaching a decision as to whether or not a case should be sent to the Crown Court, the magistrates will bear in mind the guidelines issued in *Practice Direction (Criminal Proceedings: Consolidation)* [2002] 3 All ER 904, para 51, *Mode of trial*. The purpose of the guidelines is to help magistrates decide whether or not to commit either way offences for trial in the Crown Court. Their objective is to provide guidance, not direction. They are not intended to impinge upon a magistrate's duty to consider each case individually and on its particular facts.

4.5.2 Observations in the guidelines

The following general observations are made in the guidelines.

(a)   The prosecution version of the facts should be assumed to be correct.

(b)   Where cases involve complex questions of fact or law, committal for trial should be considered.

(c)   Where two or more defendants are jointly charged with an offence each has an individual right to elect his mode of trial.

Example

Christine and Dorothy are jointly charged with assault. Both defendants indicate not guilty pleas. The magistrates are prepared to deal with the case. Christine elects trial by jury. Dorothy consents to a summary trial. According to *R v Ipswich, Justices ex p Callaghan* (1995) 159 JP 748, each defendant has the right to elect mode of trial even if it results in not guilty trials before separate courts.

(d)   The presumption is that cases will be tried summarily unless:

   (i)   one of the relevant circumstances listed below is present; and

   (ii)   the sentencing powers of the magistrates are considered insufficient.

The guidelines identify certain features of specific either way offences which may make them unsuitable for trial by magistrates.

Burglary

Burglary of dwelling-houses involving daytime entry of occupied house; night-time entry of a house normally occupied; part of a series of offences; soiling, ransacking, damage or vandalism; professional hallmarks; unrecovered property of high value (at least £10,000).

Note that if any person in the dwelling is subjected to violence or the threat of violence, the offence cannot be tried by magistrates (Magistrates' Courts Act 1980, Sch 1, para 28(c)).

Non dwellings – entry of a pharmacy or doctor's surgery; fear caused or violence done to anyone lawfully on the premises; professional hallmarks; substantial vandalism; unrecovered property of high value (at least £10,000).

Wounding/inflicting grievous bodily harm and assault occasioning actual bodily harm

Use of a weapon of a kind likely to cause serious injury; violence to the vulnerable, for example, the elderly or infirm; more than minor injury caused by kicking, headbutting; serious violence on those whose work brings them into contact with the public, for example, police, bus drivers, shopkeepers, publicans; the offence has clear racial motives.

Theft and fraud

Breach of trust by person in a position of substantial authority or in whom a high degree of trust placed; committed in a sophisticated manner; committed by an organised gang; vulnerable victim, for example, elderly or infirm; unrecovered property of high value (see 'Burglary' above).

Drugs

Class A: Supply: possession with intent to supply: these cases should be committed for trial. Possession: should be committed for trial unless the amount is consistent only with personal use.

Class B: Supply: possession with intent to supply: should be committed for trial unless where there is only small scale supply for no payment.

Possession: should be committed for trial when the quantity is not substantial and not consistent only with personal use.

4.5.3 Representations by the defence

Although the defence is given an opportunity to address the court on mode of trial, in many cases this will not be necessary. If the prosecution requests Crown Court trial and the defence agrees, then there is unlikely to be any reason to address the court. This will also be the case if the defence agrees with the prosecution's request for magistrates' court trial. Representations may be necessary if the defence does not agree with the prosecution's arguments. The defence may, for example, request that the magistrates deal with the case, whilst the prosecution requests Crown Court trial.

4.5.4 Defendant changes his mind

A defendant who consents to trial by magistrates may wish to change his mind and go to the Crown Court. This point sometimes arises where the defendant was not legally represented when he made his original decision. The magistrates have a discretion to permit the defendant to change his mind and elect for Crown Court trial at any time before the conclusion of the prosecution evidence (Magistrates' Courts Act 1980, s 25(2)). This discretion may, for example, be exercised in the defendant's favour where he did not understand his legal position or the significance of the choice which he was making. See *R v Birmingham Justices, ex p Hodgson and Another* [1985] 2 All ER 193.

4.5.5 Magistrates' discretion

The magistrates have a discretion to change from Crown Court trial to magistrates' court trial at any time before the conclusion of committal proceedings (see **Chapter 7**), provided the defendant consents (Magistrates' Courts Act 1980, s 25(3)). This is unlikely to happen very often in practice.

4.6 Advising the client

If the defendant indicates a guilty plea, the case will be dealt with in the magistrates' court and the defendant will have no choice. If the defendant indicates a not guilty plea, the decision as to whether a case will be tried in a magistrates' court or in the Crown Court will rest with the defendant if the magistrates indicate that they are prepared to deal with the matter. A defendant is entitled to expect advice from his solicitor as to the appropriate court for his case. In formulating this advice, the following factors may be relevant.

4.6.1   Factors in favour of the Crown Court

4.6.1.1   Likelihood of conviction

Whilst this is subject to knowledge of a local court, it is generally felt that there is a better chance of acquittal in the Crown Court. This may be the case where the defendant is relying on a common defence, such as 'I forgot to pay' in a theft by way of shoplifting case. Magistrates tend to hear the same stories on numerous occasions and may become 'case hardened'. Most jurors are new to the criminal justice system and may be more inclined to believe the defendant's story. If police evidence is to be challenged, magistrates may be familiar with the officer in question and the question may be better raised in the Crown Court before a jury.

4.6.1.2   Procedure for dealing with the admissibility of evidence

If the admissibility of evidence is to be challenged, the Crown Court provides the better procedure for doing so. Questions of admissibility are decided by the judge in the absence of the jury, so if evidence is ruled inadmissible, the jury will not hear it. In the magistrates' court, the justices are arbiters of fact and law, therefore they will have to hear the evidence (eg, that the defendant has made a confession) before ruling on its admissibility.

4.6.2   Factors in favour of the magistrates' court

4.6.2.1   Speed and stress

A case is likely to be dealt with more quickly in a magistrates' court. The proceedings are less formal than in the Crown Court and may, therefore, be less stressful for the defendant.

4.6.2.2   Cost

If the defendant is convicted the prosecution will apply for a contribution towards prosecution costs. A Crown Court trial is likely to be more costly than a hearing in the magistrates' court.

If the defendant is represented under a representation order the judge has the power at the conclusion of the case in the Crown Court to order a defendant to pay all or some of the costs of his defence (see **10.2.14**). No such power is available in the magistrates' court.

4.6.2.3   Sentence

Magistrates' powers of sentencing are limited. A higher sentence may be imposed in the Crown Court. However, it is also necessary to bear in mind the power of a magistrates' court to commit a defendant to the Crown Court for sentencing if the court feels that its powers of sentencing are inadequate. (As to the exercise of this power, see **10.2.16**.)

The advice given to a client as to the appropriate trial court will depend on the facts of the case and which of the factors listed above are considered to be the most important.

4.7 Further reading

See, for example:

Archbold: Criminal Pleading, Evidence and Practice (Sweet & Maxwell, 2004)

Blackstone's Criminal Practice (Oxford University Press, 2004)

John Sprack, *Emmins on Criminal Procedure* (Blackstone Press, 2002)

Chapter 5

Disclosure

5.1	Introduction	69
5.2	Duty to provide advance information	69
5.3	Duty to disclose 'unused material'	70
5.4	Primary disclosure by the prosecution (CPIA 1996, s 3)	70
5.5	Defence disclosure (CPIA 1996, ss 5 and 6)	72
5.6	Secondary disclosure by the prosecution (CPIA 1996, s 7)	73
5.7	Public interest immunity	74
5.8	Application to court for disclosure (CPIA 1996, s 8)	74
5.9	The prosecution's continuing duty of disclosure (CPIA 1996, s 9)	74
5.10	Consequences of failure to comply with disclosure requirements (CPIA 1996, ss 10 and 11)	74
5.11	Further reading	75

5.1 Introduction

In this chapter, the prosecution's duty of disclosure is considered. This duty has two purposes:

(a) the obligation to notify the defence of the evidence upon which the prosecution intend to rely ('advance information');

(b) the obligation to make available to the defence any material of relevance to the case upon which the prosecution does not intend to rely ('unused material').

Both purposes are efforts to ensure a fair trial for the defendant and to achieve 'equality of arms' as far as possible between the prosecution and the defence.

A solicitor cannot advise a defendant properly until he knows the extent of the prosecution case against the defendant. Neither is the solicitor in a position to expose the weaknesses in the prosecution case, or fully investigate the defence case, unless he has access to all the relevant material.

5.2 Duty to provide advance information

This is the obligation on the prosecution to notify the defence of its case (ie, the evidence upon which it intends to rely at trial). The duty applies to all criminal offences but the authority for such a duty and when such a duty arises depends on the classification of offence.

5.2.1 Summary offences

There is no statutory obligation on the prosecution to provide advance information for summary offences. In *R v Stratford Justices, ex p Imbert* [1999] 2 Cr App R 276, the Divisional Court stated that as a matter of good practice disclosure should normally be given. This is recognised in the Attorney-General's Guidelines on Disclosure of Information in Criminal Proceedings (29 November 2000), para 43:

> The prosecutor should ... provide to the defence all evidence upon which the Crown proposes to rely in a summary trial. Such provision should allow the accused or their

legal advisers sufficient time to properly consider the evidence before it is called. Exceptionally, statements may be withheld for the protection of witnesses or to avoid interference with the course of justice.

5.2.2 Either way offences

Under the Magistrates' Courts (Advance Information) Rules 1985, a defendant charged with an either way offence is entitled to advance information of the prosecution case. Before a decision is made as to plea before venue and mode of trial, the defence should usually request advance information from the prosecution. Advance information will usually include copies of written statements of prosecution witnesses.

If the defendant's case is to be committed to the Crown Court, the prosecution must serve copies of its evidence on the defence before the case is committed from the magistrates' court to the Crown Court.

5.2.3 Indictable only offences

If the defendant's case is sent to the Crown Court for trial, the prosecution must serve copies of its evidence on the defence at the Crown Court.

All evidence that the prosecution seek to adduce at the Crown Court trial must be disclosed to the defence.

5.3 Duty to disclose 'unused material'

This is the obligation on the prosecution under the Criminal Procedure and Investigations Act 1996 (CPIA 1996) to make available to the defence any material of relevance upon which it does not intend to rely – 'unused material'.

In order for disclosure of such prosecution 'unused material' to be effective, proper procedures must be followed during the criminal investigation so that information, documents and objects are properly recorded and retained. These procedures are set out in the Criminal Procedure and Investigations Act 1996 Code of Practice (the Code).

The Code provides that all material which is obtained in a criminal investigation and which may be relevant to the investigation is retained and revealed to the prosecution.

The Code is admissible in evidence in all criminal and civil proceedings. If a court considers that any provision of the Code or any breach of the Code is relevant to any question arising in the proceedings, the court must take that into account when deciding the question (s 23).

The scheme for disclosure is described below and diagrams illustrating disclosure of material the prosecution does not intend to rely on appear at **Appendix 1(I)** (magistrates' court) and **Appendix 1(N)** (Crown Court).

5.4 Primary disclosure by the prosecution (CPIA 1996, s 3)

The prosecution's duty of primary disclosure of 'unused material' will apply when the defendant pleads not guilty in the magistrates' court or when the defendant is committed for trial to the Crown Court or sent to the Crown Court for trial.

In such a case, the prosecution must either:

(a)   disclose to the defence any previous undisclosed prosecution material which the prosecution considers might undermine the prosecution case; or

(b   confirm in writing that there is no such material.

5.4.1   Time-limit (CPIA 1996, ss 12 and 13)

The prosecution must make disclosure as soon as is reasonably practicable after the defendant pleads not guilty in the magistrates' court or is committed to the Crown Court for trial.

Example

David is charged with theft. He intends to plead not guilty. Prior to the plea before venue and mode of trial proceedings the prosecution serves the defence with advance disclosure of the prosecution case under the Magistrates' Courts (Advance Information) Rules 1985. At plea before venue, David pleads not guilty. At mode of trial, the magistrates accept jurisdiction and David consents to summary trial. The prosecution must make primary disclosure to the defence of material it does not wish to rely on (unused material) as soon as practicable.

For cases sent to the Crown Court for trial the prosecution must make disclosure as soon as practicable after the prosecution has served its evidence on the defence (see **7.4.3**).

When the prosecutor makes primary disclosure, the prosecutor should send the defendant a notice setting out his rights and duties (Home Office Circular 11/1997, Criminal Procedure and Investigations Act 1996, paras 12 and 13). A copy of the notice of rights and duties appears at **Appendix 2(O)**.

5.4.2   Examples of matters which may fall under the duty of primary disclosure

Some examples of undermining material are found in para 7.3 of the Code:

—   records of the first description of a suspect given to the police by a potential witness, whether or not the description differs from that of the alleged offender;

—   information provided by an accused person which indicates an explanation for the offence with which he has been charged;

—   any material casting doubt on the reliability of a confession;

—   any material casting doubt on the reliability of a witness;

—   any other material which the investigator believes may fall within the test for primary prosecution disclosure in the Act.

Other examples of undermining material were given in the White Paper Disclosure (Cm 2864).

(a)   If part of the prosecution case is a statement by a witness that he saw the defendant near the scene of the crime shortly after it was committed, it will be necessary to disclose a statement by another witness that he saw a person of a different description from the defendant at the same time and place.

(b)   If the defendant has told the police in an interview that he was acting in self-defence, it will be necessary to disclose the statement of any witness who supports this but whom the prosecution does not regard as truthful.

(c)   If the victim died of a hammer blow and part of the prosecution case is a forensic test showing that the blood stains on a hammer found buried in the defendant's back garden matched those of the victim, it will be necessary to disclose a negative test showing that the fingerprints on the hammer did not match those of the defendant.

(d)   If the prosecution is aware that its main witness has a previous conviction, it must disclose it to the defence, since it may affect the weight to be placed on his testimony.

(e)   If the prosecution is in possession of a psychiatric report showing that its main witness has a history of psychiatric disorder with a tendency to fantasise, it should disclose the report since it clearly undermines the credibility of that witness.

(f)   If the prosecution is aware that a prosecution witness has applied for a reward for information leading to the conviction of a person for a criminal offence, it must disclose this to the defence.

(g   If previous versions of witness statements are inconsistent with the final version served on the defence, they must be disclosed.

Further examples are noted by Ede in his book *Active Defence* (The Law Society, 2000):

(a)   the fact of a witness having been hypnotised;

(b)   the fact of a witness having been coached or rehearsed for a TV programme;

(c)   the fact of a payment to a witness other than as a reward.

5.5   Defence disclosure (CPIA 1996, ss 5 and 6)

Where the defendant pleads not guilty at summary trial, once the prosecution has made primary disclosure the defendant may give a 'defence statement' if he wishes but he has no duty to do so.

If the case has been committed to the Crown Court for trial or sent to the Crown Court for trial, once the prosecution has made primary disclosure the defendant must give a 'defence statement'.

The defence statement must be in writing, and must:

(a)   set out in general terms the nature of the defendant's defence;

(b)   indicate the matters on which the defendant takes issue with the prosecution; and

(c)   set out, in the case of each such matter, the reason why the defendant takes issue with the prosecution.

If the 'defence statement' discloses an alibi, the defendant must give particulars of it, including:

(a)   the names and addresses of witnesses who the defendant believes are able to give evidence in support of the alibi (includes evidence of alibi given by the defendant himself); and

(b)   any information, which might help in finding an alibi witness whose name and address is not known to the defendant.

Evidence in support of an alibi is 'evidence tending to show that by reason of the presence of the accused at a particular place or in a particular area at a particular time he was not, or was unlikely to have been, at the place where the offence is alleged to have been committed at the time of its alleged commission' (s 5(8)).

If the defendant does not to give a statement, the prosecution has no duty of secondary disclosure (see **5.6**).

For additional sanctions to which the defendant will be liable if he is deficient in his duty of disclosure, see **5.10.2**.

The Bar Council has issued guidance to counsel about the circumstances which should exist before counsel agrees to draft a defence statement. These remind counsel about the significance of this document and the need to obtain the client's informed agreement before it is sent (see Bar Counsel's Guidance on Drafting Defence Statements, as approved by the Professional Conduct and Complaints Committee, 24 September 1997).

For examples of defence statements see **Appendix 2(V)** and **(W)**.

5.5.1 Time-limit

If the defendant chooses to give a statement it must be given to the prosecution and the court within 14 days of the prosecutor complying, or purporting to comply, with the obligation to provide primary prosecution disclosure (Criminal Procedure and Investigations Act 1996 (Defence Disclosure Time Limits) Regulations 1997 (SI 1997/684), reg 2)).

The period for making defence disclosure may be extended by as many days as the court specifies, but only if an application is made before the expiration of the relevant period (reg 3(2)).

An application for extension of the period must:

(a)   state that the defendant believes, on reasonable grounds, that it is not possible to give a defence statement during the relevant period;

(b)   specify the grounds for so believing; and

(c)   specify the number of days by which the defendant wishes the period to be extended (reg 3(3)).

There is no limit on the number of applications that may be made, but in each case the court may grant an extension only if satisfied that the defendant cannot reasonably give a defence statement within the relevant period (reg 4(2), (3)).

5.6 Secondary disclosure by the prosecution (CPIA 1996, s 7)

If the defendant provides a defence statement, the prosecution must either:

(a)   disclose to the defence any previously undisclosed prosecution material which might be reasonably expected to assist in the defendant's defence as revealed by the defence statement; or

(b)   confirm in writing that there is no such material.

Example

Cathryn is charged with theft. The prosecution allege that the offence took place at about 11 pm on a Saturday evening. Cathryn says nothing when interviewed by the police but the defence later send to the prosecution a 'defence statement' claiming that Cathryn has an alibi: she left her flat at 7 pm that evening to visit a friend and did not return until 3 am on the following morning. The prosecution has evidence that Cathryn was seen entering her flat at 3 am on the Sunday morning but not that she was seen leaving it earlier in the evening. The prosecution is under an obligation to disclose the evidence that Cathryn was seen entering her flat at 3 am.

5.6.1 Time-limit (CPIA 1996, ss 12 and 13)

The prosecution must make secondary disclosure as soon as practicable after the defendant gives a defence statement.

5.7 Public interest immunity

Certain material must not be disclosed to the defendant.

The most important example of this is where a court, on the application of the prosecution, has ruled that it is not in the public interest to disclose it. Such an application is likely to be on the basis that the material in question falls within one of the categories of 'sensitive' material.

Some examples of 'sensitive' material are found in para 6.12 of the Code:

(a)   material relating to national security;

(b)   material given in confidence;

(c)   material relating to informants, undercover police officers, premises used for police surveillance;

(d)   techniques used in the detection of crime;

(e)   material relating to a child witness (eg, material generated by a local authority social services department).

5.8 Application to court for disclosure (CPIA 1996, s 8)

If at any time:

(a)   the defendant has given a defence statement; and

(b)   the prosecution has complied with or failed to comply with secondary disclosure; and

(c)   the defendant has reasonable cause to believe that there is undisclosed prosecution material which might reasonably be expected to assist in his defence,

the defendant can apply to the court for an order requiring the prosecution to disclose that material.

5.9 The prosecution's continuing duty of disclosure (CPIA 1996, s 9)

This section requires the prosecution to keep under review the prosecution material and to disclose it as soon as reasonably practicable if the prosecution thinks it might undermine the prosecution case or assist the defence disclosed by the defendant. This duty continues until the trial is over (as a result of a conviction or an acquittal or the prosecutor decides not to proceed with the case).

5.10 Consequences of failure to comply with disclosure requirements (CPIA 1996, ss 10 and 11)

5.10.1 By the prosecution

If the prosecution fails to comply with the time-limit for disclosure and, because of the delay, the defendant is denied a fair trial, this could constitute grounds for staying the proceedings for abuse of process.

5.10.2 By the defendant

If the defendant:

(a   fails to make a statement when obliged to do so (see 5.5); or

(b)   does not comply with the time-limit for doing so; or

(c)   sets out inconsistent defences in the statement; or

(d) puts forward a defence at trial which is different from a defence in the statement; or

(e) adduces alibi evidence at trial without giving adequate details of the alibi or alibi witnesses in the statement,

the court, or with leave, any other party, may make such comments as appear appropriate; and the court may draw such inferences as appear proper when deciding whether the defendant is guilty.

If the defendant has put forward a defence at trial which is different from a defence in the defence statement, the court must look at the extent of the difference and whether there is any justification for it, before commenting, granting leave to comment, or drawing an inference.

Example

Melanie is charged with burglary and pleads not guilty. The prosecution makes primary disclosure. Melanie's defence statement indicates a defence of alibi and names Duncan as an alibi witness. At her trial Melanie wishes to call three witnesses Duncan, Nick and Lisa to support her alibi. As no reference was made to Nick and Lisa in her defence statement, by name or otherwise, the court, or, with leave, the prosecution, may comment on this and the court may draw such inferences as appear proper.

A defendant cannot be convicted solely on an inference drawn from his failure to comply with the disclosure provisions.

5.11 Further reading

Archbold: Criminal Pleading, Evidence and Practice (Sweet & Maxwell, 2004)

Blackstone's Criminal Practice (Oxford University Press, 2004)

Ede, *Active Defence* (The Law Society, 2000)

Chapter 6
Committal Proceedings and Sending for Trial

6.1	Introduction	77
6.2	Types of committal proceedings	77
6.3	Preliminary points	77
6.4	Committal without consideration of the evidence (Magistrates' Courts Act 1980, s 6(2))	79
6.5	Committal with consideration of the evidence (Magistrates' Courts Act 1980, s 6(1))	80
6.6	Deciding on the type of committal proceedings	81
6.7	Sending for trial procedure (Crime and Disorder Act 1998, ss 51, 52 and Sch 3)	82
6.8	Linked summary offences	84
6.9	Further reading	86

6.1 Introduction

Offences triable either way (which are not related to indictable only offences) will be the subject of committal proceedings before a magistrates' court. The purpose of committal proceedings is to ensure that there is a case for the defendant to answer in the Crown Court.

There is power to bypass committal proceedings in serious fraud cases and certain sexual or violent offences involving a child witness. Additionally, the prosecution could avoid the holding of committal proceedings by applying to a High Court judge for a voluntary bill of indictment. Such cases are beyond the scope of this book.

Important changes have been introduced by the Crime and Disorder Act 1998. Indictable only offences and related either way offences are no longer subject to committal proceedings.

6.2 Types of committal proceedings

Offences triable either way (which are not related to indictable only offences) will be subject to commital proceedings.

There are two types of committal proceedings:

(a) committal without consideration of the evidence under Magistrates' Courts Act 1980, s 6(2); and

(b) committal with consideration of the evidence under Magistrates' Courts Act 1980, s 6(1), at which the prosecution must satisfy the magistrates that there is sufficient evidence to put the defendant on trial in the Crown Court.

6.3 Preliminary points

Whichever type of committal proceedings takes place, the following points will always apply.

6.3.1 Conduct of proceedings

Proceedings may be conducted by a single magistrate.

6.3.2   Reporting restrictions (Magistrates' Courts Act 1980, s 8)

Committal proceedings usually take place in open court. The press may be present but any report is restricted to the formal part of the proceedings, that is to say, the names of the defendants and witnesses, the offence charged, and the result of the proceedings. The press are not allowed to report the evidence given at committal proceedings. The main reason for reporting restrictions is to prevent a jury from being prejudiced by what they may read in the newspapers and to attempt to ensure that they decide the case in the Crown Court on the evidence presented at the trial.

A single defendant can insist that reporting restrictions be lifted. A defendant may wish to exercise this right, for example, if publicity is needed to trace a witness whose identity is not known.

6.3.3   Evidence which is admissible at committal proceedings

Only the prosecution can adduce evidence at committal proceedings. To be admissible the evidence must fall within one of the categories set out in Magistrates' Courts Act 1980, ss 5B–5E.

6.3.3.1   Written statements under the Magistrates' Courts Act 1980, s 5B

The written statement of a prosecution witness is admissible if:

(a)   it purports to be signed by the person who made it;

(b)   it contains a declaration that it is true to the best of the maker's knowledge and belief and that it is made knowing that if it is tendered in evidence the maker would be liable to prosecution if he wilfully stated in it anything he knows to be false or did not believe to be true; and

(c)   before being tendered in evidence a copy of the statement is given to each of the other parties.

Any documents or exhibits referred to in the s 5B statements are also admissible at committal proceedings.

6.3.3.2   Depositions under the Magistrates' Courts Act 1980, s 5C

Depositions are used where a witness will not voluntarily make a written statement or produce a document or exhibit for the prosecution.

Where a magistrate considers that a person is likely to be able to make a written statement or produce a document or exhibit on behalf of the prosecution which will contain or is likely to be material evidence and the person will not do so voluntarily, the magistrate must issue a summons requiring that person to appear before him to give his evidence or produce the document or exhibit (Magistrates' Courts Act 1980, s 97A).

When that person attends court, his evidence will be taken down in writing by the magistrate in the form of a deposition. If that person fails to attend the magistrate can, in certain circumstances, issue a warrant for his arrest.

To be admissible evidence at committal proceedings, a copy of the deposition must be given to all the parties.

Any documents or exhibits included in the deposition are also admissible at committal proceedings.

6.3.3.3 Statements under the Magistrates' Courts Act 1980, s 5D

These are statements which the prosecution reasonably believes will only be admissible at trial under s 23 or s 24 of the Criminal Justice Act 1988 (see **9.6.4**).

[handwritten note: Documentary Hearsay]

In order for the statement to be admissible at committal proceedings, the prosecutor must notify the court and all the parties of his belief and provide them with a copy of the statement.

The magistrates at committal have no power to rule the statement inadmissible.

6.3.3.4 Documents under the Magistrates' Courts Act 1980, s 5E

These are documents which are admissible by some other enactment (eg, a certificate from the Driver and Vehicle Licensing Agency).

6.3.4 Defendant's right to object to written evidence being read at trial

At the same time as the prosecution serves on the defence the evidence to be adduced in committal proceedings, the prosecution must notify the defence of its right to object to written evidence which is admitted in committal proceedings being read at the Crown Court trial without further evidence (see **Appendix 2(P)**).

6.3.5 Pre-committal disclosure of unused material

The prosecution's duty of primary disclosure of 'unused material' under the Criminal Procedure and Investigations Act 1996 applies when the defendant is committed for trial or sent to the Crown Court for trial (see **7.5**). In *R v Director of Public Prosecutions, ex p Lee* [1999] 2 All ER 737, the Divisional Court held that the 1996 Act did not abolish pre-committal disclosure of 'unused material'. In most cases, prosecution disclosure can wait until after committal without jeopardising the defendant's right to a fair trial. However, the prosecutor must always be alive to the need to disclose material of which he is aware (either from his own consideration of the papers or because his attention has been drawn to it by the defence) and which he, as a responsible prosecutor, recognises should be disclosed at an earlier stage.

6.4 Committal without consideration of the evidence (Magistrates' Courts Act 1980, s 6(2))

The procedure is summarised in **Appendix 1(L)**.

6.4.1 Offer of committal

It is up to the prosecution to offer the defence a committal without consideration of the evidence.

The offer of a committal without consideration of the evidence will be made in virtually all cases and will normally be by letter. The prosecution will serve on the defence a bundle of prosecution documents complying with the requirements of ss 5B–5E of the Magistrates' Courts Act 1980. The defence solicitor will consider the statements with his client. Unless there is a good reason for asking for a committal with consideration of the evidence (see **6.6.2**), the defence will accept the prosecution's offer.

6.4.2   Procedure at committal without consideration of the evidence

The court's function is largely administrative and the proceedings will take only a few minutes.

The prosecution and defendant will attend court. A solicitor acting under a representation order will not receive payment for attending a committal without consideration of the evidence unless his presence is necessary. His presence may be necessary, for example, if there is to be a defence application for bail which will be opposed by the prosecution.

The committal proceedings commence with the charge being read to the defendant. No plea is entered as this is not a trial.

- The court clerk asks whether the defence wants reporting restrictions to be lifted (see **6.3.2**).

- The court clerk will then check that the formalities for a committal without consideration of the evidence have been complied with. The formalities are:

    (a)   that all the prosecution's evidence falls within ss 5B–5E of the Magistrates' Courts Act 1980; and

    (b)   copies of the statements and depositions have been served on the defence;

    (c)   the defendant has a solicitor acting for him (whether present in court or not); and

    (d)   the defence does not wish to make a submission of no case to answer (see **6.5.1**). If the defence does wish to make such a submission, a committal without consideration of the evidence is not appropriate.

The magistrates do not at any stage read the evidence contained in the prosecution statements.

The defendant is committed for trial to the Crown Court and reminded of his right to object to written evidence which was admitted in committal proceedings being read out at the Crown Court trial without further evidence.

A date will be set for a plea and directions hearing in the Crown Court.

- The defence will then deal with the following ancillary matters.

6.4.2.1   Representation

The defence will make an application for representation to be extended to cover the Crown Court trial. Such an application will usually be granted.

6.4.2.2   Bail

If the defendant is already on bail, it will be usual for bail to be extended until the Crown Court trial. If the defendant has been in custody until committal proceedings, the defence may be able to make a further bail application to the magistrates (see **3.4.3**).

6.5   Committal with consideration of the evidence (Magistrates' Courts Act 1980, s 6(1))

If the defendant is to be committed for trial, the prosecution must show that there is a case to answer.

6.5.1   Procedure

The procedure is summarised in **Appendix 1(M)**.

The charge is read to the defendant but no plea is taken.

* The court clerk will ask whether the defence wants reporting restrictions to be lifted.

* The prosecution evidence will either be read aloud at the hearing or, if the court directs, orally summarised. No witnesses can be called to give oral evidence.

* At the close of the prosecution case, the defence may make a submission of no case to answer. The test to be applied by the magistrates when considering a submission is laid down in the case of *R v Galbraith (George Charles)* [1981] 2 All ER 1060. The magistrates must ask themselves whether the prosecution evidence, taken at its highest, is such that a jury properly directed could not properly convict on it. The practical effect of this test was considered in Galbraith:

> ... where the prosecution evidence is such that its strength or weakness depends on the view to be taken of a witness's reliability or other matters which are generally speaking within the jury's province and where one possible view of the facts is that there is evidence on which the jury could properly convict,

then the submission of no case to answer will fail.

For a submission to succeed, therefore, the defence will have to show that the prosecution has failed to adduce evidence in support of an essential element of the offence or that, even taking the best possible view of the prosecution evidence, the case against the defendant is so unreliable that a jury could not convict on it.

If no submission is made or if the submission is rejected, the magistrates will announce that there is a case to answer and commit the defendant to the Crown Court for trial. The magistrates will then remind the defendant of his right to object to written evidence which has been adduced in committal proceedings being read out in the Crown Court without further evidence. If they uphold the submission the magistrates will announce that the submission has been upheld and discharge the defendant.

If the defendant is committed for trial, a date will be set for a plea and directions hearing at the Crown Court. Bail and representation will then be dealt with as on a s 6(2) committal.

6.5.1.1   Excluding evidence at committal

The Criminal Procedure and Investigations Act 1996 (Sch 1, paras 25 and 26) provides that the magistrates have no power to exclude prosecution evidence at committal proceedings under either s 76(2) or s 78 of the Police and Criminal Evidence Act 1984.

6.6   Deciding on the type of committal proceedings

6.6.1   Prosecution decides on committal with consideration of the evidence

If the prosecution decides to have a committal with consideration of the evidence then the defence does not have a choice.

Since the prosecution can no longer use committal proceedings to test its own witnesses by calling them to give oral evidence, it is now very unlikely ever to insist on a s 6(1) (MCA 1980) committal.

6.6.2   Prosecution decides on committal without consideration of the evidence

If the prosecution offers the defence a committal without consideration of the evidence, the choice as to the type of committal will rest with the defence. Reasons for insisting on a committal with consideration of the evidence include the following.

(a)   Making a submission of no case to answer

The circumstances in which this is a realistic possibility were discussed at **6.5.1**.

(b)   To try to persuade the court to commit the defendant for trial on a lesser charge than the one being dealt with at committal

For example, a charge of causing grievous bodily harm could be reduced to a charge of assault occasioning actual bodily harm.

If neither of the reasons described above applies to the case then a committal without consideration of the evidence is appropriate. This will be quicker than a s 6(1) committal.

Agreeing to a s 6(2) committal does not in any way prevent the defence from challenging the prosecution witnesses or the admissibility of their evidence at Crown Court.

6.7   Sending for trial procedure (Crime and Disorder Act 1998, ss 51, 52 and Sch 3)

6.7.1   Cases to which s 51 applies

Where an adult appears or is brought before a magistrates' court charged with an indictable only offence, the court must send him to the Crown Court for trial:

(a)   for that offence; and

(b)   for any either way offence or summary offence with which he is charged which fulfils the 'requisite conditions' (s 51(1)).

The 'requisite conditions' are that:

(a)   the either way or summary offence appears to the court to be related to the indictable only offence; and

(b)   in the case of a summary only offence, it is punishable with imprisonment or involves obligatory or discretionary disqualification from driving (s 51(11)).

An either way offence is related to an indictable only offence if the charge for the either way offence could be joined in the same indictment as the charge for the indictable only offence. A summary offence is related to an indictable only offence if it arises out of circumstances which are the same as or connected with those giving rise to the indictable only offence (s 51(12)).

An adult co-defendant who is charged with a related either way offence must also be sent to the Crown Court for trial (s 51(3)).

If a defendant is sent for trial for a summary offence, the trial of that offence in the magistrates' court shall be treated as if the court had adjourned it and had not fixed the time and place for its resumption (s 51(9)).

A juvenile (an offender under 18) is not liable to be sent to the Crown Court unless he is jointly charged with an indictable offence with an adult. When the adult is sent to the Crown Court under s 51, the magistrates may send the juvenile to the Crown Court as well if the magistrates consider that it is in the interests of justice for him to be tried jointly with the adult defendant. Where they do so, the magistrates may also send the juvenile to the Crown Court to be tried for related offences (s 51(5) and (6)).

6.7.2 The preliminary hearing in the magistrates' court

An adult defendant charged with an offence triable only on indictment will be sent straight to the Crown Court for trial, following a preliminary hearing in the magistrates' court. The purpose of the hearing is to determine whether there is an indictable only offence charged and whether there are related offences which should also be sent to the Crown Court. The court will also consider representation. The magistrates will set the date on which the first preliminary hearing will take place in the Crown Court and will remand the defendant in custody or on bail to appear at the Crown Court.

The preliminary hearing should be before two or more justices. The CPS must be represented by a Crown prosecutor. The preliminary hearing is likely to take place at the next available court sitting after the defendant has been charged.

Section 52(5) provides that the preliminary hearing in the magistrates' court may be adjourned but it is envisaged that, given the limited nature of the court's function under s 51, it will seldom be necessary to adjourn.

6.7.3 Representation

A magistrates' court has the power to grant a 'through representation order' (see **3.3.2.4**) for indictable only offences (and related offences or defendants) that are sent to the Crown Court under s 51.

If an application for representation has not been submitted already representation will be dealt with at the preliminary hearing. The magistrates or the justices' clerk will consider whether the case meets the interests of justice criteria and grant a representation order which covers both representation in the magistrates' court and the Crown Court.

6.7.4 Statement of means for the Crown Court

Only the interests of justice test has to be satisfied before granting a representation order: a representation order is non-means tested. At the conclusion of the case in the Crown Court the judge has the power to order a defendant to pay some or all the costs of his defence (see **10.2.14**).

When the defendant applies for representation to cover proceedings in the Crown Court, the magistrates' court will provide the defendant with Form B (see **Appendix 2(Q))**. This form should be returned to the Crown Court at least four days before the first hearing at the Crown Court which will usually be the preliminary hearing (for cases sent to the Crown Court for trial) or the plea and directions hearing (for cases committed to the Crown Court for trial). Failure to return this form, which provides details of the defendant's means and those of a partner if the defendant has one, could result in a defendant's costs order being made at the conclusion of the case for the full defence costs.

6.8 Linked summary offences

If the defendant is to be tried in the Crown Court, a question sometimes arises as to what will happen to other offences with which he is charged but which are purely summary offences.

6.8.1 Criminal Justice Act 1988, s 40(1)

A count charging a person with a summary offence to which this section applies may be included in an indictment if the charge—

(a) is founded on the same facts or evidence as a count charging an indictable offence; or

(b) is part of a series of offences of the same or similar character as an indictable offence which is also charged,

but only if (in either case) the facts or evidence relating to the offence were disclosed to a magistrates' court inquiring into the offence as examining justices or are disclosed by material which, in pursuance of regulations made under paragraph 1 of Schedule 3 to the Crime and Disorder Act 1998 (procedure where person sent for trial under section 51, has been served on the person charged).

The offences to which this section applies are: taking a conveyance, common assault, driving while disqualified and certain offences of criminal damage.

The effect of s 40 is to enable the prosecution, when drafting the indictment for trial in the Crown Court, to include a purely summary offence provided the conditions in s 40 are satisfied.

Example 1

Imran is charged with theft of goods from a motor vehicle and with taking a conveyance. The facts are that he took a vehicle without the owner's consent and stole a quantity of tapes and a radio from the car while it was in his possession. The charges are therefore founded on the same facts. Imran is committed to the Crown Court for trial on the theft charge. Under s 40, the summary offence of taking a conveyance can also be tried in the Crown Court, provided evidence in support of the charge is included in the witness statements adduced in evidence in committal proceedings.

Example 2

Sean is charged with robbery and driving whilst disqualified. The facts are that Sean pushed Susan to the ground, stole her handbag and then made his getaway by car. The charges are therefore founded on the same facts. Sean is sent to the Crown Court for trial on the robbery charge. Under s 40, the summary offence of driving while disqualified can also be tried at the Crown Court, provided evidence of the charge is included in the prosecution evidence served on the defence at the Crown Court.

If the defendant is convicted of the summary offence, the Crown Court's sentencing powers are limited to those of the magistrates.

For summary only offences that are sent to the Crown Court for trial and do not satisfy the requirements of s 40, see 7.4.6.

6.8.2 Criminal Justice Act 1988, s 41(1)

Where a magistrates' court commits a person to the Crown Court for trial on indictment for an offence triable either way or a number of such offences, it may also commit him for trial for any summary offence with which he is charged and which—

(a)   is punishable with imprisonment or involves obligatory or discretionary disqualification from driving; and

(b)   arises out of circumstances which appear to the court to be the same as or connected with those giving rise to the offence, or one of the offences, triable either way,

whether or not evidence relating to that summary offence appears on the depositions or written statements in the case;

Provided the offence committed for trial is triable either way, any summary offence which satisfies the conditions set out above may also be committed for trial.

If the defendant, on conviction for the either way offence, pleads guilty to the summary offence, the Crown Court can sentence for the summary offence, but its powers are limited to those of the magistrates. If the defendant pleads not guilty the summary offence must be remitted to the magistrates' court for trial. The Crown Court has no power to deal with the summary offence in these circumstances.

Example

Chris is committed for trial in the Crown Court on a charge of assault occasioning actual bodily harm. He also faces a charge of threatening behaviour, under the Public Order Act 1986, s 4, arising out of the same incident. This offence can be added to the indictment in the Crown Court. If Chris is convicted of the assault charge the Crown Court can sentence him for the public order offence, provided he pleads guilty. If Chris pleads not guilty to the public order offence or is acquitted on the assault charge, the Crown Court must remit the public order offence back to the magistrates.

The Crown Court is required to inform the clerk of the committing magistrates' court of the outcome of any proceedings under s 41, as proceedings in the magistrates' court in respect of the summary offence will have been adjourned.

6.8.3   Conclusion

Sections 40 and 41 are similar in that they both may allow the Crown Court to deal with linked summary offences. However, they have the following key differences.

(a)   Section 40 allows the summary offence to be tried in the Crown Court, along with the either way offence.

Section 41 only allows the Crown Court to sentence for the summary offence if the defendant pleads guilty to it. If he pleads not guilty, the trial must be held in the magistrates' court.

(b)   Section 40 applies if the defendant is committed to the Crown Court for trial for any either way offence or when an indictable offence is sent to the Crown Court for trial.

Section 41 only applies if the defendant is committed to the Crown Court for an either way offence.

(c)   Section 40 only enables the Crown Court to try a limited list of the more serious summary offences.

Section 41 may enable the Crown Court to sentence for any summary offence which is punishable with imprisonment or disqualification.

6.9 Further reading

For further discussions on criminal proceedings, see, for example:

Archbold: Criminal Pleading, Evidence and Practice (Sweet & Maxwell, 2004)

Blackstone's Criminal Practice (Oxford University Press, 2004)

John Sprack, *Emmins on Criminal Procedure* (Oxford University Press, 2002)

Ede and Edwards, *Criminal Defence* (The Law Society, 2002)

Chapter 7

Preparations for Trial on Indictment

7.1	Introduction	87
7.2	The indictment	87
7.3	Cases committed to the Crown Court for trial	87
7.4	Cases sent to the Crown Court for trial	88
7.5	Disclosure	92
7.6	Notices of further evidence	92
7.7	Preparing for the plea and directions hearing	93
7.8	Plea and directions hearing	93
7.9	Pre-trial hearings	94
7.10	Preparatory hearings	94
7.11	Briefing counsel	95
7.12	Trial on indictment	95
7.13	Further reading	96

7.1 Introduction

This chapter deals with what happens to a case after it has been either committed to the Crown Court for trial or sent to the Crown Court for trial under s 51 of the Crime and Disorder Act 1998. The major procedural steps are summarised in chart form at **Appendix 1(T)** and **Appendix 1(U)**. This chapter also deals with the main preparatory steps for Crown Court trial.

7.2 The indictment

The indictment is the formal document containing a list of charges against the defendant, to which he pleads guilty or not guilty at the beginning of the Crown Court trial. The offences alleged against the defendant are set out in separate counts of the indictment. Each count must allege only one offence. The indictment must be signed by an officer of the Crown Court. Until the indictment is signed, it is merely a 'bill of indictment'. Bills of indictment are usually drafted by the prosecution and the prosecution will have to deliver the bill to the Crown Court to be signed. Such delivery is known as 'preferment of the bill of indictment'.

The law on drafting indictments is contained principally in the Indictments Act 1915 and the Indictment Rules 1971 (SI 1971/1253). Rule 5 (as amended by the Indictments (Procedure) (Modification) Rules 1998 (SI 1998/3045)) provides that a bill of indictment must be preferred within 28 days of committal to the Crown Court or within 28 days of service of the prosecution case if the case is sent for trial. This period can be extended by application to the court.

7.3 Cases committed to the Crown Court for trial

7.3.1 Use of statements and depositions of prosecution witnesses at trial

The Criminal Procedure and Investigations Act 1996, s 68 and Sch 2, paras 1 and 2, provide that written statements and depositions which have been admitted in evidence in committal proceedings can be read at the Crown Court trial where all parties agree or where the court considers it to be in the interests of justice to do so (see **9.6.4**).

If the defendant intends to plead not guilty at the Crown Court, the defence must consider whether to object to this prosecution evidence being read to the court. Any objection to the reading out at the trial of a statement or deposition without further evidence shall be made in writing to the prosecutor and the Crown Court within 14 days of the defendant being committed for trial unless the court, at its discretion, permits such an objection to be made outside that period (Crown Court Rules 1982 (SI 1982/1109), r 22).

If the defence wishes to challenge the admissibility of the contents of the written statement or cross-examine the maker of the written statement or deposition, the defence should object.

7.3.2   First hearing

The first hearing for a defendant committed for trial at the Crown Court for an either way offence will be the plea and directions hearing (PDH) (see **7.8**). When committing a case to the Crown Court, a magistrates' court will fix a date for a PDH which must take place:

(a)   within 4 weeks of committal if the defendant is in custody; or

(b)   within 6 weeks of committal if the defendant is on bail.

(*Practice Direction (Criminal Proceedings: Consolidation)* [2002] 3 All ER 904, para 41, *Plea and directions hearings*)

7.4   Cases sent to the Crown Court for trial

7.4.1   Preliminary hearing

The first hearing for a defendant sent for trial for an indictable only offence will be a preliminary hearing. A preliminary hearing is any hearing which takes place before the prosecution has completed service of its case.

The notice specifying the charges upon which the defendant is sent for trial (required by s 51(7) of the Crime and Disorder Act 1998), together with other documents, including the charge, must be sent by the magistrates' court to the Crown Court within four days of sending a person to be tried in the Crown Court (Magistrates' Courts (Modification) Rules 1998 (SI 1998/3046)). The first Crown Court appearance must then take place:

(a)   within 8 days of receipt of that notice where the defendant is sent for trial in custody; or

(b)   within 28 days of receipt of that notice when the defendant is sent on bail.

(Crown Court (Modification) Rules 1998)

The preliminary hearing allows a defendant, who has been sent for trial in custody, to apply to the Crown Court for bail, and allows the judge, having consulted the prosecution, to set a date by which the prosecution is to serve its case on the defence and to set a date for the PDH.

There is nothing to prevent a defendant from making a bail application before the date fixed for the preliminary hearing. It is then for the Crown Court to decide when to allow an earlier hearing to determine bail. If the court so decides, it will depend on the circumstances of the case whether at that hearing it is possible for the court to determine the timetable for the case (in effect bringing forward the date of the preliminary hearing), or whether it will still be necessary to hold a hearing for that purpose on the date originally fixed. If an earlier hearing is arranged, then the s 51(7) notice and associated documents should be sent to the Crown Court in time for the hearing and the CPS should be given as much notice of the hearing as possible.

The Crown Court Rules 1982, r 27 has been modified by the Crown Court (Modification) Rules 1998 to allow the preliminary hearing to take place in chambers. *Practice Direction (Section 51 of the Crime and Disorder Act 1998 – Guidance on listing of preliminary hearings)* (22 December 1998) by the Senior Presiding Judge for England and Wales, provides that the preliminary hearing (and any others which take place before the prosecution case is served) should normally be heard in open court as chambers, with the defendant present and the court open to the public. The Crown may be represented at the hearing by a Crown prosecutor and the defence by a solicitor.

7.4.2 Depositions from reluctant witnesses

A provision equivalent to that in s 97A of the Magistrates' Courts Act 1980 (see **6.3.3.2**) is available. The procedure allows for the taking (before service of the prosecution case) of depositions from reluctant witnesses and this is taken before a magistrate, notwithstanding that the case has been sent to the Crown Court (Crime and Disorder Act 1998, Sch 3, para 4).

7.4.3 Service of prosecution case

The Attorney-General is required to make regulations for the service of documents containing the prosecution evidence on which the charge or charges are based (Crime and Disorder Act 1998, s 51(7), Sch 3, para 1). The Crime and Disorder Act 1998 (Service of Prosecution Evidence) Regulations 1998 (SI 1998/3115) set a 'long stop' date of one year from the date the case is sent, for the judge to determine the date by which the evidence is to be served.

It will generally be convenient for the evidence to be served in one bundle. In a complex case, it may be appropriate to serve evidence as it becomes available. If so, the prosecution should notify the defence that more evidence is to be served later and advise the defence once the case has been fully served.

The evidence that is served will form the prima facie case.

The date of service of the prosecution case is relevant for the timing of applications for dismissal, disclosure of evidence the prosecution do not intend to rely on and the preferment of the indictment.

There will usually be another Crown Court hearing after service of the prosecution case (or to find out why the prosecution case has not yet been served). The purpose of this hearing will be to review the case to date and confirm the PDH date. The timing of this hearing will be at the judge's discretion.

7.4.4 Applications for dismissal

Once the prosecution case has been served, the defence may make an application for dismissal (Crime and Disorder Act 1998, Sch 3, para 2). The judge shall dismiss the charge if it appears to him that the evidence against the defendant would not be sufficient for the jury to properly convict him. Detailed provision for this is made in the Crime and Disorder Act 1998 (Dismissal of Charges Sent) Rules 1998 (SI 1998/3048). The defence may give notice of intention to make an oral application, or make an application in writing (to which the prosecution may respond with a request for an oral hearing). The notice or written application, accompanied by copies of any material relied on, must be copied to the prosecution, which is allowed 14 days from receipt to make written comments or adduce further evidence. There is provision for the 14-day period to be extended.

The Rules include provision for evidence to be given orally, but only with the leave of the judge, which is to be given only when the interests of justice require.

Reporting restrictions apply which are modelled on the restrictions which apply to the reporting of committal proceedings (see **6.3.2**).

If a defendant succeeds in having the case against him dismissed, no further proceedings on the dismissed charge may be made (other than through a voluntary bill of indictment).

7.4.5   Related either way offences

Sending related either way offences for trial enables the Crown Court to deal with the indictable only offence and related either way offences in the one trial.

Where (following a successful application to dismiss or to discontinue or for any other reason) the indictable only offence which caused the case to be sent to the Crown Court in the first place is no longer on the indictment, consideration must be given to the outstanding related either way offences.

7.4.5.1   Adult defendants

The Crown Court should deal with outstanding either way offences where there is a guilty plea, or where the case appears suitable for trial on indictment, or where the defendant elects Crown Court trial.

The either way offences should be remitted to the magistrates for trial only where a not guilty plea is indicated (or no indication given), the case is suitable for summary trial and the defendant consents to be so tried (Crime and Disorder Act 1998, Sch 3, paras 7–12).

7.4.5.2   Procedure

The procedure amounts to an adapted mode of trial hearing, at which the Crown Court determines mode of trial in much the same way as magistrates would do.

(a)   The outstanding counts on the indictment that charge either way offences are read to the defendant and the court will invite him to indicate a plea, explaining that if he indicates that he would plead guilty, the court will proceed to deal with him as if the trial had started and he pleaded guilty.

(b)   If the defendant indicates that he would plead not guilty or fails to give any indication, the court must next consider whether the case is more suitable for summary trial or trial on indictment, having regard to any representations made by the prosecution or the defendant, the nature of the case, the seriousness of the offence, whether the magistrates' sentencing powers would be adequate, or any other relevant circumstances.

(c)   If the court decides that the offence is more suitable for trial on indictment, the case will proceed in the usual way. If, on the other hand, it decides that the case is more suitable for summary trial, the court must give the defendant the option of electing Crown Court trial.

(d)   If the defendant consents to summary trial, the case is remitted to the magistrates. The defendant will be remanded on bail or in custody to appear before the magistrates' court.

Example

Teja is sent for trial to the Crown Court on a robbery charge. He also faces a charge of assault occasioning actual bodily harm arising out of the same incident. This offence can be sent to the Crown Court as a related either way offence.

At the Crown Court, the robbery charge is dismissed following an application for dismissal. The court will conduct a mode of trial procedure in relation to the charge of assault occasioning actual bodily harm.

If Teja indicates a guilty plea, the court will deal with him as if the trial had started and he had pleaded guilty. The court will proceed to sentence.

If Teja indicates a not guilty plea, the court will have to decide whether the case is suitable for trial on indictment or summary trial. If the court decides that trial on indictment is more suitable, Teja has no choice; he will be tried on indictment. If the court decides that summary trial is more suitable then Teja has a choice. If he consents to summary trial, the case is remitted to the magistrates' court for trial. If not, he will be tried on indictment.

7.4.5.3   Juvenile defendants

Cases involving juveniles should be remitted to the magistrates' court unless it is necessary that they should be tried in the Crown Court. The circumstances in which the Crown Court should deal with juvenile defendants are where:

(a)   the defendant is charged with an offence which is a grave crime for the purposes of s 91 of the Powers of Criminal Courts (Sentencing) Act 2000 and the court considers that it ought to be possible for him to be sentenced under that provision; or

(b)   the juvenile is charged jointly with an adult with an either way offence and it is necessary in the interests of justice that they both should be tried at the Crown Court.

(Crime and Disorder Act 1998, Sch 3, para 13)

7.4.6   Related summary offences

Where a magistrates' court has sent a defendant for trial for offences which include a summary offence, the summary offence will not be included in the indictment and the defendant will not be asked to plead to the summary offence when the trial begins (unless the summary offence has been included in the indictment under s 40 of the Criminal Justice Act 1988, which only applies to a few summary offences; see **6.8.1**).

The Crown Court will deal with a summary offence only if the defendant pleads guilty to it and the defendant has been convicted of the indictable only offence to which it related; in so doing, the court's powers are restricted to those which would have been available to a magistrates' court. In any other circumstances, the summary offence will either be remitted to the magistrates for trial or (if the prosecution do not wish to proceed) be dismissed (Crime and Disorder Act 1998, Sch 3, para 6).

The Crown Court is required to inform the clerk of the 'sending magistrates' court' of the outcome of any proceedings in respect of the summary offence (Sch 3, para 6(7)) as proceedings in the magistrates' court in respect of the summary offence will have been adjourned.

Example

Dmitri is sent for trial in the Crown Court on a charge of robbery. He also faces a charge of threatening behavior, under the Public Order Act 1986, s 4, arising out of the same incident. The s 4 offence is sent to the Crown Court as a related summary offence. If Dmitri is convicted of the robbery charge, the Crown Court can sentence him for the public order offence, provided he pleads guilty. If he pleads not guilty to the public order offence or is acquitted of the robbery charge, the Crown Court must remit the public order offence back to the magistrates unless the prosecution decide not to proceed with the public order offence, in which case the Crown Court can dismiss the charge.

7.5 Disclosure

7.5.1 Duty to provide advance information

If the case has been committed to the Crown Court for trial, this duty is met by the papers served on the defence prior to committal to the Crown Court. For those cases sent to the Crown Court for trial, the prosecution will disclose its case at the Crown Court (see **7.4.3**). Any additional evidence which the prosecution later decide to adduce as part of the prosecution case must be brought to the defendant's attention by way of notice of further evidence (see **7.6**).

7.5.2 Duty to disclose 'unused material'

A diagram illustrating disclosure to the defence of any material of relevance to the case upon which the prosecution does not intend to rely ('unused material') in the Crown Court appears at **Appendix 1(N)**.

The prosecution's duty of primary disclosure of 'unused material' will apply where the defendant is committed for trial to the Crown Court or sent to the Crown Court for trial under s 51 of the Crime and Disorder Act 1998. The defence must give a 'defence statement' to the prosecution. If the defendant discloses inconsistent defences or a defence inconsistent with that later advanced at trial, the court or, with leave, any other party, may make such comments as appear appropriate; and the court may draw such inferences as appear proper when deciding whether the defendant is guilty.

For guidance on the drafting of defence statements, see the Professional Conduct and Complaints Committee of the Bar Council Guidance dated 24 September 1997.

7.6 Notices of further evidence

A witness may be called to give evidence for the prosecution in the Crown Court even though his statement was not served on the defence at committal stage or not served by the prosecution at the Crown Court for cases sent to the Crown Court for trial. It may be, for example, that the evidence only came to light after the plea and directions hearing in the Crown Court.

If the prosecution wishes to call additional evidence, a notice of intention to do so will be served on the defence and the Crown Court. The notice will be accompanied by a copy of the relevant witness statement.

7.7 Preparing for the plea and directions hearing

7.7.1 Guilty pleas

If a defendant intends to plead guilty, the defence solicitor should notify the Probation Service, the prosecution and the court as soon as this is known.

7.7.2 Not guilty pleas

The defence solicitor should ensure that the case is sufficiently prepared for the PDH to enable the advocate who appears at the hearing to give the judge the information required to fix a trial date. The amount of information required is such that the case has to be almost ready for a full trial unless it is very complex, in which case further PDHs may be necessary. In particular:

(a) the defence should have checked the availability of defence witnesses for the trial and served witness summonses;

(b) any evidence sought to be admitted by the defence under Criminal Justice Act 1967, s 9 should be served on the prosecution;

(c) any complex issues of law or issues of admissibility of evidence should have been identified;

(d) any factors relevant to mitigation in the event of conviction should have been identified.

A copy of the PDH: Judge's Questionnaire which has to be completed and handed in to the court prior to the commencement of the PDH appears at **Appendix 2(R)**.

7.8 Plea and directions hearing

When committing a case to the Crown Court, a magistrates' court will fix a date for a PDH in the Crown Court. A PDH must take place:

(a) within 4 weeks of committal if the defendant is in custody; or

(b) within 6 weeks of committal if the defendant is on bail.

A PDH will also take place in relation to cases sent to the Crown Court for trial.

At the PDH, a defendant will be required to plead to the charge(s) against him. A defendant who has pleaded guilty may be sentenced at the PDH. If a defendant pleads not guilty, the judge will require the following information:

(a) a summary of the issues in the case;

(b) number of witnesses to give oral evidence;

(c) number of witnesses whose evidence will be given in writing;

(d) any facts formally admitted;

(e) any alibi which should have been disclosed to the prosecution;

(f) any points of law or admissibility of evidence likely to arise at the trial;

(g) estimated length of trial;

(h) dates of availability of witnesses;

(i) dates of availability of the advocates.

See *Practice Direction (Criminal Proceedings: Consolidation)* [2002] 3 All ER 904, para 41, *Plea and directions hearings*.

If a date is not fixed for the not guilty trial, then the case will be placed in the warned list. The warned list is the list of cases awaiting a not guilty trial date. Each Crown Court will send out warned lists for the coming weeks. The Crown Court will then contact the solicitor (usually the previous afternoon) to warn the solicitor that the case will be listed for hearing the next morning.

In the majority of cases committed for trial in the Crown Court, the only pre-trial hearing will be a PDH.

7.9   Pre-trial hearings

Section 40 of the Criminal Procedure and Investigations Act 1996 allows a judge, before the trial begins, to rule on the admissibility of evidence and on any question of law relating to the case. For the purposes of this section, a trial begins when a jury is sworn or a guilty plea is accepted or a preparatory hearing starts (see 7.10).

The ruling can be made on the application of the prosecution or the defence or on the judge's own motion.

It will bind the parties at trial unless it is discharged or varied.

A ruling can be discharged or varied on the judge's own motion or on an application by the prosecution or the defence if the judge considers that it is in the interests of justice to do so. The prosecution or defence can only apply for a discharge or variation if there has been a material change of circumstances since the ruling was made.

Example

The judge could be asked to rule on the admissibility of a written statement which the prosecution or the defence seeks to adduce at trial. If the judge ruled it to be inadmissible that ruling would be binding unless it was subsequently discharged in the interests of justice.

7.10   Preparatory hearings

Part III of the Criminal Procedure and Investigations Act 1996 creates a statutory scheme of preparatory hearings (PHs) for long or complex cases which are to be tried in the Crown Court.

A judge, on his own motion, or on the application of the prosecution or the defence, can order that a PH be held if he considers that it is likely to bring substantial benefits because of the complexity or likely length of the case.

The PH will take place before the jury are sworn in and can be used for any of the following purposes:

(a)   to identify important issues for the jury;

(b)   to help the jury's understanding of the issues;

(c)   to speed up the proceedings before the jury;

(d)   to help the judge's management of the trial.

The plea will be taken at the start of the PH unless it has already been taken.

At the PH, the judge can rule on the admissibility of evidence and on any other question of law.

Under s 31 of the CPIA Act 1996, the judge can also exercise powers to help identify, simplify and narrow the issues of dispute, for example, he can require the prosecution or the defence to provide a detailed case statement.

Any order or ruling made by the judge is binding throughout the trial unless he decides on the application of the prosecution or the defence that it is in the interests of justice to vary or discharge it.

Inferences

If either party departs from the case disclosed as a result of a requirement under s 31, or fails to comply with a s 31 requirement, the judge or, with leave of the judge, any other party, may comment on this at the trial and the jury may draw such inferences from it as appear proper.

Appeals

It is possible, in certain circumstances, to appeal against the judge's ruling on the admissibility of evidence or a question of law to the Court of Appeal and then to the House of Lords.

7.11 Briefing counsel

If counsel is to be instructed in the Crown Court, a brief to counsel should be prepared and sent to counsel's clerk as soon as the case has been committed to the Crown Court or sent for trial to the Crown Court.

On receipt of the brief, counsel may require a conference. The purpose of a conference is to enable the defendant to meet and be advised by counsel. A conference:

> should normally be held in the following cases:
> – where there is a not guilty hearing;
> – where the defendant needs to be advised about please;
> – where the case is complicated by a particular factor or involves serious consequences;
> – where the case requires careful consideration of tactics, evidence, plea, experts, exhibits and witnesses.
>
> (Ede and Edwards, *Criminal Defence* (The Law Society, 2002), p 198)

An example of a brief to counsel appears as **Appendix 2(S)**. It covers counsel attending the PDH and trial. A brief should be as full as possible and should be broken down into sections:

(a) Introduction – this deals with the defendant, the charge, the history of the case, bail arrangements and which prosecution witnesses must attend the trial to give oral evidence.

(b) Prosecution case – this contains a summary of the evidence to be given by each witness.

(c) Defence case – this contains a summary of the defence evidence.

(d) Evidence – any major point likely to arise at the trial should be highlighted for the benefit of counsel.

(e) Mitigation – any facts relevant to mitigation in the event of a conviction should be mentioned.

7.12 Trial on indictment

Procedure in the Crown Court on a not guilty plea is summarised in **Appendix 1(O)**.

A trial on indictment begins with the arraignment at the PDH, which consists of putting the counts in the indictment to the defendant so that he can plead guilty or not guilty.

If there is a plea of not guilty the trial takes place before a judge and a jury in the presence of the defendant (unless, for example, he is disruptive). The order of proceedings is similar to that in a magistrates' court, except that the prosecution must make an opening speech and will also address the jury at the conclusion of the defence case before counsel for the defence. The judge will then sum up to the jury.

The judge hears argument on points of law and evidence in the absence of the jury and may direct the jury to acquit if, for example, there is a successful submission of no case to answer. The test to be applied by the judge when considering a submission is laid down in the case of *R v Galbraith (George Charles)* [1981] 2 All ER 1060 (see **6.5.1**).

The verdict whether guilty or not guilty is decided by unanimous vote of the jury, although a majority verdict of 11:1, or 10:2 will be accepted if, after two hours, unanimity is not possible. If the jury fails to agree there may be a new trial before a new jury.

The judge decides on sentence and has wider powers of sentencing than the magistrates.

7.13 Further reading

For further discussions on criminal proceedings, see, for example:

Archbold: Criminal Pleading, Evidence and Practice (Sweet & Maxwell, 2004)

Blackstone's Criminal Practice (Oxford University Press, 2004)

John Sprack, *Emmins on Criminal Procedure* (Oxford University Press, 2002)

Ede and Edwards, *Criminal Defence* (The Law Society, 2002)

Chapter 8

Summary Trial

8.1	Introduction	97
8.2	Disclosure	97
8.3	Preparing the case for trial	98
8.4	Procedure on a not guilty plea	100
8.5	Further reading	103

8.1 Introduction

Magistrates must try a summary offence and have power to try an either way offence with the defendant's consent. This chapter distinguishes the right to advance information of the prosecution case from the rules relating to disclosure of unused material by the prosecution. It explains what happens at a pre-trial review and also gives an outline of the procedure followed at a trial in the magistrates' court. The procedure on a plea of guilty in the magistrates' court is examined separately in **Chapter 10**.

The major procedural steps in relation to a summary offence are summarised in chart form at **Appendix 1(V)**.

8.2 Disclosure

8.2.1 Duty to provide advance information

This is the obligation on the prosecution to notify the defence of its case, ie, the evidence upon which it intends to rely at trial.

The Magistrates' Courts (Advance Information) Rules 1985, SI 1985/601, provide that if the defendant is charged with an offence triable either way, the prosecution must provide the defence either with copies of the prosecution witnesses' written statements or with a summary of the facts and matters about which evidence will be adduced during the course of the prosecution.

For summary only offences, it is CPS practice voluntarily to give advance information.

For more detailed information, see **5.2**.

8.2.2 Duty to disclose 'unused material'

This is the obligation on the prosecution under the Criminal Procedure and Investigations Act 1996 to make available to the defence any material of relevance to the case upon which it does not intend to rely – 'unused material'. It applies when the defendant pleads not guilty in the magistrates' court.

In the magistrates' court there is no obligation on the defendant to provide a defence statement. The advantage in providing such a statement is prosecution secondary disclosure. The chance that there may be some material available on secondary disclosure must be weighed against the inferences the court may draw if the defendant discloses inconsistent defences or a defence inconsistent with that later advanced at trial. It is probable that most defence solicitors will advise against providing a defence statement in the magistrates' court.

8.3   Preparing the case for trial

In preparing a case for trial by magistrates, the following steps should be considered.

8.3.1   Interviewing the client

Although outline instructions may have been taken at the police station or to enable a bail application or application for a representation order to be made, detailed instructions must now be taken from the defendant. A pro forma can be used to confirm the formal part of instructions such as name, address, date of birth, family details, etc, but a detailed statement will have to be taken as regards the offence. The solicitor should not be afraid to challenge the client's story in interview as it will most certainly be challenged by the prosecution at the trial.

If advance disclosure of the prosecution case has been given (as it must be with an either way offence, see 8.2.1), the statement should also include comments on the prosecution evidence. The statement should be signed and dated by the client.

8.3.2   Interviewing witnesses

The defendant will have provided the names and addresses of relevant witnesses. Witnesses should be interviewed as soon as possible and a full proof of evidence taken from them. Again, when interviewing witnesses, the solicitor should not be afraid to challenge what they say. It is important that inconsistencies be ironed out or explained at this stage rather than in court. The witness's proof of evidence should be signed by the witness and dated.

8.3.3   Writing to the prosecution

A pro forma letter can be sent to the prosecution requesting such of the following information as is appropriate to the case.

(a)   In either way offences, advance disclosure of the prosecution case. There is no statutory right to advance disclosure if the offence is summary only. However, a request for voluntary disclosure in such cases will be looked upon favourably (see 5.2.1).

(b)   Details of the defendant's criminal record. Although details will have been taken from the client, this cannot be relied upon. The prosecution will supply a copy of the record that it will be relying upon in court. This record should be checked against the information given by the client and any inconsistencies cleared up as soon as possible.

(c)   A record of any interviews with the defendant.

(d)   A copy of the custody record. In some areas the custody record is available directly from the police, but the initial approach may be to the CPS.

8.3.4   Location

If the location of the crime is important to the defence, a visit to the relevant scene should be made and plans and photographs prepared. This action may be necessary, for example, in road traffic cases and in cases where the defendant alleges that a prosecution witness, because of his position, could not possibly have seen the events which he alleges he has seen.

8.3.5 Expert evidence

If expert evidence is necessary, an expert should be instructed at the earliest possible opportunity to prepare a report. Expert evidence may be required on any technical matter that is outside the competence of the magistrates. Expert evidence should be disclosed to the prosecution before the trial. If the defendant is represented under a representation order, it is prudent to seek prior authority from the Legal Services Commission Regional Office before instructing the expert. Prior authority is sought by written application outlining the reason for instructing the expert and his fee. If prior authority is granted, the solicitor is certain to recover the cost involved from the Legal Services Commission. If prior authority is refused then the costs will still be recoverable, provided the solicitor can justify the expenditure at the end of the case.

8.3.6 Securing the attendances of witnesses

A witness summons can be issued only if the clerk to the justices or a magistrate is satisfied that a witness will not voluntarily attend or produce a document or thing (Magistrates' Courts Act 1980, s 97(1)). The magistrates' court has a discretion to refuse a witness summons if not satisfied that the application was made as soon as practicable after the defendant pleaded not guilty (Magistrates' Courts Act 1980, s 97(2B)).

Before applying for a witness summons to be issued, a witness should be asked in writing to confirm that he will attend the trial. If a negative response is received, or no response at all, this will be sufficient evidence for a witness summons to be issued. A letter to the court explaining that it has not been possible to secure the voluntary attendance of the witness will usually suffice.

A witness summons should be served personally on each witness.

If a magistrate is satisfied by evidence on oath that a witness summons is unlikely to be obeyed, he may, instead of issuing a witness summons, issue a warrant to arrest the witness (Magistrates' Courts Act 1980, s 97(2)).

8.3.7 Dispensing with attendance of witnesses

Criminal Justice Act 1967, s 9

Section 9 of the Criminal Justice Act 1967 provides that a witness's written statement is admissible at a summary trial provided that:

(a)   it is in the proper form;

(b)   a copy has been served before the hearing on each of the other parties; and

(c)   none of the parties has objected within 7 days.

The statement may only contain matters which would have been admissible if the witness had given evidence on oath.

An example of a s 9 statement illustrating the correct form is illustrated at **Appendix 2(N)**. Section 9 statements are used for matters not in dispute. If the other side wishes to challenge the admissibility of the contents of the statement or cross-examine the maker of the statement, they should object.

The s 9 procedure is available to the prosecution and defence.

Criminal Justice Act 1988, ss 23 and 24

Sections 23 and 24 of the Criminal Justice Act 1988, examined in detail at **9.6.4**, provide for the admissibility of documentary hearsay such as a witness statement with leave of the court, provided that there is a prescribed reason for not calling the witness to give evidence.

8.4 Procedure on a not guilty plea

8.4.1 Preliminary matters

8.4.1.1 Defect in process

The defendant cannot object to an information, summons or warrant on the ground of any defect in substance or form or because of any variation between it and the prosecution evidence. If the variance has misled the defendant, the court must, on his application, adjourn the hearing (Magistrates' Courts Act 1980, s 123).

The practical effect of s 123 is that trivial errors in the information or summons will have no effect at all. This will include misspellings of names or places. Where there is a substantial difference between the information or summons and the evidence to be produced, the defendant is entitled to an adjournment. An example might be an information which alleges that an offence was committed on 1 July and the defendant has alibi evidence to refute the allegation but it transpires that the prosecution evidence will show that the offence was committed on 10 July. The defendant must be allowed an adjournment to reconsider his defence.

8.4.1.2 Joinder of offences and offenders

Two or more defendants can be charged in one information with having committed an offence jointly. They will normally be tried together.

Two or more defendants charged on separate informations may be tried together if the defence agrees. The same rule applies if one defendant is charged with more than one offence. If the defence does not agree, the court has power to try two or more informations together if it is of the opinion that it is in the interests of justice to do so because they are founded on the same facts or form part of a series of offences of the same or similar character (*Chief Constable of Norfolk v Clayton (Terence Edward); Chief Constable of Norfolk v Clayton (Eileen Annie); In re Clayton* [1983] 2 AC 473).

Example 1

Julie is charged with theft, assault and burglary. The offences are unrelated. Unless Julie consents (and she is unlikely to do so), the offences must be tried individually. They do not fall within the rule in *Clayton*.

Example 2

Kathy is charged with four offences of theft. The allegations all arise from separate incidents of alleged shoplifting, on separate dates, within the same shopping precinct. These cases could be tried together as forming part of a series of offences of the same character. In reaching a decision, the magistrates will have to balance the convenience to the prosecution against the prejudice caused to Kathy.

8.4.1.3   Exclusion of witnesses

During a criminal trial, witnesses for either side should not sit in court before having been called to give evidence. The reason for this is to minimise the risk of evidence being tailored to suit testimony which has already been given. This rule does not apply to the defendant or to expert witnesses.

8.4.2   Pre-trial review

When a defendant first enters a not guilty plea, the case will usually be adjourned for a pre-trial review (PTR). At the PTR the court will set a date for trial. The court may require the following information to enable a trial date to be fixed:

(a)   a summary of the main issues in the case;

(b)   number of witnesses to give oral evidence;

(c)   number of witnesses whose evidence can be given in writing;

(d)   any facts formally admitted;

(e)   any points of law or admissibility of evidence likely to arise at the trial;

(f)   estimated length of trial; and

(g)   dates of availability of witnesses.

The PTR may be conducted by a justices' clerk.

8.4.3   A not guilty trial

The procedure in the magistrates' court in a not guilty trial is summarised in **Appendix 1(J)**.

8.4.3.1   The plea

The charge will be read to the defendant and he will be asked whether he pleads guilty or not guilty. The plea must not be equivocal, ie, ambiguous. An example is a defendant charged with theft who says, 'Guilty, but I did not intend to steal anything'. When faced with an equivocal plea, the magistrates should endeavour to explain to the defendant in simple language the nature of the charge. The charge should then be put to the defendant again. If the plea remains equivocal, the magistrates should enter a not guilty plea on behalf of the defendant.

The court has a discretion to allow a change of plea from guilty to not guilty at any time before sentence.

8.4.3.2   Prosecution's opening speech

The prosecution may state the facts of the case and indicate the issues involved and the witnesses who will be called to prove them.

8.4.3.3   Prosecution calls evidence

This may consist of oral evidence and/or written evidence under the Criminal Justice Act 1967, s 9 or the Criminal Justice Act 1988, s 23 or s 24. Witnesses who give oral evidence will be examined-in-chief, cross-examined and re-examined as described at **9.3.2**.

8.4.3.4   Submission of no case to answer

The defence may, at the end of the prosecution case, be in a position to make a submission of no case to answer. Such a submission should be made and upheld where:

(a)   there has been no evidence to prove an essential element in the alleged offence; or

(b)   the evidence adduced by the prosecution has been so discredited as a result of cross-examination or is so manifestly unreliable that no reasonable tribunal could safely convict on it.

See *Practice Direction (Submission of No Case)* [1962] 1 WLR 227.

If a submission of no case to answer is made, the prosecution has a right of reply.

If the submission is accepted, the charge against the defendant is dismissed. If the submission is rejected, the defence may then present its case and call witnesses.

8.4.3.5   Defence opening speech

The defence may address the court either before or after calling evidence, but it is more usual for the defence advocate to make a closing speech.

8.4.3.6   Defence calls evidence

Defence witnesses may be called or their statements admitted in the same way as prosecution evidence. Remember that, if the defendant does give evidence, then he must be called before any other defence witnesses unless the court 'otherwise directs' (Police and Criminal Evidence Act 1984, s 79).

8.4.3.7   Further prosecution evidence

After the close of its case, the prosecution cannot usually call further evidence without leave. The court may, for example, grant leave for the prosecution to call rebutting evidence on a matter which it could not reasonably have foreseen and of which it had no warning. Examples include alibi evidence or a defendant who adduces evidence of his own good character.

8.4.3.8   Defence final speech

The defence addresses the court if it has not already made an opening speech. The only matters which can be covered in this closing speech are matters which have been revealed by admissible evidence.

The prosecution may only address the court further with leave. The defence will always address the court last.

8.4.3.9   Points of law

Either side may address the court on matters of law at any stage in the proceedings as of right. The opponent always has a right of reply.

8.4.3.10   Verdict

The magistrates' verdict is by a majority. They may be advised by their clerk on matters of law but not on issues of fact.

If the defendant is found guilty, the court will then proceed to sentence (see **10.3**).

8.4.4   Costs

A defendant who is convicted can be ordered to pay all, or part, of the prosecution costs. If an order is made it will be for payment of a specified sum.

A defendant who is not represented under a representation order and who is acquitted should normally be awarded costs from central funds. There are exceptions, for example, a defendant who by his conduct has brought suspicion upon himself may find that costs are not awarded in his favour.

8.5 Further reading

See, for example:

Archbold: Criminal Pleading, Evidence and Practice (Sweet & Maxwell, 2004)

Blackstone's Criminal Practice (Oxford University Press, 2004)

John Sprack, *Emmins on Criminal Procedure* (Oxford University Press, 2002)

Ede, *Active Defence* (The Law Society, 2000)

Chapter 9

Criminal Evidence

9.1	Introduction	105
9.2	Preliminary points of evidence	107
9.3	Methods of proof	111
9.4	Corroboration and identification evidence	116
9.5	Particular rules of admissibility of evidence	119
9.6	Hearsay evidence	123
9.7	The defendant	134
9.8	Further reading	142

9.1 Introduction

The law of evidence regulates the way in which a criminal case may be presented to a jury or to magistrates. The rules of evidence determine whether the prosecution must prove the guilt of the defendant or whether it is for the defendant to establish his innocence, the standard of proof required and the methods of proving a case.

It is not possible to understand evidence in isolation. The first step is to appreciate how the rules of evidence to be examined in this chapter fit into the procedural progress of a trial. A summary of the general principles appears below. Each of the principles referred to is dealt with later in some detail, but an initial overview is essential.

9.1.1 Presentation of evidence – An overview

Stage A

Note that at any stage of the prosecution case, the defence can challenge the admissibility of prosecution evidence. A challenge to the admissibility of prosecution evidence is likely to be on the grounds that the evidence infringes one of the following rules:

(a)   opinion evidence (see **9.5.4**);

(b)   self-made evidence (see **9.5.3**);

(c)   the bad character and previous criminal convictions of the defendant (see **9.7.2**);

(d)   hearsay evidence including confessions made by the defendant and documentary hearsay (see **9.6**).

The court also has a general discretion to exclude prosecution evidence where its admission would have an adverse effect on the fairness of the proceedings (see **9.2.5**).

Stage B: Defence submission of no case to answer

In certain circumstances, the defence may, at the close of the prosecution case, make a submission of no case to answer. If this succeeds then the prosecution case will have failed.

Stage C

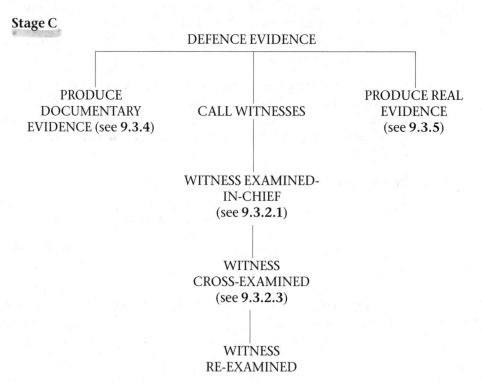

Note that at any stage of the defence case, the prosecution can challenge the admissibility of defence evidence. A challenge to the admissibility of defence evidence is likely to be on the ground that it is one of the following:

(a)   opinion evidence (see **9.5.4**);

(b)   self-made evidence (see **9.5.3**);

(c)   hearsay evidence including documentary hearsay (see **9.6**).

If the defendant gives evidence, there are restrictions on the type of question that may be put to him in cross-examination (see **9.7.5**).

Stage D: Closing speeches (and, in the Crown Court, judge's summing up)

Relevant evidential considerations include:

(a) burden and standards of proof (see **9.2.1**);

(b) evidential burden (see **9.2.2**);

(c) corroboration (see **9.4.1**);

(d) identification evidence (see **9.4.2**).

Stage E: Verdict

When studying the rules of evidence which follow, the overall framework of a criminal trial should be borne in mind and, when necessary, reference back to the above summary should be made.

9.2 Preliminary points of evidence

This section will consider:

(a) who must prove what;

(b) to what standard;

(c) whether there are any matters that a court can take into account without hearing evidence;

(d) whether the law imposes any requirements as to the amount of evidence required.

9.2.1 Burden and standards of proof

As a general rule, the prosecution is required to prove the guilt of the defendant beyond reasonable doubt. This means that at the end of a case the magistrates or jury should be told to consider all of the evidence in the case (both prosecution and defence) and to convict only if they are sure of the defendant's guilt (*Woolmington v Director of Public Prosecutions* [1935] AC 462; *Walters (Henry) v The Queen* [1969] 2 AC 26).

In exceptional cases, the burden of proof falls on the defence. For example, if a defendant wishes to plead insanity he is required to prove that fact.

If the burden of proof rests with the defence, the standard of proof required is proof on a balance of probabilities. This is a lower standard of proof than proof beyond reasonable doubt. It was explained in *Miller v Ministry of Pensions* [1947] 2 All ER 372 as simply meaning 'more probable than not'.

Subject to *Woolmington* and *Walters*, a defendant who wishes to introduce a defence to a case (eg, alibi, self-defence, mechanical defect in a vehicle) does not have the burden of proving that defence. It is for the prosecution, as part of the requirement to prove the case beyond reasonable doubt, to satisfy the magistrates or jury that the defence is not true.

9.2.2 The evidential burden

The evidential burden arises in the following ways in a criminal case.

9.2.2.1 The burden on the prosecution

It has been seen at **9.1.1** that the prosecution will present its case first. At the end of the prosecution case, the defence should consider whether the prosecution has presented sufficient evidence to justify a finding of guilt (remember that the defence will not have adduced any evidence at this stage). A submission of no case to answer can be made at this stage. Such a submission will succeed if the prosecution has failed to adduce evidence in support of a material part of the offence. For example, on a charge of theft, if no evidence has been presented to prove that the goods taken 'belonged to another', a submission should succeed.

A submission of no case to answer is made to the judge in the Crown Court and to the magistrates at summary trial.

If no submission is made, or if it fails, then the prosecution has satisfied 'the evidential burden'. This does not mean that the prosecution is entitled to a conviction at this stage. It means that the case can proceed to the next stage where the defence has an opportunity to present evidence to the court.

9.2.2.2 The burden on the defence

The defence does not have to adduce any evidence. It can simply hope that the jury or magistrates will not accept that the prosecution evidence is sufficient to prove the case beyond reasonable doubt. However, if the defendant wishes to rely on a specific defence to a charge (eg, self-defence, alibi) then some evidence of that defence must be put before the magistrates or jury. To this extent there is an evidential burden on the defence. It is important to remember that the defendant is not required to prove his defence. All that is necessary is to put some evidence before the court and the evidential burden is satisfied. The prosecution must satisfy the magistrates or jury that the defence is not true.

In certain circumstances, courts are entitled to infer a fact against the defendant. Such cases again place an evidential burden on the defendant. See further **9.2.3**.

Example

Diana is charged with theft. Evidence is adduced to show that Diana was found in possession of recently stolen property. There is now an evidential burden on Diana to give an explanation for possession of the goods. In the absence of a credible explanation, the jury or magistrates are entitled to infer that Diana is the thief.

9.2.3 Proof by evidence

In deciding whether the prosecution has proved its case beyond reasonable doubt, a jury or magistrates can only take into account a fact which has been proved by evidence.

Example

Stuart is charged with assault. No admissible evidence is put forward in support of a defence of self-defence. During his closing speech at the end of the trial, Stuart's advocate raises the issue of self-defence. This cannot be taken into account as no evidence has been adduced in support of the fact.

This rule is subject to a number of exceptions.

9.2.3.1 Facts formally admitted

In order to narrow the issues to be decided at a criminal trial, it is possible for the prosecution or defence formally to admit certain facts. For example, on a charge of theft, the sole issue to be decided may be whether the defendant was acting dishonestly. The defence can make a formal admission to the effect that the defendant appropriated goods belonging to another with the intention to permanently deprive. This relieves the prosecution of the burden of adducing evidence of these facts and the trial can proceed solely on the issue of dishonesty.

A formal admission can be made either before or at the trial. If an admission is made out of court by the defendant, it must be made in writing and made by, or be approved by, the defendant's counsel or solicitor (Criminal Justice Act 1967, s 10).

A formal admission is not to be confused with admissions made to the police by a suspect when being questioned about suspected involvement in an offence.

9.2.3.2 Judicial notice

If a court takes judicial notice of a fact then evidence of that fact will not be required.

A court is obliged by law to take judicial notice of matters of law. Thus, there is no requirement to prove the content of a public Act of Parliament.

A court may take judicial notice of matters of common knowledge, including local knowledge. An example would be the rules of the road. On a driving charge, the prosecution would not be required to prove that, in Britain, motorists should drive on the left-hand side of the road. This would be a matter of common knowledge. The distance between towns and the time taken to travel between them are matters of local knowledge and may not have to be proved by evidence.

9.2.3.3 Inferences of fact

In many criminal cases, there will be no available direct evidence from eye witnesses to support the prosecution or defence case. A court, in reaching a verdict, will be entitled to draw inferences from the existence of other proven facts. The fact that the fingerprints of the defendant were found on burgled premises and that he was seen in the vicinity of the property around the time of the crime may lead to an inference that he committed the crime.

Two common examples of inferences arising in criminal cases are as follows.

The doctrine of recent possession

A court is entitled to infer that a person found in possession of recently stolen goods is the thief or a handler. Such an inference may only be drawn in the absence of a credible explanation from the defendant. If the prosecution gives evidence of possession of recently stolen property there is an evidential burden on the defendant to put forward an explanation (see **9.2.2**).

The doctrine of continuance

If evidence is adduced to prove that a certain state of affairs existed at a particular time, a court is entitled to infer that it continued to exist at another reasonably proximate time. For example, on a charge of dangerous driving, evidence may be given that the defendant was driving at great speed 500 yards from the scene of the accident, giving rise to the charge. The court may infer that this speed continued to the scene of the accident. Again, there may be an evidential burden on the defendant if he wishes to rebut the inference that may be drawn.

9.2.4 Improperly obtained evidence

At common law, evidence illegally or unfairly obtained was admissible. Courts would not exclude evidence which was relevant simply because it had been obtained by the police as a result of an illegal search (*Kuruma v The Queen* [1955] AC 197).

In relation to evidence obtained from the defendant which was tantamount to a self-incriminatory admission (eg, a confession or evidence from an identification parade), the court has a general discretion to exclude such evidence if it had been improperly obtained (*R v Sang* [1980] AC 402).

9.2.5   Court's discretion to exclude evidence

The Police and Criminal Evidence Act 1984, s 78(1) gives criminal courts a statutory discretion to exclude prosecution evidence:

> In any proceedings the court may refuse to allow evidence on which the prosecution proposes to rely to be given if it appears to the court that, having regard to all of the circumstances, including the circumstances in which the evidence was obtained, the admission of the evidence would have such an adverse effect on the fairness of the proceedings that the court ought not to admit it.

The section has been interpreted broadly in line with the existing common law. Thus the fact that evidence has been obtained as a result of an illegal search is unlikely to be a ground for exclusion under s 78.

In *Khan v United Kingdom* [2000] Crim LR 684, the European Court of Human Rights considered the relationship between s 78 and art 6 of the European Convention on Human Rights.

The court held that since domestic law did not regulate the use of covert listening devices at the time of the applicant's conviction, the applicant's right to respect for private and family life, as guaranteed by art 8 of the Convention, had been violated.

The applicant also alleged a breach of art 6(1) of the Convention. He argued that the use, as the sole evidence in his case, of the material which had been obtained in breach of art 8 was not compatible with the 'fair hearing' requirements of art 6.

The court noted that it was not its role to determine, as a matter of principle, whether particular types of evidence, for example, unlawfully obtained evidence, might be admissible or, indeed, whether the applicant was guilty or not.

In examining whether, in all the circumstances, including the way in which the evidence was obtained, the proceedings as a whole were unfair, the court observed that the recording of the applicant's conversation had not been unlawful in the sense of being contrary to domestic criminal law, even though it had been obtained in breach of art 8.

At each level of jurisdiction the domestic courts assessed the effect of admission of the evidence on the fairness of the trial and discussed, among other matters, the nonstatutory basis for the surveillance. In the court's view it was clear that, had the domestic courts been of the view that the admission of the evidence would have given rise to substantive unfairness, they would have exercised their discretion under s 78 to exclude it. As a result, the court found that the use at the applicant's trial of the secretly taped material did not conflict with the requirements of a fair trial guaranteed by art 6(1).

There are two major areas of operation of s 78:

(a)   identification evidence; and

(b)   confessions.

Section 78 has no application to committal proceedings.

Confessions are examined at **9.6.3**; identification evidence and s 78 are discussed below.

Subjective i. argue ab personal circumstances

9.2.5.1   Identification evidence

A breach of the Code of Practice D on identification does not automatically render evidence inadmissible. It is something that a court will take into account in determining an application to exclude such evidence under s 78. Examples include: *R v Gaynor* [1988] Crim LR 242, where evidence of a group identification was excluded because insufficient effort had been made to arrange an identification parade; *R v Gall* (1990) 90 Cr App R 64, breach of the rule that an investigating officer should take no part in the parade procedure; *R v Nagah (Jasant Singh)* (1991) 92 Cr App R 334, where a confrontation identification was disallowed because the defendant had requested an identification parade and it was practicable to hold one.

If evidence is to be excluded under s 78 because of a breach of the Code D, the defence will have to show why it would be unfair to admit it. The mere fact that there has been a technical breach which does not lead to unfairness will be insufficient to exclude evidence (*R v Grannell (Robert James Lawson)* (1990) 90 Cr App R 149).

9.3   Methods of proof

Evidence may be presented by:

(a)   calling witnesses;

(b)   adducing documentary evidence;

(c)   adducing real evidence.

Usually evidence is presented by calling witnesses to give oral evidence.

A number of technical rules must be borne in mind when presenting certain types of evidence.

9.3.1   Witnesses – competence and compellability

9.3.1.1   Competence

Competence means that the witness will be permitted to testify. The general rule is that all witnesses are competent to give evidence. Only if a witness cannot understand questions asked of him in court, or cannot answer them in a way that can be understood (with, if necessary, the assistance of special measures – see **9.3.2.1**), will the witness not be able to testify (Youth Justice and Criminal Evidence Act 1999, s 54).

The only exception to the general rule relates to the defendant. The defendant is not competent to give evidence for the prosecution in his own trial, nor is any co-defendant in the proceedings (see **9.7.1**).

9.3.1.2   Determining whether a witness is competent

A witness's competence to give evidence may be challenged by the prosecution, the defence or the court itself.

In assessing the witness's competence to give evidence, the court is required to take into account any special measures it has granted, or is planning to grant, to the witness (see **9.3.2.1**).

If the witness's competence is challenged, the court will ask questions of the witness (not the party that is calling or cross-examining the witness). Any such questioning will be done in the presence of both the prosecution and the defence.

The court will be allowed to ask for expert advice about the witness's competence. It will be the responsibility of the party calling the witness to satisfy the court that the witness is competent.

9.3.1.3   Determining whether witnesses are to be sworn

References to swearing an oath include making an affirmation. The question of whether a witness is eligible to swear an oath may be raised by either the prosecution or the defence or by the court itself. The procedure used to determine this question will be the same as the procedure outlined above for determining competence (Youth Justice and Criminal Evidence Act 1999, s 55).

No witness under the age of 14 is to be sworn. A witness of 14 or over is eligible to give sworn evidence only if he understands the solemnity of a criminal trial and that taking an oath places a particular responsibility on him to tell the truth. If no evidence is offered suggesting that the witness does not understand those two matters there is a presumption that the witness is to give sworn evidence.

As with considerations of competence, the question of whether a witness should be sworn is to be considered in the absence of any jury (but in the presence of both the prosecution and the defence). Expert evidence can be received on this subject.

9.3.1.4   Unsworn evidence

Any witness who is competent to be a witness but is not allowed to give evidence on oath may give unsworn evidence (Youth Justice and Criminal Evidence Act 1999, ss 56 and 57).

9.3.1.5   Compellability

The general rule is that all witnesses can be compelled to attend court to give evidence by the service of a witness summons. The only exceptions relate to the defendant and the defendant's spouse (see **9.7.1**).

9.3.2   Oral evidence from witnesses

9.3.2.1   Special measures

There are a number of special measures available to help witnesses (other than the defendant) who might otherwise have difficulty giving evidence in criminal proceedings or who might be reluctant to do so (Youth Justice and Criminal Evidence Act 1999, ss 16–33).

The following can apply to the court for special measures to help them give evidence in court:

(a)   children under the age of 17;

(b)   those who suffer from a mental or physical disorder, or have a disability or impairment that is likely to affect their evidence; and

(c)   those whose evidence is likely to be affected by their fear or distress at giving evidence in the proceedings.

Witnesses who are alleged to be victims of a sexual offence will be considered to be eligible for help with giving evidence unless they tell the court that they do not want to be considered eligible. Otherwise, it is for the court to determine whether a witness falls into any of these categories. The court must also determine whether making particular special measures available to an eligible witness will be likely to improve the quality of the evidence given by the witness.

Both the prosecution and defence will be able to apply, normally before the trial, for the court to make a direction authorising the use of special measures for a witness they are calling. A court may also decide to make a direction even if no such application has been made.

The special measures that are available are:

(a)   screens, to ensure that the witness does not see the defendant;

(b)   allowing an interview with the witness, which has been video recorded before the trial, to be shown as the witness's evidence-in-chief at trial;

(c)   allowing a witness to give evidence from outside the court by live television link;

(d)   clearing people from the court so that evidence can be given in private;

(e)   not wearing the court dress of wigs and gowns;

(f)   allowing a witness to be cross-examined before the trial about their evidence and a video recording of that cross-examination to be shown at trial instead of the witness being cross-examined live at trial;

(g)   allowing an approved intermediary to help a witness communicate with legal representatives and the court;

(h)   allowing a witness to use communication aids.

9.3.2.2   Examination-in-chief

Leading questions

A witness is examined-in-chief by the party calling that witness. As a general rule, leading questions should not be asked on matters which are in dispute. It is, however, permissible to ask a leading question where the object is to elicit a denial of an opponent's case. For example, it would be permissible to ask a defendant, 'were you in the pub at the time of the assault?'.

A leading question is one which suggests the answer expected or assumes the existence of a fact which has not been proved.

Example

Gareth is called as a prosecution witness. He is to testify to the fact that he saw Tony, at 11 am on 6 October, steal some goods from Tescos.

The prosecutor cannot say to Gareth, 'Did you see Tony steal goods from Tescos at 11 am on 6 October?' This is a leading question.

Instead, the evidence should be elicited in this way:

Q   Where were you on 6 October at about 11 am?

A   In Tescos.

Q   Did you see anything unusual in the shop?

A   Yes, I saw Tony put some chocolate into his pocket.

Q   What happened then?

A   Tony walked out of the shop without paying for the chocolate.

Memory refreshing

A party calling a witness may apply to the court for the witness to refresh his memory in the witness-box from a document which was made or verified by him at an earlier time if—

(a)   he states in his oral evidence that the document records his recollection of the matters at that earlier time, and

(b)   his recollection of the matter is likely to have been significantly better at that time than it is at the time of his oral evidence.

(Criminal Justice Act 2003, s 139(1))

A document is made by a witness if he writes down what he saw and it is verified by him if he dictated what he saw to someone else and checked the accuracy of the document.

A document which is used to refresh the witness's memory does not become evidence in the case in its own right. However, the other party has the right to request and inspect a document used for this purpose.

Unfavourable witnesses

A witness who is called to give evidence may not give the evidence expected of him. He may be nervous, forgetful or stupid. However, if the failure to testify as expected is not deliberate, the party calling the witness is not allowed to contradict or to try to discredit that witness.

Hostile witnesses

If a witness appears to be unwilling to tell the truth on behalf of the party calling him then the party may apply to the judge or magistrates to declare that witness 'hostile'. If declared hostile, the witness may:

(a)   be cross-examined by the party calling him. Leading questions may now be asked of the witness to show that he is being untruthful; and, with leave of the court,

(b)   have any previous inconsistent statement put to him by the party calling him (Criminal Procedure Act 1865, s 3).

In practice, witnesses are commonly shown to be hostile by proving that they have made an earlier out-of-court statement from which they appear to be deliberately and dishonestly departing.

A previous inconsistent statement is not admissible to prove the truth of anything contained in the statement. Thus, it is not open to the judge or magistrates to accept the statement as true (unless the witness admits that it is true when cross-examined).

The statement can be used to undermine the credibility of the witness.

9.3.2.3   Cross-examination

Following examination-in-chief, a witness may be cross-examined by the other party (or all other parties). Leading questions may be asked.

The purposes of cross-examination include:

(a)   to put the case of the cross-examiner to the witness. A failure to challenge a witness's evidence implies acceptance of it;

(b)   to challenge the credibility of the witness;

(c)   to elicit information helpful to the cross-examiner.

9.3.2.4   Restrictions on the defendant's right to cross-examination

A defendant is prohibited from personally cross-examining witnesses in the following circumstances:

(a)   when the witness is the alleged victim of a sexual offence;

(b)   when the witness is a child who is either the alleged victim, or a witness to the commission of the alleged offence, in a case involving sexual offences, kidnapping or abduction, cruelty or physical assault. This includes child witnesses who are co-defendants;

(c)   in any other case, when the court is satisfied, upon an application or on its own initiative, that the circumstances of the case merit it.

In such circumstances, the defendant must appoint a legal representative to conduct the cross-examination on his behalf. Where the defendant refuses or fails to do so, the court must consider whether it is in the interests of justice to appoint a legal representative to test the witness's evidence (Youth Justice and Criminal Evidence Act 1999, ss 34–39).

9.3.2.5   Cross-examination as to credit — general rule

A witness called by another party may be cross-examined as to credit where it is relevant as to whether the witness's evidence should be believed. Questions as to credit may include questions as to the witness's character, criminal convictions, previous inconsistent statements and whether a witness is biased in relation to the proceedings because of, for example, a grudge or relationship with a party to the proceedings.

As a general rule, the answer given to a credit question is final. This means that the cross-examiner cannot pursue the matter raised any further by calling independent evidence to prove the fact, but there are exceptions.

9.3.2.6   Cross-examination as to credit — exceptions

With certain credit questions the answer given is not final. The cross-examining party is allowed to call other evidence to prove the matter denied by the witness in cross-examination. These exceptional cases include:

(a)   When it is alleged that a witness is biased.

(b)   When it is alleged that the witness has made a previous inconsistent statement (Criminal Procedure Act 1865, ss 4, 5). If a previous inconsistent statement is proved (either by the witness admitting that he made it or by independent evidence), it is not admissible to prove the truth of anything stated in it. Thus the trial judge or magistrates cannot accept the previous inconsistent statement as true (unless the witness admits that it is true). It is relevant only to the credibility of the witness.

(c)   When the question is to show that the witness has been convicted of a criminal offence (Criminal Procedure Act 1865, s 6). If a witness denies a conviction then it may be proved by producing a certificate signed by the clerk to the convicting court and proving that the person named in the certificate is the witness being cross-examined (Police and Criminal Evidence Act 1984, s 73).

9.3.3   Written statements from witnesses

As an alternative to a witness giving oral evidence, a written statement may be admissible in evidence. The major provisions enabling a witness statement to be admitted in evidence include:

(a)   Criminal Justice Act 1988, ss 23, 24, 30;

(b)   Criminal Procedure and Investigations Act 1996, s 68 and Sch 2, paras 1 and 2;

(c)   Criminal Justice Act 1967, s 9.

These provisions require an appreciation of the rule against hearsay and are discussed at **9.6.1**.

9.3.4 Documentary evidence

A document must be authenticated by a witness if it is to be admitted in evidence. This will usually involve calling a witness to explain to the court how the document came into existence.

By the Criminal Justice Act 1988, s 27, a copy document is admissible even though the original is still in existence.

The content of a document may be hearsay evidence. The principal provisions governing the admissibility of documentary hearsay are discussed at **9.6.4**.

9.3.5 Real evidence

Items such as objects produced in court (exhibits) and places viewed by the court, are classified as real evidence. Items produced in court may include photographs, tape recordings and video recordings. Real evidence will normally require the additional testimony of a witness to explain the relevance of the evidence to the prosecution or defence case.

9.4 Corroboration and identification evidence

9.4.1 Corroboration

In determining the guilt or innocence of the defendant, the jury or magistrates will have regard to the cogency (or weight) of evidence before them. As a general rule, the law does not give specific weight to particular types of evidence, but in certain cases there are rules relating to corroboration of a witness's evidence.

9.4.1.1 The meaning of corroboration

Corroboration is other independent evidence which supports the evidence to be corroborated in a material particular and which implicates the defendant in the crime charged (*R v Baskerville* [1916] 2 KB 658).

9.4.1.2 Examples of corroboration

(a)   The evidence of another witness.

(b)   A confession by the defendant (see **9.6.3**).

(c)   Lies told by the defendant. These are capable of amounting to corroboration provided the jury or magistrates are satisfied that:

    (i)   the lie is deliberate and relates to a material issue in the case; and

    (ii)   the lie is told because of realisation of guilt; and

    (iii)   the lie is proved by evidence independent of the witness to be corroborated. An admission by the defendant would suffice (see *R v Lucas (Ruth)* [1981] QB 720).

(d)   Circumstantial evidence, for example, possession of stolen property or forensic evidence linking the defendant to the crime, is capable of amounting to corroboration.

(e)   The refusal of a defendant, without good cause, to give an intimate body sample to the police is capable of amounting to corroboration of any other evidence in the case to which the refusal is material. In a rape case, for example, the refusal of a semen sample could corroborate the prosecution case on an issue of whether intercourse took place between the victim and the defendant. It would not provide corroboration on an issue of consent (Police and Criminal Evidence Act 1984, s 62).

(f)   The refusal of a defendant, without good cause, to stand on an identification parade is capable of amounting to corroboration of any other evidence in the case to which the refusal is material.

In the Crown Court, the judge directs the jury as to evidence which is capable, as a matter of law, of amounting to corroboration. It is for the jury to decide whether to accept or reject the evidence. In a magistrates' court, the magistrates, taking advice from their clerk if necessary, decide what is capable of amounting to corroboration. They also decide whether or not to accept the evidence.

9.4.1.3   Special rules

Cases where corroboration is essential

In a limited number of cases there cannot be a conviction on the evidence of a single witness. Corroboration is required. These include treason, perjury and the offence of speeding (unless the evidence is from a roadside camera).

If, at the close of the prosecution case, no evidence has been adduced which is capable of amounting to corroboration, a submission of no case to answer will succeed (see **9.2.2**). If there is evidence capable of amounting to corroboration then it is left to the jury or magistrates to decide, when considering their verdict, whether or not to accept the evidence as corroboration.

It is important to remember that a defendant cannot be convicted of any offence if the only evidence against him is an inference under ss 34, 36 or 37 of the Criminal Justice and Public Order Act 1994 (Criminal Justice and Public Order Act 1994, s 38(3)).

Other cases

If a judge feels that the evidence of any type of witness is suspect, for whatever reason, he may direct a jury on the special need for caution and the dangers of convicting on that evidence alone (*R v Makanjuola; R v E* [1995] 1 WLR 1348).

Examples of such cases include:

(a)   Witnesses with a purpose of their own to serve in giving false evidence. Such witnesses may be:
   (i)   other parties to the crime charged. They may be giving evidence for the prosecution (having pleaded guilty) or evidence in their own defence. In either case they may be trying to put the blame on a co-defendant or minimising their role to get a lighter sentence;
   (ii)   witnesses with a grudge against the defendant;
   (iii)   witnesses whom a defendant alleges committed the offence.
(b)   Where a prosecution witness is a mental patient (*R v Spencer (Alan Widdison); R v Smails (George Glenville)* [1986] 3 WLR 348).

In a magistrates' court, it is always open to an advocate, when making a closing speech, to address the bench on the dangers of convicting on the evidence of a 'suspect' witness alone.

9.4.2   Disputed identification evidence

Special guidelines apply when a prosecution witness's evidence visually identifies the defendant and the identification is disputed (*R v Turnbull* [1977] QB 224).

9.4.2.1   When the rules apply

The *Turnbull* guidelines apply where there is evidence that a witness visually identified the defendant. This will usually come:

(a)   from evidence that the person who committed the crime was picked out at an identification parade, group identification, video identification or confrontation; or

(b)   from evidence that the witness recognised the person who committed the crime as someone previously known to him, for example, 'It was Fred Smith'.

If the witness has simply given a description to the court of the person who committed the crime and there is no direct evidence that it was the defendant other than the fact that his physical appearance matches the description then the Turnbull guidelines do not apply.

Example 1

Joe is on trial for theft. A prosecution witness tells the court that he saw a man commit the crime and later identified Joe as that man at an identification parade.

(a)   If Joe denies being at the scene of the theft, the *Turnbull* guidelines apply.

(b)   If Joe admits to being at the scene of the theft but denies that he was the person who committed the crime, the *Turnbull* guidelines apply 'if there is a possibility of the witness being mistaken' (*R v Thornton* [1995] 1 Cr App R 598). This will depend on the facts of the case. If the defendant was the only person present then the Turnbull direction would seem to be inappropriate. If, however, there were a number of people present, the guidelines will apply (*R v Slater (Robert David)* [1995] 1 Cr App R 584).

(c)   If Joe admits taking the goods and pleads absence of *mens rea*, the *Turnbull* guidelines do not apply. The identification is not disputed.

Example 2

Jane is on trial for assault. A witness tells the court that he saw Jane commit the offence. He says that he knows Jane by sight and name as they live on the same road.

(a)   If Jane denies being at the scene of the assault, the Turnbull guidelines apply.

(b)   If Jane admits to being at the scene of the assault but claims that it was someone else who hit the victim, the Turnbull guidelines may apply (*R v Thornton* (above)).

(c)   If Jane admits hitting the victim but pleads self-defence, Turnbull does not apply as the identification is not in dispute.

Example 3

Peter is on trial for taking a conveyance. The victim of the crime tells the court that he saw a man 'about 6ft tall, with brown spiky hair and a moustache'. Peter matches this description but he was not picked out at an identification parade.

The *Turnbull* guidelines cannot apply as there is no direct evidence identifying Peter as the man who committed the offence.

9.4.2.2   The *Turnbull* guidelines — Crown Court cases

In Crown Court cases, the trial judge should assess the quality of the identification evidence, that is to say, he should look at the circumstances of the original sighting of the offender by the witness. Factors to be taken into account will include:

(a)   the length of observation;

(b)   distance;

(c)   lighting;

(d)   conditions;

(e)   whether the person identified was someone already known to the witness;

(f) how closely the description given to the police matches the appearance of the defendant.

Identification poor and without support

If the evidence is assessed as being of poor quality and without support then the judge should stop the trial at the end of the prosecution case and direct an acquittal.

Identification good

If the judge considers the quality of the initial sighting to be good, he should, when summing up the case to the jury, point out the dangers of relying on identification evidence (including the fact that it is easy for an honest witness to be mistaken) and direct the jury to take into account the factors listed above when considering the quality of the evidence.

Identification poor but supported

If the judge considers the quality of the initial sighting to be poor, but supported by other evidence, then a similar warning should be given.

Supporting evidence is some independent evidence that suggests that the identification of the defendant may be correct. It may, for example, come via a confession, possession of stolen property, or lies told by the defendant. There is no requirement that supporting evidence should fulfil all the legal criteria of corroboration. In particular, it need not be independent of the identifying witness.

9.4.2.3   The *Turnbull* guidelines – magistrates' court cases

In magistrates' court cases, the same principles apply as in Crown Court cases. Therefore:

(a)   if the case is one which appears to consist of poor quality identification evidence without support, a submission of no case to answer should be made (see **9.2.2**). This will be on the basis that the evidence is manifestly unreliable;

(b)   in any other type of case, the defence advocate is likely to deal with Turnbull in his closing speech by pointing out the unreliability of identification evidence.

9.5   Particular rules of admissibility of evidence

This paragraph is concerned with the content of evidence to be given by witnesses or which is contained in a document. Even though a witness may be competent to give evidence or a document can be authenticated, it is open to the prosecution or defence to challenge the evidence on the basis that it infringes one of the general principles of admissibility. Evidence may be inadmissible due to its being:

(a)   irrelevant;

(b)   self-made;

(c)   opinion;

(d)   privileged.

9.5.1   Challenging the admissibility of evidence

9.5.1.1   By agreement

It may be possible to agree with an opposing advocate that evidence is inadmissible. If so, such evidence will not be given at the trial and the jury or magistrates will not know about it.

9.5.1.2   By application to the court

Crown court cases

A challenge to the admissibility of evidence is made to the judge in the absence of the jury. If the challenge is on agreed facts then the advocates present legal argument to the judge who will make a ruling. If the evidence is ruled inadmissible, the jury will never hear it. If the evidence is admissible, the witness will testify in front of the jury. If there is a factual dispute involved (eg, whether the police pressured the defendant into confessing) then the judge will hear evidence from relevant witnesses for the prosecution and defence in the absence of the jury before ruling on admissibility. This procedure is known as a trial within a trial. It is commonly used to challenge the admissibility of a confession and is examined in more detail at **9.6.3.1**.

Magistrates' court cases

As magistrates are arbiters of both fact and law they must rule on the admissibility of evidence. This will often mean that the magistrates will have heard details of evidence which they find inadmissible. Such evidence should be ignored when a verdict is being considered. The special problems involved in challenging the admissibility of a confession are discussed at **9.6.3.1**.

9.5.2   Relevance

Evidence of a fact is not admissible unless that fact is relevant to an issue to be decided by the court. Relevant evidence will include direct evidence from a witness who perceived an event. It will also include circumstantial evidence from which a fact can be inferred. Even though a fact may be relevant, it can still be ruled inadmissible because it offends one of the other principles of admissibility of evidence which follow.

9.5.3   Self-made evidence

9.5.3.1   General rule

As a general rule, a witness is not allowed to support the evidence given at a trial by introducing a statement which he has made on a previous occasion. For example, if the defendant is charged with assault and gives evidence of self-defence, he will not be allowed to tell the court that, 'I told my wife the day after the incident that I was acting in self-defence'. Similarly, the wife could not testify as to what her husband told her. In either case, the evidence adds nothing to the testimony given in court. The rule against self-made evidence is subject to a number of exceptions. These include:

(a)   rebutting a suggestion of recent fabrication;

(b)   statements forming part of the *res gestae*;

(c)   exculpatory statements made to the police.

9.5.3.2 Rebutting a suggestion of recent fabrication

If, during cross-examination of a witness, it is put to a witness that he has recently concocted his testimony, evidence of previous statements can be admitted to rebut the assertion. In the example given in relation to the general rule, the defendant could call his wife to prove that he raised the issue of self-defence the day after the incident. The evidence would be admissible solely to show that the suggestion of recent fabrication was incorrect.

9.5.3.3 Statements forming part of the *res gestae*

If a statement is made 'in circumstances of spontaneity or involvement in the event so that the possibility of concoction can be disregarded' (see *Ratten (Leith McDonald) v The Queen* [1972] AC 378), it will be admissible in evidence under the *res gestae* principle. This is on the basis that a statement which is made at the time of a relevant act should be put before the court to help explain the event. The *res gestae* principle is well known in the United States by the graphic name 'the excited utterance rule'. In *R v Roberts* [1942] 1 All ER 187, the defendant testified to the fact that a gun had gone off accidentally, killing his girlfriend. He was not allowed to testify that while he was in police custody he had told his father that it was an accident. This was too far removed from the event to fall within the *res gestae* principle. The Court of Appeal held, however, that the defendant should have been allowed to call witnesses to recount the defendant's explanation which had been made contemporaneously with or within a few minutes of the shooting. Such evidence formed part of the *res gestae*. The *res gestae* principle is also an exception to the rule against hearsay.

9.5.3.4 Exculpatory statements made to the police

When being questioned by the police about an offence the defendant may put forward an explanation which, if accepted by a court, would exonerate him. Such statements are generally admissible in evidence but only to show consistency with testimony given at the trial. See *R v Pearce (David Anthony)* (1979) 69 Cr App R 365.

Example

Nicholas is charged with assault. When interviewed by the police he claims that he was elsewhere at the time of the commission of the offence. If Nicholas gives evidence at his trial in support of his alibi evidence, his statement made to the police is admissible to show consistency. If, however, he fails to testify, his statement made to the police is of no evidential value. It is not open to Nicholas to say to the court, 'my defence is in my statement to the police, please take it into account'.

Although the statement will not assist the prosecution case, as a matter of practice the interviewing officer will give evidence of the interview during the prosecution evidence and the statement will be received by the court as an exception to the rule against self-made evidence.

9.5.4 Opinion evidence

9.5.4.1 Ordinary witnesses

A witness may relate to the court any fact that he has personally perceived. Inevitably, parts of his evidence will include opinions such as the fact that a car was travelling at about 60 mph, or that a person appeared to be drunk. This is acceptable as the witness is simply relating to the court the facts as he saw them. However, the witness is not allowed to give an opinion on matters which it is the function of the court to decide. In particular, therefore, the witness cannot give his opinion on the ultimate issue to be determined, ie, the guilt or innocence of the defendant.

9.5.4.2   Expert witnesses

Expert opinion evidence is admissible in relation to matters which are outside the competence of a jury or magistrates. Examples include matters of science, medicine and technology.

It is for the judge or magistrates to decide who is an expert. There is no fixed test and the presence or absence of formal qualifications is not conclusive.

Any party to criminal proceedings in the Crown Court who proposes to adduce expert evidence at the trial is required to give advance disclosure to all other parties of the substance of the evidence as soon as practicable following committal to the Crown Court for trial or being sent to the Crown Court for trial. If advance disclosure is not given then expert evidence cannot be adduced without leave of the court (Crown Court (Advance Notice of Expert Evidence) Rules 1987 (SI 1987/716)).

The rules requiring advance notice of expert evidence have been extended to trials in the magistrates' court by the Criminal Procedure and Investigations Act 1996, s 20 and the Magistrates' Courts (Advance Notice of Expert Evidence) Rules 1997 (SI 1997/705).

Expert evidence can be difficult for a lay person to understand. To assist magistrates and juries, s 30(1) of the Criminal Justice Act 1988 provides that:

> An expert report shall be admissible as evidence in criminal proceedings, whether or not the person making it attends to give oral evidence in those proceedings.

This provision enables the jury or magistrates to have a copy of the written report by the expert in front of them as they listen to his oral evidence.

The provision is drawn widely enough to enable a written report to be admissible in the absence of the expert. Section 30(2) states that:

> If it is proposed that the person making the report shall not give oral evidence, the report shall only be admissible with the leave of the court.

Even if such leave were given, the amount of weight attached to the report is likely to be less than if the author of the report testified in person.

The written report of a prosecution expert witness is admissible at committal proceedings. No leave is required to admit it (Criminal Justice Act 1988, s 4A).

9.5.5   Privilege

9.5.5.1   Public policy privilege

As a matter of public policy, evidence which discloses the identity of a police informant is normally inadmissible. The rule extends to prevent the identification of premises used for police surveillance (*R v Rankine* [1986] 2 All ER 566). The reason for this protection is that it is in the public interest for the identity of those who help the police to be kept secret. The protection can be overridden if disclosure is necessary to show the innocence of the defendant. Thus, if the defendant alleges that he has been 'set up' by a particular person, X, the prosecution could be forced to reveal whether or not its informant was X.

9.5.5.2 Legal professional privilege

Communications between a client and his solicitor are privileged if the purpose of the communication is the giving or receiving of legal advice. In a criminal case, the practical effect of this is that letters, telephone calls, statements, etc are privileged. The defence cannot be compelled to reveal the content of such communications to any other party.

Communications between the defendant or his solicitor and a third party are also privileged, provided they are made in contemplation of pending or anticipated proceedings and the purpose, or dominant purpose, was to prepare for the litigation. Witness statements are obvious examples. The defence cannot be compelled to reveal the content of such communications to any other party.

9.5.5.3 Privilege against self-incrimination

A witness is not bound to answer a question if, in the opinion of the court, the answer would tend to expose him to proceedings for a criminal offence. This privilege is limited in the case of a defendant who elects to go into the witness box to give evidence. He will be obliged to answer questions even though the answer may tend to incriminate him as to the offence for which he is charged (Criminal Evidence Act 1898, s 1(e)).

9.6 Hearsay evidence

9.6.1 The rule against hearsay

Hearsay is:

(a)   an oral or written statement

(b)   made out of court

(c)   which is now being repeated to the court

(d)   to try to prove the truth of the matter stated out of court.

Hearsay evidence is most likely to consist of a witness giving evidence and seeking to repeat what someone else has said out of court or a party seeking to adduce a document (including a witness statement) in evidence.

Not all such evidence will be hearsay. It is necessary to consider why the party is seeking to adduce the evidence. If the purpose is to prove that anything in the statement or document is true then it will be hearsay. If it is being adduced for some other purpose, for example to show the state of mind of the maker or hearer of the statement, irrespective of its truth, then it is not hearsay (*Subramaniam v Public Prosecutor* [1956] 1 WLR 965).

Example 1

PC Smith wants to say to the court:

'I arrived at Tescos. I was met by a store detective who told me that the defendant had left the store without paying for goods.'

If the prosecution in a criminal trial for theft is asking the court to accept the truth of the store detective's statement (ie, that the defendant left the store without paying for goods) then it will be hearsay.

If, on the other hand, where the defendant is bringing a civil action for wrongful arrest against PC Smith, PC Smith is simply asking the court to accept that the statement was made to him by the store detective (thereby giving him reasonable grounds to suspect that the defendant had committed an arrestable offence) then it will not be hearsay. The court is not being asked to accept the truth of the store detective's statement.

Example 2

Michael is charged with burglary by entering a dwellinghouse as a trespasser with intent to steal. His defence is that he was simply trying to recover some of his own property in the house. The prosecution wants to call a witness to say:

'The day before the offence Michael told me that there was some valuable jewellery in the house and that he was going to steal it.'

This will not be hearsay. The court is not being asked to accept the truth of anything said by Michael (ie, that there was some valuable jewellery in the house), merely that he intended to steal. It is relevant only to his state of mind when entering the house.

Example 3

Marie makes a written statement in Suzanne's defence confirming an alibi. Marie is not available to give evidence. Marie's written statement will be hearsay as the court is being asked to accept the truth of the statement.

Example 4

Philip is charged with stealing £300 in cash from the safe at his place of work. The prosecution wishes to put in evidence a ledger compiled by a clerk showing that on the day of the offence £300 was deposited in the safe. The ledger will be hearsay as the court is being asked to accept the truth of the statement made in it, ie, that £300 was deposited.

The general rule is that hearsay evidence is not admissible. This exclusionary rule is subject to a number of exceptions. These include:

(a) *res gestae*;

(b) confessions;

(c) documentary hearsay;
Criminal Justice Act 1988, ss 23, 24 and 30 (see **9.5.4.2** for s 30);
Criminal Procedure and Investigations Act 1996, s 68, and Sch 2, para 1 and 2;
Criminal Justice Act 1967, s 9.

9.6.2 Res gestae

The principles of admissibility of a statement under the *res gestae* principle are discussed at **9.5.3.3**. Such statements are admissible as an exception to the rule against hearsay evidence.

9.6.3 Confessions

In any proceedings a confession made by an accused person may be given in evidence against him insofar as it is relevant to any matter in issue in the proceedings and is not excluded by the court in pursuance of this section. (Police and Criminal Evidence Act 1984, s 76(1))

A confession includes:

any statement wholly or partly adverse to the person who made it, whether made to a person in authority or not and whether made in words or otherwise. (Police and Criminal Evidence Act 1984, s 82(1))

Confessions can be made only by the defendant.

The most common examples of confessions will be admissions of guilt made by a defendant, orally or in writing, when being interviewed by the police. However, a confession can be made to anyone. If a defendant says to a friend, 'I did the burglary at number 10 last night', that would constitute a confession.

As a general rule, confessions are admissible in evidence (but only against the maker – they are inadmissible against anyone else implicated in the confession) as an exception to the rule excluding hearsay evidence. If a defendant says to the police, 'I stole the goods', the interviewing officer will give evidence of the defendant's statement. The court will be asked to accept the truth of that statement. It will be hearsay but admissible as an exception to the general exclusionary rule. Sometimes a confession statement will include statements which are favourable to the defendant.

Example

'I hit the victim in the face' (confession) '... but in self-defence' (favourable to the defence).

These are often referred to as 'mixed statements'. The whole statement is admissible as an exception to the rule excluding hearsay (*R v Sharp (Colin)* (1988) 86 Cr App R 274).

9.6.3.1   Challenging the admissibility of confessions

Although, as a general principle, confessions are admissible in evidence, by the Police and Criminal Evidence Act 1984, s 76(2)(a), (b):

If, in any proceedings where the prosecution proposes to give in evidence a confession made by an accused person, it is represented to the court that the confession was or may have been obtained—

(a)   by oppression of the person who made it; or

(b)   in consequence of anything said or done which was likely, in the circumstances existing at the time, to render unreliable any confession which might be made by him in consequence thereof,

the court shall not allow the confession to be given in evidence against him except insofar as the prosecution proves to the court beyond reasonable doubt that the confession (notwithstanding that it may be true) was not obtained as aforesaid.

The magistrates at committal proceedings have no power to exclude confession evidence (Police and Criminal Evidence Act 1984, s 76(9)).

Oppression

Oppression includes 'torture, inhuman or degrading treatment, and the use or threat of violence (whether or not amounting to torture)' (s 76(8)). In *R v Fulling* [1987] 2 WLR 923, the Court of Appeal considered the meaning of oppression (the statutory definition not being intended to be a complete definition). It was held that the word 'oppression' was to be given its ordinary dictionary meaning, ie, 'exercise of authority or power in a burdensome, harsh or wrongful manner; unjust or cruel treatment of subjects, inferiors, etc; the imposition of unreasonable or unjust burdens'. Deliberate police misconduct in the form of a serious breach of the Code of Practice or a course of misconduct may constitute oppression. Code C, para 11.5 provides that no police officer may try to obtain answers to questions or elicit a statement by the use of oppression.

Example

D was unlawfully held at the police station, unlawfully denied access to legal advice and questioned about an offence for which he had not been arrested. His confession was excluded on the oppression ground: *R v Davison* [1988] Crim LR 442.

The 'unreliability' ground

Under s 76(2)(b) it is necessary to consider:

(a)   the thing said or done which is the subject of the application to exclude the confession;

(b)   whether that thing said or done is likely to render any confession which might have been made by the defendant unreliable.

The thing said or done will usually involve a breach of Code C. Such breaches may include denial of access to legal advice, inducements to confess and failure to summon an independent adult in cases involving juveniles or mental disorder. However, a breach of the Code will not of itself lead to exclusion of the confession. There must be a causal link between the breach and the unreliability of any confession that might have been made. Thus, if denial of access to legal advice is relied upon, it will be difficult to establish a causal link if the defendant is an experienced criminal who says that he was fully aware of his rights. On the other hand, a young, inexperienced defendant may find it easier to establish the unreliability principle in such circumstances.

It should be noted that, in contrast to oppression, the unreliability ground need not necessarily involve any misconduct on the part of the police.

Example 1

R v Harvey [1988] Crim LR 241: H and her lesbian lover were questioned about a murder. H had a low IQ and was an alcoholic. H's lover, in the presence of H, confessed. H then made a confession exonerating her lover. The lover subsequently died and H was tried for murder, the prosecution relying on her confession. The confession was excluded on the unreliability ground, the court finding that H may well have been trying to protect her lover who had initially confessed in H's presence.

Example 2

R v Trussler (Barry) [1988] Crim LR 446: T, a drug addict, was kept in custody for 18 hours. He was interviewed several times without being given any rest and was denied access to legal advice. His confession was excluded on the unreliability ground.

Example 3

R v Alladice (Colin Carlton) (1988) 87 Cr App R 380: A was denied access to legal advice and confessed to a robbery. When giving evidence, A stated that he knew of his rights and that he understood the caution. A's application to exclude his confession was correctly rejected by the trial judge. Although there had been a serious breach of the Code of Practice, there was nothing to suggest that this might render any confession made by A unreliable.

The discretion to exclude a confession

If the prosecution fails to discharge the burden of proof imposed by the Police and Criminal Evidence Act 1984, s 76, exclusion of a confession is mandatory. The court also has a general discretion to exclude prosecution evidence under s 78 on the basis that the admission of the evidence will have an adverse effect on the fairness of the proceedings (see **9.2.5**). Again, breaches of the Code of Practice may be the basis of an application under s 78.

In *R v Canale (Ramon Michael)* [1990] 2 All ER 187, the defendant denied making certain statements attributed to him by the police. The interviewing officers had failed to make a contemporaneous note of two of the interviews and had therefore failed to give the defendant a chance to comment on the accuracy of the record of these interviews. The evidence was excluded under s 78 on the basis that its admission would be unfair to the defendant. The court had been deprived of the assistance of contemporaneous notes and had thereby lost the most cogent evidence which would have been available to resolve the conflict of evidence between the parties. As with s 76, a breach of the Code will not lead to automatic exclusion of the confession. If *Canale* had not challenged the accuracy of the officer's evidence, it is difficult to see how the absence of contemporaneous notes could have led to a successful application to exclude under s 78.

The discretion to exclude a confession has also been used where the police have misrepresented the strength of the evidence available to them and have thereby effectively tricked the defendant into confession (*R v Mason* [1988] 1 WLR 139).

The procedure for challenging the admissibility of a confession

In the Crown Court, the admissibility of a confession will be determined by the judge, in the absence of the jury, at a 'trial within a trial'. The interviewing officer will give evidence as to how the confession was obtained and the defendant will be given the opportunity of relating his version of events. The judge will then rule on admissibility. If it is ruled to be inadmissible, the confession will not be put to the jury. If it is ruled to be admissible, the interviewing officer will give evidence of it to the jury. It is open to the defence to attack the cogency of the confession in order to persuade the jury to attach no weight to it.

When challenging the admissibility of a confession, the defendant will often allege police misconduct. Since the jury will not be present at the trial within a trial, such allegations will not expose the defendant to cross-examination on any previous convictions under s 1(3)(ii) of the Criminal Evidence Act 1898 (see **9.7.5.2**) if he later gives evidence to the jury. If, however, the allegations are repeated in front of the jury s 1(3)(ii) will apply.

In the magistrates' court, a ruling as to the admissibility of the confession can be sought when the interviewing officer gives evidence (*R v Liverpool Juvenile Court, ex p R* [1988] QB 1). If the application is made under s 76, the magistrates must hold a 'trial within a trial'. There is no such obligation if the application is made under s 78. If submissions are made under both s 76 and s 78, then both applications should be examined at the same 'trial within a trial' (*Halawa v Federation Against Copyright Theft* [1995] 1 Cr App R 21). Alternatively, the question of admissibility can be left to the close of the prosecution case (if no defence evidence is required to challenge the admissibility of the confession) or to the end of the trial (before the defence closing speech). Whatever the procedure adopted, it is inevitable that the magistrates will know that a confession has been made. Furthermore, if the defendant makes allegations of police misconduct in challenging the confession, this may expose him to cross-examination on his previous convictions.

Evidence obtained in consequence of an inadmissible confession

The fact that a confession is excluded under s 76 shall not affect the admissibility in evidence of any facts discovered as a result of the confession. However, the prosecution may not call evidence that such facts were discovered as a result of a statement made by the defendant.

Example

Martin is charged with murder. As a result of statements made by him, the police are able to recover both the murder weapon and the body. If the confession is ruled inadmissible, the jury will hear evidence as to where and when these items were discovered. If his confession is ruled admissible, the jury will, in addition, hear that the defendant was able to say exactly where these items could be found.

If a confession is relevant as showing that the accused speaks, writes or expresses himself in a particular way, so much of the confession as is necessary to show that he does so will be admissible (s 76(4)–(6)).

9.6.4   Documentary hearsay

9.6.4.1   Criminal Justice Act 1988

First-hand hearsay (Criminal Justice Act 1988, s 23)

(1)   ... a statement made by a person in a document shall be admissible in criminal proceedings as evidence of any fact of which direct oral evidence by him would be admissible if—

    (i)   the requirements of one of the paragraphs of subsection (2) below are satisfied; or

    (ii)   the requirements of subsection (3) below are satisfied.

(2)   The requirements mentioned in subsection (1)(i) above are—

    (a)   that the person who made the statement is dead or by reason of his bodily or mental condition is unfit to attend as a witness;

    (b)   that—

        (i)   the person who made the statement is outside the United Kingdom; and

        (ii)   it is not reasonably practicable to secure his attendance; or

    (c)   that all reasonable steps have been taken to find the person who made the statement, but that he cannot be found.

(3)   The requirements mentioned in subsection (1)(ii) above are—

    (a)   that the statement was made to a police officer or some other person charged with the duty of investigating offences or charging offenders; and

    (b)   that the person who made it does not give oral evidence through fear or because he is kept out of the way.

The practical effect of this provision is to make first-hand documentary hearsay admissible in evidence (subject to the conditions cited below).

Example 1

Joe witnesses a crime. He makes a statement in writing, relating what he saw.

Joe's statement is first-hand hearsay. Joe is the witness as to fact and he has reduced what he said into writing.

Example 2

Joe witnesses a crime. He tells Jenny what he saw. Jenny makes a statement in writing, relating what Joe told her.

Jenny's statement is multiple hearsay. Joe's evidence has now gone through two stages of reporting.

Multiple hearsay is not covered by s 23.

Example 3

Ann deposits £300 in a safe. She records the deposit in a ledger.

Assuming that the ledger is to be adduced in evidence to prove the truth of the statement in it, ie, the deposit of £300, this would be first-hand hearsay. Ann is the witness with first-hand knowledge. The record in the ledger has gone through one stage of reporting.

Under the provisions of s 23, the evidence will be admissible only if there is a prescribed reason for not calling the maker of the statement (Joe in Example 1,

Ann in Example 3) to give evidence. The prescribed reason must be established by evidence to the appropriate standard of proof and such evidence must be admissible (*R v Acton Justices, ex p McCullen; R v Tower Bridge Magistrates Court, ex p Lawlor* (1991) 92 Cr App R 98; *R v Mattey (Jimmy Cyril); R v Queeley (Juanita Amelia)* [1995] 2 Cr App R 409).

A statement prepared for use in pending or contemplated criminal proceedings or a criminal investigation will only be admissible with leave of the court. The court should admit the statement if it is in the interests of justice to do so (s 26). Therefore, in Example 1, leave of the court will be required; in Example 3, it will not as the ledger is produced for business purposes rather than for use in criminal proceedings.

The court has a general discretion to exclude a statement otherwise admissible under s 23 (s 25).

A flowchart summarising the admissibility of evidence under s 23 is included at **Appendix 1(G).**

Hearsay in 'business documents' (Criminal Justice Act 1988, s 24)

(1) ... a statement in a document shall be admissible in criminal proceedings as evidence of any fact of which direct oral evidence would be admissible, if the following conditions are satisfied—

  (i) the document was created or received by a person in the course of a trade, business, profession or other occupation, or as the holder of a paid or unpaid office; and

  (ii) the information contained in the document was supplied by a person (whether or not the maker of the statement) who had, or may reasonably be supposed to have had, personal knowledge of the matters dealt with.

(2) Subsection (1) above applies whether the information contained in the document was supplied directly or indirectly but, if it was supplied indirectly, only if each person through whom it was supplied received it—

  (a) in the course of a trade, business, profession or other occupation; or

  (b) as the holder of a paid or unpaid office.

The practical effect of this provision is to make first-hand and multiple hearsay in certain documents admissible subject to the conditions cited below.

Example 1

Ann deposits £300 in a safe. She tells William, a clerk, who records the deposit in a ledger.

Ann .... William .... William's statement in ledger

The ledger, if adduced to prove the deposit of £300, will be multiple hearsay. As it is created by William in the course of a business, it is admissible under s 24.

Example 2

Ann deposits £300 in a safe. She tells William, a clerk. William passes on the information to Julian, who records the deposit in a ledger.

Ann .... William .... Julian .... Julian's statement in ledger

The ledger, if adduced to prove the deposit of £300, will be multiple hearsay. As the information was passed on by William in the course of a business to Julian who, also acting in the course of a business, recorded the deposit in a ledger, it is admissible under s 24.

Example 3

Sarah witnesses a crime. She tells PC Smith what she saw. PC Smith makes a statement setting out what Sarah told him but does not get her to sign it.

Sarah .... PC Smith .... PC Smith's statement

The written statement of PC Smith, if adduced to prove the truth of anything contained in it will be multiple hearsay. As PC Smith made the statement as the holder of a paid office, it is admissible under s 24.

Where the statement has been prepared for use in pending or contemplated criminal proceedings or a criminal investigation, it will be admissible only if:

(a)   there is a prescribed reason as stated in s 23 (see above) for not calling the maker of the statement; or

(b)   'the person who made the statement cannot reasonably be expected (having regard to the time which has elapsed since he made the statement and to all the circumstances) to have any recollection of the matters dealt with in the statement' (s 24(4)).

Therefore, in Examples 1 and 2 above, the ledgers will be admissible without a prescribed reason as they were not prepared for use in criminal proceedings or a criminal investigation. In Example 3, a prescribed reason is required for Sarah as the police officer's statement will have been prepared for such purpose.

Where the supplier of the information and the creator of the document are different persons, the maker of the statement is to be taken to be the person who supplied the information (*R v Derodra* [2000] 1 Cr App R 49, CA).

Leave of the court is required to admit a statement prepared for use in pending or contemplated criminal proceedings or a criminal investigation. The court should admit the statement only if it is in the interests of justice to do so (s 26).

The court has a discretion to exclude a statement otherwise admissible under s 24 (s 25).

Leave of the court (Criminal Justice Act 1988, s 26)

Where a statement which is admissible in criminal proceedings by virtue of section 23 or 24 above appears to the court to have been prepared, ... for the purposes—

(a)   of pending or contemplated criminal proceedings; or

(b)   of a criminal investigation,

the statement shall not be given in evidence in any criminal proceedings without the leave of the court, and the court shall not give leave unless it is of the opinion that the statement ought to be admitted in the interests of justice; and in considering whether its admission would be in the interests of justice, it shall be the duty of the court to have regard—

(i)   to the contents of the statement;

(ii)   to any risk, having regard in particular to whether it is likely to be possible to controvert the statement if the person making it does not attend to give oral evidence in the proceedings, that its admission or exclusion will result in unfairness to the accused or, if there is more than one, to any of them; and

(iii)   to any other circumstances that appear to the court to be relevant.

This section shall not apply to proceedings before a magistrates' court inquiring into an offence as examining justices.

An important factor to be considered is the quality of the evidence contained in the statement. In *R v Patel* (1993) 97 Cr App R 294, the Court of Appeal upheld a trial judge's decision to refuse leave under s 26 where the statement by an alibi witness was nothing more than an assertion that he could support the alibi. In contrast, in *R v Fairfax* [1995] Crim LR 949, the Court of Appeal, when upholding leave to admit identification evidence in a written statement, stressed the clarity and precision of the evidence. The court must consider whether any potential unfairness may be effectively counterbalanced by a warning to the jury that the evidence had not been tested by cross-examination and drawing attention to its possible limitations (*R v Cole* [1990] 1 WLR 866).

Where the evidence is of considerable significance implicating the defendant, the judge is entitled to take this into account in support of the admission of the statement (see *R v Fairfax; R v Batt and Batt* [1995] Crim LR 240). The fact that the absent witness provides the only significant evidence against a defendant is not sufficient to render the admission of written evidence from that witness contrary to the interests of justice per se (see *R v Grafton* [1995] Crim LR 61; *R v Fairfax* and *R v Dragic* [1996] 2 Cr App R 232). However, in *Neill v North Antrim Magistrates' Court and Others* [1992] 1 WLR 1221, the House of Lords suggested that where identification evidence forms the principal element in the prosecution case the court should, in general, be reluctant to admit it under s 23 or s 24.

The court must consider the risk of unfairness to the accused (s 25(2)(d) and s 26) and also any unfairness to the prosecution if the evidence is admitted (ie, in terms of the result of the trial rather than the prosecution as a party to the proceedings) (*R v W* [1997] Crim LR 678).

In *R v Cole* [1990] 1 WLR 866, the Court of Appeal held that the court shall take into account:

(a)   the availability for cross-examination of prosecution witnesses,

(b)   the availability of witnesses for the defence, and

(c)   the availability of the defendant himself to give evidence in support of any defence raised,

in deciding whether it is likely to be possible to controvert the statement.

The court can take into account any relevant circumstances in deciding whether to grant leave. In *R v Iqbal* [1990] 1 WLR 756, the defence disclosed the existence of their evidence some six months before the trial. The prosecution therefore had ample opportunity to investigate the circumstances and gather evidence to challenge the consistency and the credibility of the defence witnesses. The Court of Appeal held that there was no reason why the trial judge should have exercised his discretion to exclude a defence witness statement. In *R v Radak; R v Adjei; R v Butler-Rees; R v Meghjee* [1999] 1 Cr App R 187, the prosecution made an application to admit the evidence under s 23 even though it would been possible, had appropriate arrangements have been made in time, to have taken the witness's evidence on commission in the United States. Such a procedure would have given the defence the opportunity for cross-examination. The Court of Appeal held that the failure of the prosecution to explore this alternative was a factor to be taken into account under s 26 and should have led to the conclusion that the evidence should not have been admitted. It was considered that art 6 of the European Convention on Human Rights pointed to the same conclusion.

Discretion to exclude (Criminal Justice Act 1988, s 25)

(1)   If, having regard to all the circumstances [the court] ...

is of the opinion that in the interests of justice a statement which is admissible by virtue of section 23 or 24 above nevertheless ought not to be admitted, it may direct that the statement shall not be admitted.

(2) ... it shall be the duty of the court to have regard—

    (a)   to the nature and source of the document containing the statement and to whether or not, having regard to its nature and source and to any other circumstances that appear to the court to be relevant, it is likely that the document is authentic;

    (b)   to the extent to which the statement appears to supply evidence which would otherwise not be readily available;

    (c)   to the relevance of the evidence that it appears to supply to any issue which is likely to have to be determined in the proceedings; and

    (d)   to any risk, having regard in particular to whether it is likely to be possible to controvert the statement if the person making it does not attend to give oral evidence in the proceedings, that its admission or exclusion will result in unfairness to the accused or, if there is more than one, to any of them.

A flowchart summarising the admissibility under s 24 is included at **Appendix 1(H)**.

Summary

The two main types of evidence likely to be adduced under the provisions of ss 23 and 24 are:

(a)   witness statements; and

(b)   'business documents'.

Witness statements – If a statement is first-hand hearsay, it is admissible under s 23. A prescribed reason will be required for not calling the maker of the statement and leave of the court will be required.

If a statement is multiple hearsay it can only be admitted under s 24. It will be necessary:

(a)   to show that it was created or received by a person in the course of a trade, business, profession, etc;

(b)   to identify the witness with personal knowledge of the matters dealt with in the statement;

(c)   to show a prescribed reason for not calling the maker of the statement;

(d)   to obtain leave of the court.

Business documents – These will not usually have been made in anticipation of litigation. They will have been created for use in a business.

Business documents are best admitted under s 24 (whether first-hand or multiple hearsay) if:

(a)   no prescribed reason is required for not calling the maker of the statement in the document; and

(b)   leave of the court will not be required.

In *Trivedi v United Kingdom* [1997] EHRLR 521, the European Commission held that the Criminal Justice Act provisions are compatible with art 6 of the European Convention on Human Rights.

9.6.4.2   Criminal Procedure and Investigations Act 1996, s 68 and Sch 2, paras 1 and 2

    68.   Schedule 2 to this Act (which relates to the use at the trial of written statements and depositions admitted in evidence in committal proceedings) shall have effect.

SCHEDULE 2

STATEMENTS AND DEPOSITIONS

Statements

1. (1) Sub-paragraph (2) applies if—

    (a) a written statement has been admitted in evidence in proceedings before a magistrates' court inquiring into an offence as examining justices,

    (b) in those proceedings a person has been committed for trial,

    (c) for the purposes of section 5A of the Magistrates' Courts Act 1980 the statement complied with section 5B of that Act prior to the committal for trial,

    (d) the statement purports to be signed by a justice of the peace, and

    (e) sub-paragraph (3) does not prevent sub-paragraph (2) applying.

    (2) Where this sub-paragraph applies the statement may without further proof be read as evidence on the trial of the accused, whether for the offence for which he was committed for trial or for any other offence arising out of the same transaction or set of circumstances.

    (3) Sub-paragraph (2) does not apply if—

    (a) it is proved that the statement was not signed by the justice by whom it purports to have been signed,

    (b) the court of trial at its discretion orders that sub-paragraph (2) shall not apply, or

    (c) a party to the proceedings objects to sub-paragraph (2) applying.

    (4) If a party to the proceedings objects to sub-paragraph (2) applying the court of trial may order that the objection shall have no effect if the court considers it to be in the interests of justice so to order.

Depositions

2. (1) Sub-paragraph (2) applies if—

    (a) in pursuance of section 97A of the Magistrates' Courts Act 1980 (summons or warrant to have evidence taken as a deposition etc) a person has had his evidence taken as a deposition for the purposes of proceedings before a magistrates' court inquiring into an offence as examining justices,

    (b) the deposition has been admitted in evidence in those proceedings,

    (c) in those proceedings a person has been committed for trial,

    (d) for the purposes of section 5A of the Magistrates' Courts Act 1980 the deposition complied with section 5C of that Act prior to the committal for trial,

    (e) the deposition purports to be signed by the justice before whom it purports to have been taken, and

    (f) sub-paragraph (3) does not prevent sub-paragraph (2) applying.

    (2) Where this sub-paragraph applies the deposition may without further proof be read as evidence on the trial of the accused, whether for the offence for which he was committed for trial or for any other offence arising out of the same transaction or set of circumstances.

    (3) Sub-paragraph (2) does not apply if—

    (a) it is proved that the deposition was not signed by the justice by whom it purports to have been signed,

    (b) the court of trial at its discretion orders that sub-paragraph (2) shall not apply, or

    (c) a party to the proceedings objects to sub-paragraph (2) applying.

(4)   If a party to the proceedings objects to sub-paragraph (2) applying the court of trial may order that the objection shall have no effect if the court considers it to be in the interests of justice so to order.

Written statements and depositions which have been admitted as evidence in committal proceedings can be read at the trial in the Crown Court. These written statements and depositions will have been tendered by the prosecution only. This provision allows for written statements or depositions to be admitted at the Crown Court trial where all parties agree.

It is not, however, limited to cases where the parties agree. If the court considers it to be in the interests of justice, the court may order that the written statement or deposition be read at the trial.

9.6.4.3   Criminal Justice Act 1967, s 9(1), (2)

(1)   In any criminal proceedings, other than committal proceedings, a written statement by any person shall, if such of the conditions mentioned in the next following subsection as are applicable are satisfied, be admissible as evidence to the like extent as oral evidence to the like effect by that person.

(2)   The said conditions are—

(a)   the statement purports to be signed by the person who made it;

(b)   the statement contains a declaration by that person to the effect that it is true to the best of his knowledge and belief and that he made the statement knowing that, if it were tendered in evidence, he would be liable to prosecution if he wilfully stated in it anything which he knew to be false or did not believe to be true;

(c)   before the hearing at which the statement is tendered in evidence, a copy of the statement is served, by or on behalf of the party proposing to tender it, on each of the parties to the proceedings; and

(d)   none of the other parties or their solicitors, within seven days from the service of the copy of the statement, serves a notice on the party so proposing objecting to the statement being tendered in evidence under this section.

An example of the correct form of a s 9 statement is included at **Appendix 2(N)**.

In practice, the use of s 9 statements should largely be confined to evidence which is not in dispute. If the other side wishes to challenge the admissibility of the contents of the statement or cross-examine the maker of the statement, they should object.

9.7   The defendant

This paragraph deals with rules of evidence which are of particular application to the defendant.

9.7.1   Competence and compellability

9.7.1.1   The defendant as a prosecution witness

A defendant is not competent as a prosecution witness. Thus, if two defendants are jointly charged the prosecution cannot call one as a witness against the other unless he has pleaded guilty or is tried separately from the other defendant (*R v Richardson* (1967) 51 Cr App R 381). This means that at Stage A of the trial (see **9.1.1**) a defendant cannot be called to give evidence unless he pleads guilty or is tried separately.

9.7.1.2 The defendant as a defence witness

A defendant is a competent defence witness but is not compellable (Criminal Evidence Act 1898, s 1(1)).

If a defendant does give evidence then he must be called before any other witnesses for the defence, unless the court 'otherwise directs' (Police and Criminal Evidence Act 1984, s 79).

If a defendant gives evidence in his own defence and in so doing implicates a codefendant then this is admissible evidence against that co-defendant.

If the defendant does not give evidence he is likely to be subject to the provisions of s 35 of the Criminal Justice and Public Order Act 1994.

9.7.1.3 Section 35 — failure of defendant to give evidence

(1) At the trial of any person for an offence, subsections (2) and (3) below apply unless—

   (a) the accused's guilt is not in issue; or

   (b) it appears to the court that the physical or mental condition of the accused makes it undesirable for him to give evidence; ...

(2) Where this subsection applies, the court shall, at the conclusion of the evidence for the prosecution, satisfy itself (in the case of proceedings on indictment, in the presence of the jury) that the accused is aware that the stage has been reached at which evidence can be given for the defence and that he can, if he wishes, give evidence and that, if he chooses not to give evidence, or having been sworn, without good cause refuses to answer any question, it will be permissible for the court or jury to draw such inferences as appear proper from his failure to give evidence or his refusal, without good cause, to answer any question.

(3) Where this subsection applies, the court or jury, in determining whether the accused is guilty of the offence charged, may draw such inferences as appear proper from the failure of the accused to give evidence or his refusal, without good cause, to answer any question.

Thus, if the prosecution evidence has raised issues which call for an explanation from the defendant and he fails to give evidence, a court will be entitled to infer guilt from that failure.

In *R v Cowan (Donald); R v Gayle (Ricky); R v Ricciardi (Carmine)* [1995] 4 All ER 939, the Court of Appeal considered how the judge should direct the jury. It was essential that it should be made clear to the jury that:

(a) the burden of proof remained on the prosecution throughout;

(b) the defendant was entitled to remain silent;

(c) before drawing an adverse inference from the defendant's silence, they had to be satisfied that there was a case to answer on the prosecution evidence;

(d) an adverse inference from failure to give evidence cannot on its own prove guilt;

(e) no adverse inference could be drawn unless the only sensible explanation for the defendant's silence was that he had no answer to the case against him, or none that could have stood up to cross-examination.

The procedure to be adopted in relation to s 35 is found in the *Practice Direction (Criminal Proceedings: Consolidation* [2002] 3 All ER 904, para 44, *Defendant's right to give or not to give evidence).*

9.7.1.4 The defendant's spouse as a prosecution witness

A spouse is competent to give evidence for the prosecution. The spouse is not compellable except in certain specified cases (eg, where the offence involved an assault on that spouse or it was an assault or sexual offence on a person under 16) (Police and Criminal Evidence Act 1984, s 80).

This rule does not apply to a witness who has been, but is no longer, married to the defendant (s 80(5)).

9.7.1.5 The defendant's spouse as a defence witness

The defendant's spouse is always competent to give evidence on behalf of the defendant and a co-defendant.

The defendant's spouse is compellable to give evidence for the defendant.

9.7.2 Evidence of the character of the defendant

*See Handout * 1*
Replaces 9.7.2 →
9.7.5;
(Evidence of Bad
Character)

A defendant can adduce evidence of his own good character. This may be done by asking questions of a prosecution witness to establish the defendant's good character, or by the defendant's own oral evidence, or by calling character witnesses. If a defendant is of good character, this is relevant to his credibility as a witness and it may be relevant to show an absence of propensity to commit the type of offence charged.

A defendant can adduce evidence of his bad character. In *Jones v Director of Public Prosecutions; R v Jones* [1962] AC 635, the defendant, in giving evidence-in-chief, said that he had been in trouble with the police previously. The House of Lords held that cross-examination as to the earlier misconduct was permissible.

A defendant may wish to adduce evidence of the bad character of a co-defendant. Admissibility will depend entirely on the relevance of the evidence. If the evidence is relevant to an issue in the case, it will be admissible. If the evidence is relevant, it must be admitted as of right. The discretion which the judge has to exclude evidence under the Police and Criminal Evidence Act 1984, s 78 does not arise when the application to adduce the evidence is being made by a co-defendant (*R v Miller* (1952) 36 Cr App R 169, *R v Neale* (1977) 65 Cr App R 304, *R v Thompson; R v Sinclair; R v Maver* [1995] 2 Cr App R 589). For the cross-examination of one defendant by a co-defendant see **9.7.5.2**.

As a general rule, the prosecution cannot adduce evidence of a defendant's bad character and convictions. This common law prohibition prevents evidence of bad character from being adduced as part of the prosecution evidence. It is not to be confused with the separate statutory provisions (which are dealt with later) governing the cross-examination of a defendant on his convictions.

There are a number of exceptions to this rule. They include:

(a)   rebutting an assertion of good character;

(b)   similar fact evidence.

9.7.3 Rebutting an assertion of good character

If the defence has adduced evidence of the defendant's good character (by asking questions of a prosecution witness to establish the defendant's good character, or by the defendant's own oral evidence, or by calling character witnesses), the prosecution may adduce evidence in rebuttal. The prosecution may, with leave of the court, reopen its case at the conclusion of the defence case and adduce its own evidence of the defendant's convictions.

9.7.4   Similar fact evidence

This topic is dealt with in outline only.

As a general rule, the prosecution cannot adduce evidence of the previous behaviour of the defendant if the purpose in so doing is simply to show a disposition to commit offences similar to the offence being tried. For example, if the defendant is on trial for theft by way of shoplifting, evidence cannot usually be adduced of the fact that the defendant has committed this kind of offence before.

Problems can arise when the prosecution seeks to adduce evidence of the defendant's behaviour on other occasions for some reason other than to show a general disposition to commit the offence in question. It should be noted that it is the conduct behind the offence which is relevant, not the fact of a criminal conviction.

In *R v Lunt* (1987) 85 Cr App R 241, the Court of Appeal laid down guidelines for the correct approach to 'similar fact' evidence as follows.

(a)   'Similar fact' evidence will be admissible only if it goes beyond showing a 'tendency to commit the crime charged' and is 'positively probative' of an issue in the case.

(b)   In determining the admissibility of 'similar fact' evidence, it is first necessary to identify the issue in the case to which the evidence is directed and then to decide whether or not it is positively probative of that issue and does more than simply reveal the defendant's bad character.

In *R v Lunt*, it was stressed that examples of properly admitted similar fact evidence will be rare.

The essential feature is that the probative force of the evidence 'is sufficiently great to make it just to admit the evidence, notwithstanding that it is prejudicial to the accused in tending to show that he was guilty of another crime' (*Director of Public Prosecutions v P (A Father)* [1991] 3 All ER 337).

Examples of issues to which similar fact evidence may be relevant include the following.

9.7.4.1   Identification

In *R v Straffen* [1952] 2 QB 911, the defendant, who had escaped from Broadmoor, was accused of strangling a girl. Evidence was admitted of the fact that the defendant had strangled two other girls and that the features of the two previous crimes were very similar to the offence charged. Because of this, the 'similar fact' evidence was admitted, not to show that the defendant had a disposition to commit murder but because the features of the cases provided a very strong indication that the defendant was guilty of the offence charged.

9.7.4.2   Plausibility of the defendant's explanation

In *R v Smith* (1915) 11 Cr App R 229, the defendant was charged with murdering his wife who was found drowned in a bath. Smith had insured her life for a large amount of money. His defence was that his wife had died of natural causes. Evidence was admitted to show that Smith had 'married' two other women and that they too had been found dead in their bath with Smith due to gain from their life assurance policies. As in *Straffen*, the evidence was not admitted to show that Smith had a disposition to commit murder. Its probative force was directed at the plausibility of the defence.

9.7.5 Cross-examining the defendant

9.7.5.1 Criminal Evidence Act 1898, s 1

(1)   A person charged in criminal proceedings shall not be called as a witness in the proceedings except on his own application.

(2)   A person charged in criminal proceedings who is called as a witness in the proceedings may be asked any question in cross-examination notwithstanding that it would tend to criminate him as to any offence with which he is charged in the proceedings.

A defendant is not obliged to give evidence. If he chooses to do so then he is liable to be cross-examined in the same way as any other witness. This includes cross-examination on any previous inconsistent statement that may have been made.

9.7.5.2 Criminal Evidence Act 1898, s 1(3)

A person charged in criminal proceedings who is called as a witness in the proceedings shall not be asked, and if asked shall not be required to answer, any question tending to show that he has committed or been convicted of or been charged with any offence other than one with which he is then charged, or is of bad character unless—

(i)   the proof that he has committed or been convicted of such other offence is admissible evidence to show that he is guilty of an offence with which he is then charged; or

(ii)   he has personally or by his advocate asked questions of the witnesses for the prosecution with a view to establish his own good character, or has given evidence of his good character, or the nature or conduct of the defence is such as to involve imputations on the character of the prosecutor or the witnesses for the prosecution, the deceased victim of the alleged crime; or

(iii)   he has given evidence against any other person charged in the same proceedings.

Section 1(3)(i) enables the prosecution to cross-examine the defendant on the facts behind previous criminal conduct to help prove the offence charged. It is rarely relied on in practice but if it is used it is likely to be in 'similar fact' evidence cases. Before relying on s 1(3)(i) the prosecution must have called evidence of the similar facts as part of its case. If such evidence has been called then the defendant can be cross-examined on those offences if he gives evidence.

Section 1(3)(ii) is largely self-explanatory. If a defendant, while testifying, has put evidence before the court that he is of good character then the prosecution is allowed to cross-examine the defendant on his previous convictions. Such cross-examination is limited to the court, date of conviction and the nature of the conviction. The facts of the previous conviction should not be referred to as they are not relevant. The object of the cross-examination is to rebut the untrue assertion of good character.

Character is indivisible. This means that, if the defendant gives evidence about one aspect of his character, that will allow the prosecution to examine him on other aspects.

Example

Joe is charged with assault. He says in evidence that he is a mild and peace-loving man. This is evidence of good character. The prosecution is permitted to cross-examine Joe about past convictions for dishonesty.

There is obviously an overlap between the common law provisions (see 9.7.3) and s 1(3)(ii). Two examples will serve to illustrate the point.

Example 1

Alan is on trial for theft. He does not give evidence himself. However, he calls a character witness.

Here, the prosecution will have to call rebutting evidence. The prosecution cannot rely on s 1(3)(ii) as the defendant has not gone into the witness-box to give evidence. Therefore, he cannot be cross-examined.

Example 2

John is charged with an assault occasioning actual bodily harm. He gives evidence of his own good character.

Here, the prosecution could call rebutting evidence but, it will not normally be necessary. John is in the witness-box. He has given evidence-in-chief and can therefore be cross-examined. By giving evidence of his own good character he has lost the basic s 1(3) protection and can therefore be cross-examined on his previous convictions.

Section 1(3)(ii) also provides that 'the nature or conduct of the defence is such as to involve imputations on the character of the prosecutor, the deceased victim of the alleged crime or the witnesses for the prosecution'.

This may arise when prosecution witnesses are being cross-examined or when the defendant gives evidence. For example, the defendant may:

(a)   allege that a prosecution witness is biased; or

(b)   allege that police witnesses are fabricating evidence; or

(c)   cross-examine prosecution witnesses on their previous criminal convictions.

If the judge or magistrates find that the attack on the character of a prosecution witness comes within s 1(3)(ii) then the defendant can be cross-examined on his previous convictions.

In *R v Taylor (Nicholas Jones); R v Goodman (Donald Walter)* [1999] Crim LR 407, the Court of Appeal provided guidance on the procedure to be adopted when an accomplice gives evidence for the Crown. An accomplice is a participant in the crime alleged.

Example

John and Warren are jointly charged with an assault occasioning actual bodily harm. Both have previous convictions. John pleads guilty and is now competent and compellable to give evidence for the prosecution at Warren's trial.

At Warren's trial, unless there is a specific request from the defence to refrain, the prosecution ought to read out John's convictions at the beginning of the trial. If the defence then proceed to cross-examine John on his previous convictions, such a cross-examination would not lead to the loss of Warren's shield under s 1(3)(ii) of the Criminal Evidence Act 1898. This is probably on the basis that nothing new has been revealed to the jury by cross-examining on such admitted facts. However, if the defence goes further and alleges that John has a grudge against Warren or accuses John of fabricating evidence, then the defence has cast imputations on the character of a prosecution witness. The prosecution can then apply to the court for leave to cross-examine Warren on his previous convictions.

Such cross-examination may include the court, date of conviction and the nature of conviction. In *R v McLeod* [1995] 1 Cr App R 591, CA, the court said that similarities in previous defences, rejected by juries in the past (eg an alibi defence) and whether or not the defendant pleaded guilty or not guilty or was disbelieved on oath were also proper matters for cross-examination. The object of crossexamination is to show the court the type of person making the attack on the character of a prosecution witness, that is to say, it is relevant only to the credibility of the defendant as a witness. Hence, previous convictions for offences of dishonesty are, in principle, more damaging than offences of violence (even if the present charge is for an offence of violence).

If cross-examination under this section is permitted, the jury or magistrates should be told that they should not infer guilt from the fact that the defendant is of bad character and that the convictions are relevant only to the credibility of the defendant as a witness.

Section 1(3)(iii) provides that the defendant 'has given evidence against any other person charged in the same proceedings'.

This provision will arise where two defendants are on trial together. One defendant, in giving evidence in his own defence, may implicate the other. This may be either through a direct accusation of guilt of the co-defendant or may be evidence that undermines the co-defendant's defence. (*R v Varley* [1982] 2 All ER 519).

The co-defendant is permitted to cross-examine the defendant giving evidence on his previous convictions. If the co-defendant chooses not to exercise this right then the prosecution may do so instead. Cross-examination under s 1(3)(iii) is subject to the same limitations as s 1(3)(ii) but, unlike s 1(3)(ii), the convictions may be relevant to the credibility of the defendant as a witness and also as to whether the defendant is guilty of the offence (*R v Randall* [2004] 1 All ER 467, HL).

The discretion to prevent cross-examination

Even if the prosecution can show that cross-examination under s 1(3) is permissible, the judge or magistrates can exercise a discretion to prevent cross-examination of the defendant on his previous convictions (*Selvey v DPP* [1970] AC 304 and the Police and Criminal Evidence Act 1984, s 78).

The use of questioning under s 1(3)(ii) was considered by the Court of Appeal in *R v McLeod* [1995] 1 Cr App R 591.

(a)   The judge has to weigh the prejudicial effect of the questions put to the defendant against the damage done by the attack on the prosecution's witnesses and has to exercise his discretion so as to secure a fair trial for both the prosecution and defence.

(b)   In the Court of Appeal, it is not enough that the court thinks it would have exercised its discretion differently. It will only interfere with the trial judge's decision if the judge erred in principle or if there was no material on which he could have properly arrived at his decision.

(c)   The primary purpose of cross-examination on previous convictions and on the bad character of the defendant is to show that he is not worthy of belief. It is not, and should not be, to show he has a predisposition to commit the type of offence with which he is charged. However, the mere fact that the previous offences were of a similar type to that charged and may suggest a tendency to commit the offence charged will not make the questioning improper.

(d) Prolonged cross-examination on previous offences is undesirable. Unless admissible as similar fact evidence, the prosecution should not seek to emphasise similarities between the previous offences and the present offence.

(e) Similarities of defences rejected by the court on previous occasions could be legitimate questions if they were central to credibility, for example, false alibis, a defence that an incriminating substance had been planted, and whether or not the defendant pleaded guilty or was disbelieved having given evidence on oath.

(f) If the underlying facts show a particularly bad character, the judge should balance the gravity of the attack on the prosecution against the prejudice to the defendant resulting from the disclosure of the facts.

(g) Objection to a particular line of questioning about underlying facts should be taken early, as this will not normally be a ground for discharging a jury. While it is the judge's duty to keep cross-examination within proper bounds, it will be difficult to contend that there has been an improper exercise of discretion if no objection is taken at the time.

(h) In every case where the defendant has been cross-examined as to character and convictions, the judge should, in summing up, tell the jury that the purpose of the questioning goes only to credit and that they should not consider that it showed a propensity to commit the offence they were considering.

There is no discretion to prevent cross-examination of one defendant by a co-defendant under s 1(3)(iii) (*Murdoch v Taylor* [1965] AC 574).

9.7.5.3 Spent convictions

The Rehabilitation of Offenders Act 1974 provides that after a prescribed period of time certain convictions are spent. This means that the convicted person is to be treated as never having been convicted of the spent offence.

The rehabilitation periods vary with the sentence:

Absolute discharge	6 months
Conditional discharge	1 year or period of order if longer
Attendance centre order	1 year after expiry of order
Fine or community sentence	5 years
Custodial sentence of up to 6 months	7 years
Custodial sentence of between 6 and 30 months	10 years

A conviction for an offence which was punished by a custodial sentence exceeding 30 months cannot become spent.

The Act does not apply to evidence admitted in criminal proceedings. Instead, the matter is governed by *Practice Direction (Criminal Proceedings: Consolidation* [2002] 3 All ER 904, para 6, *Spent Convictions*). This provides that a spent conviction should be referred to only if it is in the interests of justice to do so. If a defendant has convictions which are not spent, it will usually be unnecessary to refer to spent convictions. If a defendant has previous convictions which are spent, he may, with the leave of the court, be entitled to put himself forward as a person of previous good character (*R v Bailey* [1989] Crim LR 723).

9.8 Further reading

Textbooks dealing with the general principles of criminal evidence include:

Peter Murphy, *Murphy on Evidence* (Oxford University Press, 2003)

Richard May, *Criminal Evidence* (Sweet & Maxwell, 2004)

Chapter 10

Sentencing

10.1	Introduction	143
10.2	The powers of the court	143
10.3	Sentencing procedure	160
10.4	The plea in mitigation	162
10.5	Sentencing guidelines	165
10.6	Further reading	166

10.1 Introduction

This chapter deals with the law, practice and procedure of sentencing of offenders who are aged 18 or older. Offenders under the age of 18 are dealt with in the youth court. A brief outline of the sentencing powers of the youth court is contained in **Chapter 11**.

A large part of a solicitor-advocate's time is taken up with the sentencing process, either following a guilty plea by his client or on conviction at a summary trial. Solicitors also have limited rights of audience in the Crown Court on sentencing matters (see **1.4.2**) and in any event must brief counsel who is appearing in the Crown Court on any matter that will be relevant to sentence in the event of the client pleading guilty or being convicted by a jury.

This chapter deals with:

(a)   powers of the court;

(b)   procedure on sentencing; and

(c)   mitigation.

10.2 The powers of the court

The Powers of Criminal Courts (Sentencing) Act 2000 (PCC(S)A 2000) provides a structured approach to sentencing. The standard penalty is a fine. If the offence is too serious for a fine a 'community sentence' will be given (eg, community punishment orders or community rehabilitation orders). If the offence is considered too serious for a community sentence, then, and only then, should a custodial sentence be imposed. A diagram illustrating the PCC(S)A 2000 sentencing scheme appears at **Appendix 1(P)**.

In deciding the seriousness of the offence, the court may take into account:

(a)   the present offence;

(b)   any associated offences (as defined below);

(c)   previous convictions (see below); and

(d)   racial or religious aggravation (see below).

Associated offences

An associated offence is one in which the defendant has been convicted in the same proceedings or sentenced at the same time, or an offence which the defendant has asked the court to take into consideration when passing sentence (see **10.3.2.3** for offences taken into consideration).

Example

Courtney is convicted of three offences of theft. In applying the seriousness test, the court will look at the most serious offence first. If only a custodial sentence is justified for this offence then the seriousness test is satisfied. If one offence alone is not serious enough for a custodial sentence then the court may look at all three offences together in deciding whether only a custodial sentence is justified.

Previous convictions

By PCC(S)A 2000, s 151(1):

> In considering the seriousness of any offence, the court may take into account any previous convictions of the offender or any failure of his to respond to previous sentences.

Example

James is convicted of theft from an employer. He has two previous convictions for similar offences and committed the current offence while on a community rehabilitation order.

The court may take previous convictions and the failure to respond to the community rehabilitation order into account in determining seriousness.

Section 151(2) also provides that:

> In considering the seriousness of any offence committed while the offender was on bail, the court shall treat the fact that it was committed in those circumstances as an aggravating factor.'

Racial or religious aggravation

If an offence is 'racially or religiously aggravated' the court must treat that fact as an aggravating factor and must state in open court that the offence was so aggravated (PCC(S)A 2000, s 153).

The Crime and Disorder Act 1998, s 28(1) provides that an offence is racially or religiously aggravated if:

(a)   at the time of committing the offence, or immediately before or after doing so, the offender demonstrates towards the victim of the offence hostility based on the victim's membership (or presumed membership) of a racial or religious group; or

(b)   the offence is motivated (wholly or partly) by hostility towards members of a racial or religious group based on their membership of that group.

'Membership' includes association with members of that group.

'Racial group' means a group of persons defined by reference to race, colour, nationality (including citizenship) or ethnic or national origins (s 28(4)). 'Religious group' means a group of persons defined by reference to religious belief or lack of religious belief (s 28(5)).

Section 153 of the PCC(S)A 2000 will not apply if the defendant has been charged with one of the racially aggravated offences under ss 29–32 of the Crime and Disorder Act 1998 (assault, criminal damage, public order offences and harassment).

10.2.1 Absolute or conditional discharge (PCC(S)A 2000, ss 12–15)

In order to impose either an absolute or conditional discharge, the court must be satisfied that, having regard to the circumstances and nature of the offence and character of the defendant, punishment is inexpedient. A conditional discharge may be imposed, for example, where a person of previous good character commits a petty theft. The court may feel that a court appearance with the attendant publicity is punishment enough. An absolute discharge is sometimes imposed where the court feels that the defendant, although technically guilty of an offence, is morally blameless.

A person can be conditionally discharged for a period not exceeding 3 years. If he commits any offence during that time he may be sentenced for the original offence.

10.2.2 Fines (PCC(S)A 2000, ss 126–129 and 135–142)

Where the Crown Court or magistrates' court decides that a fine is the appropriate sentence for an offence, PCC(S) A 2000, s 128 provides that:

(1)   Before fixing the amount of any fine ..., a court shall inquire into the financial circumstances of the offender.

(2)   The amount of any fine fixed by a court shall be such as, in the opinion of the court, reflects the seriousness of the offence.

(3)   In fixing the amount of any fine ..., a court shall take into account the circumstances of the case including, among other things, the financial circumstances of the offender so far as they are known, or appear, to the court.

(4)   Subsection (3) above applies whether taking into account the financial circumstances of the offender has the effect of increasing or reducing the amount of the fine.

The court has power to order an offender to provide a statement of means before passing sentence.

10.2.3 Community sentences (PCC(S)A 2000, ss 33–36)

A community sentence is a sentence composed of one or more of the following orders:

–   Community rehabilitation orders
–   Community punishment orders
–   Community punishment and rehabilitation orders
–   Drug treatment and testing orders
–   Curfew orders
–   Attendance centre orders (offenders under 21 only).

Before imposing a community sentence, the court must consider that:

(a)   the offence (or combination of the offence and one or more associated offences) is serious enough to warrant it; and

(b)   the order or orders are the most suitable for the offender; and

(c)   the restrictions on the offender's liberty imposed by the order or orders are commensurate with the seriousness of the offence or the combination of the offence and other offences associated with it.

Community sentences may be an effective way of dealing with offenders convicted of crimes against property and less serious offences of violence. As a general principle, a court must be satisfied that the offence is too serious for a financial penalty.

10.2.4 Community rehabilitation orders (Criminal Justice and Court Services Act 2000, s 43, PCC(S)A 2000, ss 41–45 and Schs 2 and 3)

A community rehabilitation order is likely to be appropriate where an offender needs advice and assistance to overcome the reasons for offending. The offender is placed under the supervision of a probation officer and 'additional requirements' can be imposed. These include requirements to undergo treatment for psychiatric problems or alcohol dependency. The offender can be required to live in a particular place, including an approved hostel or other institution, which will provide close supervision. Attendance at a community rehabilitation centre can also be required. Such centres help the offender face up to the consequences of offending.

A court may place the defendant on a community rehabilitation order from 6 months to 3 years for any offence where it considers it desirable in the interests of:

(a)   securing the offender's rehabilitation; or

(b)   protecting the public from harm from the offender; or

(c)   preventing the commission of further offences by the offender.

The defendant must consent to the community rehabilitation order if the proposed order imposes a requirement for psychiatric treatment or alcohol dependency treatment.

A community rehabilitation order may be combined with a fine but not with imprisonment, immediate or suspended.

10.2.5 Community punishment orders (Criminal Justice and Court Services Act 2000, s 44, PCC(S)A 2000, ss 46–50 and Sch 3)

A community punishment order (CPO) requires an offender to participate in community projects of various kinds, supervised by the Probation Service. The maximum number of hours that can be imposed is 240. The minimum number of hours is 40. A CPO may be appropriate where the court feels that the offender should be deprived of leisure time or should make reparation to the community for his offending.

A community punishment order can be imposed only if:

(a)   the defendant has been convicted of an imprisonable offence; and

(b)   the court is satisfied that the offender is a suitable person to do the work and that appropriate work is available.

A suspended sentence of imprisonment should not be imposed as well as a CPO, but a defendant given a CPO may also be fined.

10.2.6 Community punishment and rehabilitation orders (Criminal Justice and Court Services Act 2000, s 45, PCC(S)A 2000, s 51 and Sch 3)

A community punishment and rehabilitation order is an order which requires the defendant to be under the supervision of a probation officer for a minimum period of 12 months and a maximum period of 3 years and to perform unpaid work for a minimum of 40 hours and a maximum of 100 hours.

A community punishment and rehabilitation order may be suitable where the court feels that an offender should be punished by deprivation of leisure time and given assistance in overcoming the root cause of his offending.

The defendant must have been convicted of an imprisonable offence and the court must consider that a community punishment and rehabilitation order is desirable in the interests of:

(a)   rehabilitating the defendant; or

(b)   protecting the public from harm; or

(c)   preventing the commission of further offences.

10.2.7   Drug treatment and testing orders (PCC(S)A 2000, ss 52–58 and Sch 3)

This order is available for defendants aged 16 or over and can last from 6 months to 3 years. The court can make the order if it is satisfied that the defendant is dependent on drugs and is susceptible to treatment. The defendant must consent to the order. (Remember that refusal of consent is a ground for imposition of a custodial sentence.) A treatment provider's assessment must accompany or be incorporated into the pre-sentence report. The court has to be satisfied that the defendant is susceptible to treatment and that there is a place on a treatment programme.

The court can require the defendant to submit to treatment to reduce or eliminate his dependency, for example, by attending a clinic or taking methadone. The court can impose a testing requirement specifying how many tests the defendant must submit to each month. The tests will be taken by the treatment provider who will submit the results to the supervising probation officer, who will report them to the court.

The court can review the defendant's progress no more frequently than once a month. At each review, the court will receive a written report from the offender's probation officer which will include drug test results. The court may amend the order at a review hearing with the defendant's consent. If the defendant does not consent, the court may revoke the order and re-sentence the offender.

10.2.8   Curfew orders (PCC(S)A 2000, ss 37–40 and Sch 3)

A curfew order is an order requiring the defendant to stay for specified periods in specified places. It can last for a maximum period of 6 months. If the defendant is aged under 16, the maximum period is 3 months. A period of curfew cannot last for less than 2 hours or more than 12 hours during any one of the days specified. An example would be an order requiring the defendant to stay indoors at home between the hours of 8 pm and 6 am. This may be appropriate, for example, to keep the offender out of public houses or night clubs. If a curfew order is made, the court will appoint a person to monitor the defendant's whereabouts.

A curfew order can be imposed if the defendant has been convicted of any offence (it need not be imprisonable). A court cannot make a curfew order unless it is situated in an area with facilities for monitoring the whereabouts of the offender.

Section 38 of the PCC(S)A 2000 provides that a curfew order may, in addition, include requirements for securing electronic monitoring ('tagging') of the defendant's whereabouts during the curfew period specified in the order.

10.2.9 Attendance centre orders (PCC(S)A 2000, ss 60–62 and Sch 5)

An attendance centre order requires the offender to attend a specified place and take part in supervised activities.

A typical order will require the offender to attend a centre for 3 hours on a number of Saturday afternoons, depriving him of leisure time.

The consent of the defendant is not required and the sentence is only available for an offender under the age of 21.

10.2.10 Breach of a community sentence and re-offending (PCC(S)A 2000, ss 39, 43, 48, 51, 56 and Sch 3, paras 3–6 and 10–14)

10.2.10.1 Breach of community sentence – by failure to comply

Breach is confined to a failure to comply with the terms of the community sentence.

Failure to comply with community sentence requirements (eg, not turning up for work on a community punishment order) can lead to the court punishing the breach and allowing the order to continue or revoking the order and re-sentencing for the offence.

Magistrates may deal with breach of a community sentence imposed by any magistrates' court. Breach of a Crown Court community sentence must be dealt with by the Crown Court.

10.2.10.2 Further offence during community sentence

Commission of a further offence during the period of a community sentence does not amount to breach of that sentence.

The new offence must be dealt with according to its own seriousness. Once sentence for that offence has been decided upon then the court should consider the effect of the new sentence on the existing community sentence.

'Existing' means still in existence at the time the new offence is disposed of. Thus, if the community sentence, which was in existence when the new offence was committed, has subsequently expired or been completed, then it is no longer existing and the court has no power to deal with it.

All magistrates' courts have the power to allow the community sentence to continue or revoke the community sentence without re-sentencing the defendant for the original offence. If the same magistrates' court imposed the community sentence, then the court has the power to revoke the community sentence and re-sentence for the original offence.

The Crown Court can deal with a community sentence made either by a magistrates' court or a Crown Court. The court has the power to allow the community sentence to continue, revoke without re-sentencing or revoke and re-sentence for the original offence.

10.2.11 Custodial sentences

Offenders aged 18–21 are sent to young offender institutions. Offenders aged 21 or above are sent to prison.

Where the court intends to impose a sentence of imprisonment for the first time or impose detention in a young offender institution, the offender must be legally represented at the time of sentence unless he has been given the opportunity to apply for representation and has failed to do so.

10.2.11.1 Qualification for a custodial sentence (PCC(S)A 2000, s 79)

The court cannot impose a custodial sentence unless one of the following applies.

The seriousness test

A court may impose a custodial sentence if it considers that the offence (or the combination of the offence and one or more offences associated with it) is so serious that only a custodial sentence can be justified for it.

In *R v Howells and Others* [1999] 1 Cr App R (S) 335, the Court of Appeal gave some guidance on the interpretation of the seriousness test when approaching cases which are on or near the custody threshold. In such cases, the courts would usually find it helpful to begin by considering the nature and extent of the defendant's criminal intention and of any injury or damage caused. Other things being equal, an offence which was deliberate and premeditated would be more serious than one which was not. An offence resulting in physical or mental trauma would generally be more serious than one that resulted in financial loss. Previous convictions and failure to respond to non-custodial sentences may be taken into account and the commission of an offence whilst on bail is to be treated as an aggravating factor (see below). In deciding whether to impose a custodial sentence in a borderline case, the court would ordinarily take account of matters relating to the offender, such as:

(a)   an admission of guilt;

(b)   hard evidence of remorse (shown, for example, by an expression of regret to the victim and the offer of compensation);

(c)   evidence of a determination to take steps to deal with an addiction to drink or drugs;

(d)   youth and immaturity;

(e)   previous good character (absence of a criminal record);

(f)   positive good character (such as solid employment record or faithful discharge of family duties);

(h)   physical or mental disability;

(i)   whether or not the offender had previously served a custodial sentence.

Courts should always bear in mind that criminal sentences in almost every case are intended to protect the public, whether by punishing the offender or reforming him, or by deterring him and others, or all of these things. The sentence imposed should be no longer than is necessary to meet the penal purpose which the court had in mind.

The above guidelines are useful but it cannot be said that they offer a test to determine when the custody threshold has been reached in individual circumstances. Guidance on this question must still be found in decisions of the Court of Appeal in particular kinds of cases.

Violent and sexual offences

The second ground for qualification for a custodial sentence is that the offence is a violent or sexual offence and the court considers that only a custodial sentence would be adequate to protect the public from serious harm from the defendant. This means that the court considers that unless the defendant is imprisoned he is likely to commit further offences which would lead to death or serious physical or psychological injury to a member of the public.

The previous convictions of the defendant may be relevant on this ground in showing, for example, a history of violent or sexual offences of increasing severity. This may lead the court to the conclusion that the ground of protection of the public is satisfied. Because protection of the public is likely to require a long custodial sentence, the ground is unlikely to be used by magistrates.

Refusal of a community sentence

A custodial sentence may be imposed if the defendant refuses to consent to a community sentence where his consent is required.

10.2.11.2   Aggravating and mitigating factors

In applying the seriousness test, the court must also have regard to any aggravating and mitigating factors about the offence and (in the case of violent and sexual offences) the offender (PCC(S)A 2000, s 81(4)).

10.2.11.3   Criteria for deciding length of term of imprisonment (PCC(S)A 2000, s 80)

The sentence must be:

(a)   for such term as the court considers is commensurate with the seriousness of the offence or the combination of the offence and one or more offences associated with it; or

(b)   where the offence is a violent or sexual offence, for such longer term as the court considers necessary to protect the public from serious harm from the defendant. (This cannot exceed the statutory maximum for the offence.)

Any aggravating or mitigating factors will also be taken into account in determining length of sentence (PCC(S)A 2000, s 81(4)).

A person aged 21 or over may be sentenced to imprisonment:

(a)   by the Crown Court up to the maximum fixed by statute;

(b)   by a magistrates' court for up to 6 months, unless statute fixes a lower maximum. Magistrates may, however, impose consecutive sentences up to a maximum of 12 months in aggregate when dealing with two or more either way offences (Magistrates' Courts Act 1980, ss 31, 133(2)).

The maximum sentence in a young offender institution for a person aged between 18 and 21 is the same as for imprisonment.

10.2.12   Suspended sentence of imprisonment (PCC(S)A 2000, ss 118–125)

The Crown Court may suspend a term of imprisonment not exceeding 2 years for between 1–2 years inclusive ('the operational period').

A magistrates' court may suspend imprisonment for the same operational period, but the term will be subject to their maximum.

It is not possible to suspend detention in a young offender institution.

A suspended sentence can be imposed only if the court first decides to imprison but then feels that it can be suspended because of the exceptional circumstances of the case. This is a very important principle. A suspended sentence should not be used in an attempt to frighten a petty offender who does not qualify for imprisonment. The decision of the sentencing court should be that the defendant qualifies for imprisonment, but because of the exceptional circumstances of the case the sentence may be suspended.

Frequently invoked mitigating circumstances cannot be regarded as exceptional. In *R v Okinikan* (1993) 14 Cr App R (S) 453, the Court of Appeal held that:

> taken on their own, or in combination, good character, youth and an early plea are not exceptional circumstances justifying a suspended sentence.... They may amount to mitigation sufficient to persuade the court that a custodial sentence should not be passed or reduce its length.

Decisions where the Court of Appeal has held that exceptional circumstances exist include *R v Cameron (John McDougal)* (1993) 14 Cr App R (S) 801 (assault occasioning actual bodily harm on son by father; local authority supported their being reunited), *R v French (Julie Ann)* (1994) 15 Cr App R (S) 194 (fraud; severe financial and emotional difficulties; psychiatric care), *R v Khan (Ashraf Ullah)* (1994) 15 Cr App R (S) 320 (fraud; paranoid psychosis) and *R v Weston (Arnold)* [1996] 1 Cr App R (S) 297 (indecent assault on young girl; arthritic defendant in early retirement with disabled and depressed wife).

Where a court passes a suspended sentence for a term of more than 6 months, the court may make a suspended sentence supervision order. This is an order placing the offender under the supervision of a supervising officer (usually a member of the Probation Service) for a period which is specified in the order and does not exceed the operational period of the order (PCC(S)A 2000, s 122).

10.2.12.1 Activation of a suspended sentence

If an offender is subsequently convicted of an imprisonable offence committed during the operational period, the suspended sentence must normally be ordered to take effect with the original term unaltered. The court must normally activate the suspended sentence in full, unless it is of the opinion that it would be unjust to do so in view of the circumstances which have arisen since the sentence was passed, including the facts of the subsequent offence (s 119).

If the court is of the opinion that it would be unjust to activate the suspended sentence in full, there is power to activate the suspended sentence:

(a)   for a lesser period;

(b)   to vary the length of the operational period (so that it lasts until a date not more than two years from the date of variation); or

(c)   to make no order at all.

Relevant factors that may be taken into account by a court include: whether the new offence before the court is both trivial in nature and unconnected with the original offence that led to the imposition of the suspended sentence; and whether the new offence has been committed towards the end of the operational period.

If activated, the original sentence will normally run consecutively to any term imposed for the second offence. If not activated in full, the reasons for the court's decision must be given.

Magistrates may deal with breach of a suspended sentence imposed by any magistrates' court. If the suspended sentence was imposed by the Crown Court, only the Crown Court may deal with the matter.

10.2.13 Motoring penalties

10.2.13.1 Endorsement of driving licences (Road Traffic Offenders Act 1988, s 44)

Dangerous driving, careless driving and aggravated vehicle-taking all carry obligatory endorsement of the driving licence with particulars of the conviction.

The licence must also be endorsed with the appropriate number of penalty points, unless at the same time the defendant is disqualified from driving.

Where a licence is ordered to be endorsed, particulars of the endorsement are recorded on the licence and also recorded centrally at the Driver and Vehicle Licensing Agency (DVLA) at Swansea.

Where the defendant is convicted of two or more endorsable offences committed on the same occasion the court will endorse the highest number of points unless it thinks fit to order otherwise (Road Traffic Offenders Act 1988, s 28(4)). In such circumstances, the court must state its reasons in open court.

> #### Example
> Peter is convicted of speeding (3 to 6 penalty points) and using a vehicle with defective brakes (3 penalty points), both offences being committed on the same occasion. The court takes the view that the speeding offence merits 6 points. Only 6 points will go on his driving licence unless the court thinks fit to order otherwise. The court may endorse points for both offences if it is satisfied that Peter has been driving with defective brakes for a number of months.

10.2.13.2 Disqualification for the offence itself (Road Traffic Offenders Act 1988, s 34)

Obligatory disqualification

A number of offences, including dangerous driving and aggravated vehicle-taking, carry obligatory disqualification. Where an offence carries obligatory disqualification the court must generally order the defendant to be disqualified from driving for at least 12 months.

Discretionary disqualification

Where an offence carries discretionary disqualification for committing the offence itself, the court may order the defendant to be disqualified for such period as it thinks fit. Careless driving, taking a conveyance and theft of a motor vehicle carry discretionary disqualification.

Interim disqualification

Section 26 of the Road Traffic Offenders Act 1988 enables a magistrates' court, when committing a defendant to the Crown Court under certain statutory provisions for sentencing, deferring sentence or adjourning for sentence, to impose an interim period of disqualification from driving for an offence involving obligatory or discretionary disqualification. This can last until the case is concluded.

Disqualification under PCC(S)A 2000, s 146

Where a defendant is convicted of any offence, the court may order him to be disqualified from driving for such period as it thinks fit. That no vehicle was used in the commission of the offence is irrelevant. The disqualification may be in addition to dealing with him in any other way or may be instead of any other sentence.

Disqualification under PCC(S)A 2000, s 147

Where a defendant is convicted on indictment of an offence carrying imprisonment of 2 years or more, or is committed for sentence, under s 38 or s 38A of the Magistrates' Courts Act 1980 to be sentenced for such an offence, the Crown Court may disqualify him for such period as it thinks fit if satisfied that a motor vehicle was used in committing the offence. This applies even if the offence is not endorsable and even if the defendant disqualified had not himself used the vehicle (ie, it was used by an accomplice).

10.2.13.3 Disqualification under the penalty points system (Road Traffic Offenders Act 1988, Part II)

A defendant will be liable to disqualification for at least 6 months if the penalty points to be taken into account number 12 or more.

Where the defendant is convicted of an offence which carries obligatory endorsement the penalty points to be taken into account are:

(a) any points attributed to the offence of which he is convicted, disregarding any offence in respect of which an order for disqualification for committing the offence itself is made (see above); *plus*

(b) any points previously endorsed on his licence in respect of offences committed within the 3 years immediately preceding the commission of the most recent offence.

Note that any penalty points endorsed on the defendant's licence prior to a previous disqualification under the points system must be ignored. Only a disqualification for accumulating 12 or more penalty points has the effect of 'wiping the slate clean', ie, removing all existing penalty points from the licence; all other disqualifications leave them undisturbed.

Example 1

Raj is convicted of careless driving. The offence was committed on 1 April 2003. He has the following endorsement on his licence: careless driving committed on 31 March 2001, 5 points.

If Raj is disqualified for the offence itself, his licence will not be endorsed with any penalty points. If he is not disqualified for the offence itself, between 3 and 9 points will be awarded. If the number of points awarded are 7 or more, Raj is liable to be disqualified under the points system.

Example 2

Sameira is convicted of careless driving. The offence was committed on 1 June 2004. She has the following endorsements on her licence:

Offence	Date of Offence	Sentence
Speeding	1 October 2003	4 points
Speeding	1 March 2003	(disqualified for 6 months under penalty points system)
Careless driving	1 July 2002	8 points
Speeding	1 July 2001	3 points

If Sameira is disqualified for the current offence of careless driving itself, her licence will not be endorsed with any penalty points. If she is not disqualified for the offence itself, she will be awarded 3 to 9 points. The only relevant points on the licence to date which are to be taken into account are the 4 points awarded on 1 October 2003. Although all the other points were awarded for offences committed within three years of the date of commission of the current offence, they are not taken into account as Sameira was disqualified for these under the penalty points system. Therefore, if the number of points awarded for the current offence of careless driving is 8 or more, Sameira is liable to be disqualified under the points system.

The disqualification under the points system must be for a minimum period. If the defendant has no previous disqualification of 56 days imposed within three years of the commission of the most recent offence for which penalty points are to be taken into account, then the period is six months. If there is one such disqualification in the three years, the period is a minimum of one year. If there are two or more such disqualifications imposed within three years of the most recent offence, then the minimum period is two years. Disqualifications under the Road Traffic Offenders Act 1988, s 26, the PCC(S)A 2000, s 147 and those imposed for theft of a motor vehicle or taking a conveyance without the consent of the owner are not to be taken into account.

The Road Traffic (New Drivers) Act 1995 provides a 'probationary period' for a newly qualified driver of two years, beginning with the day on which he becomes a newly qualified driver. If such drivers accumulate 6 or more penalty points during that period, the court notifies the DVLA. The DVLA then issues a notice of revocation of the driving licence and requires the surrender of the existing driving licence, if still in the driver's possession. The driver is invited to apply for a provisional licence. A full driving licence may not be granted until the driver has passed another driving test.

10.2.13.4 Relationship between disqualification for the offence itself and disqualification under the penalty points system

It is not possible to be disqualified under both provisions for the one offence.

The court will consider penalty points disqualification before discretionary disqualification for the one offence unless the court is unable to disqualify the defendant under the penalty points system (Road Traffic Offenders Act 1988, s 34(2)).

It has yet to be authoritatively decided as to whether disqualification can arise under both provisions when the defendant is being dealt with for more than one offence.

10.2.13.5 Avoiding disqualification or endorsement

Obligatory disqualification or obligatory endorsement arising out of the offence itself

Obligatory penalties can be avoided if the defendant can show the existence of 'special reasons'. Special reasons may avoid endorsement or disqualification or secure a reduced period. There is no statutory definition of special reasons. A special reason is one that is:

(a)   a mitigating circumstance;

(b)   which does not constitute a defence to the charge;

(c)   connected with the commission of the offence not personal to the offender; and

(d)   which the court ought properly to take into account when considering sentence

(*R v Crossan* [1939] NI 106; *Whittall v Kirby* [1946] 2 All ER 552; *R v Wickins* (1958) 42 Cr App R 236).

Therefore, the fact that the defendant was driving dangerously because of an emergency may constitute a special reason. The fact that the defendant would lose his job if disqualified is not a special reason: it is personal to the offender and is not connected with the commission of the offence itself.

It is possible for the court to find the reasons special enough to avoid obligatory disqualification but not special enough to avoid obligatory endorsement. If that is the case, the court will endorse the defendant's driving licence with penalty points. If the defendant already has sufficient penalty points on his driving licence, then he may find himself liable to be disqualified under the penalty points system.

Example

Elaine is charged with driving with excess alcohol which carries an obligatory disqualification. She argues special reasons. The court finds the reasons special enough to avoid obligatory disqualification but not special enough to avoid obligatory endorsement. Elaine already has 9 points on her licence and so is liable to be disqualified under the penalty points system as 3–11 points must be endorsed on her driving licence for the offence.

The defendant must prove special reasons exist on the balance of probabilities. If the court finds special reasons, they must be stated in open court (and in magistrates' courts, recorded in the court register) (Road Traffic Offenders Act 1998, s 47(1)).

Discretionary disqualification for the offence itself

Whenever the court has a discretion to disqualify, mitigating factors can be put to the court with a view to avoiding disqualification or reducing the period. Mitigating factors are any factors which are relevant to the offence before the court. They can be connected with the circumstances of the offence itself or be personal to the offender. Therefore, unlike special reasons, factors such as loss of job on disqualification can be taken into account.

Disqualification under the points system

If the court is satisfied that there are mitigating circumstances, it may decide not to disqualify under the points system or to reduce the period. All circumstances can be taken into account (both those connected with the offence and those personal to the offender) except:

(a)   the triviality of the present offence;

(b)   hardship (unless it is exceptional);

(c)   mitigating circumstances taken into account to avoid disqualification (or reduce the period) under the points system within the preceding three years (Road Traffic Offenders Act 1988, s 35(4)).

Example 1

Himesh is liable to disqualification under the points system. He puts forward the fact that if disqualified he will lose his job. This can be taken into account only if the court is satisfied that loss of his job would constitute exceptional hardship.

Example 2

Joan is liable to disqualification under the points system. She avoided a points disqualification 18 months ago on the basis that disqualification would cause exceptional hardship due to the fact that she lives in an isolated area, with no public transport, and suffers from arthritis, making walking difficult. She cannot put forward these factors again at the current hearing.

The defendant must prove mitigating circumstances exist on the balance of probabilities. If the court finds mitigating circumstances, they must be stated in open court (and in the magistrates' court recorded in the court register) (Road Traffic Offenders Act 1988, s 47(1)).

10.2.14   Ancillary orders

A court has power to make the following ancillary orders.

10.2.14.1   Compensation orders (PCC(S)A 2000, ss 130–134)

The defendant can be ordered to pay compensation to the victim of an offence. Compensation cannot normally be ordered in respect of motoring offences. Magistrates can make an order of up to £5000 per offence. There is no limit in the Crown Court, but the court must have regard to the defendant's means.

10.2.14.2   Forfeiture orders (PCC(S)A 2000, ss 143–145)

A court may order forfeiture of any property which was in the defendant's possession or control at the time of apprehension if the property was used for committing or facilitating any offence or was intended by him to be so used or was in his unlawful possession.

An order for the forfeiture and destruction of a controlled drug is made under s 27 of the Misuse of Drugs Act 1971.

10.2.14.3   Confiscation orders (Crime and Disorder Act 1998, s 3)

A magistrates' court has the power to make a confiscation order in respect of the proceeds of crime if it commits a defendant to the Crown Court for sentence under s 3 or s 4 of the PCC(S)A 2000. The Crown Court may make a confiscation order in respect of the proceeds of crime (Proceeds of Crime Act 2002). This is subject to detailed conditions beyond the scope of this book.

10.2.14.4   Prosecution costs (Prosecution of Offences Act 1985, s 18)

If the defendant is convicted of any offence, the court may order the defendant to pay to the prosecution such costs as are just and reasonable and must specify the amount.

10.2.14.5   Defence costs (Access to Justice Act 1999, s 17 and the Criminal Defence Service (Recovery of Defence Costs Orders) Regulations 2001, SI 2001/856)

A defendant who is not represented under a representation order and who is acquitted should normally be awarded costs from central funds (Prosecution of Offences Act 1985, s 16). There are exceptions, for example, a defendant who by his conduct has brought suspicion upon himself, and has misled the prosecution into thinking that the case against him is stronger than it is, may find that costs are not awarded in his favour. (See further *Practice Direction (Crime: Costs)* [1991] 1 WLR 498, as amended by *Practice Direction (Costs in Criminal Proceedings) (No 2)* [2000] 1 Cr App R 60.)

At the conclusion of a case in the Crown Court the judge has the power to order a defendant who is represented under a representation order to pay some or all the costs of his defence (a recovery of defence costs order (RDCO)).

The judge has to consider making an RDCO at the end of the case and after all other financial orders and penalties that may be made. An RCDO should be made against every defendant who is convicted and has the means to pay. However, the order is not dependent on the defendant being convicted, although an order against an acquitted defendant would be exceptional. The order can be for any amount up to the full costs incurred in representing the defendant and can include costs incurred in other courts.

An RDCO may not be made against a defendant who:

(a)   only appears in the magistrates' court;

(b)   has been committed for sentence to the Crown Court;

(c)   is appealing against sentence in the Crown Court;

(d)   has been acquitted other than in exceptional circumstances.

The defendant must complete Form B (see **Appendix 2(Q)**) and return it to the Crown Court at least four days before the first hearing at the Crown Court. The Crown Court will then refer the financial resources of the defendant to the Legal Services Commission who will prepare a report for the judge outlining the income and capital available to the defendant. The report will also be made available to the defence. The judge will then consider the report at the conclusion of the case and determine whether to make an RDCO. The judge may require the solicitor representing the defendant to provide an estimate of the costs likely to be incurred in the proceedings. If it later turns out that the actual costs incurred were less than the amount of the RDCO, then the balance must be repaid.

In deciding how much should be paid under an RDCO the judge will take into account the resources of the defendant together with the resources of his partner. The resources of other people who have been making funds available to the defendant can also be considered. Generally an order will not be made against the first £3000 of any capital available. The defendant's main dwelling may be treated as capital for the purposes of an RDCO but the first £100,000 of any equity (ie, the market value less any outstanding mortgages) in that property will be disregarded. In most cases, RDCOs will be made on the basis of capital rather than income. Income will only be taken into account if the defendant's gross annual income exceeds £24,000.

The Crown Court has the power to make an order freezing the defendant's assets where it is appropriate to do so in support of the RDCO provisions. An RDCO may provide for payment to be made forthwith or by instalments. Payments are made to the Legal Services Commission. The Legal Service Commission may enforce an order as if it was a civil debt.

10.2.15   Deferment of sentence (PCC(S)A 2000, ss 1 and 2)

A court may defer sentence for up to six months. When the defendant appears to be sentenced, the court has the same powers of sentence as it had on conviction. If the defendant is convicted of any offence during the period of deferment, he may be sentenced for the deferred sentence at the same time.

This is a useful provision and can be used, for example, where the defendant claims that a recent change in circumstances in his life will mean that he is unlikely to offend again. If he has the offer of a job, or is about to be married, the court may decide to defer sentence for a period of up to six months to see how the defendant reacts to the change in his circumstances. If the reaction is favourable, a custodial sentence should not normally be imposed at the end of the period of deferment.

When imposing a deferred sentence, the court should specify what conduct is expected of the defendant and what sentence it is minded to impose if he does not comply. The court can defer sentence only once.

10.2.16 Committal to the Crown Court for sentence

10.2.16.1 PCC(S)A 2000, s 3

A magistrates' court may commit an offender of 18 years of age or above to the Crown Court for sentence if:

(a)   it has convicted him of an offence triable either way; and either

(b)   the offence (or the combination of the offence and one or more associated offences) was so serious that greater punishment should be inflicted for the offence than the court has power to impose; or

(c)   in the case of a violent or sexual offence, a prison sentence or a term longer than the court has power to impose is necessary to protect the public from serious harm from him.

The Crown Court may then deal with the defendant as if he had been convicted on indictment.

At plea before venue, the defendant is asked to indicate a plea.

If the defendant indicates a guilty plea, the magistrates may still commit the defendant to the Crown Court for sentence if they consider their sentencing powers inadequate.

> #### Example 1
>
> Kevin is charged with assault occasioning actual bodily harm. He indicates a guilty plea. The plea before venue procedure comes to an end and the magistrates proceed to sentence.
>
> When the prosecution summarise the facts, the magistrates learn that the defendant attacked a bus driver who sustained extensive injuries. Kevin may be committed to the Crown Court for sentence.
>
> #### Example 2
>
> Sheila is charged with theft. She indicates a guilty plea. The plea before venue procedure comes to an end and the magistrates proceed to sentence.
>
> The prosecutor hands into the court a list of Sheila's previous convictions. She has numerous previous convictions for dishonesty offences. This may now be a suitable case for committal for sentence to the Crown Court.

In *R v Warley Magistrates' Court, ex p DPP; R v Staines Magistrates' Court, ex p DPP; R v North East Suffolk Magistrates' Court, ex p DPP; R v Lowestoft Justices, ex p DPP* [1998] 2 Cr App R 307, the Divisional Court considered the plea before venue procedure and committal for sentence. In deciding whether the powers of punishment were adequate, the magistrates should take into account the sentencing discount granted on a guilty plea. Where it was obvious that the gravity of the offence required punishment that would exceed the magistrates' powers, they should commit to the Crown Court without seeking any pre-sentence report or hearing mitigation. The defence should, however, be allowed to make a brief submission in opposition to this course of action and the prosecution should be allowed to reply.

If the defendant indicates a not guilty plea, the magistrates hear representations from the prosecution and the defence as to mode of trial. If the offence is so serious that the magistrates do not have sufficient sentencing powers, this will usually be revealed at the mode of trial enquiry and the magistrates will commit to the Crown Court for trial. A decision to commit for sentence is likely to be based on factors which were unknown at the mode of trial enquiry.

Example 3

Andrew indicates a not guilty plea, the magistrates accept jurisdiction, and Andrew consents to summary trial. Having been convicted he asks for 16 other offences to be taken into consideration (TIC) (see **10.3.2.3**). The TICs were not known at the mode of trial enquiry. Andrew may be committed to the Crown Court for sentencing.

Example 4

Having indicated a not guilty plea, Paul is convicted by the magistrates. At the mode of trial enquiry, it appeared that the offence involved unoccupied premises. It later transpires that part of the premises consisted of a dwelling and the victim was frightened by Paul. This may now be a suitable case for committal for sentence to the Crown Court.

10.2.16.2   PCC(S)A 2000, s 4

This provision deals with the situation where the magistrates' court has committed a defendant for trial for some offences, but has to deal with him for other related either way offences. In this context, one offence is related to another if they can both be tried on the same indictment. If the defendant committed for trial has indicated an intention to plead guilty to those related offences, he must, by virtue of the mode of trial procedure, be treated as if he has pleaded guilty to them (see **4.4**). Section 4 gives the magistrates power to commit the defendant to the Crown Court for sentence for the related offences, even if they do not meet the requirements laid down in s 3, ie, that the offence is so serious that the magistrates' powers of punishment are inadequate or (in the case of a violent or sexual offence) that a longer sentence than they have power to impose is necessary to protect the public from serious harm from him.

Example

Imogen is charged with aggravated vehicle-taking and theft of a radio cassette player from the same vehicle.

At plea before venue, she indicates a plea of not guilty to the theft charge and the magistrates proceed to mode of trial. The magistrates accept jurisdiction and Imogen elects trial by jury.

She indicates a guilty plea to the aggravated vehicle-taking charge which means that the magistrates will proceed to sentence.

Instead of sentencing her, the magistrates can commit Imogen for sentence for the aggravated vehicle-taking charge under s 4 even though it does not meet the requirements for committal for sentence under s 3.

The powers of the Crown Court to sentence the defendant for the offence committed under s 4 depend on whether it convicts him of the original offence, ie, the theft offence in the above example. If it convicts him of the original offence, then the Crown Court will have the power to impose any sentence which it would have power to impose if the defendant had been convicted on indictment. If not, the Crown Court's powers to deal with the defendant in respect of offences for which he has been committed for sentence are limited to those of the magistrates.

10.2.16.3   Committal for sentence — bail or custody

In most cases where a plea of guilty is made at the plea before venue, it will be unusual to alter the position as regards bail or custody. When a defendant who has been on bail pleads guilty at the plea before venue, the practice should normally be to continue bail, even if it is anticipated that a custodial sentence will be imposed at the Crown Court, unless there are good reasons for remanding the defendant in custody. If the defendant is in custody, then after entering a plea of guilty at the plea before venue, it will be unusual, if the reasons for remanding in custody remain unchanged, to alter the position (*R v Rafferty* [1999] 1 Cr App R 235).

10.3 Sentencing procedure

Following a guilty plea or conviction of the defendant, it will often be necessary for the court to adjourn for reports to be prepared to assist the court in sentencing.

10.3.1 Pre-sentence reports

Pre-sentence reports are ordered by the court and made by a probation officer or social worker. The purpose of the report is to assist the court in deciding the most suitable method of dealing with the offender. If a custodial sentence is being considered by the court, the report should contain detailed information about how the offender could be punished in the community.

Pre-sentence reports will often be ordered before:

(a)   imposing any custodial sentence unless the offence (or an associated offence) is triable only on indictment and the court is of the opinion that it is unnecessary;

(b)   making a community rehabilitation order with additional requirements (see **10.2.4**);

(c)   making a community punishment order;

(d)   making a community punishment and rehabilitation order;

(e)   making a drug treatment and testing order.

A court need not obtain a pre-sentence report if it considers that it is unnecessary to do so. There will be cases, for example, when a custodial sentence is inevitable irrespective of the content of a pre-sentence report. A court may feel that a report is, therefore, not necessary. Courts are unlikely to impose a community sentence without a pre-sentence report because of the need to consult with the agencies responsible for supervision of the sentence (eg, the Probation Service).

Copies of a pre-sentence report should be given by the court to the offender or his solicitor and to the prosecutor.

10.3.2 Procedure

Magistrates' court sentencing procedures are illustrated in a flowchart at **Appendix 1(Q)**.

Unless the defendant pleaded not guilty and sentencing is following immediately after trial, the prosecution will summarise the facts of the case.

10.3.2.1 Victim impact statement

This statement, which will be referred to by the prosecutor, gives a victim of crime a formal opportunity to say how the crime has affected him. It may identify a need for protection or support and can be taken into account when sentencing. (See *Practice Direction (Criminal Proceedings: Consolidation)* [2002] 3 All ER 904, para 28, *Personal statements of victims*.)

10.3.2.2 'Newton hearing'

Although the defendant pleads guilty, he may still dispute some prosecution allegations. If the dispute is substantial the court must either accept the defence account, and sentence accordingly, or give the parties the opportunity of calling evidence so that the dispute may be resolved (*R v Newton (Robert John)* (1983) 77 Cr App R 13). If evidence is called this is known as a *Newton* hearing.

Example

Fred pleads guilty to s 47 actual bodily harm. The prosecution alleges that he was the aggressor and launched an unprovoked attack. Fred says that he only attacked the other man after being subjected to racial abuse. The difference would have a major effect on the sentence the court would impose and so the court must either hold a *Newton* hearing or accept Fred's account as true.

The prosecution will present details of the defendant's background and a record of his previous convictions to the court. When considering the seriousness of the offence, the court can take into account any previous convictions of the offender or any failure of his to respond to previous sentences. If the offence was committed whilst on bail, the court must treat that as an aggravating factor.

10.3.2.3 Offences taken into consideration (TICs)

The prosecution will give details of other offences to be taken into consideration. In addition to the offence or offences charged, the defendant may have committed a number of other crimes. It is likely to be in the defendant's interest that all matters outstanding against him should be dealt with at the same time. The defendant can ask a court to take other offences into consideration on sentence. These should be offences of a similar or less serious nature. When sentencing the defendant, the court has the power to sentence only in respect of the offences with which he is convicted. The effect of asking for other offences to be taken into consideration is that the court is entitled to take them into account when passing sentence. If the defendant qualifies for a custodial sentence (see **10.2.11**), a number of TICs may increase the length of the sentence. In practice, the overall effect on the sentence is unlikely to be great, particularly when the offence charged is the most serious one.

If an offence is taken into consideration the defendant cannot subsequently be prosecuted for it. It is not a conviction but compensation can be awarded to the victim of a 'TIC' offence.

The practice involved in asking for other offences to be taken into consideration is that the defendant will be given a form by the police giving details of the various offences. He will sign the form and will be asked to admit before the court that he wishes the other offences to be taken into consideration on sentence. An example of a 'TIC' form appears at **Appendix 2(T)**.

10.3.2.4 Pre-sentence report and means enquiry form

If a report has been ordered it will now be made available to the court. In a magistrates' court, the defence will also have to produce a completed means enquiry form. This will be used by the court if a financial penalty is being considered.

The defence speech in mitigation is presented to the court (see 10.4). Sentence is passed.

10.4   The plea in mitigation

10.4.1   The purpose of the plea in mitigation

The role of the defence solicitor in presenting a plea in mitigation to the court is either to reduce the severity of the sentence to be passed or, in appropriate cases, to persuade the court that punishment, as such, would be inexpedient and that a sentence which will help the defendant should be passed. The objective of the plea in mitigation is to ensure that a sentence is passed by the court which is appropriate both to the circumstances of the offence and to the circumstances of the defendant. The aim is to obtain the most lenient punishment which can reasonably be imposed.

10.4.2   Assessing the likely sentence

A common fault of young solicitor advocates is to 'talk up' a sentence. In other words, the advocate has not made any attempt to assess the likely range of penalties to be imposed for the offence and addresses the court on potential penalties which may be wholly inappropriate. The starting point for any plea in mitigation is to attempt to make a realistic assessment of the likely range of sentences which will be in the mind of the court.

A useful starting point in the magistrates' court is to consult the Magistrates' Association Sentencing Guidelines. If more than one offence is being dealt with, it is also necessary to bear in mind that the overall sentence should be kept in proportion to the 'totality' of the offending behaviour. This simply means that care should be taken in sentencing for several minor offences to avoid an overall sentence that would be more appropriate to a much more serious crime.

Extracts from the Sentencing Guidelines appear in **Appendix 3**, and should be consulted when a plea in mitigation is being prepared.

10.4.3   The plea in mitigation

When making a plea in mitigation, the advocate should address the court on the circumstances of the offence, the circumstances of the offender and the sentence he is seeking to persuade the magistrates to impose. An effective plea in mitigation will try to 'sell' a particular sentence by reference to the mitigating factors available. Whatever the advocate says about the offence and the offender should be designed to persuade the magistrates to impose a particular sentence.

The court may have ordered a pre-sentence report. The advocate should note any comments contained in the report about the offence, the defendant's background and any recommendation on sentence.

The court may hear character witnesses or receive letters or references on the defendant's behalf.

When the defendant wishes to avoid obligatory disqualification or endorsement for a driving offence, he will give evidence on oath of special reasons or mitigating circumstances.

The following are matters commonly dealt with by the advocate in his plea in mitigation.

10.4.3.1   The offence

Aggravating features

The advocate should identify any aggravating features which would normally encourage a court to take the view that a sentence at the higher end of the scale should be appropriate and see if it is possible to disassociate the defendant's case from those features.

Under the PCC(S)A 2000, failure to respond to previous sentences may be taken into account when considering the seriousness of the offence and if the offence is committed whilst on bail the court must treat that as an aggravating factor. The court 'should identify any convictions relevant for this purpose and then consider to what extent they affect the seriousness of the present offence' (Magistrates' Association Sentencing Guidelines, para 2). Offences of a similar nature are therefore liable to weigh more heavily against the defendant than those of a different character.

It may therefore be necessary for the advocate to explain the circumstances of the previous offences and the defendant's failure to respond to previous sentences.

Mitigating features

The advocate should identify whether there are any mitigating factors which should be brought to the attention of the court to reduce the seriousness of the offence. For example, if the offence is an offence against the person, provocation can be relevant mitigation.

10.4.3.2   The offender

The Magistrates' Association Sentencing Guidelines set out some examples of offender mitigation but there are frequently others to be considered in individual cases.

Age

The younger the offender, the more likely a court will be to pass a sentence designed to help the offender rather than punish him. Equally, a defendant of advanced age may receive more sympathetic treatment than would otherwise be the case.

Health (physical or mental)

One of the most common explanations given to a court for criminal conduct is that the defendant was under the effects of drink or drugs. As a basic rule, the voluntary ingestion of drink or drugs will not be good mitigation. If, on the other hand, there is evidence that the defendant is an alcoholic or a drug addict, this may point towards the need for a sentence which will overcome these problems, as opposed to the imposition of a punitive penalty.

Co-operation with the police

If a defendant has assisted the police with their enquiries by naming others involved in the crime or by revealing the whereabouts of stolen property which is subsequently recovered, this may be effective mitigation.

The fact that the defendant confessed when being questioned by the police can also be presented in a favourable light as the defendant has not wasted time during the investigation process.

Voluntary compensation

A defendant who voluntarily makes good the damage which has been caused, or who makes voluntary payments of compensation may get credit from the court for this. The motive behind the reparation is obviously important. It is far easier for a wealthy person to make voluntary payments of compensation than for a person of limited means. The court will therefore look not only at whether reparation has been made but also the reasons for it.

Remorse

Evidence of remorse is undoubtedly effective mitigation in many cases. The fact that an advocate apologises to the court on behalf of his client is unlikely to have any great effect. The court is likely to be more impressed with tangible signs of remorse, for example, the defendant taking positive steps to tackle the problems which led him to commit the offence.

Other offender mitigation

The defendant's advocate will explain to the court the defendant's reasons for committing the offence. If the offence is one involving dishonesty, the fact that the defendant was in serious financial difficulty can be put forward, although it must be appreciated that a mere plea 'that the defendant found it difficult to live on benefit' is unlikely to meet with any sympathy. A stressful home background which has driven the defendant to committing an offence can validly be put forward.

The advocate should explain why the defendant committed the offence in a way that puts the offence in the context of the defendant's life generally. The court will want to try and understand the defendant and why he committed the offence.

If the defendant has been convicted following a plea of not guilty, it will not usually be appropriate to then explain to the court why the defendant committed the offence.

A person of previous good character should be given credit for this fact. The defendant should be given some credit if he has no previous convictions for the kind of offence for which he has been convicted. For example, the advocate might say in mitigation that, although the defendant has a record for dishonesty offences, he has no history of violence so that, in relation to the assault, he should be treated as a person of good character. The defendant should also be given some credit if there has been a substantial gap between the present offence and the last one, indicating that the offender has made a genuine attempt to 'go straight'.

The defendant's present situation is of great importance. The court will be looking for evidence of the defendant's stability, a regular home and job, and people who will be supportive to the defendant. The advocate will need to compare the defendant's present situation with the time the offence was committed.

The mere fact that the defendant or his family will be upset by the imposition of a custodial sentence is unlikely to have any effect on the court. If, however, it can be shown that there are exceptional circumstances, the effect of imprisonment can, in appropriate cases, be effective mitigation. If the defendant's partner is seriously ill, for example, a court may decide not to impose an immediate custodial sentence. This, of course, will depend on the nature of the offence. It must be appreciated that some offences are so serious that custody is inevitable.

If conviction will result in dismissal from employment, this factor may be taken into account by the court, although if the offence is related to the defendant's employment it will be less effective mitigation.

In driving offences, the loss of licence will inevitably lead to hardship and this can be taken into account to avoid discretionary disqualification for the offence but not to avoid disqualification under the points system unless such hardship is exceptional.

When a fine is a possibility, the advocate will need to obtain considerable detail about the defendant's financial position (eg, income after tax, outgoings out of income, any capital) in order to help the court fix the fine at a proper level. In the magistrates' court, the defence will have to produce a completed means enquiry form. The advocate will also need to take the defendant's instructions on how much time the defendant will need to pay any fine imposed and the level of weekly instalments he could meet.

10.4.3.3 Sentence

The PCC(S)A 2000, s 152 requires a court to take into account in deciding the sentence to pass on an offender who has pleaded guilty:

(a)   the stage in the proceedings for the offence at which the offender indicated his intention to plead guilty; and

(b)   the circumstances in which the indication was given.

The object of this provision is to save court time and spare, for example, victims of crime the anxiety of giving evidence. Section 152 may result in a discount being given on a custodial sentence or the number of hours to be served under a community punishment order being reduced.

Example 1

Alyona is arrested at the scene of a burglary. She is caught 'red handed' by the police. The circumstances of the case make it unlikely that any credit will be given for a guilty plea. A guilty plea is almost inevitable on the facts.

Example 2

Peter is arrested for theft. The evidence against him is largely circumstantial. He makes a full confession to the police and, on his first appearance before a court, indicates his intention to plead guilty. Peter will get full credit for his early guilty plea in these circumstances.

The possible sentencing options should be addressed and the advocate should identify the advantages of the sentence he is arguing for and any detrimental effects of those he is arguing against.

The advocate should also deal with any ancillary orders, for example, compensation, forfeiture and costs, which the prosecution may have applied for.

The mitigating factors which are set out above are not exhaustive but are some of the most commonly used.

10.5 Sentencing guidelines

Under s 80 of the Crime and Disorder Act 1998, the Court of Appeal can give guidance on sentences imposed for indictable offences. A duty is imposed on the Court of Appeal to consider whether to frame guidelines, or to revise existing guidelines. In considering guidelines, the Court of Appeal must have regard to the need to promote consistency in sentencing, the pattern of sentencing for similar offences, the cost and effectiveness of different offences and the need to promote public confidence in the criminal justice system. This duty is supplemented by the creation of the Sentencing Advisory Panel, which, on its own initiative, may propose to the Court of Appeal that guidelines for particular categories of offence be adopted or revised and must do so if directed by the Home Secretary. In either situation, it will consult, consider and formulate views and furnish information to the Court of Appeal. The Panel was appointed by the Lord Chancellor.

For offences sentenced in the magistrates' court, the Magistrates' Association has issued guidelines.

Extracts from the Magistrates' Association Sentencing Guidelines are set out in **Appendix 3**.

10.6 Further reading

See, for example:

Archbold: Criminal Pleading, Evidence and Practice (Sweet & Maxwell, 2004)

Blackstone's Criminal Practice (Oxford University Press, 2004)

John Sprack, *Emmins on Criminal Procedure* (Oxford University Press, 2002)

Wallis and Halnan, *Wilkinson's Road Traffic Offences* (Sweet and Maxwell, 2003)

Chapter 11

The Youth Court

11.1	General	167
11.2	Sentencing	167
11.3	Further reading	169

11.1 General

Under the Magistrates' Courts Act 1980, s 24, defendants under the age of 18 must be dealt with in the youth court unless:

(a) they are charged with homicide, in which case they must be sent to the Crown Court;

(b) they are charged jointly with an adult and the court considers it necessary in the interests of justice for both to be tried in the Crown Court; or

(c) a defendant aged 10–17 inclusive is charged with indecent assault or an offence which carries a maximum penalty of 14 years or more for an adult; or the defendant is aged 14–17 inclusive and is charged with causing death by dangerous driving, or causing death by dangerous driving whilst under the influence of drink or drugs, and the court considers that, if he or she is convicted, no disposal would be appropriate other than a term of detention under PCC(S)A 2000, s 91, in which case the matter should be sent to the Crown Court. (Section 91 of the PCC(S)A 2000 permits a period of detention in excess of the normal maximum that can be imposed on an offender aged under 18, ie, 24 months.)

11.2 Sentencing

A detailed consideration of sentencing in the youth court is beyond the scope of this book. For the most part, sentencing principles are similar to the sentencing principles that apply in the adult court.

11.2.1 Detention and training orders (PCC(S)A 2000, ss 100–107)

A detention and training order requires the offender to be subject to a period of detention and training followed by a period of supervision. The court will be able to impose a detention and training order on those aged 15–17 inclusive, convicted of an imprisonable offence sufficiently serious to justify custody, and on those aged 12–14 inclusive, convicted of an imprisonable offence sufficiently serious to justify custody who are, in the opinion of the court, persistent offenders.

Subject to the limitation as to overall length, the period of a detention and training order shall be 4, 6, 8, 10, 12, 18, or 24 months. The total length of the order (comprising both the period of detention and training and also the period of supervision) may not exceed the maximum term of imprisonment that a Crown Court could impose on an adult offender (PCC(S)A 2000, s 101(2)).

11.2.2 Community sentences

11.2.2.1 Community rehabilitation orders (Criminal Justice and Court Services Act 2000, s 43, PCC(S)A 2000, ss 41–45 and Schs 2 and 3)

A community rehabilitation order is available for offenders of a minimum age of 16.

11.2.2.2 Community punishment Orders (Criminal Justice and Court Services Act 2000, s 44, PCC(S)A 2000, ss 46–50 and Sch 3)

Community punishment orders are available for offenders aged at least 16.

11.2.2.3 Community punishment and rehabilitation orders (Criminal Justice and Court Services Act 2000, s 45, PCC(S)A 2000, s 51 and Sch 3)

Community punishment and rehabilitation orders are available for defendants aged at least 16.

11.2.2.4 Curfew orders (PCC(S)A 2000, s 37 and Sch 3)

Curfew orders are available for offenders of a minimum age of 10.

11.2.2.5 Drug treatment and testing orders (PCC(S)A 2000, ss 52–58 and Sch 3)

Drug treatment and testing orders are available for defendants aged 16 or over.

11.2.2.6 Attendance centre orders (PCC(S)A 2000, ss 60–62 and Sch 5)

Attendance centre orders are available for offenders of a minimum age of 10.

11.2.2.7 Action plan orders (PCC(S)A 2000, ss 69–72 and Sch 7)

These are designed to give the offender a short but intensive programme of work to tackle the causes of offending at an early age. The court can impose such an order where it thinks that this will prevent re-offending or will rehabilitate the offender. The offender must comply with a 3-month action plan. The plan will impose certain requirements regarding the offender's behaviour and whereabouts. The order cannot be combined with custody or any other community sentence. Action plan orders are available for offenders aged 10 to 17 inclusive.

11.2.2.8 Supervision orders (PCC(S)A 2000, ss 63–68 and Sch 7)

A supervision order may be made on an offender aged under 18, placing him under the supervision of a local authority or a probation officer or a member of a youth offending team. In many ways, a supervision order is the equivalent for children or young persons of a community rehabilitation order. The basic supervision order may be supplemented, where appropriate, with various requirements, for example, making reparation to a specified person. It is not possible, however, to combine a reparation order (see below) with a supervision order. If an offender is suitable to be made the subject of a supervision order, a reparation element should form a requirement of such an order. Before making such requirements, the court should consider the views of the victim. There is no specified minimum period to a supervision order and the maximum period is 3 years.

11.2.3 Reparation orders (PCC(S)A 2000, ss 73–75 and Sch 8)

A reparation order may require an offender to, inter alia, write a letter of apology to the victim, apologise to the victim in person, or repair criminal damage. This is not a community sentence. It cannot be combined with custody or a community sentence but can be made a requirement of a supervision order (see above). If, in any case, the court has power to make a reparation order but does not do so, it shall give reasons as to why it does not make the order. It is intended that courts consider the making of the order in any case in which a compensation order is not imposed.

11.2.4 Fines and discharges

Fines and discharges are available in the youth court. Parents may be ordered to pay fines imposed in respect of offenders under the age of 18 (PCC(S)A 2000, s 137).

11.2.5 Referrals to youth offender panels (PCC(S)A 2000, ss 16–32 and Sch 1)

Referral to a youth offender panel is available for young people convicted for the first time. Its primary aim is to prevent re-offending. The youth offender panel is composed of people with an interest or expertise in dealing with young people.

The youth offender panel will work with the young offender and his family to establish a programme of behaviour for the young offender to follow. The programme will be guided by the following three principles:

(a)   making reparation to the victim;

(b)   achieving reintegration into the law-abiding community;

(c)   taking responsibility for the consequences of offending behaviour.

11.3 Further reading

See, for example:

Archbold: Criminal Pleading, Evidence and Practice (Sweet & Maxwell, 2004)

Blackstone's Criminal Practice (Oxford University Press, 2004)

John Sprack, *Emmins on Criminal Procedure* (Oxford University Press, 2002)

Chapter 12

Appeals

12.1	Appeals from the magistrates' court and youth court	171
12.2	Appeals from the Crown Court	172
12.3	Further reading	172

12.1 Appeals from the magistrates' court and youth court

A flowchart summarising appeals from the magistrates' court and youth court appears at **Appendix 1(R)**.

12.1.1 Appeals to the Crown Court

 The defendant may appeal against conviction or sentence, but if he pleaded guilty he may only appeal against sentence unless he claims his plea was equivocal (Magistrates' Courts Act 1980, s 108).

If the Crown Court is satisfied that the plea was equivocal, it will remit the case to the magistrates' court with a direction that a plea of not guilty be entered.

Notice of appeal must be given both to the justices' clerk and the prosecution within 21 days of sentence. The Crown Court has power to grant leave to appeal out of time, but this is rarely exercised. An example of a notice of appeal appears at **Appendix 2(U)**.

Appeals against conviction and/or sentence will be heard by a Crown Court judge or a recorder sitting with between two and four magistrates. The appeal will take the form of a re-hearing. If the appeal is against conviction, all of the evidence will be heard again. If the appeal is against sentence, the prosecution will outline the facts of the case to the court who will decide what the appropriate sentence is.

On an appeal to the Crown Court, the court may:

(a)   confirm, reverse or vary the magistrates' decision; or

(b)   remit the matter (eg, on an equivocal plea) with its opinion thereon to the magistrates; or

(c)   make such other order in the matter as the court thinks just and by such order exercise any power which the magistrates might have exercised. This means, for example, that orders for costs and compensation can be made.

The Crown Court may issue any sentence, which may be heavier or lighter than that of the magistrates, provided the sentence is one which the magistrates' court had power to issue. It is important, therefore, to point out to a defendant who wishes to appeal to the Crown Court that his sentence could be increased up to the maximum sentencing powers of the magistrates' court which originally dealt with the case.

12.1.2 Appeals to the High Court (Queen's Bench Division) by case stated

Either the defence or the prosecution may appeal from the decision of a magistrates' court to the High Court (Queen's Bench Division). The right of appeal is available where the magistrates' decision is wrong in law or was given in excess of the magistrates' jurisdiction (Magistrates' Courts Act 1980, s 111). The High Court may affirm, reverse or vary the decision of the magistrates or remit the case to the magistrates' court with its opinion. The procedure for the appeal is not a re-hearing. The appeal will be decided after hearing arguments on points of law put forward by the parties.

12.2 Appeals from the Crown Court

A flowchart summarising appeals from the Crown Court following a trial on indictment appears at **Appendix 1(S)**.

A defendant may appeal against conviction to the Court of Appeal only with leave of the Court of Appeal or where the trial judge has issued a certificate of fitness for appeal. This applies whether the appeal is on a question of fact, a question of law or a mixed question of fact and law (Criminal Appeals Act 1995, s 1).

The test for granting leave to appeal is whether the court feels that the conviction is unsafe. In practice, this comes down to the question of whether there is a real danger that the defendant might have been prejudiced.

As a result of the decision in *Condron and Another v United Kingdom* (see **2.9.6**) where the procedure at trial is held to be in violation of art 6 of the European Convention on Human Rights (right to a fair trial), a conviction will be deemed unsafe.

A defendant may appeal his sentence with leave of the Court of Appeal. The Court of Appeal cannot increase the sentence but may either confirm or reduce it.

The prosecution cannot appeal to the Court of Appeal against the acquittal of a defendant or against the sentence imposed on the defendant. However, if it appears to the Attorney-General that the sentencing of a person in the Crown Court has been unduly lenient he may, with the leave of the Court of Appeal, refer the case to the Court of Appeal to review the sentencing of that person. On such a referral, the Court of Appeal may quash any sentence passed on the defendant and, in place of it, pass such sentence as it thinks appropriate for the case and in accordance with the powers which the Crown Court had in dealing with that person.

12.3 Further reading

See, for example:

Archbold: Criminal Pleading, Evidence and Practice (Sweet & Maxwell, 2004)

Blackstone's Criminal Practice (Oxford University Press, 2004)

John Sprack, *Emmins on Criminal Procedure* (Oxford University Press, 2002)

APPENDICES

Appendix 1   Procedural Charts and Diagrams

Appendix 2   Documents

Appendix 3   Magistrates' Association Sentencing Guidelines

Appendix 4   Police Station Advice: Advising on Silence

Appendix 5   Law Commission Guidance for Bail Decision-makers and their Advisers

Appendix 6   PACE Codes

Appendix 1

Procedural Charts and Diagrams

(A)	An overview of criminal procedure	177
(B)	Police ranks	178
(C)	Police station procedure	179
(D)	The detention process	180
(E)	Commencement of criminal proceedings	181
(F)	Contested bail application procedure	182
(G)	Documentary hearsay (CJA 1988, s 23)	183
(H)	Documentary hearsay (CJA 1988, s 24)	184
(I)	Disclosure in the magistrates' court of material the prosecution does not intend to rely on	185
(J)	Magistrates' court procedure: Not guilty plea	186
(K)	Plea before venue and mode of trial procedure	187
(L)	Committal without consideration of the evidence (MCA 1980, s 6(2))	188
(M)	Committal with consideration of the evidence (MCA 1980, s 6(1))	189
(N)	Disclosure in the Crown Court of material the prosecution does not intend to rely on	190
(O)	Crown Court procedure — Not guilty plea	191
(P)	The Powers of Criminal Courts (Sentencing) Act 2000: Sentencing scheme for adult offenders	192
(Q)	Magistrates' court sentencing procedures	193
(R)	Summary trials: Appeals	194
(S)	Trial on indictment: Appeals	195
(T)	Committal proceedings to Crown Court trial	196
(U)	Sending for trial to Crown Court	197
(V)	Summary trial: Summary offence	198

(A)   An overview of criminal procedure

(B) Police ranks

SUPERINTENDENT

↑

CHIEF INSPECTOR*

↑

INSPECTOR

↑

SERGEANT

↑

CONSTABLE

* Not a significant rank under PACE 1984

(C)   Police station procedure

(D)   The detention process

Hours

0.00   *Arrival at the police station.* Detention clock begins (but see s 41 for exceptional cases involving arrest outside England and Wales).

0.10   *Detention authorised.* Insufficient evidence to charge detention necessary to secure or preserve evidence or obtain such evidence by questioning the suspect (s 37(2)). Review clock begins.

6.10   Latest time for *first review of detention.* Carried out by inspector. Suspect, or solicitor if available, must be given chance to make representations (s 40). Must be noted in custody record.

15.10   Latest time for *second review of detention.* Must be noted in custody record. Thereafter at 9-hourly intervals (s 40).

24.00   *Suspect to be released (with or without bail) or charged* unless superintendent has reasonable grounds for believing:

    (a)   detention grounds in s 37(2) still exist; and

    (b)   offence for which suspect arrested is an arrestable offence; and

    (c)   investigation conducted diligently and expeditiously.

    Authorisation cannot be granted before second review or after 24 hours (s 42).

36.00   *Superintendent's authority expires.* Suspect to be released (with or without bail) or charged unless extension of warrant of further detention obtained from magistrates' court. A warrant of further detention is only available if the offence is a serious arrestable offence and the grounds in s 43 are satisfied.

72.00   *Maximum period warrant can authorise expires.* Suspect to be released (with or without bail) or charged unless extension of warrant obtained from magistrates (s 43).

96.00   *Absolute maximum period of detention.* Suspect to be released (with or without bail) or charged.

(E) Commencement of criminal proceedings

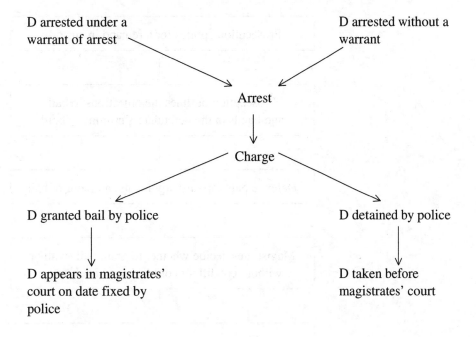

D arrested under a warrant of arrest

D arrested without a warrant

Arrest

Charge

D granted bail by police

D detained by police

D appears in magistrates' court on date fixed by police

D taken before magistrates' court

OR

Information laid by prosecution

Summons issued for offence

Summons served on D

D appears in magistrates' court in answer to summons

(F)   Contested bail application procedure

* *Note*:   If the magistrates require a surety, the surety will have to enter into his/her recognisance before the defendant is released.

(G)   Documentary hearsay (CJA 1988, s 23)

WRITTEN STATEMENT

YES   NO——→NOT ADMISSIBLE
UNDER s 23

FIRST-HAND HEARSAY

YES   NO ——→NOT ADMISSIBLE
UNDER s 23

IS THERE A PRESCRIBED REASON?

(i)   DEAD/UNFIT TO ATTEND

(ii)   OUTSIDE UK AND NOT REASONABLY PRACTICABLE TO
SECURE ATTENDANCE

(iii)   DISAPPEARED

(iv)   FEAR (WHERE STATEMENT MADE TO PC)

YES   NO —→NOT ADMISSIBLE
UNDER s 23

PREPARED FOR CRIMINAL PROCEEDINGS

YES   NO

ADMISSIBLE WITH LEAVE   ADMISSIBLE SUBJECT TO A
(court admits the   GENERAL DISCRETION TO
statement if in the interests   EXCLUDE (s 25)
of justice (s 26))

(H)   Documentary hearsay (CJA 1988, s 24)

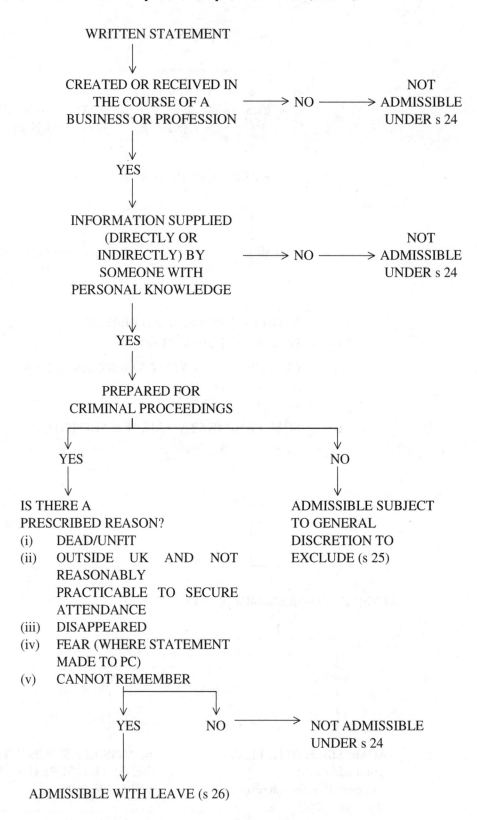

(I) Disclosure in the magistrates' court of material the prosecution does not intend to rely on

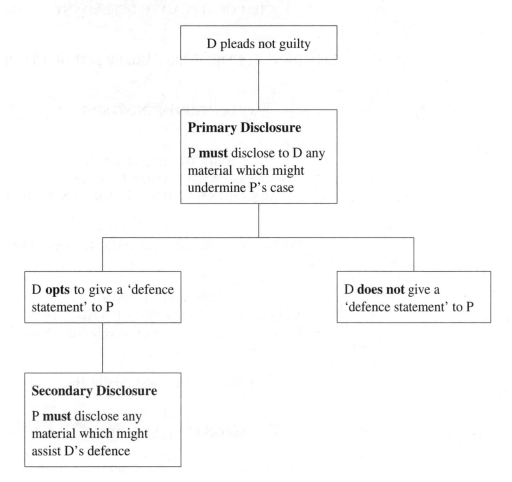

(J)   Magistrates' court procedure: Not guilty plea

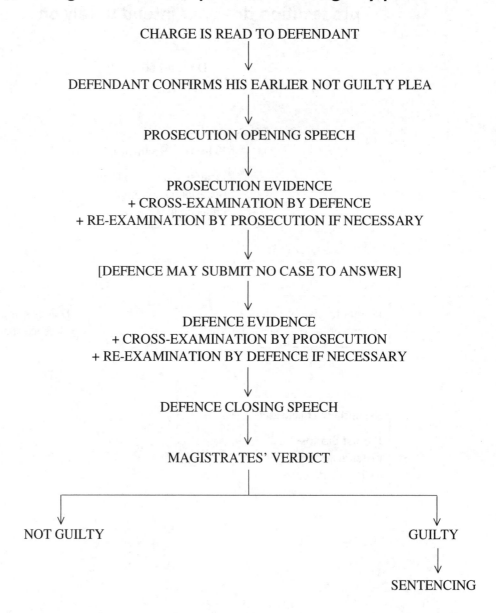

CHARGE IS READ TO DEFENDANT

DEFENDANT CONFIRMS HIS EARLIER NOT GUILTY PLEA

PROSECUTION OPENING SPEECH

PROSECUTION EVIDENCE
+ CROSS-EXAMINATION BY DEFENCE
+ RE-EXAMINATION BY PROSECUTION IF NECESSARY

[DEFENCE MAY SUBMIT NO CASE TO ANSWER]

DEFENCE EVIDENCE
+ CROSS-EXAMINATION BY PROSECUTION
+ RE-EXAMINATION BY DEFENCE IF NECESSARY

DEFENCE CLOSING SPEECH

MAGISTRATES' VERDICT

NOT GUILTY   GUILTY

SENTENCING

(K)   Plea before venue and mode of trial procedure

P63/64

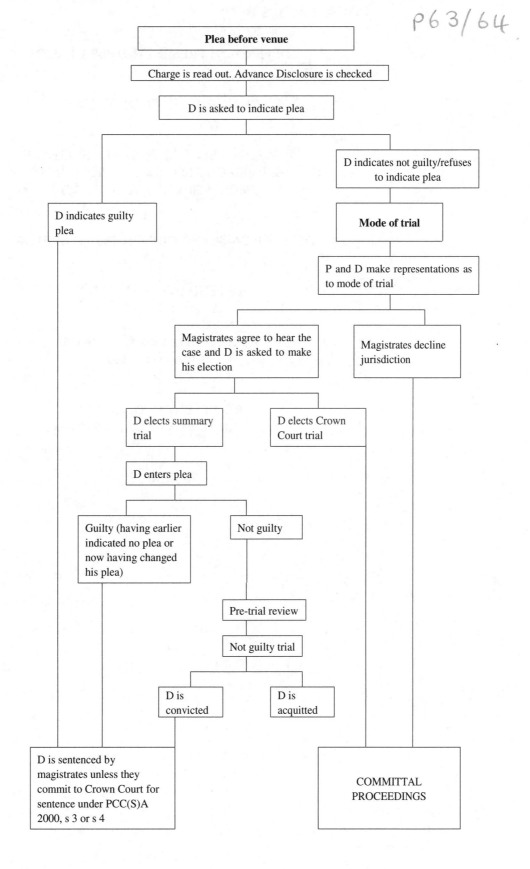

(L) Committal without consideration of the evidence (MCA 1980, s 6(2))

DEFENDANT PRESENT (NO PLEA TAKEN)

↓

CHARGE READ TO DEFENDANT

↓

JUSTICES' CLERK CHECKS ALL EVIDENCE
SERVED ON DEFENDANT'S SOLICITOR
(MCA 1980, s 5B STATEMENTS)

↓

DEFENCE RAISES NO OBJECTIONS TO EVIDENCE

↓

DEFENDANT COMMITTED

↓

WRITTEN EVIDENCE WARNING
(CPIA 1996, s 68)

↓

REPRESENTATION ORDER
(EXTEND TO COVER CROWN COURT)

↓

BAIL

(M) Committal with consideration of the evidence (MCA 1980, s 6(1))

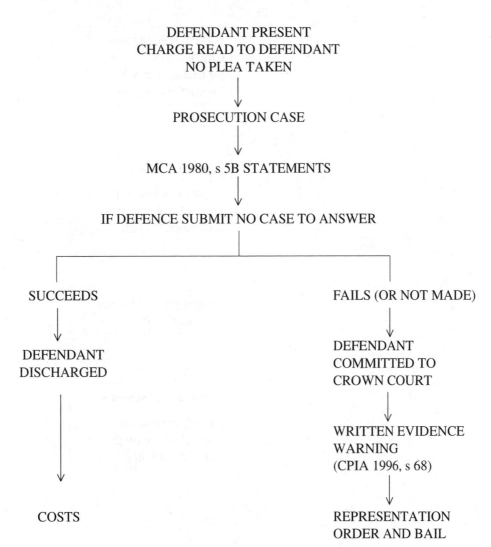

DEFENDANT PRESENT
CHARGE READ TO DEFENDANT
NO PLEA TAKEN

↓

PROSECUTION CASE

↓

MCA 1980, s 5B STATEMENTS

↓

IF DEFENCE SUBMIT NO CASE TO ANSWER

SUCCEEDS   FAILS (OR NOT MADE)

↓   ↓

DEFENDANT   DEFENDANT
DISCHARGED   COMMITTED TO
                                                    CROWN COURT

                                                    ↓

                                                    WRITTEN EVIDENCE
                                                    WARNING
                                                    (CPIA 1996, s 68)

                                                    ↓

COSTS   REPRESENTATION
                                                    ORDER AND BAIL

(N) Disclosure in the Crown Court of material the prosecution does not intend to rely on

(O)   Crown Court procedure: not guilty plea

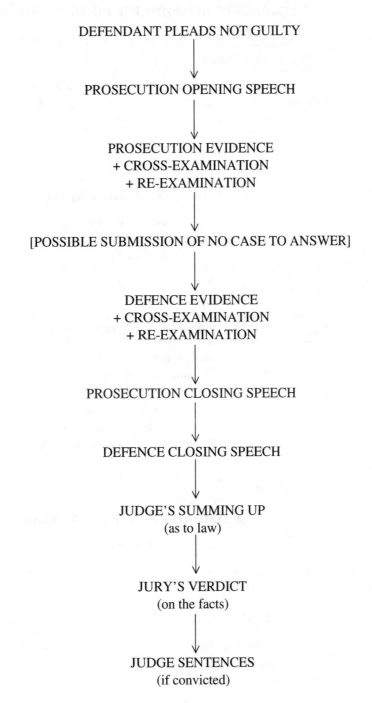

DEFENDANT PLEADS NOT GUILTY

↓

PROSECUTION OPENING SPEECH

↓

PROSECUTION EVIDENCE
+ CROSS-EXAMINATION
+ RE-EXAMINATION

↓

[POSSIBLE SUBMISSION OF NO CASE TO ANSWER]

↓

DEFENCE EVIDENCE
+ CROSS-EXAMINATION
+ RE-EXAMINATION

↓

PROSECUTION CLOSING SPEECH

↓

DEFENCE CLOSING SPEECH

↓

JUDGE'S SUMMING UP
(as to law)

↓

JURY'S VERDICT
(on the facts)

↓

JUDGE SENTENCES
(if convicted)

(P)   The Powers of Criminal Courts (Sentencing) Act 2000: Sentencing scheme for adult offenders

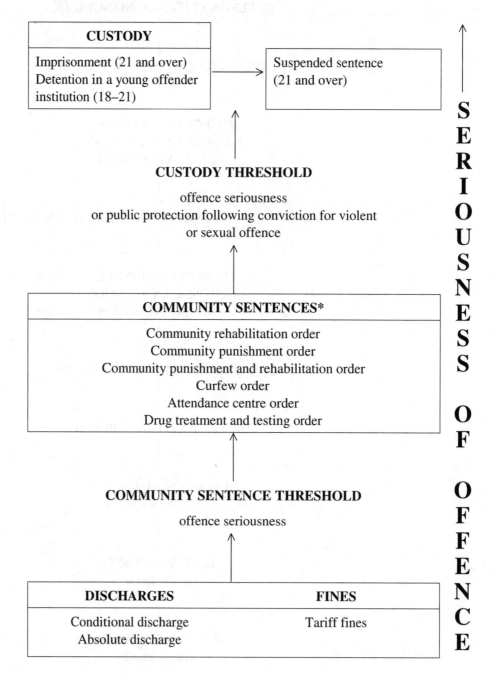

* Selection of particular community sentences requires justification in terms of both 'suitability' and 'seriousness of offence'.

(Q) Magistrates' court sentencing procedures

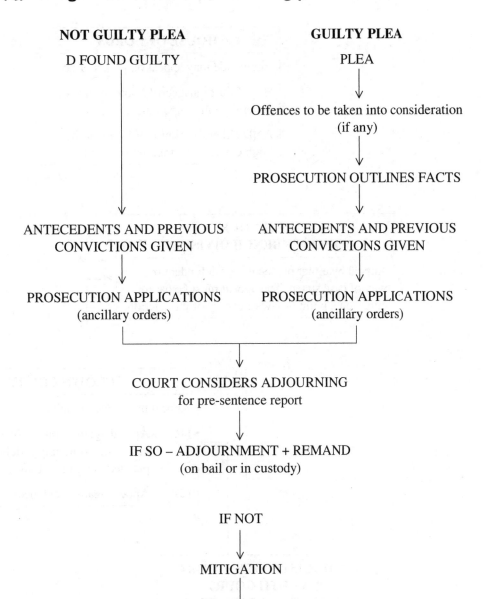

NOT GUILTY PLEA	GUILTY PLEA
D FOUND GUILTY	PLEA

Offences to be taken into consideration
(if any)

PROSECUTION OUTLINES FACTS

ANTECEDENTS AND PREVIOUS CONVICTIONS GIVEN	ANTECEDENTS AND PREVIOUS CONVICTIONS GIVEN
PROSECUTION APPLICATIONS (ancillary orders)	PROSECUTION APPLICATIONS (ancillary orders)

COURT CONSIDERS ADJOURNING
for pre-sentence report

IF SO – ADJOURNMENT + REMAND
(on bail or in custody)

IF NOT

MITIGATION

SENTENCE

(R)   Summary trials: Appeals

(S)   Trial on indictment: Appeals

HOUSE OF LORDS

Appeal on points of law only

Court of Appeal must certify point of law of general public importance; AND Court of Appeal or House of Lords must grant leave to appeal.

Either side may appeal.

(Attorney-General's references may reach House of Lords.)

(Attorney-General's references on sentence may also reach House of Lords.)

↑

COURT OF APPEAL (CRIMINAL DIVISION)

Appeal by defendant only

(1)   against conviction – on a point of law or fact or mixed law and fact – leave required (unless trial judge has issued certificate of fitness for appeal).

(2)   against sentence – leave required (unless trial judge has issued certificate of fitness for appeal).

[Following an acquittal in the Crown Court, the Attorney-General may refer a point of law for clarification to Court of Appeal – but this does not affect the acquittal (Criminal Justice Act 1972, s 36).]

Where the Attorney-General believes that the trial judge has imposed a sentence which is unduly lenient (in certain serious offences) he may refer the case to the Court of Appeal where the sentence can be replaced by one the Court of Appeal considers to be more appropriate (Criminal Justice Act 1988, ss 35, 36).

↑

CROWN COURT

Trial on indictment before judge and jury

(T)   Committal proceedings to Crown Court trial

(U)   Sending for trial to Crown Court

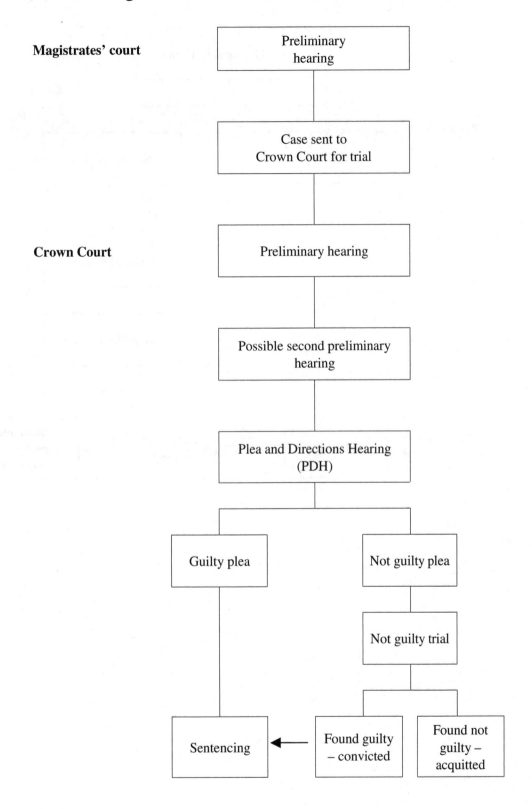

(V)   Summary trial: Summary offence

Appendix 2

Documents

(A)   Custody record   201
(B)   Volunteer's notice   205
(C)   Notice to detained person   206
(D)   Notice of entitlements   207
(E)   Record of tape-recorded interview   209
(F)   Written statement under caution   211
(G)   Solicitor's record of attendance at police station   212
(H)   Identification parade record   217
(I)   Charge sheet   226
(J)   Summons   228
(K)   Application for the right to representation in criminal proceedings:
       Magistrates' court or Crown Court (Form A)   230
(L)   Representation order: Magistrates' court   236
(M)   Record of decision to grant or withhold bail and certificate as to
       hearing on application for bail   237
(N)   Witness statement   238
(O)   Criminal Procedure and Investigations Act 1996 Part I:
       Disclosure — Rights and duties of accused persons   240
(P)   Notice to accused: Right to object to written statement or deposition   243
(Q)   Statement of means for right to representation in criminal
       proceedings in the Crown Court (Form B)   244
(R)   Plea and directions hearing: Judge's questionnaire   252
(S)   Brief to counsel   256
(T)   'TIC' Form   258
(U)   Notice of appeal   260
(V)   Defence statement   261
(W)   Defence statement   262

(A) Custody record

B L A N K S H I R E   P O L I C E

CUSTODY RECORD

Station: WEYFORD	EM No:		Custody No:	WE	17963	9

1. Reasons for Arrest: TAKING A CONVEYANCE – s12(1) THEFT ACT 1968, THEFT OF £750 – s1(1) THEFT ACT 1968

2. † Comment made by person if present when facts of arrest explained
Yes ☐   No ☑   If "Yes" record on Log of Events

3. Place of Arrest: 123 SOMERSET AVENUE, WEYFORD

4.

	Time	Date
Arrested at:	20.45	30/7/00
Arrived at Station:	21.00	30/7/00
Relevant Time:	21.00	30/7/00

Condition on Arrival: ....

Relevant time not applicable ☐ ✓ if appropriate

5. DETENTION DECISION   *Delete as appropriate

A. Detention authorised*:

B. Detention not authorised*:

Signature: John Platt

Name: JOHN PLATT

Time: 21.10   Date: 30/7/00

REASON FOR DETENTION:

(i)   To charge .... ☐

&/or (ii) Other authority (state authority) .... ☐

&/or (iii) Other secure or preserve evidence.......... ☐

&/or (iv) To obtain evidence by questioning .... ☑

Record grounds for detention – MUST complete for (iii) and (iv).
ARRESTED IN POSSESSION OF PROPERTY STOLEN FROM MOTOR VEHICLE, DETENTION NECESSARY TO OBTAIN EVIDENCE BY QUESTIONING

Person present when grounds recorded: Yes ☑ : No ☐ x
Person informed of grounds: Yes ☑ : No ☐ x
x : If 'No', in either case, record reason(s) in Log of Events

6. † Comment made by person when informed of detention
Yes ☐   No ☑   If "Yes" record on Log of Events

7. Drugs Referral Information leaflet issued:
Time: .... Date: ..../......../........

OFFICER OPENING CUSTODY RECORD
Signature: John Platt
Name: JOHN PLATT
Rank/No: SGT 3456
Time: 21.10   Date: 30/7/00

11.97

8. PERSONAL DETAILS

Surname: EVERETT

Forename(s): RONALD EDWIN

Address: 123 SOMERSET AVENUE, WEYFORD, BLANKSHIRE

Telephone No: 01730 400902 Post Code WE2 1AE

Occupation: LABOURER

Age: 43   Date of Birth: 25/6/57

Height: 1M 80   Sex: Male/Female

Ethnic Origin: GB

Place of Birth: GB

9. Arresting Officer: ALAN BROWN
Rank: DC   No: 2907   Stn: WEYFORD

10. Officer in the case: ALAN BROWN
Rank: DC   No: 2907   Stn: WEYFORD

11. DETAINED PERSON'S RIGHTS
An extract from a notice setting out my rights has been read to me and I have been given a copy. I have also been provided with a written notice setting out my entitlements while in custody.
Signature: R Everett
Time: 21.10   Date: 30/7/00

LEGAL ADVICE REQUESTED
I want to speak to a solicitor as soon as practicable:
Signature: R Everett
Time: 21.10   Date: 30/7/00

LEGAL ADVICE DECLINED
I have been informed that I may speak to a solicitor IN PERSON or ON THE TELEPHONE:
Signature: ....
Time: .... Date: ..../......../........
I DO NOT WANT TO SPEAK TO A SOLICITOR at this time:
Signature: ....
Time: .... Date: ..../......../........
† Reasons, if given, for not wanting legal advice:
....

Notification of named person: Requested   Yes ☐ : No ☑
Nominated person: ....
Detainees signature: ....

12. APPROPRIATE ADULT   **INTERPRETER**
Yes ☐ : No ☑   Yes ☐ : No ☑
Notices served, rights and grounds for detention explained in presence of Appropriate Adult/Interpreter.
Signature of A/Adult: ....
Time: .... Date: ..../......../........
Signature of Interpreter: ....
Time: .... Date: ..../......../........

13. FOREIGN NATIONALS
Embassy/Consulate informed: Yes ☐ : Not Applicable ☑
(Record details in Log of Events)
Force Immigration Dept informed: Yes ☐ : Record on 7K

RECORD OF RIGHTS

Surname EVERETT   Custody Record No. WE | 17963 | 9

Interpreter present   Yes ☐   No ☑   Detained person informed of rights   Yes ☑   No ☐
                                           (If No, record reason on detention log)

> "You have the right to have someone informed that you have been detained. You have the right to consult privately with an independent solicitor either in person, in writing or on the telephone. Independent legal advice is available from the duty solicitor free of charge. You also have the right to consult a copy of the Codes of Practice covering police powers and procedures. You may do any of these things now, but if you do not you may still do so at any time whilst detained at the police station."

Solicitor requested   Yes ☑   No ☐
(If No, remind the person of the right to speak to a solicitor, in person, or on the telephone)

Solicitor requested   Yes ☑   No ☐
(If No, ask for and if applicable, record reason)

Name of solicitor requested   MR. ANDREW CRAWFORD

Reason, if given, for not
wanting legal advice

Notification of named person requested   Yes ☐   No ☑

Details of nominated person (if appropriate)

Name
Address

Telephone number

Details of appropriate adult (if appropriate)

Name
Address

Telephone number

An extract from a notice setting out a detained person's rights has been read to me and I have been given a copy. I have been provided with a written notice setting out a detained person's entitlements while in custody.

I ~~do~~/ do not .... want a person informed.

I understand that my right to speak to a solicitor includes the right to speak on the telephone.

I do /~~do not~~ want to speak to a solicitor at this time.

Signature *Everett*   Time 21.10   Date 30/7/00

DETENTION LOG

Surname EVERETT   Custody Record No. WE | 17963 | 9

Date	Time		Signed
30/7/00	21.10	Detention authorised for questioning. Everett informed of rights. Requested access to solicitor but no notification to a third party.	JPlatt
30/7/00	21.15	Search of Everett. Wallet marked 'A' containing £10 retained.	JPlatt
30/7/00	21.20	Telephoned Mr. Andrew Crawford, Solicitors at Everett's request. Consultation on telephone between Everett and Solicitor. Mr. Crawford asked note to be made that travelling to station to see Everett.	JPlatt
30/7/00	21.30	Everett taken cup of tea and placed in cell.	JPlatt
30/7/00	21.45	Mr. Crawford, Solicitor arrived to see Everett. Everett taken from cell to interview room by PC Smith. Private consultation with solicitor.	JPlatt
30/7/00	22.30	Everett transferred to custody of Inspector Kingston for identification parade.	Platt
30/7/00	23.05	Everett transferred to my custody by Inspector Kingston who confirmed all provisions of Identification Code complied with.	JPlatt
30/7/00	23.15	Everett transferred to custody of DC Brown. Taken to interview room. Interviewed by DC Brown in presence of WDC Carpenter and Mr Crawford, Solicitor.	JPlatt
30/7/00	23.45	Everett returned to my custody by DC Brown who stated to me that all provisions of Detention Code complied with.	JPlatt
30/7/00	23.55	Sufficient evidence to charge Everett. Everett placed in cell by PC Smith while papers prepared.	JPlatt
31/7/00	00.20	Everett charged. Copy charge supplied.	JPlatt
31/7/00	00.25	Authorised Everett to be kept in custody on grounds I believed that he would not answer bail. Informed Everett and Mr. Crawford accordingly.	JPlatt
31/7/00	00.55	Everett returned to his cell by PC Smith. Given snack and cup of tea.	Platt
31/7/00	01.00	Visited. Everett awake. Detention reviewed. No representations. Ground for detention unchanged.	JPlatt

DETENTION LOG

Surname	EVERETT	Custody Record No.	WE	17963	9

Date	Time		Signed
31/7/00	02.00	Visited. Asleep.	J Platt
31/7/00	03.00	Visited. Asleep.	J Platt
31/7/00	04.00	Visited. Asleep.	J Platt
31/7/00	05.00	Visited. Asleep.	J Platt
31/7/00	06.00	Visited. Asleep.	J Platt
31/7/00	07.00	Everett given breakfast.	J Platt
31/7/00	08.30	Transferred to custody of Group 4 Security to take to Weyford Magistrates' Court.	J Platt

(B)   Volunteer's notice

BLANKSHIRE POLICE

PERSON ATTENDING VOLUNTARILY AT POLICE STATION AND NOT UNDER ARREST

You can speak to a solicitor at the police station at any time, day or night. It will cost you nothing.

If you do not know a solicitor, or you cannot contact your own solicitor, ask for the duty solicitor. He or she is nothing to do with the police. Or you can ask to see a list of local solicitors.

You can talk to the solicitor in private on the telephone, and the solicitor may come and see you at the police station.

If the police want to question you, you can ask for the solicitor to be there. If there is a delay ask the police to contact the solicitor again. You can ask the police to wait for the solicitor to be at the interview.

The Law Society   **The Criminal Defence Service**

(C)   Notice to detained person

BLANKSHIRE POLICE

Notice to Detained Person

> The section in capital letters is to be read to the detained person by the custody officer before giving the notice to the detained person.

YOU HAVE THE RIGHT TO:

(1)   SPEAK TO AN INDEPENDENT SOLICITOR FREE OF CHARGE

(2)   HAVE SOMEONE TOLD THAT YOU HAVE BEEN ARRESTED

(3)   CONSULT THE CODES OF PRACTICE COVERING POLICE POWERS AND PROCEDURES.

YOU MAY DO ANY OF THESE THINGS NOW, BUT IF YOU DO NOT, YOU MAY STILL DO SO ANY TIME WHILST DETAINED AT THE POLICE STATION.

If you are asked questions about a suspected offence, you do not have to say anything. But it may harm your defence if you do not mention when questioned something which you later rely on in court. Anything you do say may be given in evidence.

Free Legal Advice

You can speak to a solicitor at the police station at any time, day or night. It will cost you nothing.

Access to legal advice can only be delayed in certain circumstances (see Annex B of Code of Practice C).

If you do not know a solicitor, or you cannot contact your own solicitor, ask for the duty solicitor. He or she is nothing to do with the police. Or you can ask to see a list of local solicitors.

You can talk to the solicitor in private on the telephone, and the solicitor may come to see you at the police station.

If the police want to question you, you can ask for the solicitor to be there.

If there is a delay, ask the police to contact the solicitor again. Normally, the police must not question you until you have spoken to the solicitor. However, there are certain circumstances in which the police may question you without a solicitor being present (see paragraph 6.6 of Code of Practice C).

If you want to see a solicitor, tell the custody officer at once. You can ask for legal advice at any time during your detention. Even if you tell the police you do not want a solicitor at first, you can change your mind at any time.

Your right to legal advice does not entitle you to delay procedures under the Road Traffic Act 1988 which require the provision of breath, blood and urine specimens.

THE LAW SOCIETY   The Criminal Defence Service

The right to have someone informed of your detention.

You may on request have one person known to you, or who is likely to take an interest in your welfare, informed at public expense as soon as practicable of your whereabouts. If the person you name cannot be contacted you may choose up to two alternatives. If they too cannot be contacted the custody officer has discretion to allow further attempts until the information can be conveyed. This right can only be delayed in exceptional circumstances (see Annex B of Code of Practice C).

The right to consult the Codes of Practice.

The Codes of Practice will be made available to you on request. These Codes govern police procedures. The right to consult the Codes of Practice does not entitle you to delay unreasonably any necessary investigative and administrative action, neither does it allow procedures under the Road Traffic Act of 1988 requiring the provision of breath, blood or urine specimens to be delayed.

The right to a copy of the Custody Record.

A record of your detention will be kept by the custody officer. When you leave police detention or are taken before a court, you and your legal representative or the appropriate adult shall be supplied on request with a copy of the custody record as soon as practicable. This entitlement lasts for 12 months after your release from police detention.

(D) Notice of entitlements

BLANKSHIRE POLICE

NOTICE OF ENTITLEMENTS

This notice summarises provisions contained in Codes C and D of the Codes of Practice regarding your entitlements whilst in custody. The letters and numbers in brackets relate to the appropriate Code and paragraph references. If you require more detailed information please ask to consult the Codes.

All detainees should read parts A and B of the notice. Part C explains provisions which apply to juveniles and persons suffering from a mental disorder or are mentally vulnerable and Part D explains additional provisions which apply to citizens of independent commonwealth countries and nationals of foreign countries.

PART A – GENERAL ENTITLEMENTS

Whilst in custody you are entitled to the following:–

1. **Visits and contact with outside persons**
    In addition to your rights to have someone informed of your arrest, and legal advice, you may receive visits, at the custody officer's discretion. Unless certain conditions apply you may also make one telephone call, and be supplied with writing materials ('C'5.4 and 5.6).

2. **Reasonable Standards of Physical Comfort**
    Where practicable you should have your own cell ('C'8.1), which is clean, heated, ventilated and lit ('C'8.2). Bedding should be clean and serviceable ('C'8.3).

3. **Adequate Food and Drink**
    Three meals per day. Drinks with and, upon reasonable request, between meals ('C' 8.6).

4. **Access to Toilets and Washing Facilities** ('C' 8.4).

5. **Replacement Clothing**
    If your own clothes are taken from you, you must be given replacements that are clean and comfortable ('C'8.5).

6. **Medical Attention**
    You may ask to see the police surgeon (or other doctor at your own expense) for a medical examination, or if you require medication. You may also be allowed to take or apply your own medication at appropriate times, but in the case of controlled drugs the police surgeon will supervise you when doing so ('C'9.8– 'C'9.12).

7. **Exercise**
    Where practicable, brief outdoor exercise every day ('C'8.7).

8. **If in 'Police Detention' to make representations when your detention is reviewed**
    When the grounds for your detention are periodically reviewed, you have a statutory right to say why you think you should be released, unless you are unfit to do so because of your condition or behaviour ('C'15.3 and 15.3B).

PART B – CONDUCT OF INTERVIEWS

1. Interview rooms should be adequately heated, lit and ventilated ('C'12.4).

2. Persons being interviewed should not be required to stand ('C'12.6).

3. In any 24 hour period you must be allowed at least 8 hours rest, normally at night 'C'12.2).

4. Breaks should be made at recognised meal times, and short breaks for refreshments should normally be made at intervals of approximately two hours ('C'12.7).

5. Interviewing officers should identify themselves by name and rank (or by warrant number in terrorism cases) ('C'12.7).

PART C – APPROPRIATE ADULTS

If you are under 17 years of age or suffering from a mental disorder or are mentally vulnerable, you should be assisted by an 'appropriate adult' as explained in Code C, paragraph 1.7. A solicitor present at the station in a professional capacity may not be the appropriate adult ('C' Note 1F). The appropriate adult will be present when you are:

1. informed of and served with notices explaining the rights of detained persons, and when informed of the grounds for detention ('C'3.17);

2. interviewed (except in urgent cases), or provide or sign a written statement ('C'11.12);

3. intimately searched ('C' Annex A, paragraph 5);

4. cautioned ('C'10.12);

5. given information, asked to sign documentation, or asked to give consent regarding any identification procedure ('D'2.12–2.14); or

6. charged ('C'16.1); or

7. when the grounds for detention are periodically reviewed ('C'15.3).

PART D – FOREIGN NATIONALS/COMMONWEALTH CITIZENS

If you are a citizen of a foreign or commonwealth country, you are entitled to the following:

1. To communicate at any time with your High Commission, Embassy or Consulate, and have them told of your whereabouts and the grounds for your detention ('C'7.1).

2. To private visits from a consular officer to talk, or to arrange for legal advice ('C'7.3).

(E)   Record of tape-recorded interview

BLANKSHIRE POLICE

RECORD OF TAPE RECORDED INTERVIEW

Name of person interviewed Ronald E. Everrett _____ at _____ Weyford _____ Police Station

Date of interview 30.7.0- _____ Time commenced ___ 22.30 _____ Time concluded ___ 22.45 _____

Interviewing Officer(s) ____ DC 2907 Brown _____ Tape Reference _ 9_/WPS/1697 _____

Other Person(s) Present ____ Donald Crawford Solicitor _____ Exhibit Number _____ AB/2 _____

This record consisting of   2   pages is the exhibit referred to in the statement made and signed by me. The interviewee has been cautioned
by me and informed that at the end of the interview a notice will be given to him/her about what will happen to the tapes

Signature *Alan Brown*

Signature of officer preparing record   _____
(if different from above)

Tape Times		
50		Introductions. Caution.
		You have been positively identified as the man who took away a Jaguar
		from New Street this afternoon. What do you have to say?
	R	He's wrong. It wasn't me.
	2907	Well, he's certain about it. There was £750 stolen from that car and
		in your flat there is very nearly £750 in cash. How do you
		account for that?
	R	I've saved it. We're trying to buy a house.
30	2907	And the leather jacket is just a coincidence?
	R	I've told you. I don't know anything about any of it - lots of people
		have leather jackets.
00	2907	Was your wife with you this afternoon?
	R	Yes.
	2907	She remembers it differently from you.
	R	How do you mean?
	2907	She told us all about it - that you and she took the car and stole
		the money.
	R	You're lying.
	2907	No. It's written down. Want to think again?
	R	We didn't do it.
	2907	So she's lying

CONTINUATION OF RECORD OF TAPED INTERVIEW OF   Ronald E. Everett   **PAGE**

Tape Times	
R	[No reply]
2907	Well
R	We didn't do it. It's nothing to do with us. That's final.

Signature of officer preparing record   *Alan Brown*

(F)   Written statement under caution

<u>**BLANKSHIRE POLICE**</u>

STATEMENT

Commenced: 12.15
Finished: 12.45

WEYFORD Division
G Station

23 August 200-

I make this statement of my own free will. I understand that I need not say anything unless I wish to do so but that it may harm my defence if I do not mention now something which I later rely on in court. I also understand that anything I do say may be given in evidence.

(Signed)   *June South*

I had run out of food this morning and as a friend was coming to tea this evening I had to go to the shops. I took the children on the bus into Weyford. I went to Tescos. The kids played in the shop and made a lot of noise. I decided to buy some salmon for tea. I picked out as well some toothpaste for everyone, and some bread and margarine and other things. I paid for everything in the basket but did not pay for the salmon and toothpaste. I must have put the other things into my bag by mistake as I meant to pay for them because I had enough money. I was stopped outside the shop by a store detective and taken back inside. I never meant to steal anything.

(Signed)   *June South*

Statement and signatures witnessed by A. Butchers DC 1007

(G)   Solicitor's record of attendance at police station

POLICE STATION ATTENDANCE FORM			
UFN:		Book no:	
Date:		Own/Duty	
CLIENTS DETAILS			
Name:		Address:	
Date of birth:			
Tel:			
Referral from third party: Yes/No			
Name:		Tel:	
Address:		Relationship to client:	
ARREST DETAILS			
Police station:		Custody no: Arrest/Voluntary	
Tel:		Officer in case:	
Time & Date of arrest:		Relevant time:	
Allegation (Including date):			
	F/E		**F/E**
Time of first call:		Time of request for attendance:	
Time of first contact with client:		Time of attendance:	
Time between call & contact: mins		Time between request & attendance: mins	
Delay in contact/attendance: Yes/No		If yes, reason:	
Access to client delayed: Yes/No		Extent of delay: hours	
Reason:			
Representation made: Yes/No			
Appropriate adult required: Yes/No		Name:	
Address:		Relationship to client:	
		Police contacted AA: Yes/No	
Tel:		Client advised on AA's role: Yes/No	
Attendance required because of interview/ID parade/complaint: Yes/No			
If no attendance, reason:			
If attendance, sufficient benefit test met: Yes/No			

NAME:
UFN:

TELEPHONE CALLS						
Date	Time	R/A	Person spoken to	F/E	Instructions / Advice / Action	Duration

INFORMATION FROM POLICE

Inspected custody record: Yes/No

Search of client: Yes/No Tick if intimate	Client's consent given: Yes/No

Legal authority & reason:

Evidence obtained:

Search of premises: Yes/No	Address

Legal authority & reason   S.32/S.18

Evidence obtained:

Samples taken: Yes/No	Client's consent given: Yes/No
Type: Intimate/non-intimate	Refusal implications explained: Yes/No

Legal authority & reason:

Previous questioning/interview: Yes/No

Details:

Previous attendance at police station: Yes/No	Was legal advice received: Yes/No
	Was it sought: Yes/No

Client fit for interview: Yes/No	FME called/attended: Yes/No

Co-accused: Yes/No

Name	Solicitor	Known to client?	In custody?	Conflict?

Significant statement or silence: Yes/No	Advised client to comment on this in interview: Yes/No

Consultation with officer	Name:

CONSULTATION WITH CLIENT

Previous convictions/cautions: Yes/No	
Details	

Outstanding criminal cases/on bail: Yes/No	
Details	

Health problems: Yes/No	
Details (including nature & effect of illness, & medication taken):	

FME called: Yes/No	Note in custody record: Yes/No

Other vulnerabilities (e.g. language): Yes/No	
Details	

Injuries: Yes/No	
Details (including description & cause):	

Witness to injuries: Yes/No	Name:
FME called: Yes/No	Affects fitness for IV: Yes/No
Note on custody record: Yes/No	Photographs required: Yes/No

Searches made/samples taken: Yes/No	Consent given: Yes/No

Witness(es): Yes/No	
Name & Address:	
Alibi: Yes/No	
Where & when:	
Name & Address of alibi witness:	

Advised client on implications from silence under   s34: Yes/No   s36: Yes/No   s37: Yes/No
Advised client to answer questions/remain silent/issued prepared statement Reasons:
In interview, client answered questions/remained silent/issued statement/mixed

Complaint against police: Yes/No	Advised client on procedure for
Make complaint prior to release: Yes/No	complaint: Yes/No

Note: attach clients instructions on substance of allegations and issues in dispute.
Include instructions on role of co-suspects; and anything said by them.
Keep full note of any interview.

IDENTIFICATION PROCEDURES

Obtained original description provided by each witness: Yes/No	
Advised client on methods of identification & procedure: Yes/No	
Advised client of right of refusal & implications thereof: Yes/No	
Advised client to consent to:	
Client consented to:	Representation made:
Date of ID procedure:	Place: Type:
Result:	

Witness	Identified?	Witness remarks
1.	Yes/No	
2.	Yes/No	
3.	Yes/No	
4.	Yes/No	

Make full note separately of procedure used and checks made

ATTENDANCE DETAILS

Date of attendance	Outcome (enter bail to return/place: date: time)	Fee earner attending
1.		
2.		
3.		
4.		

OUTCOME

No further action: Yes/No	
Caution/warning/reprimand: Yes/No	Advised client of implications: Yes/No
Charge: Yes/No	
Advised client on implications of reply to charge & inference from silence: Yes/No	
Advise to client: reply to charge/remain silent	
Reasons:	
Time of charge:	Reply:
Advised client on prints, photos & DNA: Yes/No	
Bail refused: Yes/No	Representations made: Yes/No
Procedure for future application explained: Yes/No	Prospects of success: low/medium/high
Bail granted: Yes/No	Explained consequences of FTA: Yes/No
Conditions:	Explained consequences of breach: Yes/No
Charge (including date):	

Court:	Venue:	Date:	Time:
File allocated to			
Costs form completed: Yes/No			

(H) Identification parade record

Name: RONALD EDWIN EVERRETT   Age   43

Address: 123, SOMERSET AVENUE,
                        WEYFORD.

I have read this notice.

I am [willing] [not willing] to attend an identification parade.
    [My reasons for not wishing to attend are:]

I am [willing] [not willing] to attend an group identification.
    [My reasons for not wishing to attend are:]

I would like the following to attend:

        Name of solicitor: MR DONALD CRAWFORD

        Address: HERRICK-BROWN & CO, 7 HIGH STREET,
                        WEYFORD, BLANKSHIRE

        Name of friend:

        Address:

        Name of parent/guardian
        or appropriate adult:

        Address:

                                Signed: Ronald E. Everett.
                                Date: 30/7/0—   Time: 22.0⁵
To be signed by the appropriate adult in the case of a juvenile or pers
who is mentally ill or mentally handicapped.

                                Signed:
                                Date: Time:

Officer serving Notice

                                Signed: Brian Kingston
                                Date: 30/7/0—   Time: 22.06

One copy should be retained and attached to the report of the
identification parade if one is held subsequently.

FORM B

REPORT OF IDENTIFICATION PARADE OR GROUP IDENTIFICATION[BOTH HEREINAFTER
REFERRED TO AS "PARADE"]

(see Notes below)

Part I

Station: WEYFORD

Place held: WEYFORD POLICE STATION

Date held: 30/7/0—

Screen used: ~~YES~~/NO   Photographed: ~~YES~~/NO

If screen used: ~~[video recorded] or~~
                        ~~[solicitor] friend] appropriate adult] present~~ — ~~Name:~~

Name of suspect: RONALD   EDWIN   EVERRETT

Offence(s) with which charged or suspected:

TAKING A CONVEYANCE WITHOUT CONSENT CONTRARY
TO S12(1) THEFT ACT 1968

THEFT OF £750 CONTRARY TO S1 THEFT ACT 1968

Notes:

1.   If the space is insufficient for the reply to any question, attach a
     continuation sheet.

2.   Form C will be completed as a record of persons forming the parade
     where their names are known to the police.

3.   All copies of Form C will then be attached to this report, together
     with a copy of Form A.

Part 1 (contd)   FORM B (contd)

Provision for a suspect who is mentally ill, mentally handicapped or a
juvenile.

Age:

Name of appropriate adult:

Address:

Relationship:

Provision for attendance of solicitor or friend.

QUESTION TO SUSPECT:

"Do you wish to have your solicitor or any friend present at this parade?"

ANSWER:

Steps taken to comply with suspect's request (to include the name and
address of solicitor/friend and the time he attended and if it was not
possible for request to be complied with, the reason for this):

MR DONALD CRAWFORD, SOLICITOR, MERRICK-BROWN + CO,
7 HIGH STREET, WEYFORD, BLANKSHIRE WAS ALREADY
PRESENT.

Note:

If the colicitor/friend is already present this should be recorded, with
his/her name and address.

I confirm immediately before the parade that the suspect had received a
Notice to the Suspect on identification parades. At 22:15 (time) on
30/7/0-. (date) I again explained to him the procedures which would be
followed during the parade and I advised him that he did not have to say
anything unless he wished to do so but that anything he did say in the
course of the parade would be recorded and might be given in evidence in
subsequent court proceedings.

Identification Officer INSPECTOR   Time: 22.19
                        KINGSTON   Brian Kingston

Witnesses will be kept in a place where they cannot see the parade or the
suspect, or hear any of the proceedings, and will be introduced one at a
time. Witnesses who have previously seen a photograph etc. or desription of
the suspect should not be shown the photograph etc. or description again
before inspecting parade.

Part 1 (contd)   FORM B (contd)

While waiting to attend the parade they should be prevented from talking with each other.

On leaving they will not be allowed to communicate with witnesses still waiting to view.

Where was the suspect placed before the parade was held and how was he introduced?

SUSPECT HELD IN INTERVIEW ROOM BEFORE PARADE

Description of the suspect and clothing:-

1m 80cm. WHITE. CLEAN SHAVEN. SHORT BROWN HAIR. WEARING OPEN NECK BLUE SHIRT AND BLUE DENIM JEANS.

Where were the witnesses placed before the parade was held and who was posted with them?

IN THE FINGERPRINT ROOM. PC SMITH WAS POSTED WITH HIM.

SKETCH PLAN

To show rooms or areas witnesses and persons standing on the parade were kept prior to their introduction to the parade.

Part II   FORM B (contd)

Time parade began: 22.20
_____

QUESTION TO SUSPECT(S)
"Do you object to any of the persons paraded?"

ANSWER (A):   NO

~~ANSWER (B):~~

State arrangements made in consequence of any objection and if any person
is replaced, cross through his name on Form C. All copies of Form C are to
be attached to the final report and not destroyed:
_____

State names of all police officers and other persons present during the
parade showing in the case of police officers, whether under instruction or
connected with the investigation of the above offence:

        INSPECTOR KINGSTON
        DC BROWN
        WDC CARPENTER   } SUBSEQUENTLY LEFT — SEE BELOW
        DONALD CRAWFORD
        PC SMITH
_____

QUESTION TO SUSPECT(S):
"Do you object to any of the other persons being present who are not on the
parade or to any of the arrangements for the parade?"

ANSWER (A):   YES, I DO NOT WISH DC BROWN OR WDC
               CARPENTER TO BE PRESENT

~~ANSWER (B):~~

Steps taken to comply with any objection:

        DC BROWN & WDC CARPENTER WERE ASKED
        TO LEAVE THE ROOM WHICH THEY DID.

Explain to your suspect(s) before the witness appears "You may select any place you like among the persons paraded." Show opposite, as is facing the parade, the position of members of the parade marking the suspect(s) as X (and Y), and giving the other participants the numbers they have on Form C. Delete excess numbers.

1	2	3	4	5	6	7	8	9	10	11	12	13	14	15	16
			X												

LEFT   RIGHT

Name of witness: JAMES WRIGHT

Address: 22, THE AVENUE, WEYFORD, BLANKSHIRE

Who ushered witness in?   PC 609 SMITH

(a) ADDRESS TO EACH WITNESS BY OFFICER IN CHARGE:

The officer should identify the occasion on which the witness saw the person whom he has come to identify and should explain to the witness that the person who he saw at the scene of the crime is not necessarily amongst those paraded. The following words are an example of those which might be used, adapted as necessary.

"Mr/Mrs/Miss/Ms ....

You have been asked here today to see if you can pick out the person whom you saw on .... at .... in .... (doing) ....

The person(s) you saw may or may not be amongst those on this parade and if you cannot make a positive identification you should say so.

I am going to ask you in a moment to walk along the line at least twice, taking as much time and care as you wish. When you have done so, I shall ask you whether the person(s) you saw on.............. is (are) here, and that if the person(s) is (are), you should indicate to me the number of the person(s) concerned."

The conduct of each witness's inspection of the parade must be reported on Part III(c). If there is more than one witness, additional copies of Part III(c) are to be attached.

Describe what witness does and says e.g. walked L to R along front, reverse at rear. If identification made, how was it made?
WALKED L to R ALONG FRONT. WALKED R TO L ALONG REAR. WHEN ASKED IF HE COULD MAKE AN IDENTIFICATION WITNESS WALKED L TO R ALONG FRONT AND SAID "I THINK IT IS NUMBER 4."

FORM B (contd)

Describe what parade was asked to do at request of witness, if applicable
e.g. walk, speak, remove hat, etc. (see Notes below)

(A) Was (Suspect) RONALD EDWIN EVERRETT.... identified?   YES

    Did he/~~she~~ say anything? (if identified) ~~If Yes, what~~ ...NO.........

(B) Was ....* identified?

    Did he/she say anything? (if identified) If Yes, what ....

    * Insert name(s) of suspect(s)

Any comments made by suspect after witness left:

    SUSPECT SAID "HE'S WRONG."

Where was the witness taken after the parade, who escorted him there and
who was posted with him?

WITNESS TAKEN BACK TO FINGERPRINT ROOM BY PC SMITH
WHO REMAINED WITH HIM THERE UNTIL PARADE
WAS CONCLUDED

               Signed: Brian Kingston   Time: 22.28

               Identification Officer

Notes:

It may sometimes happen that a witness desires to see the suspect with a
hat on or off and there is no objection to the persons paraded thereupon
being asked to wear or remove hats. If a witness asks to hear members of
the parade speak or see them move, he should be asked whether he can first
identify any persons on the parade on the basis of appearance only, and his
reply should be noted. When the request is to hear members of the parade
speak, he should be reminded that the participants in the parade have been
chosen on the basis of physical appearance only. Members of the parade may
then be asked to comply with the witness's request to hear them speak or
see them move. Full details of the incident, including the stages at which
any identification was made, should be recorded.

To be completed for each witness inspecting the parade

After the last witness has left:

QUESTION TO SUSPECT(S)

"Do you wish to make any comments on the conduct of this parade?"

ANSWER (A):   NO

~~ANSWER (B):~~

Time parade finished: 22:30

Remarks on any point not already covered:

I certify that the above parade took place in accordance with the code of practice. I am not involved with the investigation of the case.

Signature and rank of Identification Officer: Brian Kingston
                                                        INSPECTOR

Date signed: 30/7/0—   Time: 22:32

Attach completed Form C and a copy of Form A.

RECORD OF PERSONS FORMING IDENTIFICATION PARADE ~~OR GROUP IDENTIFICATION~~

DATE HELD: 30/7/0 —

Name(s) of suspect(s): RONALD EDWIN EVERETT   Ref No:

Details of persons forming the parade
N.B. For parade not videoed or photographed include age, height, and dress.

	Signature for Expenses
1. Name MICHAEL JAMES WRIGHT Address Age 35 Height 1m 85 Dress BLUE JEANS, WHITE SHIRT	MJ Wright
2. Name HENRY PHILIP JONES Address Age 38 Height 1m 99 Dress BLUE JEANS, GREY SHIRT	HP Jones
3. Name DAVID BERTRAM RICHARDS Address Age 44 Height 1m 82 Dress BLUE JEANS, BLUE T SHIRT	David Richards
4. Name MAURICE ALAN HARMER Address Age 41 Height 1m 85 Dress BLUE JEANS BLUE SHIRT	Maurice A Harmer
5. Name WAYNE JEROME BINDMAN Address Age 39 Height 1m 80 Dress BLUE JEANS, YELLOW SHIRT	Wayne Bindman.
6. Name CHARLES EDWARD SORWIND Address Age 32 Height 1m 83 Dress BLUE JEANS, PINK SHIRT	Charles Sorwind.
7. Name DAMIAN LITTLETON Address Age 40 Height 1m 78 Dress BLUE JEANS, WHITE SHIRT	Damian Littleton
8. Name CHRISTOPHER EDWARD HILL Address Age 34 Height 1m 74 Dress BLUE JEANS, YELLOW SHIRT	CHill

Note: (Continue overleaf if necessary)

1.   If the suspect objects to any of the persons forming the parade, that person should not be used and his name and details should be crossed through.
2.   If a parade is held without a solicitor or friend of the suspect being present, a colour photograph of the parade shall be taken unless any member of the parade objects. A copy of the photograph shall be supplied on request to the suspect of his solicitor within a reasonable time.
3.   When a group identification is held in a public place, it will not normally be practicable to note the details of persons involved or to take a photograph.

(I)   Charge sheet

COURT COPY

Police Station	WEYFORD	Custody No	WGG/0-/33
Station Code	WFF		
Charged Persons Surname	DOE	Title	MR
Forenames	JOHN		
Place of Birth	GUILDFORD	Date of Birth	01/02/34
Address	NO FIXED ABODE		
	WOODBRIDGE MEADOWS		
	WEYFORD WE1 1AA		

You are charged with the offence/s shown below.
You do not have to say anything. But it may harm your defence if you do not mention anything now something which you later rely on in court.
Anything you do say may be given in evidence.

Page 1 of 1

No: 1   Crime No: WG/0-/1234   Local Code: C203

ON MONDAY 15TH MAY 200- AT WEYFORD IN THE COUNTY OF BLANKSHIRE STOLE AN AIRMAIL LETTER OF A VALUE UNKNOWN BELONGING TO CHARLES BLAKE

CONTRARY TO SECTION 1(1) OF THE THEFT ACT 1968

Reply to charges

None

Charged Persons Signature _JDoe_

Person Charging Name
Signature _____

Officer Charging Name
Signature _____   PS/333/DICKSON

Officer In Case   INSP/N/MEAD

Charged 17/6/0-
Time 10.30 am
Date

CHARGE RECORD

DETAINEE COPY

Police Station	WEYFORD	Custody No	WGG/0-/33
Station Code	WFF		
Charged Persons Surname	DOE	Title	MR
Forenames	JOHN		
Place of Birth	GUILDFORD	Date of Birth	01/02/34
Address	NO FIXED ABODE		
	WOODBRIDGE MEADOWS		
	WEYFORD WE1 1AA		

You are charged with the offence/s shown on the charge sheet.

You do not have to say anything. But it may harm your defence if you do not mention anything now something which you later rely on in court.
Anything you do say may be given in evidence.

YOU ARE REQUIRED TO ATTEND COURT

at WEYFORD MAGS CT

on 20/06/0-   at 10.00am.

If you fail without reasonable cause to surrender to the Court at the appointed place and time, you commit an offence for which you may be fined, imprisoned or both.

LEGAL AID

IF YOU REQUIRE LEGAL REPRESENTATION AT COURT AND CANNOT AFFORD A SOLICITOR YOU MAY BE ENTITLED TO LEGAL AID. IF YOU WISH TO APPLY FOR LEGAL AID A SPECIAL FORM IS OBTAINABLE FROM ANY POLICE STATION, MAGISTRATES CLERKS OFFICE, OR A SOLICITOR DEALING IN CRIMINAL LEGAL AID CASES.

YOU SHOULD MAKE YOUR APPLICATION IMMEDIATELY

THE COURT WILL NOT AUTOMATICALLY ADJOURN THE CASE WHEN THERE HAS BEEN A DELAY IN APPLYING FOR LEGAL AID.

PRODUCTION OF DRIVING LICENCE

If the offence with which you have been charged is one for which your driving licence may be endorsed (and the Inspector or Sergeant on duty at the station will advise you) you are required to have your driving licence at Court when you appear. If you are convicted you may be required to produce the licence.
FAILURE TO PRODUCE IT IS AN OFFENCE AND THE LICENCE IS AUTOMATICALLY SUSPENDED UNTIL IT IS PRODUCED.

(Section 101(4), Road Traffic Act, 1988).

Custody Officer	PS/333/DICKSON
Signature	

(J)   Summons

In Blankshire

Petty Sessional Division of Weyford

To: James Baker..the Defendant

of   18 Dorset Avenue   Date of Birth: 20.8.1958

Weyford   Unemployed

Blankshire   being the last known or usual place of above

BE1 8BT

THE INFORMATION of Barry Williams Sgt 891 of Blankshire Constabulary this day laid before me that you the Defendant, on 20th August 200–, at Station Road, Weyford in the said County drove a Ford Contrary to s. 2 Road Traffic Act 1988

Barry Williams

YOU THE DEFENDANT ARE THEREFORE HEREBY SUMMONED to appear on 1st November 200–, at 10.00 before the Magistrates' Court sitting at The Law Courts, The Civic Centre, Weyford, Blankshire to answer the said information.

DATED this 25th September 200–

Paul French

Justice of the Peace

LEGAL AID:— If you require details you should immediately communicate with the Clerk to the Justices at the address on the notice herewith.

CERTIFICATE OF SERVICE
(Magistrates' Courts Rules, 1981, Rule 67(2))

Defendant ___JAMES   BAKER_____

I HEREBY CERTIFY that I this day served the within-named defendant with a document of which this is a true copy, in the manner shown a (a) below.

(a)   By sending it by post to him in a prepaid recorded delivery letter posted by me on   5-10-200—
at the   WEYFORD   Post Office situated at   HIGH STREET, WEYFORD
addressed as overleaf being his last known place of abode.

(b)   Delivering to him personally.

(c)   By leaving it for him with a person at the address overleaf, being the defendant's last known place of abode.

(d)   By sending it by post in a prepaid recorded delivery letter posted by me on
at the   Post Office situated at
to the registered office of the defendant company.

Dated this   5th   day of OCTOBER   20 0 —

_____J.C. Waiter_____ Signature

(K)   Application for the right to representation in criminal proceedings: Magistrates' court or Crown Court (Form A)

Application for the Right to Representation in Criminal Proceedings: Magistrates' Court or Crown Court

Form A

I apply for the right to representation for the purposes of proceedings before the   Crown Court ☐   Magistrates' court ☑   Youth court ☐

I. Personal details

Ia	Surname	PRESCOTT
Ib	Forename(s)	JAKE
Ic	Title *Mr, Mrs, Miss, Ms, or another*	MR

Id Date of birth   17.06.1983

Ie Home address
10 AGRARIA ROAD
WEYFORD
WE2 7AF

If Present address
If different from above

2. Case details

2a What charges have been brought against you? *Describe briefly what it is that you are accused of doing. For example, theft of £10 worth of CDs, or assault on a neighbour.*

ROBBERY OF A GAMEBOY ADVANCE MACHINE FROM A 14 YEAR OLD BOY IN A PEDESTRIAN SUBWAY DURING THE HOURS OF DARKNESS.

2b Are there any co-defendants in this matter?

No ☐   Yes ☑ If **Yes**, give their names

NOEL ALEXANDER

2c Give reasons why you and your co-defendants cannot be represented by the same solicitors

THERE IS A CONFLICT OF INTEREST. HE CLAIMS THAT I TOOK PART IN THE ROBBERY AND FORCED HIM TO PARTICIPATE. I DENY BEING PRESENT.

3. The Court Proceedings

3a I am due to appear before

> The NEWTOWN   magistrates'court [✓] youth court [ ]
>
> **or**
>
> Date 21.01.200—   at 10 am / ~~pm~~

3b I appeared before

> The   magistrates'court [ ] youth court [ ]
>
> Date   at   am / pm

and

Tick whichever applies

> My case has been sent to the Crown Court for trial under Section 51 of the Crime and Disorder Act 1998 [ ]
>
> My case has been transferred to the Crown Court for trial [ ]
>
> I was convicted and committed for sentence to the Crown Court [ ]
>
> I was convicted and/or sentenced and I wish to appeal against the conviction/sentence [ ]

4. Outstanding matters

If there are any other **outstanding** criminal charges or cases against you, give details including the court where you are due to appear

> N/A

5. Reasons for wanting representation

To avoid the possiblity of your application being delayed, or publicly funded representation being refused because the court does not have enough information about the case, you must complete the rest of this form.

When deciding whether to grant publicly funded representation, the court will need to know why it is in the interests of justice for you to be represented.

If you need help in completing the form you should speak to a solicitor.

Details	Reason(s) for grant or refusal **For court use only**
5a It is likely that I will lose my liberty *You should consider seeing a solicitor before answering this question*	I HAVE PREVIOUS CONVICTIONS FOR OFFENCES OF VIOLENCE AND DISHONESTY. THE VICTIM WAS A SCHOOLBOY, ALONE IN A PEDESTRIAN SUBWAY DURING THE HOURS OF DARKNESS.

5. Reasons for wanting representation *continued*

Details

Reason(s) for grant or refusal
For court use only

5b I am currently subject to a sentence that is suspended or non-custodial that if breached may allow the court to deal with me for the original offence
Please give details

> PROBATION ORDER FOR THEFT, IMPOSED BY WESTVILLE MAGISTRATES' COURT FOR 2 YEARS ON _____ .

5c It is likely that I will lose my livelihood

5d It is likely that I will suffer serious damage to my reputation

5e A substantial question of law is involved
You will need the help of a solicitor to answer this question

> *Please give authorities to be quoted with law reports' references* CASE INVOLVES:
> • DISPUTED IDENTIFICATION (TURNBULL GUIDELINES APPLY)
> • CHALLENGING ADMISSIBILITY OF CONFESSION (ss 76 + 78 PACE)
> • ADVERSE INFERENCES (s 34 CJPO ACT 1996)

5f I shall be unable to understand the court proceedings or state my own case because:
  i)   My understanding of English is inadequate
  ii) I suffer from a disability

5g Witnesses have to be traced and/or interviewed on my behalf
State the circumstances

> AT THE TIME OF THE ALLEGED OFFENCE, I WAS IN AN AMUSEMENT ARCADE. AS WELL AS A FRIEND WHO WAS WITH ME, THERE MAY BE OTHER WITNESSES WHO SAW ME THERE.

5h The case involves expert cross examination of a prosecution witness
Give brief details

> THE POLICE OFFICER WHO INTERVIEWED ME AS TO BREACHES OF PACE AND THE CODES, THE VICTIM AS TO MISTAKEN IDENTIFICATION. MY CO-ACCUSED AS TO IMPLICATING ME.

5. Reasons for wanting representation *continued*

Details

5i   It is in someone else's interests that I am represented

> IT IS NOT APPROPRIATE THAT A SCHOOLBOY BE CROSS-EXAMINED IN PERSON BY ONE OF HIS ALLEGED ATTACKERS.

5j   Any other reasons
Give full particulars

> I INTEND TO PLEAD NOT GUILTY AND THE TRIAL WILL TAKE PLACE AT NEWTOWN CROWN COURT.

6. Legal representation

a)   If you do not give the name of a solicitor, the court will select a solicitor for you.

b)   You must tell the solicitor that you have named him.

c)   If you have been charged together with another person or persons, the court may assign a solicitor other than the solicitor of your choice.

The solictor I wish to act for me is:

> JOHN SMITH

Give the firm's name and address (if known)

> COLLANS SOLICITORS, 14 THE HIGH STREET, NEWTOWN NA17 2BA

Declaration to be completed on behalf of the solicitor named above

i)   I certify that the named solicitor above has a crime franchise contract or a general criminal contract, or an individual case contract.

ii)   I understand that only firms with a general criminal contract or individual case contract may provide representation in the magistrates' court.

Signed_____   Date_____

7. Declaration

> If you knowingly make a statement which is false, knowingly withhold information, you may be prosecuted.
>
> If convicted, you may be sent to prison for up to three months or be fined or both (*section 21 Access to Justice Act 1999*)

I apply for representation for the charge(s) that are currently before the court.

I understand that should my case proceed to the Crown Court or any higher court, the court may order that I pay for some or all of the costs of representation incurred in the proceedings by way of a Recovery of Defence Costs Order.

I understand that should my case proceed to the Crown Court or any higher court, I will have to furnish details of my means to the court and/or the Legal Services Commission.

Signed _Jake Prescott_   Date _14·01·0—_

For Court use only

Any additional factors considered when determining the application, including any information given orally

Decision on Interests of Justice Test

I have considered all available details of all the charges and it /it is not in the interests of justice that representation be granted for the following reasons:

Signed _____ Appropriate officer

Date | | | | | | | |

To be completed where the right to representataion extends to the Crown Court

Statement of Means Form B given to the defendant on *(date)*_____

Indicate type of case:

Indictable only   Yes ☐   No ☐

Section 51 offence   Yes ☐   No ☐

Either-way offence and
elected/not suitable for summary trial   Yes ☐   No ☐

First date of hearing at the Crown Court   _____

(L)   Representation order: Magistrates' court

WEYFORD MAGISTRATES' COURT

Court Code: 2936
Reference: LA/2936/00/1341
Date of Hearing: –

REPRESENTATION ORDER (MAGISTRATES' COURT)

In accordance with the Access to Justice 1999 the Court now grants representation to   for the following purpose:

Delete (1) to (4) as necessary.

(1)   Proceedings before a Magistrates' Court in connection with

(2)   Appealing to Crown Court against a decision of the Magistrates' Court on

(3)   Resisting an appeal to the Crown Court against a decision of the Magistrate Court

(4)   Proceedings for (both a Magistrates' Court and *) the Crown Court in connection with   including in the event of his being convicted or sentenced in those proceedings, advice and assistance in regard to the making of an appeal to the Criminal Division of the Court of Appeal.

The representation granted shall consist of the following:—

Magistrates' Court proceedings*—

Solicitor
Solicitor and Junior Counsel

Crown Court proceedings*—

Solicitor
Solicitor and Junior Counsel
Solicitor and Queen's Counsel (only available where the offence charged is murder)
Solicitor, Junior Counsel and Queen's Counsel (only available where prosecution brought by Serious Fraud Office)

including advice on the preparation of the case for the proceedings.

The Solicitor/Counsel assigned is
of

The assisted person has been committed to   prison/released on bail and may be communicated with at

...............................(signed)   ....(dated)

* Delete as necessary

(M) Record of decision to grant or withhold bail and certificate as to hearing on application for bail

WEYFORD MAGISTRATES' COURT

Date 31/7/2000   Accused RONALD EDWIN EVERETT   Date of birth 25/6/1943

Alleged offence(s) TAKING A CONVEYANCE , THEFT

BAIL

The accused is granted bail (subject to the conditions set out below) with a duty to surrender to the custody of

☑ WEYFORD   Magistrates'/~~Youth~~ Court at Weyford

on Monday -day the 14ᵗʰ August   at 9.45 am/~~pm~~

☐ the Crown Court at Guildford/   at 10am on   or on such a day and at such a time and place as may be notified to the accused by the appropriate officer of that court

N.B. If you fail to surrender to bail or to comply with bail conditions you may be arrested and taken into custody.

Failure to surrender to bail is an offence punishable with imprisonment and/or a fine.

Conditions to be complied with

Before release

☑ To provide   1   suret(y)~~(ies)~~ in the sum of £ 500   ~~(each)~~   ☐ To surrender passport to police

☐ To provide a security in the sum of £   to be deposited with the court

After release

☐ To live and sleep each night at   ☐ To abide by the rules of the hostel

☐ To remain indoors at   between the hours of

☐ To report to Weyford   Police Station each Wednesday and Saturday   between 1900 — 2100 hours

☐ Not to go

except to see solicitor by prior written appointment or to attend court

☐ To make himself available as and when required to enable pre-sentence/medical report to be prepared

☐ Not to contact directly or indirectly

☐

☐

The reasons for imposing conditions are to ensure that the accused:-

☑ surrenders to custody   ☐ does not commit an offence while on bail

☐ does not interfere with witnesses or obstruct the course of justice

☐ is available to enable enquiries or a report to be made   ☐ goes to see his solicitor (legal representative)

CUSTODY

The court withholds bail, having found the exception(s) to the right to bail specified in the first column of the schedule hereto (and applying the exception(s) for the reasons specified in the second column)

☐ The accused is remanded in custody for appearance before WEYFORD Magistrates'/Youth Court at Weyford   at 10 am on

☐ The accused is committed in custody for appearance before the Crown Court at Weyford on   at 10 am or on such a day and at such a time and place as may be notified to the accused by the appropriate officer of that court

☐ The accused has consented to the hearing and determination in his absence of future applications for remand in custody and the notice overleaf applies

SCHEDULE

EXCEPTIONS TO THE RIGHT TO BAIL - SCHED. 1	REASONS FOR APPLYING EXCEPTIONS (pt I, paras 2, 2A)
Indictable/either-way cases (Part I, para 2A)	☐ Nature and seriousness of offence and likely conclusion
☐ Alleged offence committed while on bail	☐ Character, antecedents and lack of community ties
Imprisonable (Part I, paras 2(a)-(c), 5, 7)	☐ Accused's record under previous grants of bail
☐ Belief would fail to surrender	☐ Strength of evidence against accused
☐ Belief would commit offence while on bail	☐
☐ Belief would interfere with witnesses or obstruct the course of justice	☐
☐ Insufficient information for bail decision	
☐ Otherwise impracticable to complete enquiries or make report	**CERTIFICATE OF FULL ARGUMENT**
All cases (Pt I, paras 3, 4, 6; Pt II, paras 3, 4, 5)	I hereby certify that at the hearing today the court heard full argument on application for bail by or on behalf of accused and
☐ Serving a custodial sentence	☐ that the court has not previously heard full argument in these proceedings (except at the last hearing)
☐ For accused's (protection) (welfare) (youths only)	☐ that the following new considerations/change in circumstances apply
☐ Arrested for absconding or breaching bail conditions	
Non-imprisonable (Part II, para 2)	
☐ Previous failure to answer bail and belief would fail to surrender to custody	Signed Ian Gallagher Clerk of the Court present during the proceedings

| Solicitor | FEB 2000 |

(N)   Witness statement

BLANKSHIRE POLICE

Statement or Section	WEYFORD	Division	G
		Date	23rd August 200-

Statement of (name of witness) _____ IAN GOVERN
(In full - Block Letters)

Date and place of birth   25.8.1954   Cardiff

This statement, (consisting of   1   pages each signed by me), is true to the best of my knowledge and belief and I make it knowing that, if it is tendered in evidence, I shall be liable to prosecution if I wilfully stated in it anything which I know to be false or do not believe to be true.

Dated the   23rd   day of   August   20 0-

Signature ...*Ian Govern*...

.... being unable to read the above statement I ....
of ....read it to him before he signed it.

Dated the   day of   20

I am the manager of Tesco Supermarket, Oxford Street, Weyford. At about 11.15 a.m. on Monday 23rd August I was called to my office by Mr. Astor Teck who is employed as a security officer by Tesco Limited. A woman I now know to be Mrs. June South was in the office with her three children. In my presence Mr. Teck went through the cash receipt and checked it against the items in Mrs South's shopping bag.   Five items appeared not to have been paid for, two 7 oz tins of John West Salmon and three large tubes of Gibbs S.R. Toothpaste. These I identified as coming from this store by the price ticket on them. The goods were recovered from Mrs. South No one has authority to take items from this store without payment.

Signature ...*Ian Govern*..........................

Taken by ...*A.Butchers PC 1007*...............

(continued overleaf)

Address 2A, The Parade, Weyford
Blankshire   WE9 6BB

Telephone Number W 686872   Occupation Retail Manager

Dates to avoid:
18-12-0- -- 8-1-0

(O) Criminal Procedure and Investigations Act 1996 Part I: Disclosure — Rights and duties of accused persons

(Home Office Circular 11/1997)

1.   The Criminal Procedure and Investigations Act 1996 makes important changes to the law on prosecution and defence disclosure in criminal cases. This notice sets out your rights and duties under the relevant provisions. Please read it carefully and show it to your solicitor if you have one.

2.   Although this notice is sent to you by the prosecutor, he cannot advise you on its contents and you should not approach him for advice.

Disclosure by the accused

3.   Before the trial begins, the prosecutor must disclose to you prosecution material which he thinks might undermine the case against you. If there is no such material, he must write to you to say so. In either case, he must also send you a schedule of non-sensitive material at the same time.

4.   If your case is to be tried in the Crown Court, you must give the prosecutor and the court a 'defence statement' containing certain information about your defence. This must –
    (a)   set out in general terms the nature of your defence, ie the reasons for your intention to plead not guilty,
    (b)   state the matters on which you disagree with the prosecution, and
    (c) state in each case the reason why you disagree.

5.   If you have an alibi, you must give details of the alibi in the defence statement, including –
    (a)   if you know it, the name and address of any witness you believe is able to give evidence in support of the alibi, or
    (b)   any information you may have which might be useful in finding any such witness.

'Evidence in support of an alibi' means 'evidence tending to show that by reason of the presence of the accused at a particular place or in a particular area at a particular time he was not, or was unlikely, to have been at the place where the offence is alleged to have been committed at the time of its alleged commission'.

6.   You may give the defence statement within 14 days of the prosecutor making disclosure to you. The 14-day period starts on the date when the prosecutor writes to you, not the day when you receive his letter. If you cannot give a defence statement within 14 days, you may ask the court for more time. The court will want to know why you cannot do so, and how much more time you need. If you apply for more time, you must –
    (a)   do so before the 14 days are up, and
    (b)   give the pprosecutor a copy of your application.

7.   Section 11 of the Act says that if you fail to comply with these requirements, certain consequences follow. You fail to comply with these requirements if you:
    (a)   do not give a defence statement, or
    (b)   give a defence statement after the end of the 14-day period, or after the end of any longer period of time allowed by the court, or
    (c)   set out inconsistent defences in the defence statement, or

(d)   put forward a defence at trial which is different from any defence set out in the defence statement, or

(e)   put forward evidence in support of an alibi at trial, without giving details of the alibi in the defence statement, or

(f)   call a witness in support of an alibi at trial without giving details of the witness in the defence statement.

8.   If you fail to comply with these requirements, the court (or, if the court allows, any other party) may comment on the failure to comply, and the jury may draw such inferences as appear proper in deciding whether you are guilty.

9.   If you put forward a defence at trial which is different from any defence set out in the defence statement, then (when deciding whether to comment on the failure to comply) the court must consider the extent of the difference in the defences, and whether there is any justification for it.

10.   You cannot be convicted solely on the basis of an inference drawn from a failure to comply with these requirements.

11.   If your case is to be tried in a magistrates' court, you may give a defence statement if you wish (for example, to get further prosecution disclosure) but you are not required to do so. If you do not give a defence statement, no inference may be drawn. If you do give a defence statement the same procedures apply as if your case was being tried in the Crown Court (paragraphs 4–10 above), except that there is no jury but the court may draw inferences from a failure to comply with the relevant requirements.

12.   If you decide not to give a defence statement, your case may come to court more quickly if you tell the court and the prosecutor before the end of the 14-day period.

Right of accused person to apply for additional prosecution disclosure

13.   If you give a defence statement, the prosecutor must then disclose to you any additional prosecution material which might reasonably be expected to assist the defence which you disclosed in your defence statement. If there is no such material, he must write to you to say so.

14.   After this, if you have reason to believe that there is more prosecution material which has not been disclosed to you and which might reasonably be expected to assist the defence which you disclosed in your defence statement, you may apply to the court for an order to disclose it. You must –

(a)   identify the material you need, and

(b)   tell the court why you think it might assist your defence.

If you apply to the court, you must give the prosecutor a copy of your application. If you contact the prosecutor first, you may be able to obtain the material you need without having to apply to the court.

Right of accused person to apply for review of a non-disclosure ruling

15.   If the prosecutor has material which he ought to disclose to you, but which is sensitive for some reason, he may apply to the court for a ruling that on balance it is not in the public interest to disclose it.

16.   If the court rules against disclosure, you may ask the court to review its ruling. If you do so, you must –

(a)   say why you think the ruling should be reviewed, and

(b)   give the prosecutor a copy of your application.

Duty to disclose material in confidence

17.   You may use material disclosed to you for the purposes of your trial, or (if you are convicted) in connection with any appeal. If you want to use the material for any other purpose, you must first apply to the court for permission to do so, and say why you want to use it. You must also give a copy of your application to the prosecutor.

18.   If you use the material for any other purpose without getting the permission of the court, you may be liable to proceedings for contempt of court. If the court finds you guilty of contempt, it may commit you to custody for a specified period or fine you or both.

(P) Notice to accused: Right to object to written statement or deposition

FORM 14A

Notice to accused: right to object to written statement or deposition being read out at trial without further proof (CPI Act 1996, s 68, Sch 2, paragraphs 1(3)(c) and 2(3)(c): MC Rules 1981, r 4B (as inserted by MC (Amendment) Rules 1997)

To AB, of

If you are committed for trial, the Crown Court may try you in respect of the charge or charges on which you are committed or in respect of any other charge arising out of the same transaction or set of circumstances which may, with leave of the Court, be put to you.

[Written statements] [and] [depositions] have been made by the witness named below and copies of their [statements] [and] [depositions] are enclosed. Each of these [statements] [and] [depositions] will be read out at the trial without oral evidence being given by the witness who has made the [statement] [or] [deposition] unless you want that witness to give oral evidence and to be cross-examined on such oral evidence. If you want any of these witnesses to give oral evidence, and be cross-examined if necessary, you should inform the Crown Court and me in writing within 14 days of being committed for trial. If you do not do so you will lose your right to prevent the [statement] [or] [deposition] being read out without any oral evidence being given by the witness in question and to require the attendance of that witness unless the Court gives you leave to do so, but that will not prevent the prosecutor from exercising his discretion to call that witness to give oral evidence, and be cross-examined, at the trial if the prosecutor so wishes.

[* [Pre-paid] reply forms [and pre-paid envelopes] are enclosed and if you object to any [statement] [or] [deposition] being read out at the trial without oral evidence being given by the witness who made it you must let the Crown Court and myself know within 14 days of being committed for trial, and at the same time indicate which of these witnesses you want to give oral evidence at the trial.

If you have a solicitor acting for you in your case you should hand this notice and the [statements] [and] [depositions] to him at once, so that he may deal with them].

Names of witnesses whose [statements] [and] [depositions] are enclosed:–

Address any reply to:–

(Signed) ....

[On behalf of the Prosecutor]

* Omit if documents are sent to accused's solicitor.

(Q)   Statement of means for right to representation in criminal proceedings in the Crown Court (Form B)

Statement of Means for
Right to Representation in
Criminal Proceedings in the Crown Court

Form B

Reference

Now that you have been granted publicly funded representation in the Crown Court you must complete this form and return it to the court at least **4 days** before your first hearing at the Crown Court. If you do not comply, the judge may make a Court Order against you requiring you to pay for all costs incurred in your defence.

If you or your partner are receiving one of the following benefits, you are only required to complete Parts 1 and 2A of this form:

■ Income-based Job Seeker's Allowance
■ Income Support
■ Working Families' Tax Credit
■ Disabled Person's Tax Credit

If you indicate one of the above, and no further enquiries are made of you or your partner, only this information will go before the judge to consider whether to make a Recovery of Defence Costs Order.

A partner is a person with whom the applicant lives as a couple and includes a person with whom the person concerned is not currently living but from whom he or she is not living separate and apart.

You should inform the Court if your circumstances change once you have completed this form and returned it to the Crown Court.

See the Declaration at the end of this form for enquiries that can be made about the information you provide.

Part 1 - Personal details

1a	Surname	PRESCOTT
1b	Surname at birth *If different*	
1c	Title *Mr/Mrs/Miss/Ms/other*	MR
1d	Date of birth	17 · 06 · 198—
1e	Forename(s)	JAKE
1f	Home address *Including postcode*	10 KERARIA ROAD WEYFORD WE2 7AF
1g	Address where we can contact you *If different from above*	

1h   Marital status
Tick as appropriate

Single ✓   Cohabiting ☐   Widowed ☐

Married ☐   Married but separated ☐   Divorced ☐

Part 2 - Financial position

Part A - Benefits

If you or your partner receive Income-based Job Seeker's Allowance, Income Support, Working Families' Tax Credit or Disabled Person's Tax Credit, please provide the following details:

(i) The address of the Social Security Office or Jobcentre or Tax Credit Office that is dealing with you or your partner's claim

> 1 HIGH STREET
> NEWTOWN
> NE 19 2BX

(ii) National Insurance number of the person claiming benefit.

This is required so that we can verify your, or your partner's, claim with the Benefits Agency or Inland Revenue

> NA 37 81 26 X

(iii) Name of Benefit

> JOB SEEKER'S ALLOWANCE

(iv) Name of recipient of Benefit

> JAKE PRESCOTT

(v) Date of birth of recipient of Benefit

> 17 . 06 . 198—

Please go to the end of the form and sign the Declarations if you have completed this section.

Part B - Income from work

In this section you are asked to give details of the money you receive.

You should answer these questions with annual amounts. Where you are paid monthly, multiply the amount by 12 or where you are paid weekly, multiply the amount by 52.

	You	Your partner	Additional details	Court use
1 Provide details of gross earnings, including bonuses, overtime or commission				
Do you or your partner receive benefits from work that are not money? *For example: luncheon vouchers, company car, free health insurance etc. Please specify*	Yes ☐ No ☐	Yes ☐ No ☐		
Employer's name and address				
2 Are you or your partner, self-employed / in partnership?	Yes ☐ No ☐	Yes ☐ No ☐	(i) Turnover	
Indicate nature of work for you and/or your partner			(ii) Business expenses (not taken out for personal use)	
Indicate you and/or your partner's role in company			(iii) Net profit (Turnover minus business expenses) (iv) Period of trading	

Part B - Income (continued)

		You		Your partner		Additional details	Court use
3	Part-time work : gross earnings including bonuses, commission and overtime						
	Employer's name and address						
4	Are you or your partner a shareholder in a private limited company, or are you or your partner a company director?	Yes ☐	No ☐	Yes ☐	No ☐	Provide details for you and/or your partner.	
5	Is anybody else, including a company or other body, supporting either you or your partner financially or making resources available to either of you?	Yes ☐	No ☐	Yes ☐	No ☐	Examples of non-financial support may include the following: Do you live in someone else's house or drive someone else's car? Indicate the nature of the support and what period this support covered. Provide details of connection to individual or company, and name the individual or company.	
6	Do you receive any other income not mentioned in any of the above questions?	Yes ☐	No ☐	Yes ☐	No ☐	Indicate the nature of this income. For example, an allowance or income from trust. Indicate how often this income is received.	
7	Do you receive any income from state benefits? *Give details of benefit received, how much and how often*	Yes ☐	No ☐	Yes ☐	No ☐		

Part C - Capital and Savings
Please provide details of all your capital and savings.

		You	Your partner	Additional details	Court use
1	**Main dwelling** Do you and/or your partner own the house/property that you treat as your main dwelling?	Yes ☐ No ☐	Yes ☐ No ☐	If **Yes**, please provide the following details: i) What is the outstanding mortgage on your property? ii) What is its current market value? iii) What share do you own in this property and if not shared with your partner, who do you own this property with? iv) What type of property is this? *For example, flat* v) How many bedrooms does this property have?	
2	**Other property** Do you and/or your partner own any other property?	Yes ☐ No ☐	Yes ☐ No ☐	If **Yes**, provide the following details: i) What is the outstanding mortgage on this property? ii) What is its current market value? iii) What share do you own in this property and if not with your partner, who do you own this property with? iv) What type of property is this? *For example, flat* v) How many bedrooms does this property have?	

Part C - Capital and Savings (continued)

		You	Your partner	Additional details	Court use
3	Savings *Please provide details of savings, including money in the bank, building society, or at home or in current accounts, National Savings Certificates, ISA's.*			If you have savings certificates, provide details of the issue and how many units you have	
4	Do you and/or your partner own any stocks or shares? *Include Unit Trusts, PEPs or ISAs.*	Yes ☐ No ☐	Yes ☐ No ☐	If **Yes**, please provide details of the company and name of the fund if appropriate. Also provide the present value and the amount of the yearly dividend	
5	Do you and/or your partner have any rights under a trust fund?	Yes ☐ No ☐	Yes ☐ No ☐	If **Yes**, what are the details of the fund and what rights do you have?	
6	Articles of value *Please provide details of any articles of value that you and/or your partner own, and their approximate value.*			Include antiques, jewellery, art etc.	
7	Do you or your partner have any other capital assets that you have not indicated above?	Yes ☐ No ☐	Yes ☐ No ☐	If **Yes**, please provide details of the same	

Part D - Financial commitments

		You		Your partner		Additional details	Court use
1	Do you have any dependants who live with you?	Yes ☐	No ☐	Yes ☐	No ☐	If **Yes**, please provide details of how many, their relationship and their ages.	
2	Do you and/or your partner have any financial orders that this court should know about?	Yes ☐	No ☐	Yes ☐	No ☐	If **Yes**, please indicate the nature of the order(s) and the amount(s).	
3	How much do you and/or your partner pay in housing costs?					Provide details of rent or mortgage on your main dwelling. Indicate the period that this amount covers.	

Part E - Further information

		You		Your partner		Additional details	Court use
1	Has any other person been paying towards your legal costs and expenses in these or any other proceedings prior to your grant of representation?	Yes ☐	No ☐			If **Yes**, please provide details of the amount and from whom this support came. Indicate their relationship.	
2	Are any of your and/or your partner's assets subject to a mareva injunction or freezing order?	Yes ☐	No ☐	Yes ☐	No ☐	If **Yes**, please provide details of the nature of the assets, the value of the order and whose order or injunction it is.	

Part E - Further information

	You		Your partner		Additional details	Court use
3 Do you and/or your partner have interests in any business abroad?	Yes ☐	No ☐	Yes ☐	No ☐	If **Yes**, please provide details of the nature of the business, its name and address and your and/or your partner's interest in it.	
4 Are you and/or your partner currently bankrupt or subject to bankruptcy proceedings or subject to an Individual Voluntary Arrangement?	Yes ☐	No ☐	Yes ☐	No ☐	If **Yes**, please provide full details	

Is there any other information that you feel is relevant to the Court or the Legal Services Commission which should be taken into account when considering your means?

Please provide details where relevant.

Declaration

1. I declare that to the best of my knowledge and belief, I have given a complete and correct statement of my income and/or savings and/or capital and those of my partner.

2. I understand I may be required to provide evidence to support the information I have supplied on this form.

3. I authorise such enquiries as are considered necessary to enable the Court or the Legal Services Commission to ascertain mine and/or my partner's income, outgoings, savings, business interests.

4. I consent to the disclosure of any information by other parties that may assist in their enquiries.

5. I authorise the Court or the Legal Services Commission to make such enquiries to the Benefits Agency, Tax Credit Office or Inland Revenue as they feel necessary and I consent to the disclosure of information to confirm that I am in receipt of such benefits as I have stated.

6. I understand that the Court and the Legal Services Commission can provide a report on my financial position to the trial judge and my representative, with a view to a Recovery of Defence Costs Order being made for up to the full amount of the costs incurred in defending me in the proceedings, in this and any other court.

7. I understand that if I knowingly make a statement which is false or knowingly withhold information I may be prosecuted. If convicted of such an offence I may be sent to prison for up to three months or fined or both (section 21 Access to Justice Act 1999).

8. I understand that I must co-operate fully and immediately with any enquiry into my financial circumstances by the Court or Legal Services Commission, and that if the information I have provided is not correct or complete, then an Order may be made against me requiring me to pay all costs incurred in defending me in the proceedings, in this and any other court.

Signature	Jake Prescott	Date	14-01-0-

Full name in Block Capitals	JAKE PRESCOTT

Declaration and authority by person receiving the benefit

This additional declaration should be signed by the person receiving the benefit if they are not the person applying for publicly funded representation.

I consent to the Court or Legal Services Commission disclosing information about me to the Department of Social Security and making such enquiries as may be necessary to check the information provided in this application. The Department of Social Security may carry out such processing as is necessary to check this information remains correct and may inform the Court or Legal Services Commission of any relevant changes.

Signature		Date	

(R)   Plea and directions hearing: Judge's questionnaire

Plea and Directions Hearing

Judge's Questionnaire

In accordance with the practice rules issued by the Lord Chief Justice.

A copy of this questionnaire, completed as far as possible with the agreement of both advocates, is to be handed in to the court prior to the commencement of the Plea and Directions Hearing.

The Crown Court at
Case No. **T**
PTI URN
R v
Date of PDH
Name of Prosecution Advocate at PDH
Name of Defence Advocate at PDH

1	a	Are the actual/proposed not guilty pleas definitely to be maintained through to a jury trial?	Yes ☐ No ☐
	b	Has the defence advocate advised his client of section 152 Powers of Criminal Courts (Sentencing) Act 2000? *(Reductions in sentence for guilty pleas)*	Yes ☐ No ☐
	c	Will the prosecution accept part guilty or alternative pleas?	Yes ☐ No ☐
2		How long is the trial likely to take?	
3	a	Are there Human Rights issues to be relied upon?	Yes ☐ No ☐
		If **Yes**, what are the Human Rights issues?	
	b	What are the other issues in the case?	
4		Issues as to the mental or medical condition of any defendant or witness.	
5		Prosecution witnesses whose evidence will be given. Can any statement be read instead of calling the witnesses?	To be read (number) ☐ To be called (number) ☐ Names:

6	a	Number of Defence witnesses whose evidence will be placed before the Court.	Defendant + [ ]
	b	Any whose statements have been served which can be agreed and accepted in writing.	

7	Is the prosecution intending to serve any further evidence?	Yes ☐ No ☐
	If **Yes**, what area(s) will it cover?	
	What are the witnesses' names?	

8	Facts which are admitted and can be reduced into writing. *(s10(2)(b) CJA 1967)*	

9	Exhibits and schedules which are to be admitted.	

10	Is the order and pagination of the prosecution papers agreed?	

11	Any alibi which should have been disclosed in accordance with CJA 1967?	Yes ☐ No ☐

12	a	Any points of law likely to arise at trial?	
	b	Any questions of admissibility of evidence together with any authorities it is intended to rely upon.	

13	a	Has the defence notified the prosecution of any issue arising out of the record of interview? *(Practice Direction Crime: Tape Recording of police interview 26 May 1989)*	Yes ☐ No ☐
	b	What efforts have been made to agree verbatim records or summaries and have they been successful?	

14		Any applications granted / pending for:	
	(i)	evidence to be given through live television links?	Yes ☐ No ☐
	(ii)	evidence to be given by pre-recorded video interviews with children?	Yes ☐ No ☐
	(iii)	screens?	Yes ☐ No ☐
	(iv)	the use of video equipment during the trial?	Yes ☐ No ☐
	(v)	use of tape playback equipment?	Yes ☐ No ☐

15	Any other significant matter which might affect the proper and convenient trial of the case? *(e.g. expert witnesses or other cases outstanding against the defendant)*	

16	Any other work which needs to be done. *Orders of the Court with time limits should be noted on page 4.*	Prosecution
		Defence

17	a	Witness availability and approximate length of witness evidence.	Prosecution
			Defence
	b	Can any witness attendance be staggered?	Yes ☐ No ☐
		If **Yes**, have any arrangements been agreed?	Yes ☐ No ☐

18	Advocates' availability?	Prosecution
		Defence

Case listing arrangements

Name of Trial Judge:

Custody Cases *Fix or warned list within 16 weeks of committal*

Fixed for trial on

Place in warned list for trial   for week beginning

Further directions fixed for

Not fixed or put in warned list within
16 weeks because:

Date of expiry of custody time limit

Application to extend custody time limit?   Yes ☐   Extended to

                                              No ☐

Bail Cases

Further directions fixed for

Fixed for trial on

Fixed as a floater / backer on

Place in a reserve/warned list for trial   for week beginning

List officer to allocate   ☐ within [   ] days / weeks

                                             ☐ before

Sentence

Adjourned for sentence on

(to follow trial of R v

Other directions, orders, comments

Signed: *Judge*   Date:

(S)   Brief to counsel

IN THE CROWN COURT

AT GUILDFLEET

REPRESENTATION ORDER

Case No.0–/1732

REGINA

v

ALAN TRIP

**BRIEF TO COUNSEL ON BEHALF OF THE DEFENDANT
TO APPEAR AT THE PDH ON 7 NOVEMBER 200– AT 10.30 AND AT
THE TRIAL ON A DATE TO BE FIXED**

Counsel has copies of the following –

1. Statements of Alan Trip (including comments on prosecution statements)
2. Bundle of prosecution witness statements
3. Custody record of Alan Trip
4. List of Alan Trip's previous convictions
5. Representation Order
6. Indictment
7. Bail notice
8. Primary disclosure by the prosecution under the Criminal Procedure and Investigations Act 1996 ('the 1996 Act')
9. 'Defence statement' under the 1996 Act
10. Secondary disclosure by the prosecution under the 1996 Act

INTRODUCTION

Counsel is instructed on behalf of Alan Trip of 1 Oakwell Terrace, Guildfleet. The defendant is on bail and charged with theft of a gold ring to the value of £225, the property of Cedric Mane, contrary to s 1 Theft Act 1968. The defendant will plead not guilty. He was committed under s 6(2), Magistrates' Courts Act 1980 to Guildfleet Crown Court for trial by Guildfleet Magistrates on 30th September 200–. All prosecution witnesses should attend the trial to give oral evidence. There are no defence witnesses other than the defendant.

The prosecution and defence have complied with the disclosure provisions of the 1996 Act. The prosecution has confirmed in writing that there is no material which might undermine the prosecution case; instructing solicitors have set out in the 'defence statement' the general nature of the defence and the matters on which the defence takes issue with the prosecution and the reasons for doing so; the prosecution has confirmed in writing that there is no prosecution material which assists in the defendant's defence.

THE PROSECUTION CASE

The prosecution case is that the defendant took the ring from 6 Marchant Crescent, Guildfleet, a property belonging to Mr. Mane, on 3rd May 200–. The defendant was a lodger at 6 Marchant Crescent from 2nd January 200– to 3rd May 200–. On the morning of 3rd May, following a row with Mr. Mane, the defendant was asked to leave. Mr. Mane will say that he left the ring on the coffee table in the lounge when he left for work on 3rd May at approximately 8.30 a.m. At this time the defendant was still packing his bags prior to leaving. When Mr. Mane returned home from work at 5.30 p.m. both the defendant and the ring had gone. There was no sign of a forcible entry into the property and nothing else had been taken. Peter Plant, a friend of Mr. Mane's will say that the defendant offered him a gold ring for £50 in the Cat and Lion Public House, Guildfleet, on the evening of 3rd May. Plant allegedly refused the offer but informed Mr. Mane on hearing of the theft. The defendant was arrested on 6th May. Counsel will note from the custody record that he did not, on arrival at the police station, ask for a solicitor. The defendant was interrogated by D.C. Blakeway and D.C. Hind and made both oral and written confessions of guilt.

THE DEFENCE CASE

The defendant denies all knowledge of the ring. He claims that Mr. Mane is making allegations of theft against him to 'get even' following their row. The defendant admits talking to Peter Plant in the Cat and Lion Public House but denies offering him a ring. Whilst the defendant cannot put forward any real motive for Plant lying, he suspects that Mane has some 'hold' over Plant and is forcing him to give false testimony. There is no dispute that the defendant confessed his guilt but he claims that he did so only after being denied access to a solicitor and being threatened with physical violence.

EVIDENCE

Counsel's attention is particularly drawn to the following points of evidence:-

The confession - the admissibility of the defendant's confession should be challenged under s.76 and s.78 Police and Criminal Evidence Act 1984. The threats of violence, if accepted by the judge, may constitute oppression and Counsel will be aware of a number of recently reported cases in which denial of access to a solicitor has led to exclusion of a confession under s.78. Although the defendant did not request a solicitor on arrival at the police station he claims that he did so prior to being interrogated. Under the Code of Practice dealing with detention and interrogation the defendant is entitled to request a solicitor at any time. The custody record is silent on the issue and it would appear that the police will deny all knowledge of the request.

The defendant's previous convictions - Counsel will note that the defendant has six previous convictions for theft. In view of the allegations being made against Mr. Mane and the police (if the confession is admitted) it would seem likely that the defendant will be cross-examined on the convictions under s.1(3)(ii) Criminal Evidence Act 1898. Instructing solicitors have explained this to Mr. Trip.

MITIGATION

Instructing solicitors have considered the question of a plea in mitigation if the defendant is convicted. Mr. Trip is a single man, aged 23, and has been unemployed since leaving school at 16. Counsel will note that the present offence was allegedly committed three months into the operational period of a suspended sentence imposed for theft. If the defendant is convicted, a custodial sentence would seem to be inevitable.

Counsel is requested to advise in conference, attend the PDH, represent the defendant at the trial on a plea of not guilty and, if necessary, to make a plea in mitigation and advise on the prospects of an appeal.

(T)   'TIC' Form

BLANKSHIRE POLICE

WEYFORD	STATION
G	DIVISION
23/8/0–	DATE

OTHER OFFENCES

To: ......Jayne Jones..

charged with)   Theft ....
indicated   )

for   (hearing)   at ..Weyford Magistrates' Court.. on ...27th August 200–

MEMORANDUM FOR THE INFORMATION OF THE ACCUSED

(1)   The list on the back hereof gives particulars of _____ FIVE _____
other offences with which you are charged.

    In the event of you(r) **being found guilty / convicted** of any offence of which you are **charged /
indicted** it will be open to you, before **the court makes an order / sentence is passed,** to admit all or
any of the other offences, and you may thereupon ask that any of these other offences which you have admitted
may be taken into consideration in any **order the court may make / sentence the court may pass upon you.**

(2)   Please sign the receipt below, and retain for your own information the copy of this document.

(3)   If you wish now to volunteer any statement concerning any of these other offences, or to ask
for any further information in respect thereto, you may do so in writing, either in the space at the foot of this
document or in a separate letter. Or, if you prefer, you may ask for a Police Officer to take any statement you
may wish to give.

FORM OF RECEIPT TO BE SIGNED BY THE ACCUSED

I have received a copy of this document.

                    Signed ....
                    Date ....
        In the presence of ....

SPACE FOR ANY STATEMENT THE ACCUSED MAY WISH TO VOLUNTEER

                    Signed ....
                    Date ....
        In the presence of ....

CHARGES OUTSTANDING AGAINST _____   Jane Jones

No.	Crime Ref.	Place of Offence	Date of Offence	Details of Offence	Name and Address of Victim	Remarks
1		Weyford	6.6.0–	Stole a packet of frozen peas valued a £1.77 Contrary to s.1(1) Theft Act 1968	Tesco Ltd. 88 High Street, Weyford	
2		Weyford	6.6.0–	Stole a tube of toothpaste valued at £0.70 Contrary to s.1(1) Theft Act 1968	Boots Ltd 84 High Street, Weyford	
3		Weyford	6.6.0–	Stole some writing paper valued at £1.50 Contrary to s.1(1) Theft Act 1968	W.H. Smith Ltd 86 High Street, Weyford	
4		Weyford	10.7.0–	Stole coffee, butter, sardines, and chocolate valued at £5.50 Contrary to s.1(1) Theft Act 1968	Tesco Ltd 88 High Street, Weyford	
5		Weyford	24.7.0–	Stole toothpaste, baked beans and tea valued at £2.10 Contrary to s.1(1) Theft Act 1968	Keymarkets Ltd 98 High Street, Weyford	

A. Butchers DC 1007

(U) Notice of appeal

MAGISTRATES' COURT

NOTICE OF APPEAL TO CROWN COURT, AGAINST CONVICTION

To the Justices' Clerk of the Magistrates' Court sitting at Weyford

AND TO the Crown Prosecution Services, Weyford Branch Office, 9 Guildfleet Road, Weyford, Blankshire WE7 5XX

TAKE NOTICE THAT I, Barry Jones of 42 Murdstone Close Weyford, Blankshire WE4 2AF

intend to appeal to the Crown Court at Weyford against my conviction on 11 November 200– by Weyford Magistrates' Court for the offence of driving a Ford Escort motor car Reg. No L207 LBP on Hamilton Avenue, Weyford without due care and attention Contrary to Section 3 Road Traffic Act 1988.

The basis of my appeal is that the magistrates' decision was wrong and contrary to the evidence. I am not guilty of the offence.

Dated 18 November 200–

Signed *Barry Jones*

Case Reference Number WE 24105

(V) Defence statement

DEFENCE STATEMENT

To: Crown Prosecution Service, 2 Crown Buildings, Newtown.

To: The Crown Court at Newtown

Name of Accused: Terry Ball

Charge: Assault occasioning actual bodily harm contrary to section 47 Offences Against the Person Act 1861

Date of next hearing: 26 February 200–

Name and address of solicitors for the accused:

Collaws Solicitors, 14 The High Street, Newtown NT17 2BA.   Reference JD/1620

Date: 16 February 200–

1.   The nature of the accused's defence is that he acted in self-defence at common law and to prevent a crime under section 3 Criminal Law Act 1967 and to effect a citizen's arrest at common law and under section 24 Police and Criminal Evidence Act 1984. The accused was acting pursuant to the policy of his then employer, Studio 10 Club.

2.   The accused takes issue with the prosecution in relation to the following matters:

(i)   The statement of Kubar Singh.

(ii)   The statement of Neil McInnes.

3.   The accused takes issue with the prosecution about these matters because the accuracy of the prosecution witnesses' accounts is not accepted. The credibility of witnesses may be questioned.

4.   The accused requests the disclosure of the following material as it might undermine the prosecution case or might reasonably be expected to assist the defences disclosed by this written statement:

Item Number 3 on Schedule: Interview records made at Studio 10 Club on questioning staff and customers.

This material will disclose the names of potential witnesses for the defence.

(W) Defence statement

IN THE CROWN COURT AT NEWTOWN Case No. 2456/200–

REGINA

v

JAKE PRESCOTT

DEFENCE STATEMENT

1. The nature of the accused's defence to the charge of robbery contrary to section 8 Theft Act 1968 is alibi.

2. The matters on which the accused takes issue with the prosecution are:
   (i) the allegation that the accused was in the Newtown precinct at approximately 5 pm on 12 December 200–;
   (ii) the allegation that the accused was in the Market Street subway at approximately 5 pm on 12 December 200–;
   (iii) the allegation that the accused threatened the complainant;
   (iv) the allegation that the accused robbed the complainant of a Gameboy Advance games machine.

3. The reason why the accused takes issue with the prosecution about these matters is that the allegations are untrue.

4. The particulars of the alibi are that at about 5 pm on 12 December 200– the accused was at the Newtown Amusement Arcade. The accused will call a witness in support of this alibi. The name of the witness is Peter Storey. The address of the witness is currently unknown. His last known address was 61 Poplar Avenue, Newtown NE19 5BA.

Dated the 1 March 200–

Collaws Solicitors
14 The High Street
Newtown NT172BA

Reference JD/ 1675

Solicitors for the defendant

Appendix 3

Magistrates' Association Sentencing Guidelines

Introduction

These Sentencing Guidelines cover offences with which magistrates deal regularly and frequently in the adult criminal courts. They provide a sentencing structure which sets out how to:

- establish the seriousness of each case
- determine the most appropriate way of dealing with it.

The Sentencing Guidelines provide a method for considering individual cases and a guideline from which discussion should properly flow; but they are not a tariff and should never be used as such. **The guideline sentences are based on a first-time offender pleading not guilty.**

Using the sentencing structure

The sentencing structure used for these Guidelines was established by the Criminal Justice Act 1991. This reaffirms the principle of 'just deserts' so that any penalty must reflect the seriousness of the offence for which it is imposed and the personal circumstances of the offender. Magistrates must always start the sentencing process by taking full account of all the circumstances of the offence and making a judicial assessment of the seriousness category into which it falls. It is important that the court makes clear the factual basis on which the sentence is based.

In every case, the Criminal Justice Act 1991 requires sentencers to consider:

- Is discharge or a fine appropriate?
- Is the offence serious enough for a community penalty?
- Is it so serious that only custody is appropriate?

If the last, in either way cases, justices will also need to consider if magistrates' courts' powers are sufficient.

The format of the Sentencing Guidelines

1.   CONSIDER THE SERIOUSNESS OF THE OFFENCE

Magistrates must always make an assessment of seriousness following the structure of the Criminal Justice Act 1991. **The guideline sentences are based on a first-time offender pleading not guilty**.

Where this guideline is discharge or fine, a suggested starting point guideline fine is also given. Refer to the guidance on pages 85–87 and 101–102.

Where the starting point guideline is a community penalty, refer to the guidance on pages 91 and 92.

Where the starting point guideline is custody, think in terms of weeks and credit as appropriate for a timely guilty plea.

For some either way offences the guideline is 'are your sentencing powers sufficient?'. This indicates that magistrates should be considering whether the seriousness of the offence is such that six months (or 12 months in the case of two or more offences) is insufficient, so that the case must be committed to the Crown Court (consult the legal adviser with regard to Crown Court sentencing and guideline cases). If the case is retained in the magistrates' court a substantial custodial sentence is likely to be necessary.

It should be noted that if magistrates consider (say) nine months to be the appropriate sentence, to be reduced for a timely guilty plea to six months, then the case falls within their powers and must be retained. Subject to offender mitigation, six months would appear to be the appropriate sentence. However, if sentence is passed on this basis the court should specifically say so in its reasons.

2.   CONSIDER AGGRAVATING AND MITIGATING FACTORS

Make sure that all aggravating and mitigating factors are considered. The lists in the Sentencing Guidelines are neither exhaustive nor a substitute for the personal judgment of magistrates. **Factors which do not appear in the Guidelines may be important in individual cases**.

If the offence was racially or religiously aggravated, the court must treat that fact as an aggravating factor under statute (s.153 of the Powers of Criminal Courts (Sentencing) Act 2000). Refer to page 98 for further guidance.

If the offence was committed while the offender was on bail, the court must treat that as an aggravating factor under statute (s.151 Powers of Criminal Courts (Sentencing) Act 2000).

Consider previous convictions, or any failure to respond to previous sentences, in assessing seriousness. Courts should identify any convictions relevant for this purpose and then consider to what extent they affect the seriousness of the present offence.

3.

TAKE A PRELIMINARY VIEW OF SERIOUSNESS, THEN CONSIDER OFFENDER MITIGATION

When an initial assessment of the seriousness of the offence has been formed, consider the offender.

The Guidelines set out some examples of offender mitigation but there are frequently others to be considered in individual cases. Any offender mitigation that the court accepts must lead to some downward revision of the provisional assessment of seriousness, although this revision may be minor. **Remember, however, that the guideline sentences are based on a first-time offender pleading not guilty.**

A previous criminal record may deprive the defendant of being able to say that he is a person of good character.

4.

CONSIDER YOUR SENTENCE

The law requires the court to consider reducing the sentence for a timely guilty plea. Credit for a timely guilty plea may result in a sentencing reduction of up to one-third but the precise amount of credit will depend upon the facts of each case and a last minute plea of guilty may attract only a minimal reduction.

Credit may be given in respect of the amount of a fine or periods of community service or custody. Periods of mandatory disqualification or mandatory penalty points cannot be reduced for a guilty plea.

5.

DECIDE YOUR SENTENCE

Remember that magistrates have a duty to consider the award of compensation in all appropriate cases, and to give reasons if compensation is not awarded. See pages 89–90, Section Three.

Agree the form of words that the Chairman will use when announcing sentence.

Assault – actual bodily harm

Offences Against the Person Act 1861 s.47
Triable either way – see Mode of Trial Guidelines
Penalty: Level 5 and/or 6 months

CONSIDER THE SERIOUSNESS OF THE OFFENCE
(INCLUDING THE IMPACT ON THE VICTIM)

IS DISCHARGE OR FINE APPROPRIATE?

IS IT SERIOUS ENOUGH FOR A COMMUNITY PENALTY?

GUIDELINE: → IS IT SO SERIOUS THAT ONLY CUSTODY IS APPROPRIATE?

ARE YOUR SENTENCING POWERS SUFFICIENT?

THIS IS A GUIDELINE FOR A FIRST-TIME OFFENDER PLEADING NOT GUILTY

 ### CONSIDER AGGRAVATING AND MITIGATING FACTORS AND THE WEIGHT TO ATTACH TO EACH

for example	for example
Abuse of trust (domestic setting)	Minor injury
Deliberate kicking or biting	Provocation
Extensive injuries (may be psychological)	Single blow
Headbutting	*This list is not exhaustive*
Group action	
Offender in position of authority	
On hospital/medical or school premises	
Premeditated	
Victim particularly vulnerable	
Victim serving the public	
Weapon	
This list is not exhaustive	

If offender is on bail, this offence is more serious
If offender has previous convictions, their relevance and any failure to respond to previous sentences should be considered – they may increase the seriousness. The court should make it clear, when passing sentence, that this was the approach adopted.

TAKE A PRELIMINARY VIEW OF SERIOUSNESS, THEN CONSIDER OFFENDER MITIGATION

for example
    Age, health (physical or mental)
    Co-operation with police
    Evidence of genuine remorse
    Voluntary compensation

CONSIDER YOUR SENTENCE

Compare it with the suggested guideline level of sentence and reconsider your reasons carefully if you have chosen a sentence at a different level. Consider a reduction for a timely guilty plea.

DECIDE YOUR SENTENCE
NB. COMPENSATION – Give reasons if not awarding compensation

Breach of a community order	Criminal Justice Act 1991 sch. 2 A fine – maximum £1,000 A Community Punishment Order (up to 60 hours) In certain circumstances, an Attendance Centre Order Revocation of Order and re-sentence for original offence Commit a Crown Court Order to be dealt with at Crown Court

CONSIDER THE EXTENT OF THE BREACH

 ## CONSIDER AGGRAVATING AND MITIGATING FACTORS AND THE WEIGHT TO ATTACH TO EACH

for example No attempt to start the sentence Unco-operative *This list is not exhaustive*	**for example** Completed a significant part of the order *This list is not exhaustive*

CONSIDER OFFENDER MITIGATION
(including timely admission)

DECIDE IF THE ORDER SHOULD CONTINUE

IF THE ORDER SHOULD CONTINUE

    Is a fine appropriate? (Starting Point B)

    Is a community punishment order appropriate?

    Where the order is a community rehabilitation order, is an attendance centre order appropriate?

    Is a curfew order appropriate?

IF THE ORDER SHOULD NOT CONTINUE AND IT IS A MAGISTRATES' COURT ORDER:

    Revoke and re-sentence for original offence (see relevant guideline)

NB. IF THE ORDER WAS MADE BY THE CROWN COURT, MAY FINE AND ALLOW ORDER TO CONTINUE, OR COMMIT TO CROWN COURT TO BE DEALT WITH (CONSULT LEGAL ADVISER)

Burglary (dwelling)	Theft Act 1968 s.9 Triable either way – see Mode of Trial Guidelines Penalty: Level 5 and/or 6 months

CONSIDER THE SERIOUSNESS OF THE OFFENCE
(INCLUDING THE IMPACT ON THE VICTIM)

IS DISCHARGE OR FINE APPROPRIATE?
IS IT SERIOUS ENOUGH FOR A COMMUNITY PENALTY?
IS IT SO SERIOUS THAT ONLY CUSTODY IS APPROPRIATE?
GUIDELINE: →   *ARE YOUR SENTENCING POWERS SUFFICIENT?*

THIS IS A GUIDELINE FOR A FIRST-TIME OFFENDER PLEADING NOT GUILTY

 ## CONSIDER AGGRAVATING AND MITIGATING FACTORS AND THE WEIGHT TO ATTACH TO EACH

for example
    Force used or threatened
    Group enterprise
    High value (in economic or sentimental terms) property stolen
    More than minor trauma caused
    Professional planning/organisation/ execution
    Significant damage or vandalism
    Victim injured
    Victim present at the time
    Vulnerable victim
IF ANY of the above factors are present you should commit for sentence.

for example
    First offence of its type AND low value property stolen AND no significant damage or disturbance AND no injury or violence
    Minor part played
    Theft from attached garage
    Vacant property
ONLY if one or more of the above factors are present AND none of the aggravating factors listed are present should you consider NOT committing for sentence.

If racially or religiously aggravated, or offender is on bail, this offence is more serious
If offender has previous convictions, their relevance and any failure to respond to previous sentences should be considered – they may increase the seriousness. The court should make it clear, when passing sentence, that this was the approach adopted.

TAKE A PRELIMINARY VIEW OF SERIOUSNESS, THEN CONSIDER WHETHER THE CASE SHOULD BE COMMITTED FOR SENTENCE, THEN CONSIDER OFFENDER MITIGATION

for example
    Age, health (physical or mental)
    Co-operation with police
    Evidence of genuine remorse
    Voluntary compensation

CONSIDER COMMITTAL OR YOUR SENTENCE

Compare it with the suggested guideline level of sentence and reconsider your reasons carefully if you have chosen a sentence at a different level.
Consider a reduction for a timely guilty plea.

DECIDE YOUR SENTENCE
NB. COMPENSATION – Give reasons if not awarding compensation

Theft Act 1968 s.9 Triable either way – see Mode of Trial Guidelines Penalty: Level 5 and/or 6 months	Burglary (non-dwelling)

CONSIDER THE SERIOUSNESS OF THE OFFENCE
(INCLUDING THE IMPACT ON THE VICTIM)

IS DISCHARGE OR FINE APPROPRIATE?
GUIDELINE: →   IS IT SERIOUS ENOUGH FOR A COMMUNITY PENALTY?
IS IT SO SERIOUS THAT ONLY CUSTODY IS APPROPRIATE?
ARE YOUR SENTENCING POWERS SUFFICIENT?

THIS IS A GUIDELINE FOR A FIRST-TIME OFFENDER PLEADING NOT GUILTY

CONSIDER AGGRAVATING AND MITIGATING FACTORS
AND THE WEIGHT TO ATTACH TO EACH

for example	for example
Forcible entry Group offence Harm to business Occupants frightened Professional operation Repeat victimisation School or medical premises Soiling, ransacking, damage *This list is not exhaustive*	Low value Nobody frightened No damage or disturbance *This list is not exhaustive*

If racially or religiously aggravated, or offender is on bail, this offence is more serious
If offender has previous convictions, their relevance and any failure to respond to previous
sentences should be considered – they may increase the seriousness. The court should make
it clear, when passing sentence, that this was the approach adopted.

TAKE A PRELIMINARY VIEW OF SERIOUSNESS, THEN
CONSIDER OFFENDER MITIGATION

for example
> Age, health (physical or mental)
> Co-operation with police
> Evidence of genuine remorse
> Voluntary compensation

CONSIDER YOUR SENTENCE

Compare it with the suggested guideline level of sentence and reconsider
your reasons carefully if you have chosen a sentence at a different level.
Consider a reduction for a timely guilty plea.

DECIDE YOUR SENTENCE
NB. COMPENSATION – Give reasons if not awarding compensation

Common assault	Criminal Justice Act 1988 s.39 Triable only summarily Penalty: Level 5 and/or 6 months

CONSIDER THE SERIOUSNESS OF THE OFFENCE
(INCLUDING THE IMPACT ON THE VICTIM)

IS DISCHARGE OR FINE APPROPRIATE?

GUIDELINE: → *IS IT SERIOUS ENOUGH FOR A COMMUNITY PENALTY?*

IS IT SO SERIOUS THAT ONLY CUSTODY IS APPROPRIATE?

THIS IS A GUIDELINE FOR A FIRST-TIME OFFENDER PLEADING NOT GUILTY

 ## CONSIDER AGGRAVATING AND MITIGATING FACTORS AND THE WEIGHT TO ATTACH TO EACH

for example
Abuse of trust (domestic setting)
Group action
Injury
Offender in position of authority
On hospital/medical or school premises
Premeditated
Spitting
Victim particularly vulnerable
Victim serving the public
Weapon
This list is not exhaustive

for example
Impulsive
Minor injury
Provocation
Single blow
This list is not exhaustive

If offender is on bail, this offence is more serious
If offender has previous convictions, their relevance and any failure to respond to previous sentences should be considered – they may increase the seriousness. The court should make it clear, when passing sentence, that this was the approach adopted.

TAKE A PRELIMINARY VIEW OF SERIOUSNESS, THEN CONSIDER OFFENDER MITIGATION

for example
Age, health (physical or mental)
Co-operation with police
Evidence of genuine remorse
Voluntary compensation

CONSIDER YOUR SENTENCE

Compare it with the suggested guideline level of sentence and reconsider your reasons carefully if you have chosen a sentence at a different level. Consider a reduction for a timely guilty plea.

DECIDE YOUR SENTENCE
NB. COMPENSATION – Give reasons if not awarding compensation

Drugs: Class A – possession	Misuse of Drugs Act 1971 s.5 Triable either way – see Mode of Trial Guidelines Penalty: Level 5 and/or 6 months

CONSIDER THE SERIOUSNESS OF THE OFFENCE

IS DISCHARGE OR FINE APPROPRIATE?
GUIDELINE: →   IS IT SERIOUS ENOUGH FOR A COMMUNITY PENALTY?
IS IT SO SERIOUS THAT ONLY CUSTODY IS APPROPRIATE?
ARE YOUR SENTENCING POWERS SUFFICIENT?

THIS IS A GUIDELINE FOR A FIRST-TIME OFFENDER PLEADING NOT GUILTY

 ## CONSIDER AGGRAVATING AND MITIGATING FACTORS
AND THE WEIGHT TO ATTACH TO EACH

for example
   An amount other than a very small
   quantity
   This list is not exhaustive
	for example
	   Very small quantity
	   This list is not exhaustive

If offender is on bail, this offence is more serious
If offender has previous convictions, their relevance and any failure to respond to previous
sentences should be considered – they may increase the seriousness. The court should make
it clear, when passing sentence, that this was the approach adopted.

TAKE A PRELIMINARY VIEW OF SERIOUSNESS, THEN
CONSIDER OFFENDER MITIGATION

for example
   Age, health (physical or mental)
   Co-operation with police
   Evidence of genuine remorse

CONSIDER YOUR SENTENCE

Compare it with the suggested guideline level of sentence and reconsider
your reasons carefully if you have chosen a sentence at a different level.
Consider a reduction for a timely guilty plea. Consider forfeiture and destruction.

DECIDE YOUR SENTENCE

Misuse of Drugs Act 1971 s.4 Triable either way – see Mode of Trial Guidelines Penalty: Level 5 and/or 6 months	Drugs: Class A – production, supply

CONSIDER THE SERIOUSNESS OF THE OFFENCE
(INCLUDING THE IMPACT ON THE VICTIM)

IS DISCHARGE OR FINE APPROPRIATE?

IS IT SERIOUS ENOUGH FOR A COMMUNITY PENALTY?

IS IT SO SERIOUS THAT ONLY CUSTODY IS APPROPRIATE?

GUIDELINE: →   *ARE YOUR SENTENCING POWERS SUFFICIENT?*

THIS IS A GUIDELINE FOR A FIRST-TIME OFFENDER PLEADING NOT GUILTY

 ## CONSIDER AGGRAVATING AND MITIGATING FACTORS AND THE WEIGHT TO ATTACH TO EACH

for example
- Commercial production
- Deliberate adulteration
- Quantity
- Sophisticated operation
- Supply to children
- Venue, eg prisons, educational establishments
- *This list is not exhaustive*

for example
- Small amount
- *This list is not exhaustive*

If offender is on bail, this offence is more serious
If offender has previous convictions, their relevance and any failure to respond to previous sentences should be considered – they may increase the seriousness. The court should make it clear, when passing sentence, that this was the approach adopted.

TAKE A PRELIMINARY VIEW OF SERIOUSNESS, THEN CONSIDER WHETHER THE CASE SHOULD BE COMMITTED FOR SENTENCE, THEN CONSIDER OFFENDER MITIGATION

for example
- Age, health (physical or mental)
- Co-operation with police
- Evidence of genuine remorse

CONSIDER COMMITTAL OR YOUR SENTENCE

Compare it with the suggested guideline level of sentence and reconsider your reasons carefully if you have chosen a sentence at a different level. Consider a reduction for a timely guilty plea. Consider forfeiture and destruction.

DECIDE YOUR SENTENCE

Drugs: Class B and C – possession	Misuse of Drugs Acts 1971 s.5 Triable either way – see Mode of Trial Guidelines Penalty: Level 4 and/or 3 months

CONSIDER THE SERIOUSNESS OF THE OFFENCE

GUIDELINE: →

IS DISCHARGE OR FINE APPROPRIATE?
IS IT SERIOUS ENOUGH FOR A COMMUNITY PENALTY?
IS IT SO SERIOUS THAT ONLY CUSTODY IS APPROPRIATE?
ARE YOUR SENTENCING POWERS SUFFICIENT?

THIS IS A GUIDELINE FOR A FIRST-TIME OFFENDER PLEADING NOT GUILTY

GUIDELINE FINE – STARTING POINT B

CONSIDER AGGRAVATING AND MITIGATING FACTORS AND THE WEIGHT TO ATTACH TO EACH

for example Large amount *This list is not exhaustive*	**for example** Small amount *This list is not exhaustive*

If offender is on bail, this offence is more serious
If offender has previous convictions, their relevance and any failure to respond to previous sentences should be considered – they may increase the seriousness. The court should make it clear, when passing sentence, that this was the approach adopted.

TAKE A PRELIMINARY VIEW OF SERIOUSNESS, THEN CONSIDER OFFENDER MITIGATION

for example
Age, health (physical or mental)
Co-operation with police
Evidence of genuine remorse

CONSIDER YOUR SENTENCE

Compare it with the suggested guideline level of sentence and reconsider your reasons carefully if you have chosen a sentence at a different level. Consider a reduction for a timely guilty plea. Consider forfeiture and destruction.

DECIDE YOUR SENTENCE

Misuse of Drugs Act 1971 s.4 Triable either way – see Mode of Trial Guidelines Penalty: Level 5 and/or 6 months	**Drugs: Class B and C – supply, possession with intent to supply**

CONSIDER THE SERIOUSNESS OF THE OFFENCE
(INCLUDING THE IMPACT ON THE VICTIM)

IS DISCHARGE OR FINE APPROPRIATE?

IS IT SERIOUS ENOUGH FOR A COMMUNITY PENALTY?

IS IT SO SERIOUS THAT ONLY CUSTODY IS APPROPRIATE?

GUIDELINE: →   *ARE YOUR SENTENCING POWERS SUFFICIENT?*

THIS IS A GUIDELINE FOR A FIRST-TIME OFFENDER PLEADING NOT GUILTY

 ## CONSIDER AGGRAVATING AND MITIGATING FACTORS AND THE WEIGHT TO ATTACH TO EACH

for example	for example
Commercial supply Deliberate adulteration Large amount Sophisticated operation Supply to children Venue, eg prisons, educational establishments *This list is not exhaustive*	No commercial motive Small amount *This list is not exhaustive*

If offender is on bail, this offence is more serious
If offender has previous convictions, their relevance and any failure to respond to previous sentences should be considered – they may increase the seriousness. The court should make it clear, when passing sentence, that this was the approach adopted.

TAKE A PRELIMINARY VIEW OF SERIOUSNESS, THEN CONSIDER WHETHER THE CASE SHOULD BE COMMITTED FOR SENTENCE, THEN CONSIDER OFFENDER MITIGATION

for example
   Age, health (physical or mental)
   Co-operation with police
   Evidence of genuine remorse

CONSIDER COMMITTAL OR YOUR SENTENCE

Compare it with the suggested guideline level of sentence and reconsider your reasons carefully if you have chosen a sentence at a different level. Consider a reduction for a timely guilty plea. Consider forfeiture and destruction.

DECIDE YOUR SENTENCE

Theft Act 1968 s.15 Triable either way – see Mode of Trial Guidelines Penalty: Level 5 and/or 6 months	**Obtaining by deception**

CONSIDER THE SERIOUSNESS OF THE OFFENCE
(INCLUDING THE IMPACT ON THE VICTIM)

IS DISCHARGE OR FINE APPROPRIATE?

GUIDELINE: →　　*IS IT SERIOUS ENOUGH FOR A COMMUNITY PENALTY?*

IS IT SO SERIOUS THAT ONLY CUSTODY IS APPROPRIATE?

ARE YOUR SENTENCING POWERS SUFFICIENT?

THIS IS A GUIDELINE FOR A FIRST-TIME OFFENDER PLEADING NOT GUILTY

CONSIDER AGGRAVATING AND MITIGATING FACTORS AND THE WEIGHT TO ATTACH TO EACH

for example	**for example**
Committed over lengthy period Large sums or valuable goods Two or more involved Use of stolen credit/debit card, cheque 　books, or giros Victim particularly vulnerable *This list is not exhaustive*	Impulsive action Short period Small sum *This list is not exhaustive*

If offender is on bail, this offence is more serious
If offender has previous convictions, their relevance and any failure to respond to previous
sentences should be considered – they may increase the seriousness. The court should make
it clear, when passing sentence, that this was the approach adopted.

TAKE A PRELIMINARY VIEW OF SERIOUSNESS, THEN CONSIDER OFFENDER MITIGATION

for example
　　Age, health (physical or mental)
　　Co-operation with police
　　Evidence of genuine remorse
　　Voluntary compensation

CONSIDER YOUR SENTENCE

Compare it with the suggested guideline level of sentence and reconsider
your reasons carefully if you have chosen a sentence at a different level.
Consider a reduction for a timely guilty plea.

DECIDE YOUR SENTENCE
NB. COMPENSATION – Give reasons if not awarding compensation

Racially or religiously aggravated assault – actual bodily harm

Offences Against the Person Act 1861 s.47
Crime and Disorder Act 1998 s.29
Anti-Terrorism, Crime and Security Act 2001
Triable either way – see Mode of Trial Guidelines
Penalty: Level 5 and/or 6 months

CONSIDER THE SERIOUSNESS OF THE OFFENCE
(INCLUDING THE IMPACT ON THE VICTIM)

IS DISCHARGE OR FINE APPROPRIATE?
IS IT SERIOUS ENOUGH FOR A COMMUNITY PENALTY?
IS IT SO SERIOUS THAT ONLY CUSTODY IS APPROPRIATE?
GUIDELINE: →   *ARE YOUR SENTENCING POWERS SUFFICIENT?*

THIS IS A GUIDELINE FOR A FIRST-TIME OFFENDER PLEADING NOT GUILTY

CONSIDER AGGRAVATING AND MITIGATING FACTORS AND THE WEIGHT TO ATTACH TO EACH

for example	for example
Deliberate kicking or biting	Minor injury
Extensive injuries (may be psychological)	Provocation
Group action	Single blow
Headbutting	*This list is not exhaustive*
Motivation for the offence was racial or religious	
Offender in position of authority	
On hospital/medical or school premises	
Premeditated	
Setting out to humiliate the victim	
Victim particularly vulnerable	
Victim serving the public	
Weapon	
This list is not exhaustive	

If offender is on bail, this offence is more serious
If offender has previous convictions, their relevance and any failure to respond to previous sentences should be considered – they may increase the seriousness. The court should make it clear, when passing sentence, that this was the approach adopted.

TAKE A PRELIMINARY VIEW OF SERIOUSNESS, THEN CONSIDER WHETHER THE CASE SHOULD BE COMMITTED FOR SENTENCE, THEN CONSIDER OFFENDER MITIGATION

for example
   Age, health (physical or mental)
   Co-operation with police
   Evidence of genuine remorse
   Voluntary compensation

CONSIDER COMMITTAL OR YOUR SENTENCE

Compare it with the suggested guideline level of sentence and reconsider your reasons carefully if you have chosen a sentence at a different level. Consider a reduction for a timely guilty plea.

DECIDE YOUR SENTENCE
NB. COMPENSATION – Give reasons if not awarding compensation

Criminal Justice Act 1988 s.39 Crime and Disorder Act 1998 s.29 Anti-Terrorism, Crime and Security Act 2001 Triable either way – see Mode of Trial Guidelines Penalty: Level 5 and/or 6 months	**Racially or religiously aggravated common assault**

CONSIDER THE SERIOUSNESS OF THE OFFENCE
(INCLUDING THE IMPACT ON THE VICTIM)

IS DISCHARGE OR FINE APPROPRIATE?

IS IT SERIOUS ENOUGH FOR A COMMUNITY PENALTY?

GUIDELINE: → IS IT SO SERIOUS THAT ONLY CUSTODY IS APPROPRIATE?

ARE YOUR SENTENCING POWERS SUFFICIENT?

THIS IS A GUIDELINE FOR A FIRST-TIME OFFENDER PLEADING NOT GUILTY

 ## CONSIDER AGGRAVATING AND MITIGATING FACTORS AND THE WEIGHT TO ATTACH TO EACH

for example	for example
Group action Injury **Motivation** for the offence was racial or religious Offender in position of authority On hospital/medical or school premises Premeditated Setting out to humiliate the victim Victim particularly vulnerable Victim serving the public Weapon *This list is not exhaustive*	Impulsive Minor injury Provocation Single blow *This list is not exhaustive*

If offender is on bail, this offence is more serious
If offender has previous convictions, their relevance and any failure to respond to previous sentences should be considered – they may increase the seriousness. The court should make it clear, when passing sentence, that this was the approach adopted.

TAKE A PRELIMINARY VIEW OF SERIOUSNESS, THEN CONSIDER OFFENDER MITIGATION

for example
> Age, health (physical or mental)
> Co-operation with police
> Evidence of genuine remorse
> Voluntary compensation

CONSIDER YOUR SENTENCE

Compare it with the suggested guideline level of sentence and reconsider your reasons carefully if you have chosen a sentence at a different level. Consider a reduction for a timely guilty plea.

DECIDE YOUR SENTENCE
NB. COMPENSATION – Give reasons if not awarding compensation

Racially or religiously aggravated wounding – grievous bodily harm	Offences Against the Person Act 1861 s.20 Crime and Disorder Act 1998 s.29 Anti-Terrorism, Crime and Security Act 2001 Triable either way – see Mode of Trial Guidelines Penalty: Level 5 and/or 6 months

CONSIDER THE SERIOUSNESS OF THE OFFENCE
(INCLUDING THE IMPACT ON THE VICTIM)

IS DISCHARGE OR FINE APPROPRIATE?

IS IT SERIOUS ENOUGH FOR A COMMUNITY PENALTY?

IS IT SO SERIOUS THAT ONLY CUSTODY IS APPROPRIATE?

GUIDELINE: →   *ARE YOUR SENTENCING POWERS SUFFICIENT?*

THIS IS A GUIDELINE FOR A FIRST-TIME OFFENDER PLEADING NOT GUILTY

 ## CONSIDER AGGRAVATING AND MITIGATING FACTORS AND THE WEIGHT TO ATTACH TO EACH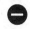

for example	for example
Deliberate kicking/biting Extensive injuries Group action **Motivation** for the offence was racial or religious Offender in position of authority On hospital/medical or school premises Premeditated Setting out to humiliate the victim Victim particularly vulnerable Victim serving the public Weapon *This list is not exhaustive*	Minor wound Provocation *This list is not exhaustive*

If offender is on bail, this offence is more serious
If offender has previous convictions, their relevance and any failure to respond to previous sentences should be considered – they may increase the seriousness. The court should make it clear, when passing sentence, that this was the approach adopted.

TAKE A PRELIMINARY VIEW OF SERIOUSNESS, THEN CONSIDER WHETHER THE CASE SHOULD BE COMMITTED FOR SENTENCE, THEN CONSIDER OFFENDER MITIGATION

for example
    Age, health (physical or mental)
    Co-operation with police
    Evidence of genuine remorse
    Voluntary compensation

CONSIDER COMMITTAL OR YOUR SENTENCE

Compare it with the suggested guideline level of sentence and reconsider your reasons carefully if you have chosen a sentence at a different level.
Consider a reduction for a timely guilty plea.

DECIDE YOUR SENTENCE
NB. COMPENSATION – Give reasons if not awarding compensation

56   Issued October 2003 for implementation 1 January 2004

Theft	Theft Act 1968 s.1 Triable either way – see Mode of Trial Guidelines Penalty: Level 5 and/or 6 months May disqualify where committed with reference to the theft or taking of a vehicle

CONSIDER THE SERIOUSNESS OF THE OFFENCE
(INCLUDING THE IMPACT ON THE VICTIM)

IS DISCHARGE OR FINE APPROPRIATE?

GUIDELINE: →   *IS IT SERIOUS ENOUGH FOR A COMMUNITY PENALTY?*

IS IT SO SERIOUS THAT ONLY CUSTODY IS APPROPRIATE?

ARE YOUR SENTENCING POWERS SUFFICIENT?

THIS IS A GUIDELINE FOR A FIRST-TIME OFFENDER PLEADING NOT GUILTY

 ## CONSIDER AGGRAVATING AND MITIGATING FACTORS AND THE WEIGHT TO ATTACH TO EACH

for example High value Planned Sophisticated Adult involving children Organised team Related damage Vulnerable victim *This list is not exhaustive*	**for example** Impulsive action Low value *This list is not exhaustive*

If racially or religiously aggravated, or offender is on bail, this offence is more serious
If offender has previous convictions, their relevance and any failure to respond to previous
sentences should be considered – they may increase the seriousness. The court should make
it clear, when passing sentence, that this was the approach adopted.

TAKE A PRELIMINARY VIEW OF SERIOUSNESS, THEN CONSIDER OFFENDER MITIGATION

for example
Age, health (physical or mental)
Co-operation with police
Evidence of genuine remorse
Voluntary compensation

CONSIDER YOUR SENTENCE

Compare it with the suggested guideline level of sentence and reconsider
your reasons carefully if you have chosen a sentence at a different level.
Consider a reduction for a timely guilty plea.

DECIDE YOUR SENTENCE
NB. COMPENSATION – Give reasons if not awarding compensation

Theft Act 1968 s.1 Triable either way – see Mode of Trial Guidelines Penalty: Level 5 and/or 6 months	Theft in breach of trust

CONSIDER THE SERIOUSNESS OF THE OFFENCE
(INCLUDING THE IMPACT ON THE VICTIM)

IS DISCHARGE OR FINE APPROPRIATE?

IS IT SERIOUS ENOUGH FOR A COMMUNITY PENALTY?

GUIDELINE: → *IS IT SO SERIOUS THAT ONLY CUSTODY IS APPROPRIATE?*

ARE YOUR SENTENCING POWERS SUFFICIENT?

THIS IS A GUIDELINE FOR A FIRST-TIME OFFENDER PLEADING NOT GUILTY

 ## CONSIDER AGGRAVATING AND MITIGATING FACTORS
AND THE WEIGHT TO ATTACH TO EACH

for example Casting suspicion on others Committed over a period High value Organised team Planned Senior employee Sophisticated Vulnerable victim *This list is not exhaustive*	**for example** Impulsive action Low value Previous inconsistent attitude by employer Single item Unsupported junior *This list is not exhaustive*

If racially or religiously aggravated, or offender is on bail, this offence is more serious
If offender has previous convictions, their relevance and any failure to respond to previous sentences should be considered – they may increase the seriousness. The court should make it clear, when passing sentence, that this was the approach adopted.

TAKE A PRELIMINARY VIEW OF SERIOUSNESS,
THEN CONSIDER OFFENDER MITIGATION

for example
Age, health (physical or mental)
Co-operation with police
Evidence of genuine remorse
Voluntary compensation

CONSIDER YOUR SENTENCE

Compare it with the suggested guideline level of sentence and reconsider your reasons carefully if you have chosen a sentence at a different level. Consider a reduction for a timely guilty plea.

DECIDE YOUR SENTENCE
NB. COMPENSATION – Give reasons if not awarding compensation

Wounding – grievous bodily harm	Offences Against the Person Act 1861 s.20 Triable either way – see Mode of Trial Guidelines Penalty: Level 5 and/or 6 months

CONSIDER THE SERIOUSNESS OF THE OFFENCE
(INCLUDING THE IMPACT ON THE VICTIM)

IS DISCHARGE OR FINE APPROPRIATE?
IS IT SERIOUS ENOUGH FOR A COMMUNITY PENALTY?
IS IT SO SERIOUS THAT ONLY CUSTODY IS APPROPRIATE?
GUIDELINE: → **ARE YOUR SENTENCING POWERS SUFFICIENT?**

THIS IS A GUIDELINE FOR A FIRST-TIME OFFENDER PLEADING NOT GUILTY

 ## CONSIDER AGGRAVATING AND MITIGATING FACTORS AND THE WEIGHT TO ATTACH TO EACH

for example	for example
Abuse of trust (domestic setting) Deliberate kicking/biting Extensive injuries Group action Offender in position of authority On hospital/medical or school premises Premeditated Prolonged assault Victim particularly vulnerable Victim serving the public Weapon *This list is not exhaustive*	Minor wound Provocation *This list is not exhaustive*

If offender is on bail, this offence is more serious
If offender has previous convictions, their relevance and any failure to respond to previous sentences should be considered – they may increase the seriousness. The court should make it clear, when passing sentence, that this was the approach adopted.

TAKE A PRELIMINARY VIEW OF SERIOUSNESS, THEN CONSIDER WHETHER THE CASE SHOULD BE COMMITTED FOR SENTENCE, THEN CONSIDER OFFENDER MITIGATION

for example
Age, health (physical or mental)
Co-operation with police
Evidence of genuine remorse
Voluntary compensation

CONSIDER COMMITTAL OR YOUR SENTENCE

Compare it with the suggested guideline level of sentence and reconsider your reasons carefully if you have chosen a sentence at a different level.
Consider a reduction for a timely guilty plea.

DECIDE YOUR SENTENCE
NB. COMPENSATION – Give reasons if not awarding compensation

Seriousness

Establishing the Seriousness of the Offence

In establishing the seriousness of the case before them, courts should:

- make sure that all factors which aggravate or mitigate the offence are considered. The lists in the *Guidelines* are neither exhaustive nor a substitute for the personal judgment of magistrates. Factors which do not appear in the *Guidelines* may be important in individual cases;
- consider the various seriousness indicators, remembering that some will carry more weight than others;
- take into account, as a seriousness factor, the impact of the offence upon the victim;
- note that, by statute, racial and religious aggravation increases the seriousness of any offence – s.153 Powers of Criminal Courts (Sentences) Act 2000 – but see the note on specific racially aggravated offences created under ss.29-32 of the same Act on page 98;
- always bear in mind that, by statute, the commission of an offence on bail aggravates its seriousness;
- consider the effect of using previous convictions, or any failure to respond to previous sentences, in assessing seriousness. Courts should identify any convictions relevant for this purpose and then consider to what extent they affect the seriousness of the present offence;
- note that, when there are several offences to be sentenced, the court must have regard to the totality principle. This means that the overall effect of the sentence must be commensurate with the total criminality involved.

When the court has formed an initial assessment of the seriousness of the offence(s), consider any offender mitigation.

Victim personal statements

A victim personal statement gives victims a formal opportunity to say how a crime has affected them. Where the victim has chosen to make such a statement, a court should consider and take it into account prior to passing sentence. (LCJ Practice Direction made 16 October 2001.)

Evidence of the effects of an offence on the victim must be in the form of a s.9 witness statement or expert's report and served on the defence prior to sentence.

Except where inferences can properly be drawn from the nature or circumstances surrounding the offence, a sentencer must not make assumptions unsupported by evidence about the effects of an offence on the victim.

The court must pass what it judges to be the appropriate sentence having regard to the circumstances of the offence and of the offender, taking into account, so far as the court considers it appropriate, the consequences to the victim.

The opinions of the victim or the victim's close relatives as to what the sentence should be are not relevant.

Reduction in sentence for guilty pleas

(Section 152, Powers of Criminal Courts (Sentencing) Act 2000)

In deciding what sentence to pass on a person who has pleaded guilty the court has to take into account the stage in the proceedings at which that plea was indicated and the circumstances in which the indication was given. If the court imposes a less severe penalty than it would have given, it must state this in open court. It would be a matter of good practice for the court to say how much credit has been given, with a brief reason for the decision.

The principles of 'discount' apply as much to magistrates' courts as they do to Crown Courts. A timely guilty plea may attract a sentencing reduction of up to a third but the precise amount will depend on the facts of each case. A change of plea on the day set down for trial may attract only a minimal reduction in sentence; the court must still consider whether credit should be given.

Reductions apply to fines, periods of community sentences and custody. An early guilty plea may also affect the length of a disqualification or the number of penalty points. However, minimum periods of disqualification and mandatory penalty points cannot be reduced for a guilty plea. Reasons should be given for decisions.

Pre-sentence reports

(See also the section on *community sentences* on pages 91 and 92.)

The purpose of all reports is to provide information to help the court decide on the most suitable sentence. They are required in most cases where the threshold of 'serious enough' (community penalties) or 'so serious' (custody) is reached – and should only be sought in such cases. They can be in the form of a PSR (pre-sentence report) or SSR (specific sentence report).

PSRs are written reports to assist the courts in determining sentence. In accordance with National Standards 2002 they contain:

- a full risk assessment;
- a proposal for sentence commensurate with the risk of harm, likelihood of re-offending, the nature of the offence and the suitability of the offender.

A PSR must be provided within 15 working days or any agreed shorter period.

SSRs

An SSR is a PSR for legal purposes as it meets the definition of section 162 of the Powers of Criminal Courts (Sentencing) Act 2000. SSRs are designed to speed up the provision of information to courts to allow sentencing without delay in relatively straightforward cases. They are a specific limited enquiry undertaken at the request of the court into an offender's suitability for a particular community sentence.

They are designed to be available on the day requested (or next morning). If there is doubt about a defendant's suitability for a specific sentence report the probation officer may recommend an adjournment for a full PSR.

Giving reasons

Magistrates should normally give reasons for their findings and decisions; this is obligatory under the Human Rights Act.

- The offender should be told the reasons for the decision.
- The victim will want to know the reasons for the decision.
- The public are entitled to know what is going on in the criminal justice system, and to have confidence in it.
- If a sentence is unusual the importance of giving reasons is greater.
- Ill-informed criticism in the media may be reduced if reasons have been given in public and recorded.
- In preparing an SSR or a PSR, or in implementing a community sentence, the probation service must know what the magistrates had in mind and what findings of fact they made.
- If a case has to be adjourned, and a differently constituted bench sits next time, the later bench must know the reasons for the decisions and findings of the earlier bench.

And:

- The reasons will be necessary if there is an appeal by way of case stated.

There are now many instances where the giving of reasons is required by law.

- Why bail is refused.
- Why the offence is so serious as to justify prison.
- Why a defaulter is being sent to prison.
- If a compensation order is not awarded.
- If a sentence is reduced because of a guilty plea.
- If the court does not disqualify the driver or endorse his licence for 'special reasons'.
- If the court does not impose a 'totting up' disqualification.

Having reached their findings through a structured approach, it is perfectly proper for the magistrates to seek the advice and assistance of the legal adviser in how best to formulate and articulate their reasons for the purpose of the pronouncement.

It is the responsibility of the legal adviser to provide the justices with any advice they require properly to perform their functions, whether or not the justices have requested that advice. The Practice Direction on the functions and responsibilities of Justices' Clerks and authorised legal advisers, made by the Lord Chief Justice on 2 October 2000, makes it clear that this responsibility extends to giving advice on the appropriate decision-making structure to be applied in any given case, reminding the bench of the evidence, and assisting the court, where appropriate as to the formulation of reasons and the recording of those reasons.

Financial penalties

Fining

Fines are suitable as punishment for cases which are not serious enough to merit a community penalty, nor so serious that a custodial sentence must be considered.

The aim should be for the fine to have equal impact on rich or poor and before fixing the amount of a fine, the court must enquire into the offender's financial circumstances, preferably using a standard means form.

A fine must not exceed the upper statutory limit. Where this is expressed in terms of a 'level' the maxima are:

Level 1	£200
Level 2	£500
Level 3	£1,000
Level 4	£2,500
Level 5	£5,000

The fine must reflect the seriousness of the offence and must be proportionate to the offender's means.

A reduction must be considered for a guilty plea – up to a third if the plea was timely (see page 82), and the appropriate announcement made.

Where compensation and costs are in issue (see pages 88–90) then the order of priorities is compensation – fine – costs. The totality of the financial penalty must be considered in reaching a decision on the level of fine.

Where a defendant is to be fined for several offences and his means are limited it may be better to fix the relevant fine level for the most serious offence and order 'no separate penalty' on the lesser matters.

The suggested fines in these *Guidelines* are given as either A, B or C . These represent 50%, 100% and 150% of the defendant's weekly take home pay/benefit. (Weekly take home pay or benefit means weekly income after all deductions made by an employer (take home pay) or the amount of weekly benefit payment.) These levels take into account ordinary living expenses. This guidance should not be used as a tariff and every offender's means must be individually considered.

The defendant should be given a document which sets out the total fines, rate of payment, date of first payment and place of payment before leaving the court.

Assessing means

Before fixing the amount of any fine the Powers of Criminal Courts (Sentencing) Act 2000, section 128 requires the court to enquire into the financial circumstances of the offender so far as they are known. Defendants should be asked to complete a means form to provide this information.

The first figure needed is take home pay/benefit which is used to ensure the fairest approach to those in different financial circumstances – the guideline fines (which are only a starting point) are based on this income and reflect ordinary living expenses.

The court should be aware of other information including:

- whether the offender has savings or other disposable or realisable capital assets;
- liability to pay outstanding fines;
- level of outgoings.

And should in every case consider individual circumstances, but outgoings will only be relevant if they are out of the ordinary and substantially reduce ability to pay, leading to undue hardship.

The financial circumstances of third parties, eg other members of the family, are irrelevant, save insofar as the offender derives income or benefit from such persons, or he is thereby relieved of a proportion of household expenses.

If for any reason the magistrates are not satisfied with the information they have received, and they feel they cannot sentence until they have such information, they may adjourn the case for further information to be supplied, and they may make a financial circumstances order requiring a statement of means to be provided, Powers of the Criminal Courts (Sentencing) Act 2000, section 126.

The fine is payable in full on the day and the defendant should always be asked for immediate payment. If periodic payments are allowed, the fine should normally be payable within a maximum of 12 months. It should be remembered however, that for those on very low incomes it is often unrealistic to expect them to maintain weekly payments for as long as a year.

The fine should be a hardship, depriving the offender of the capacity to spend the money on 'luxuries', but care should be taken not to force him or her below a reasonable 'subsistence' level.

Fining in the defendant's absence

If, having been given a reasonable opportunity to inform the court of his means, the offender refuses or fails to do so, the magistrates may draw such inference as to means as they think just in the circumstances, using all available information. It is inappropriate simply to fine the maximum level.

For further advice on the fines procedure, see the flowchart on the next page and the guidance on fine enforcement on page 101.

1. DECIDE SENTENCING BAND ACCORDING TO SERIOUSNESS

Consider the aggravating and mitigating features of the offence, plus any personal mitigation relating to the offender – decide that a fine is appropriate

2. DECIDE LEVEL OF FINE ACCORDING TO SERIOUSNESS

Taking the above factors into account, decide on the level of fine
(A, B or C) that reflects those factors

3. OBTAIN FINANCIAL INFORMATION

The court is required by statute to enquire into financial circumstances and to take them into account so far as they are known. Full information (from means form/questioning in court) should cover income, savings (if any) and outgoings including other court fines.

4. SET FINE

A fine is meant to have an equal impact on rich and poor. To ensure a fair approach the starting point in all cases should be **weekly take home pay/weekly benefit payment.**

Select level A (50%), level B (100%) or level C (150%) of this weekly amount according to decision on seriousness (see 2 above).
NB these levels already take into account ordinary living expenses.

5. CONSIDER FACTORS **RELEVANT TO INDIVIDUAL CASE**

OUTGOINGS: *These are only relevant if they are out of the ordinary and substantially reduce ability to pay, leading to undue hardship.*

TIMELY GUILTY PLEA: give credit where appropriate.

COMPENSATION/COSTS: If these are applicable then total financial penalty must be considered in relation to known means, including savings. If means insufficient for all three elements, apply usual priority of compensation – fine – costs.

CONFIRM ORIGINAL FIGURE OR JUSTIFY ANY CHANGE

6. ANNOUNCE AMOUNT OF FINE: SEEK IMMEDIATE PAYMENT

If payment in full not possible, seek immediate part payment
If time is asked for, consider all information above in setting
level of payments/time to clear total sum

Costs

The following guidance was given by the Court of Appeal in *R. v. Northallerton Magistrates' Court ex parte Dove*:

1. An order for costs to the prosecutor should never exceed the sum which, having regard to the defendant's means and any other financial order imposed upon him, he is able to pay and which it is reasonable to order him to pay.

2. Such an order should never exceed the sum which the prosecutor had actually and reasonably incurred.

3. The purpose of the order is to compensate the prosecutor and not to punish the defendant.

4. The costs ordered to be paid should not in the ordinary way be grossly disproportionate to the fine imposed for the offence. If the total of the proposed fine and the costs sought by the prosecutor exceeds the sum which the defendant could reasonably be ordered to pay, it was preferable to achieve an acceptable total by reducing the sum of costs ordered, rather than by reducing the fine.

5. It is for the defendant to provide the justices with such data relevant to his financial position as would enable them to assess what he could reasonably afford to pay, and if he fails to do so the justices are entitled to draw reasonable inferences as to his means from all the circumstances of the case.

6. It is incumbent on any court which proposed to make any financial order against a defendant to give him a fair opportunity to adduce any relevant financial information and to make any appropriate submissions.

Compensation orders

The Legal Framework

As well as assessing the seriousness of the offence, including the impact on the victim, and any mitigating factors affecting the offender, the court is under a duty to consider compensation in every case where loss, damage or injury has resulted from the offence, whether or not an application has been made (Powers of Criminal Courts (Sentencing) Act 2000, s.130).

Priorities

If the sentence is to be financial, then the order of priorities is compensation, fine, costs. If the sentence is to be a community penalty, the court should consider carefully the overall burdens placed on the offender if a compensation order is to be made too. If the sentence is to be custody, then a compensation order will be unlikely unless the offender has financial resources available with which to pay immediately or on release.

Giving Reasons

If, having considered making a compensation order, the court decides that it is not appropriate to make one, it has a statutory duty to give its reasons for not ordering compensation.

Limitations on Powers

Magistrates have the power to award compensation for personal injury, loss or damage up to a total of £5,000 for each offence. An exception is where the injury, loss or damage arises from a road accident: a compensation order may not be made in such a case unless there is conviction of an offence under the Theft Act or if the offender is uninsured and the Motor Insurers' Bureau will not cover the loss. If in doubt, seek advice from the legal adviser. Compensation should only be awarded in fairly clear, uncomplicated cases: if there are disputes and complications, the matter should be left to the civil courts.

No Double Compensation

Any victim may bring a civil action for damages against the offender: if that action is successful, the civil court will deduct the amount paid by the offender under a compensation order. In this way, there should be no double compensation. The same applies where the victim receives a payment under the Criminal Injuries Compensation Scheme. The magistrates' court should therefore take no account of these other possibilities.

Criminal Injuries Compensation Scheme

The Criminal Injuries Compensation Scheme provides state compensation for the victims of crimes of violence, particularly those who are seriously injured. The minimum award is currently £1,000. Courts are encouraged to make compensation orders, whether or not the case falls within the Criminal Injuries Compensation Scheme, in order to bring home to offenders themselves the consequences of their actions.

The Purpose of Compensation Orders

The purpose of making a compensation order is to compensate the victim for his or her losses. The compensation may relate to offences taken into consideration, subject to a maximum of £5,000 per charge. Compensation for personal injury may include compensation for terror, shock or distress caused by the offence. The court must have regard to the means of the offender when calculating the amount of the order.

The Approach to Compensation

In calculating the gross amount of compensation, courts should consider compensating the victim for two types of loss. The first, sometimes called 'special damages', includes compensation for financial loss sustained as a result of the offence – eg the cost of repairing damage, or in cases of injury, any loss of earnings or dental expenses. If these costs are not agreed, the court should ask for evidence of them. The second type of loss, sometimes called 'general damages', covers compensation for the pain and suffering of the injury itself and for any loss of facility.

Calculating the Compensation

The amount of compensation should be determined in the light of medical evidence, the victim's sex and age, and any other factors which appear to the court to be relevant in the particular case. If the court does not have sufficient information, then the matter should be adjourned to obtain more facts.

The Table below gives some general guidance on appropriate starting points for general damages for personal injuries.

Once the court has made a preliminary calculation of the appropriate compensation, it is required to have regard to the means of the offender before making an order. Where the offender has little money, the order may have to be scaled down significantly. However, even a compensation order for a fairly small sum may be important to the victim.

Type of injury	Description	Starting point
Graze	Depending on size	Up to £75
Bruise	Depending on size	Up to £100
Black eye		£125
Cut: no permanent scar	Depending on size and whether stitched	£100-£500
Sprain	Depending on loss of mobility	£100-£1,000
Finger	Fractured little finger, recovery within month	£1,000
Loss of non-front tooth Loss of front tooth	Depending on cosmetic effect	£500-£1,000 £1,500
Eye	Blurred or double vision	£1,000
Nose Nose Nose	Undisplaced fracture of nasal bone Displaced fracture of bone requiring manipulation Not causing fracture but displaced septum requiring sub-mucous resection	£1,000 £1,500 £2,000
Facial scar	However small, resulting in permanent disfigurement	£1,500
Wrist Wrist	Closed fracture, recovery within month Displaced fracture, limb in plaster, recovery in 6 months	£3,000 £3,500
Leg or arm	Closed fracture of tibia, fibula, ulna or radius, recovery within month	£3,500
Laparotomy	Stomach scar 6-8 inches (resulting from operation)	£3,500

Community sentences

The purpose of a community sentence is to provide a rigorous and effective punishment for an offender whose offence requires more than a financial penalty but is not so serious as to necessitate imprisonment. A community sentence has three principal elements: restriction of liberty, reparation and prevention of re-offending.

Community sentences include:

- attendance centre orders;
- community rehabilitation orders with or without special requirements;
- community punishment orders;
- community punishment and rehabilitation orders;
- curfew orders;
- drug treatment and testing orders.

The restrictions on liberty imposed by the sentence must be commensurate with the seriousness of the offence and the order must be the one most suitable for the offender.

It is generally good practice to require a pre-sentence or specific sentence report when considering whether to impose a community sentence. Where a report is considered necessary the shorter report should be requested whenever this will be sufficient, to enable the case to be finalised more speedily. In ordering such a report the court should indicate any relevant findings of fact, view of the level of seriousness and the aim of the sentence. In pronouncing sentence the court should stress the need of the offender to co-operate and the consequences of breach.

Penalties for breach of a community sentence are:

- a fine of up to £1,000, the order to continue;
- community punishment of up to 60 hours, the order to continue;
- revocation and re-sentencing for the original offence (in which case the probable sentence will be custody);
- attendance centre order.

See the revised National Standards and the new inter-agency publication *Towards Good Practice – Community Sentences and the Courts.*

The court may ask to be kept informed of the offender's progress under the order.

Electronic monitoring of curfew orders

Curfew orders enforced by electronic monitoring are available for offenders aged ten and over.

The curfew order is a community sentence requiring an offender to remain at a specified place from 2 to 12 hours a day on from 1 to 7 days a week, for a maximum period of six months. The court must obtain and consider information about the proposed curfew address including the attitude of others affected by the order. The order must take account of religious beliefs, employment, education and the requirements of other community orders.

The offender's consent is not required.

The aims of the order are:

- to restrict liberty in a systematic controlled way;
- to make it harder for the offender to commit further crimes;
- to interrupt the pattern of offending by removing the offender from the circumstances of his/her offending;
- provide clear evidence of curfew compliance.

The order can be used as a stand alone order, in combination with any other community order, or can be added to a pre-existing community order.

When considering whether to impose an order the offence must be assessed by the court to be 'serious enough' for a community penalty. When ordering a pre-sentence report the court should specifically ask the probation service to carry out a curfew assessment in all appropriate cases.

Breach of court orders

The breach of court orders should never be treated lightly. They should be rigorously enforced. In making any pronouncement on sentence the breach should be given special mention.

A failure by the court to respond effectively to a breach can:

- erode public confidence in the courts;
- undermine the work of the agency supervising the order;
- allow the offender to feel he has 'got away with it'.

The offender should be clearly told of the seriousness of the offence and, if the court decides to allow an order to continue, be told what is expected of him/her and the likely consequence of any further breach.

In the case of community sentences there are National Standards revised in April 2002 which lay down strict enforcement requirements for the probation service.

Racially or religiously aggravated offences

There are special provisions on racial and religious aggravation, under the Crime and Disorder Act 1998 as amended. There are two forms of aggravation: an offence is racially or religiously aggravated EITHER if it is racially or religiously motivated, OR if in committing the offence the offender demonstrates racial or religious hostility (eg by making a racist remark). The guideline case for sentencing for these offences is *Kelly and Donnelly 2001*, and three situations should be treated separately:

i)   there are a few specific racially or religiously aggravated offences in the Crime and Disorder Act, which have higher maximum penalties than the non-aggravated versions of those offences (eg common assault, abh, criminal damage, etc). Where a defendant is convicted of one of these special offences, the court should determine its sentence for the basic offence (such as criminal damage or assault), and then decide how much to add for the racial or religious aggravation. When the sentence is announced, the court should state how much it added to the basic offence in order to reflect the racial or religious aggravation.

ii)   most offences do not have a specific racially or religiously aggravated version, however. Here, the general principle applies, which is that racial or religious aggravation is a factor that should increase the severity of the sentence.

iii) where an offender is convicted of an offence which has a racially or religiously aggravated version, but is convicted only of the basic offence, it is wrong in principle to pass a higher sentence on racial or religious grounds. If the racially or religiously aggravated version of the offence is not charged or not proved, that is the end of the matter.

Stating the reasons for sentence

1. We are dealing with an offence of:

   ....

2. We have considered the impact on the victim which was ....

   ....

3. We have taken into account these features which make the offence more serious:

   ....

   ....

4. We have taken into account these features which make the offence less serious:

   ....

   ....

5. (where relevant) We have taken into account that the offence was:
   racially and/or religiously aggravated
   committed on bail

6. We have taken into account your previous record, specifically the offences of.........................
   .... and your failure to respond to the sentences imposed.

7. We have taken into account what we have heard in your favour about the offence and about you:

   ....

   ....

8. We have taken into account the fact that you pleaded guilty [at an early stage] [but not until ....] and we have reduced the sentence by [state how much].

9. And, as a result, we have decided that the most appropriate sentence for you is:

   ....

10. (where relevant) We have decided not to award compensation in this case because:

   ....

Appendix 4

Police Station Advice: Advising on Silence

Criminal Practitioners' Newsletter, Special Edition, No 54, October 2003

© The Law Society

The legal position

Changes to the silence provisions

Sections 34, 36 and 37 of CJPOA 1994 have been amended by s 59 of the Youth Justice and Criminal Evidence Act 1999 so that inferences cannot be drawn where the accused was at a police station or other authorised place of detention at the time of failure to mention a relevant tact (or failure to account), and he or she had not been allowed an opportunity to consult a solicitor prior to being questioned, charged or informed that they may be prosecuted. This includes cases where the suspect has had their right of access to a solicitor delayed under the Police and Criminal Evidence Act 1984 (PACE) s 58(8) 2000 or the Terrorism Act Sch 8 para 8, but also where (exceptionally) the police can interview a suspect who has asked for legal advice before he or she has received it.[1] As a result, PACE Code of Practice C (the revised version of which came into force on 1 April 2003) now provides that in circumstances where inferences cannot be drawn as a result of these amendments, a different caution must be administered. This caution, and guidance on when it should be administered, are set out in a new Annex C to Code C.

'Silence' on its own cannot prove guilt

In this guidance the term 'silence' is used to mean failure to mention a fact subsequently relied upon by the accused in his or her defence, or failure to account for an object substance or mark etc. under CJPOA 1994 s 36, or failure to account for presence under s 37.

It is important to remember that inferences may be drawn under s 34 in circumstances where the accused did answer police questions, if the accused relies on facts at trial that he or she did not tell the police about in interview or on being charged eg, where the accused lied to police.

It remains the case, however, that silence cannot, by itself, prove guilt (CJPOA 1994 s 38), and inferences can only be drawn if the court or jury first finds that the other evidence establishes a prima facie case or is 'sufficiently compelling to call for an answer' from the accused.[2] However, this does not mean that in order for inferences to be drawn the police must disclose evidence amounting to a prima facie case prior to questioning the suspect.

Despite the inherent unfairness, the courts have consistently held that the police are **not** under a general duty to disclose evidence to the suspect at the police station.[3]

Conditions for drawing inferences

It has been held that the silence provisions of the CJPOA 1994 do not, in themselves, contravene the right to fair trial under art 6 of the European

Convention on Human Rights. The courts have given some guidance on the conditions that must be satisfied in order for inferences to be possible under s 34:[4]

1. **The silence provisions only apply in criminal proceedings.**

2. **The alleged failure to mention facts subsequently relied upon must occur before charge or on being charged.** Where there is more than one interview, inferences may be drawn from failure to mention relevant facts in one interview even if they were mentioned in a subsequent interview. Similarly, inferences may be drawn from failure to mention facts in an interview even though they were mentioned at charge, or from failure to mention facts on being charged even though no inference could be drawn from failure to mention facts in interview.[5] However, the prosecution must establish that the accused knew, or must have known, of the facts at the relevant time.[6]

3. **The suspect must have been cautioned** (Code C para 10.1 (caution at interview), Code C para 16.2 (caution at charge)). Minor variations in the wording of the caution are permissible provided that the sense of the caution is preserved. For inferences under ss 36 or 37, the accused must have been arrested and must also have been given a special warning prescribed by Code C para 10.11.

4. **The questioning must be directed to trying to discover whether or by whom the alleged offence was committed** (inferences under s 34(1((a) only). Inferences cannot be drawn if the police have already made up their mind to charge before commencing the interview.[7] However, inferences can be drawn if a court is persuaded that the police still had an open mind even if there was sufficient evidence to charge prior to the interview starting.[8]

5. **The failure of the accused must be to mention any fact relied on in his or her defence in those proceedings** (s 34 only). A defendant may be treated as relying on facts even if they do not give evidence where, for example, cross-examination of prosecution witnesses allows reliance on facts to be inferred.[9] A hypothesis proffered by the accused does not amount to a reliance on facts, and neither does a bare admission made in cross-examination, but an assertion that *something is actually the case'* (eg, an explanation given by the accused for his or her relationship with alleged co-conspirators) can amount to assertion of a fact.[10] An oral assertion of facts in interview (even though police questions are not answered), or the handing in of a written statement, can amount to the assertion of facts so that, if accepted by a court, inferences could not be drawn.[11] It was held in *R v Knight*,[12] in respect of a written statement handed to the police, that the purpose of the 'silence' legislation was to encourage early disclosure of the defence not the scrutiny and testing of the defence by police in interview. Note that inferences under ss 36 and 37 do not depend upon the facts put forward by the accused at trial since it is the mere failure or refusal to provide an account to the police that is relevant.

6. **The accused could reasonably be expected, in the circumstances existing at the time, to have mentioned the facts relied on at trial** (s 34 only).

    'Circumstances existing at the time' is to be widely interpreted, and includes:

    •   what disclosure had been made to the suspect, or their lawyer, by the police

    •   what information the prosecution can demonstrate the suspect knew at the time of questioning or charge

- the condition and circumstances of the suspect
- any legal advice that the suspect received.

What is reasonable is a question of fact for the court or jury. Note that there is no reasonableness requirement under ss 36 and 37.

The effect of legal advice

The fact that an accused was advised by their lawyer not to mention facts or advised not to provide an account to the police does not, of itself, prevent inferences from being drawn.[13] In *Condron v UK*[14] the European Court of Human Rights (ECtHR) made it clear that legal advice is an important safeguard in the context of Article 6 and held that the fact that an accused is advised by their lawyer to remain 'silent' must be given appropriate weight by the trial court.

This was given domestic effect by the Court of Appeal in *R v Betts and Hall*[15] in which it was held that:

> If it is a plausible explanation that the reason for not mentioning facts is that the particular appellant acted on the advice of his solicitor and not because he had no or no satisfactory answer to give then no inference can be drawn.
>
> That conclusion does not give a licence to a guilty person to shield behind the advice of his solicitor. The adequacy of the explanation advanced may well be relevant as to whether or not the advice was truly the reason for not mentioning the facts. A person, who is anxious not to answer questions because he has no or no adequate explanation to offer, gains no protection from his lawyer's advice because that advice is no more than a convenient way of disguising his true motivation for not mentioning facts.
>
> In the instant case, we were of the view that the jury had failed to appreciate on the directions given that they could only draw inferences against the appellants if they were sure that their failure to mention facts was not merely as a result of the advice, however adequate or inadequate that explanation might be, and could only do so if they were sure that the particular applicant had not at that stage any explanation to offer or none that he believed would stand up to questioning or investigation.

Betts and Hall appears to hold that legal advice to remain 'silent' will prevent inferences from being drawn provided that the court or jury is satisfied that this is a genuine reason for failure to mention the relevant facts. The fact that such advice was given will not, however, prevent inferences from being drawn if the court or jury is sure that the real reason the accused remained silent was because they had no innocent explanation to give or none that would stand up to questioning. In deciding whether legal advice was the real reason for silence the court may take account of the adequacy of the explanation put forward for remaining silent.

The effect *of Betts and Hall* is not completely clear because, of course, an accused may have a number of reasons for remaining silent one of which is the advice they received. The Judicial Studies Board Specimen Directions deal with this by advising judges to direct juries as follows:

> [Having decided that the accused relied on legal advice to remain silent, and taken into account the fact that he or she can accept or reject such advice] decide whether the defendant could reasonably have been expected to mention the facts on which he now relies. If, for example, you considered that he had or may have had an answer to give, but reasonably relied on the legal advice to remain silent, you should not draw any conclusion against him. But if, for example, you were sure that the defendant had no answer, and merely latched onto the legal advice as a convenient

shield behind which to hide, you would be entitled to draw a conclusion against him... (para 40.5)

Unfortunately, the effect of legal advice on the drawing of inferences was confused rather than clarified by the Court of Appeal decision in *R v Howell*,[16] which held that even if a court or jury were satisfied that legal advice was a genuine reason for silence, this would not prevent inferences from being drawn. The court went on to state that there *'must always be soundly based objective reasons for silence',* but it did not set out a definitive list of what it believes to be 'objective' reasons for advice to remain silent.

Until the court is able to provide clear and consistent guidance on what it believes are relevant factors justifying advice to remain silent, solicitors should approach the issue of advising clients on silence with extreme caution and should explain to clients that the fact that they are advising them to remain silent will not necessarily prevent inferences from being drawn. Whilst solicitors must have proper regard for the decisions of the courts, if there are cogent reasons for silence solicitors must not flinch from advising accordingly, whilst ensuring that their clients are made aware of the risks of following that advice.

Advising the client

Deciding what advice to give

In deciding what advice to give solicitors will, as before, need to balance the risks of answering police questions against the risks of not answering police questions. In doing so, the following factors will be relevant (although in any particular case, some factors may be more important than others, and other factors may also be relevant):

1. **The level of disclosure**

    It has been held that the fact that the police have disclosed little or nothing of the case against the suspect, so that the solicitor cannot usefully advise the client, can be a 'good' reason for advising silence.[18] However, the fact that the police do not have a written statement from the complainant was held in *Howell* not to be a 'good' reason for advice to remain silent. Solicitors should keep a careful record of what has been disclosed by the police prior to each interview, and should ask the interviewing officer or officer in the case whether they have any information that they have not disclosed. Particular care should be taken where the police are using the tactic of 'phased disclosure', reconsidering the advice on each occasion that further disclosure is given.

2. **The nature of the case**

    Advice to remain silent is likely to be justified where the material in the hands of the police is so complex, or relates to matters so long ago, that no sensible immediate response is appropriate.[18] Advice must be reviewed if the police give the suspect the time and opportunity to consider the allegation, to review relevant documents, etc.

3. **The circumstances of the suspect**

    The courts have recognised that advice to remain silent may be appropriate where the suspect's condition is such that a response in interview would not be advisable. Relevant factors here include ill-health, mental disorder or vulnerability, confusion, intoxication, shock, etc.[19] Where possible, evidence of the condition of the suspect, from a doctor or other health care practitioner, should be obtained and, in any event, the solicitor should make a careful record of the relevant condition.

4. **The apparent strength of the police case**

If the prosecution evidence is, or is likely to be, strong a court is likely to take the view that this is a situation calling for an explanation from the suspect. Considering the strength of the evidence will involve an assessment of the likely admissibility of the evidence concerned. In *Howell* the court held that the possibility that the complainant may withdraw the complaint was not a 'good' reason for remaining silent. Nevertheless, it may still be appropriate to advise silence in such circumstances since if the complainant does withdraw their complaint, there may be insufficient evidence for a successful prosecution. Further, the court in *Howell* stated that the fact that the lawyer believed that the suspect would be charged whatever he said in interview was also not a 'good' reason. However, it has been held in other cases that inferences should not be drawn in such circumstances.[20] The solicitor should, where relevant, ask the police in advance of an interview what their intentions are once the interview has been conducted. If they believe that the interview and/or detention is unlawful or contrary to Code C, the lawyer should make representations and request that they be noted on the custody record together with the police response.

5. **The client's instructions**

If, having obtained instructions, the solicitor concludes that the client is guilty of the suspected offence, s/he should consider the strength of the police evidence.

If the police evidence is strong, the solicitor should consider the potential advantages of making admissions, including any possible effect on sentence or on alternatives to prosecution eg caution, final warning or reprimand. If the police evidence is weak, or the solicitor is unclear of the strength of the police case, the solicitor should consider the advantages (and disadvantages) of remaining silent at this stage.

Remember that if the client has admitted their guilt, the solicitor cannot go into the police interview with them in the knowledge that the client is going to assert their innocence, but it is proper for the solicitor to accompany the client in the police interview if the client does not answer questions.

If the client has a defence, the solicitor should consider the dangers of not putting it forward in interview (especially in terms of credibility and the damage from inferences), but should also consider what strategy (eg, answering questions or making a written statement) would be most appropriate. Answering police questions may be the most persuasive evidence of the veracity of the defence, but there are risks attached to putting forward a defence in a police interview even though it is genuine.

In deciding what advice to give it is important that solicitors remember that their principal professional obligation is to advise, and to act, in their client's best interests. This may mean advising silence even in the absence of reasons recognised by the courts as 'good' reasons.

Waiver of privilege

Consultations between solicitors and their clients are normally covered by legal professional privilege, so that an accused may not be asked, and if asked, cannot be required to state, what passed between them and their lawyer. There are special difficulties, however, in relation to advice not to answer questions because mere evidence of that advice may not be enough to prevent inferences from being drawn. The following principles can be drawn from the cases:

- If the accused simply gives evidence that he or she was advised by their solicitor to remain silent, this will not amount to waiver of privilege (but is also unlikely to be very persuasive).[21]

- If the accused, or his or her lawyer, tells the police of the reasons for the advice, or gives evidence of the basis or reasons for the advice, this is likely to amount to waiver of privilege.[22] Note that a lawyer's opening statement in a police interview can be adduced as evidence by the prosecution at trial.[23]

- Waiver of privilege is indivisible, so that if privilege is waived, the accused (and his or her lawyer if giving evidence) may be asked what else was said in consultation, and whether there were other reasons for advice to remain silent.

Normally, therefore, the solicitor should not tell the police nor state in the police interview the reason(s) for advice given to the client. Although there is no specific authority on the point, it should **not** amount to a waiver of privilege where the solicitor tells the police that they have advised their client not to answer questions, and separately informs them of facts relevant to that decision, eg, a belief on the part of the lawyer that the detention or interview is unlawful or contrary to Code C. Similarly, it should **not** amount to a waiver of privilege if the solicitor states in the police interview 'I now advise my client not to answer questions because....', **provided** that no reference is made to information obtained or advice given in privileged circumstances.

The need to keep proper records

It is essential that solicitors keep a full, clear and contemporaneous record of the information obtained, prevailing circumstances and advice given at the police station. In any particular case, the solicitor may be required to give evidence of the advice given and the reasons for it, and are open to significant judicial criticism if their records are found to be inadequate. Furthermore, since the evidence of a solicitor may be crucial in the decision whether to draw inferences, such a failure may do a considerable disservice to a client which could amount to inadequate professional service or, in an extreme case, a disciplinary offence.

A careful note, together with relevant times, should be taken of the following:

- the physical and mental state of the client
- the general conduct of the police and the 'atmosphere' in which the investigation is conducted
- what the police allege has been said by the client prior to the solicitor's attendance
- what the police assert has been said to the suspect by the police eg. a request to account for an object etc., and what reply, if any, was made
- what information is disclosed to the solicitor by the police
- what requests for information and disclosure are made to the police by the solicitor
- any request for information to be recorded in the custody record, and any representations made to the custody officer
- what information and instructions are given to the solicitor by the client
- the suspect's apparent understanding of the significance of the allegation, and the significance of his or her replies or failure to respond

- what advice the solicitor gives to the client, and the reasons for that advice
- the wording of any caution or special warning given to the client, and of any explanation of the caution or special warning
- what was said during the course of a police interview
- what was said at the time of charge/report for summons.

Strategies where the client is not answering police questions

Where the suspect is not going to answer police questions in interview, either as a result of advice given or of their own volition, the solicitor should consider and advise upon the appropriate strategy to adopt.

1. **Informing the police**

    The solicitor should normally make an opening statement at the beginning of a police interview setting out:

    - their role in the interview
    - the advice given not to answer questions (if appropriate)
    - the disclosure given to the solicitor by the police (if appropriate)
    - the circumstances in which the lawyer will intervene.

    The solicitor should inform the police that their client is not going to answer police questions, but should not normally state the reasons for any advice (see above). If, for example, the solicitor believes the detention and/or interview to be unlawful or contrary to Code C, he or she should inform the custody officer prior to the interview, and repeat it at the beginning of the interview. The interviewing officer may, following *Howell,* try to undermine the solicitor's advice by telling the suspect that they are not obliged to accept advice to remain silent. The solicitor should deal with this possibility in the following way:

    - Prior to the interview, warn the client that the interviewing officer may use this tactic, explaining the officer's aim – to make the client lose faith in the legal advice given and what the solicitor will do if the officer attempts to do so.
    - During the interview, if the officer attempts to use this tactic intervene immediately to inform the officer that (a) should the case go to trial, it will be for the court to decide on the merits of the legal advice given to the client and the client's decision, and (b) the court will draw its own conclusions as to the appropriateness of the officer's conduct.

2. **Handing in a statement**

    Handing a statement to the police setting out the relevant facts has been treated by the courts as 'mentioning' facts for the purposes of the silence provisions, and the same principle should apply to providing an account for the purposes of ss 36 and 37 CJPOA 1994.[24] This strategy should be considered where there are good reasons for informing the police of facts that are likely to relied upon by the defence at trial (or for providing an account), whilst not wanting to place the client at risk of 'cross-examination' by the police (eg, because they are nervous or because police disclosure has been limited). However, note that handing in a statement will 'fix' the suspect with the defence, and may have the effect of providing the police with sufficient evidence to charge.

    It was held in *R v Knight*[25] that handing in a statement does not 'in itself' prevent inferences from being drawn. If the defendant relies on facts at trial that were not mentioned in the statement, inferences can still be drawn from failure to mention those facts. Therefore, the statement should set out the facts that have been disclosed by the police, and cover the essential features of the defence in as much detail as possible having regard to the prosecution case as far as it is known. Care must be taken to anticipate the facts that are likely to be relied on at trial, and also to anticipate any request to account under ss 36 or 37 CJPOA 1994, and to deal with these in the statement. If there is more than one interview, the statement should be reviewed in the light of any information disclosed by the police during the course of a prior interview, or between interviews, and consideration given to handing in a supplementary statement.

A statement should normally be handed to the police at the beginning of an interview, whilst telling the police that the client does not intend to answer questions. Provided that the facts subsequently relied upon at trial are adequately covered, it should have the effect of avoiding inferences under s 34(1)(a) (or under ss 36 and 37), but will not prevent inferences under s34(1)(b). The latter could be particularly relevant if information is disclosed by the police during the interview that is not adequately covered in the statement. In these circumstances, as noted above, the solicitor should consider whether a supplementary statement should be handed to the police.

3.   **Taking a statement that is not handed to the police**

This will not prevent all inferences, but may avoid an inference that facts put forward by the defence at trial have been fabricated since the police interview.[26] If, at trial, the prosecution argue recent fabrication, the statement becomes admissible to rebut the inference. However, if the prosecution do not assert recent fabrication but, for example, seek to persuade the court or jury that an innocent person would have wanted to assert their innocence to the police, the statement will be inadmissible as a self-serving statement. Nevertheless, taking a statement that is not handed in may be an appropriate strategy where there are good reasons not to hand a statement in, and there is a real possibility that the prosecution will argue recent fabrication.

4.   **Answering some questions and not others**

This is not normally an appropriate strategy because of the adverse effects on credibility of the defence at trial. It would normally be more advisable to hand in a statement covering the relevant facts.

5.   **Refusal to be interviewed**

It is not normally appropriate to advise a client to refuse to be interviewed unless, for example, the solicitor is strongly of the view that they are not fit to be interviewed. However, clients do, on occasion, decide that they are not prepared to leave their cell for the purpose of an interview. Such a refusal may have the effect of preventing a police interview from taking place, although note Code C para 12.5 which sets out the actions that the police may take, including interviewing the suspect in their cell.

References

1   For circumstances where the police can proceed with an interview in the absence of advice that has been requested. see Code C Annex B.

2   There has been some differences of opinion on this, but see the Judicial Studies Board Specimen Directions, para 40

3   See *R v Imran and Hussein* [1997] Crim LR 754.

4   See, in particular, *R v Argent* (1997) 2 Cr App R 27, [1997] Crim LR 346.

5   *R v Dervish* [2002] 2 Cr App R 6.

6   *R v N* [1999] Crim LR 61 and *R v B (MT)* [2000] Crim LR 181.

7   *R v Pointer* [1997] Crim LR 676.

8   *R v McGuinness* [1999] Crim LR 318. *R v Elliott* [2002] EWCA Crim 931, *R v Howell* [2003] Crim LR 405.

9   *R v Bowers* [1998] Crim LR 817, *R v Ashton and others* [2002] EWCA Crim 2782.

10   *R v N* [1999] Crim LR 61, *R v Betts and Hall* [2001] Crim LR 754, *R v Milford* [2001] Crim LR 330.

11   *R v McGarry* [1998] 3 All ER 805, *R v Ashton and others* [2002] EWCA Crim 2782.

12   [2003] EWCA Crim 1977.

13   *R v Condron* [1997] 1 Cr App R 185.

14   [2000] Crim LR 679

15   [2001] 2 Cr App R 257.

16   [2003] Crim LR 405.

17   *R v Argent and R v Roble* [1997] Crim LR 449.

18   *See R v Roble and R v Howell* (n 16).

19   See *R v Howell* (n 16).

20   See, for example, *R v Pointer* (n 7).

21   See *R v Condron* (n 14), and *R v Quang Van Bui* [2001] EWCA Crim 1.

22   *R v Bowden* [1999] 4 All ER 43.

23   *R v Fitzgerald* [1998] 6 June (CA, unreported).

24   See *R v McGarry* [1999] Crim LR 316 and *R v Ali* [2001] EWCA Crim 863.

25   [2003] EWCA Crim 1977.

26   *R v Condron* (n 13].

Appendix 5

Law Commission Guidance for Bail Decision-makers and their Advisers

Note: Paragraphs 2A and 6 of Part 1 of Schedule 1 to the Bail Act 1976, referred to in the Guidance, have been repealed and replaced by new paras 2A and 6 (see **3.4.3.4**).

In June 2001, the Law Commission published Bail and the Human Rights Act 1998 (Paper No 269) accompanied by the Guidance. The Guidance has been disseminated to the judiciary and justices' clerks and is here reproduced in full.

General principles applicable to the refusal of bail

1. Any decision to refuse bail should only be taken where this can be justified both under domestic legislation, principally the Bail Act 1976 (the Act), and under the European Convention on Human Rights (the Convention), as interpreted by the European Court of Human Rights (Strasbourg jurisprudence).

2. Accordingly, a defendant should only be refused bail where this is necessary for a purpose that is recognised by Strasbourg jurisprudence applying Article 5(3) of the Convention. That is where detention is necessary to avoid a real risk that, were the defendant released,

   (1) he or she would

      (a) fail to attend trial; or

      (b) interfere with evidence or witnesses, or otherwise obstruct the course of justice; or

      (c) commit an offence while on bail; or

      (d) be at risk of harm against which he or she would be inadequately protected; or

   (2) a disturbance to public order would result.

3. Detention will only be necessary if the risk could not be adequately addressed by the imposition of appropriate bail conditions that would make detention unnecessary.

4. Any court refusing bail should give reasons that explain why detention is necessary. Those reasons should be closely related to the individual circumstances of the defendant.

The exceptions to the right to bail in English law

5. Some of the exceptions to the right to bail found in the Act correlate so closely with the above purposes recognised by the Strasbourg jurisprudence that there is no need to consider separately how they should be applied in a way that complies with the Convention. These are the exceptions in paragraph 2(a) (fail to surrender to custody) and (c) (interfere with witnesses or otherwise obstruct the course of justice) and paragraph 7 (impracticable to complete inquiries or report without keeping defendant in custody) of Part I, and paragraph 2 of Part II (also based on failure to surrender to custody), of Schedule 1 to the Act.

6. In respect of the remaining exceptions to the right to bail we offer the following guidance as an aid to compliance with the Convention.

The risk of offending on bail

7.   The decision-taker must consider whether it may properly be inferred from any previous convictions and other circumstances relating to the defendant that there is a real risk that the defendant will commit an offence if granted bail, and that the defendant therefore falls within paragraph 2(b) of Part I of Schedule 1 to the Act. Provided that a decision to withhold bail is a necessary and proportionate response to a *real risk* that, if released, the defendant would commit an offence while on bail, such a decision will comply with the Convention.

Defendant on bail at the time of the alleged offence

8.   The factor in paragraph 2A of Part I of Schedule 1 to the Act (a defendant who commits an indictable offence whilst on bail) does not, in itself, establish any Article 5(3) purpose.

9.   Consequently, a court should not base a decision to withhold bail solely on paragraph 2A. To do so would infringe Article 5 and would be unlawful under sections 3 and 6 of the Human Rights Act 1998 (HRA)

10.   That factor may, however, be relevant to a decision whether to withhold bail on the basis of another relevant exception, for example the risk that the defendant will commit an offence while on bail.

Detention for the defendant's own protection

11.   A decision to refuse bail to a defendant under the exception in paragraph 3 of Part I of Schedule 1 to the Act, that is for the defendants own protection (from self-harm or harm from others) would comply with the Convention, where

      (1)   detention is *necessary* to address a *real risk* that, if granted bail, the defendant would suffer harm, against which detention could provide protection; and

      (2)   there are exceptional circumstances in the nature of the alleged offence and/or the conditions or context in which it is alleged to have been committed.

12.   A decision of a court to order detention because of a risk of *self*-harm may be compatible with the ECHR even where the circumstances giving rise to the risk are unconnected with the alleged offence, provided that the court is satisfied that there is a real risk of self-harm, and that a proper medical examination will take place rapidly so that the court may then consider exercising its powers of detention under the Mental Health Act 1983.

Detention because of a lack of information

13.   The refusal of bail under paragraph 5 of Part I of Schedule 1 to the Act, where it has not been practicable to obtain sufficient information for the taking of a full bail decision for want of time since the institution of proceedings against the defendant, would be compatible with Article 5 provided that

      (1)   detention is for a short period, which is no longer than necessary to enable the required information to be obtained, and

      (2)   the lack of information is not due to a failure of the prosecution, the police, the court or another state body to act with 'special diligence'.

14.   There is no need in such a case for the court to be satisfied of any of the recognised purposes set out in paragraph 2 above.

15.   After the initial short period of time has passed, a lack of information that is not due to a failure of a state body to act with 'special diligence' may be taken

into account as a factor militating in favour of detention on *another* Convention compliant ground for detention.

Detention following arrest under section 7

Paragraph 6 of Part I and paragraph 5 of Part II of Schedule 1

16. The broad provisions in paragraph 6 of Part I and paragraph 5 of Part II of Schedule 1 to the Act, that a defendant arrested pursuant to section 7 need not be granted bail, should be read subject to the narrower provisions governing bail following a section 7(3) arrest, set out in section 7(5) of the Act. That provision requires that bail should again be granted unless the justice is of the opinion that the defendant is not likely to surrender to custody, or has broken or is likely to break any condition of bail. Detention on one of these grounds will comply with the Convention only where this is necessary for one or more of the recognised purposes set out above in paragraph 2.

Section 7(5) hearings

17. At the hearing of section 7(5) proceedings there is no requirement that oral evidence should be heard in every case, but account should be taken of the quality of material presented. The may range from mere assertion to documentary proof. If the material includes oral evidence, the defendant must be given an opportunity to cross-examine. Likewise, a defendant should be permitted to give relevant oral evidence if he or she wishes to do so.

Section 25 of the Criminal Justice and Public Order Act 1994

18. The expression 'exceptional circumstances' in section 25 of the Criminal Justice and Public Order Act 1994 should be construed so that it encompasses a defendant who, if released on bail, would not pose a real risk of committing a serious offence. This construction achieves the purpose of Parliament to ensure that, when making bail decisions about defendants to whom section 25 applies, decision-takers focus on the risk the defendant may pose to the public by re-offending.

19. It is possible that's some other circumstance might constitute 'exceptional circumstances'. Even if 'exceptional circumstances' do exist, bail may, nonetheless, be withheld on a Convention-compatible ground if this is deemed to be necessary in the individual case.

Conditional bail

Conditional bail as an alternative to custody

20. A defendant must be released, if need be subject to conditions, unless:
    (1) that would create a risk of the kind which can, in principle, justify pretrial detention (set out above in paragraph 2), and
    (2) that risk cannot, by imposing suitable bail conditions, be averted, or reduced to a level at which it would not justify detention.

Conditional bail as an alternative to unconditional bail

21. A court should only impose bail conditions for one of the purposes which Strasbourg jurisprudence recognises as capable of justifying detention (set out above in paragraph 2).

22. A bail condition should only be imposed where, if the defendant were to break that condition or be reasonably thought likely to do so, it may be

necessary to arrest the defendant in order to pursue the purpose for which the condition was imposed.

Reasons for imposing conditions

23.   Decision-takers should state their reasons for imposing bail conditions and specify the purposes for which any conditions are imposed.

24.   Decision-takers should also be alert to ensure that any bail conditions they impose do not violate the defendants other Convention rights, such as those protected by Articles 8–11 of the Convention (the right to respect for family life, freedom of thought, conscience and religion, freedom of expression and freedom of assembly and association).

Giving reasons for bail decisions

25.   It is of particular importance that decision-takers or their clerks make, and retain for the file, a note of the gist of the arguments for and against the grant of bail, and the oral reasons given by the tribunal for their decision.

26.   Standard forms should be completed accurately to show that a decision has been taken in a way that complies with the Convention.

Participation of the defendant

27.   Strasbourg jurisprudence recognises it as sufficient participation of the defendant in bail proceedings if, where necessary, he or she participates through a legal representative. Nevertheless, a domestic court should not hear a bail application to a conclusion in the absence of a defendant where the defendant's presence is essential to fair proceedings.

Form of evidence

28.   It is not necessary to hear sworn evidence in the great majority of cases. Courts should, in particular cases, consider whether fairness requires the calling of evidence on oath for the determination of the application, as a failure to call such evidence may cause a particular decision to fall foul of Article 5(4).

29.   A court hearing bail proceedings should take account of the quality of the material presented. It may range from mere assertion to documentary proof. If the material includes sworn oral evidence, the defendant must be given an opportunity to cross-examine. Likewise, the defendant should be permitted to give relevant oral evidence if he or she wishes to do so.

Disclosure

30.   *Ex parte Lee* recognises an ongoing duty of disclosure from the time of arrest. The Court of Appeal emphasised that at the stage before committal, there are continuing obligations on the prosecutor to make such disclosure as justice and fairness may require in the particular circumstances of the case, that is, where it could reasonably be expected to assist the defence when applying for bail. This will ensure that the defendant enjoys 'equality of arms' with the prosecution.

31.   Compliance with this requirement, together with those imposed by the Attorney-General's guidelines to prosecutors, should ensure compliance with the Convention. This will apply equally to hearings pursuant to s.7(5). (see above).

32.   The duty of disclosure does not require that the whole of the prosecution file be disclosed to the defence prior to the hearing. It is sufficient if disclosure is provided of the material the defendant needs in order to enjoy 'equality of

arms' with the prosecution in relation to the matter to be decided by the court.

Public hearing

33.   Where normally the hearing would be in chambers, if the defendant requests that the bail hearing be held in public, it should be held in public unless there is a good reason not to do so.

The right to challenge pre-trial detention

34.   The Convention gives a detained person the right to make further court challenges to the legality of his or her detention despite having already made one or more such challenges, where for example, with the passage of time, the circumstances which once were considered by a court to justify detention may have changed.

35.   To ensure compliance with the Convention, Part 11A of Schedule I to the Act should be applied on the basis that courts should be willing, at intervals of 28 days, to consider arguments that the passage of time constitutes, in the particular case, a change in circumstances relevant to the need to detain the defendant, so as to require the hearing of all the arguments on the question of bail. It may be, for example, that the time served on remand may have reduced the risk of the defendant absconding.

36.   If the court finds that the passage of time does amount to a relevant change of circumstances then a full bail application should follow in which all the arguments, old and new, could be put forward and taken into account.

Appendix 6

PACE Codes

Police and Criminal Evidence Act 1984 (PACE)

Code C

Code of practice for the detention, treatment and questioning of persons by police officers

Commencement — Transitional Arrangements

This Code applies to people in police detention after midnight on 31st March 2003, notwithstanding that their period of detention may have commenced before that time.

1 General

1.1   All persons in custody must be dealt with expeditiously, and released as soon as the need for detention no longer applies.

1.1A A custody officer must perform the functions in this Code as soon as practicable. A custody officer will not be in breach of this Code if delay is justifiable and reasonable steps are taken to prevent unnecessary delay. The custody record shall show when a delay has occurred and the reason. See *Note 1H*

1.2   This Code of Practice must be readily available at all police stations for consultation by:
- police officers
- detained persons
- members of the public.

1.3   The provisions of this Code:
- include the *Annexes*
- do not include the *Notes for Guidance*.

1.4   If an officer has any suspicion, or is told in good faith, that a person of any age may be mentally disordered or otherwise mentally vulnerable, in the absence of clear evidence to dispel that suspicion, the person shall be treated as such for the purposes of this Code. See *Note 1G*

1.5   If anyone appears to be under 17, they shall be treated as a juvenile for the purposes of this Code in the absence of clear evidence that they are older.

1.6   If a person appears to be blind, seriously visually impaired, deaf, unable to read or speak or has difficulty orally because of a speech impediment, they shall be treated as such for the purposes of this Code in the absence of clear evidence to the contrary.

1.7   'The appropriate adult' means, in the case of a:

(a)   juvenile:

   (i)   the parent, guardian or, if the juvenile is in local authority or voluntary organisation care, or is otherwise being looked after under the Children Act 1989, a person representing that authority or organisation;

   (ii) a social worker of a local authority social services department;

(iii) failing these, some other responsible adult aged 18 or over who is not a police officer or employed by the police.

(b) person who is mentally disordered or mentally vulnerable: See Note 1D

(i) a relative, guardian or other person responsible for their care or custody;

(ii) someone experienced in dealing with mentally disordered or mentally vulnerable people but who is not a police officer or employed by the police;

(iii) failing these, some other responsible adult aged 18 or over who is not a police officer or employed by the police.

1.8 If this Code requires a person be given certain information, they do not have to be given it if at the time they are incapable of understanding what is said, are violent or may become violent or in urgent need of medical attention, but they must be given it as soon as practicable.

1.9 References to a custody officer include those performing the functions of a custody officer.

1.9A When this Code requires the prior authority or agreement of an officer of at least inspector or superintendent rank, that authority may be given by a sergeant or chief inspector authorised to perform the functions of the higher rank under the Police and Criminal Evidence Act 1984 (PACE), section 107.

1.10 Subject to *paragraph 1.12*, this Code applies to people in custody at police stations in England and Wales, whether or not they have been arrested, and to those removed to a police station as a place of safety under the Mental Health Act 1983, sections 135 and 136. *Section 15* applies solely to people in police detention, e.g. those brought to a police station under arrest or arrested at a police station for an offence after going there voluntarily.

1.11 People in police custody include anyone detained under the Terrorism Act 2000, Schedule 8 and section 41, having been taken to a police station after being arrested under the Terrorism Act 2000, section 41. In these cases, reference to an offence in this Code includes the commission, preparation and instigation of acts of terrorism.

1.12 This Code's provisions do not apply to people in custody:

(i) arrested on warrants issued in Scotland by officers under the Criminal Justice and Public Order Act 1994, section 136(2), or arrested or detained without warrant by officers from a police force in Scotland under section 137(2). In these cases, police powers and duties and the person's rights and entitlements whilst at a police station in England or Wales are the same as those in Scotland;

(ii) arrested under the Immigration and Asylum Act 1999, section 142(3) in order to have their fingerprints taken;

(iii) whose detention is authorised by an immigration officer under the Immigration Act 1971;

(iv) who are convicted or remanded prisoners held in police cells on behalf of the Prison Service under the Imprisonment (Temporary Provisions) Act 1980;

(v) detained for examination under the Terrorism Act 2000, Schedule 7 and to whom the Code of Practice issued under that Act, Schedule 14, paragraph 6 applies;

(vi) detained for searches under stop and search powers except as required by Code A.

The provisions on conditions of detention and treatment in *sections 8* and *9* must be considered as the minimum standards of treatment for such detainees.

1.13 In this Code:

(a) 'designated person' means a person other than a police officer, designated under the Police Reform Act 2002, Part 4 who has specified powers and duties of police officers conferred or imposed on them;

(b) reference to a police officer includes a designated person acting in the exercise or performance of the powers and duties conferred or imposed on them by their designation.

1.14 If a power conferred on a designated person:

(a) allows reasonable force to be used when exercised by a police officer, a person exercising that power has the same entitlement to use force;

(b) includes power to use force to enter any premises, that power is not exercisable by that designated person except:

(i) in the company, and under the supervision, of a police officer;

(i) for the purpose of:

• saving life or limb; or

• preventing serious damage to property.

1.15 Nothing in this Code prevents the custody officer, or other officer given custody of the detainee, from allowing civilian support staff who are not designated persons to carry out individual procedures or tasks at the police station if the law allows. However, the officer remains responsible for making sure the procedures and tasks are carried out correctly in accordance with the Codes of Practice. Any such civilian must be:

(a) a person employed by a police authority maintaining a police force and under the control and direction of the Chief Officer of that force;

(b) employed by a person with whom a police authority has a contract for the provision of services relating to persons arrested or otherwise in custody.

1.16 Designated persons and other civilian support staff must have regard to any relevant provisions of the Codes of Practice.

1.17 References to pocket books include any official report book issued to police officers or civilian support staff.

Notes for guidance

1A *Although certain sections of this Code apply specifically to people in custody at police stations, those there voluntarily to assist with an investigation should be treated with no less consideration, e.g. offered refreshments at appropriate times, and enjoy an absolute right to obtain legal advice or communicate with anyone outside the police station.*

1B *A person, including a parent or guardian, should not be an appropriate adult if they:*

• *are*

— *suspected of involvement in the offence*

— *the victim*

— *a witness*

— *involved in the investigation*

• *received admissions prior to attending to act as the appropriate adult.*

Note: If a juvenile's parent is estranged from the juvenile, they should not be asked to act as the appropriate adult if the juvenile expressly and specifically objects to their presence.

1C *If a juvenile admits an offence to, or in the presence of, a social worker or member of a youth offending team other than during the time that person is acting as the juvenile's appropriate adult, another appropriate adult should be appointed in the interest of fairness.*

1D   *In the case of people who are mentally disordered or otherwise mentally vulnerable, it may be more satisfactory if the appropriate adult is someone experienced or trained in their care rather than a relative lacking such qualifications. But if the detainee prefers a relative to a better qualified stranger or objects to a particular person their wishes should, if practicable, be respected.*

1E   *A detainee should always be given an opportunity, when an appropriate adult is called to the police station, to consult privately with a solicitor in the appropriate adult's absence if they want.*

1F   *A solicitor or independent custody visitor (formerly a lay visitor) present at the police station in that capacity may not be the appropriate adult.*

1G   *'Mentally vulnerable' applies to any detainee who, because of their mental state or capacity, may not understand the significance of what is said, of questions or of their replies. 'Mental disorder' is defined in the Mental Health Act 1983, section 1(2) as 'mental illness, arrested or incomplete development of mind, psychopathic disorder and any other disorder or disability of mind'. When the custody officer has any doubt about the mental state or capacity of a detainee, that detainee should be treated as mentally vulnerable and an appropriate adult called.*

1H   *Paragraph 1.1A is intended to cover delays which may occur in processing detainees e.g. if:*

- *a large number of suspects are brought into the station simultaneously to be placed in custody;*
- *interview rooms are all being used;*
- *there are difficulties contacting an appropriate adult, solicitor or interpreter.*

1I   *The custody officer must remind the appropriate adult and detainee about the right to legal advice and record any reasons for waiving it in accordance with section 6.*

2 Custody records

2.1   A separate custody record must be opened as soon as practicable for each person brought to a police station under arrest or arrested at the station having gone there voluntarily. All information recorded under this Code must be recorded as soon as practicable in the custody record unless otherwise specified. Any audio or video recording made in the custody area is not part of the custody record.

2.2   If any action requires the authority of an officer of a specified rank, subject to *paragraph 2.6A*, their name and rank must be noted in the custody record.

2.3   The custody officer is responsible for the custody record's accuracy and completeness and for making sure the record or copy of the record accompanies a detainee if they are transferred to another police station. The record shall show the:

- time and reason for transfer;
- time a person is released from detention.

2.4   A solicitor or appropriate adult must be permitted to consult a detainee's custody record as soon as practicable after their arrival at the station and at any other time whilst the person is detained. Arrangements for this access must be agreed with the custody officer and may not unreasonably interfere with the custody officer's duties.

2.4A   When a detainee leaves police detention or is taken before a court they, their legal representative or appropriate adult shall be given, on request, a copy of the custody record as soon as practicable. This entitlement lasts for 12 months after release.

2.5 The detainee, appropriate adult or legal representative shall be permitted to inspect the original custody record after the detainee has left police detention provided they give reasonable notice of their request. Any such inspection shall be noted in the custody record.

2.6 Subject to *paragraph 2.6A*, all entries in custody records must be timed and signed by the maker. Records entered on computer shall be timed and contain the operator's identification.

2.6A Nothing in this Code requires the identity of officers or civilian support staff to be recorded or disclosed:

(a) in the case of enquiries linked to the investigation of terrorism; or

(b) if the officer or civilian support staff reasonably believe recording or disclosing their name might put them in danger.

In these cases, they shall use their warrant or other identification numbers and the name of their police station. See *Note 2A*

2.7 The fact and time of any detainee's refusal to sign a custody record, when asked in accordance with this Code, must be recorded.

Note for guidance

2A   The purpose of paragraph 2.6A(b) is to protect those involved in serious organised crime investigations or arrests of particularly violent suspects when there is reliable information that those arrested or their associates may threaten or cause harm to those involved. In cases of doubt, an officer of inspector rank or above should be consulted.

3 Initial action

(a) Detained persons — normal procedure

3.1 When a person is brought to a police station under arrest or arrested at the station having gone there voluntarily, the custody officer must make sure the person is told clearly about the following continuing rights which may be exercised at any stage during the period in custody:

(i) the right to have someone informed of their arrest as in *section 5*;

(ii) the right to consult privately with a solicitor and that free independent legal advice is available;

(iii) the right to consult these Codes of Practice. See *Note 3D*

3.2 The detainee must also be given:

• a written notice setting out:

— the above three rights;

— the arrangements for obtaining legal advice;

— the right to a copy of the custody record as in *paragraph 2.4A*;

— the caution in the terms prescribed in *section 10*.

• an additional written notice briefly setting out their entitlements while in custody, see *Notes 3A* and *3B*.

Note: The detainee shall be asked to sign the custody record to acknowledge receipt of these notices. Any refusal must be recorded on the custody record.

3.3 A citizen of an independent Commonwealth country or a national of a foreign country, including the Republic of Ireland, must be informed as soon as practicable about their rights of communication with their High Commission, Embassy or Consulate. See *section 7*

3.4 The custody officer shall:

• note on the custody record any comment the detainee makes in relation to the arresting officer's account but shall not invite comment. If the custody officer authorises a person's detention the detainee must be informed of the grounds as soon as practicable and before they are questioned about any offence;

- note any comment the detainee makes in respect of the decision to detain them but shall not invite comment;

- not put specific questions to the detainee regarding their involvement in any offence, nor in respect of any comments they may make in response to the arresting officer's account or the decision to place them in detention. Such an exchange is likely to constitute an interview as in *paragraph 11.1A* and require the associated safeguards in *section 11*.

See *paragraph 11.13* in respect of unsolicited comments.

3.5   The custody officer shall:

(a)   ask the detainee, whether at this time, they:

    (i)   would like legal advice, see *paragraph 6.5*;

    (ii)   want someone informed of their detention, see *section 5*;

(b)   ask the detainee to sign the custody record to confirm their decisions in respect of (*a*);

(c)   determine whether the detainee:

    (i)   is, or might be, in need of medical treatment or attention, see *section 9*;

    (ii)   requires:

- an appropriate adult;

- help to check documentation;

- an interpreter;

(d)   record the decision in respect of (*c*).

3.6   When determining these needs the custody officer is responsible for initiating an assessment to consider whether the detainee is likely to present specific risks to custody staff or themselves. Such assessments should always include a check on the Police National Computer, to be carried out as soon as practicable, to identify any risks highlighted in relation to the detainee. Although such assessments are primarily the custody officer's responsibility, it may be necessary for them to consult and involve others, e.g. the arresting officer or an appropriate health care professional, see *paragraph 9.13*. Reasons for delaying the initiation or completion of the assessment must be recorded.

3.7   Chief Officers should ensure that arrangements for proper and effective risk assessments required by *paragraph 3.6* are implemented in respect of all detainees at police stations in their area.

3.8   Risk assessments must follow a structured process which clearly defines the categories of risk to be considered and the results must be incorporated in the detainee's custody record. The custody officer is responsible for making sure those responsible for the detainee's custody are appropriately briefed about the risks. If no specific risks are identified by the assessment, that should be noted in the custody record. See *Note 3E* and *paragraph 9.14*

3.9   The custody officer is responsible for implementing the response to any specific risk assessment, e.g.:

- reducing opportunities for self harm;

- calling a health care professional;

- increasing levels of monitoring or observation.

3.10   Risk assessment is an ongoing process and assessments must always be subject to review if circumstances change.

3.11 If video cameras are installed in the custody area, notices shall be prominently displayed showing cameras are in use. Any request to have video cameras switched off shall be refused.

(b) Detained persons — special groups

3.12 If the detainee appears deaf or there is doubt about their hearing or speaking ability or ability to understand English, and the custody officer cannot establish effective communication, the custody officer must, as soon as practicable, call an interpreter for assistance in the action under *paragraphs 3.1–3.5*. See *section 13*

3.13 If the detainee is a juvenile, the custody officer must, if it is practicable, ascertain the identity of a person responsible for their welfare. That person:

- may be:
  - the parent or guardian;
  - if the juvenile is in local authority or voluntary organisation care, or is otherwise being looked after under the Children Act 1989, a person appointed by that authority or organisation to have responsibility for the juvenile's welfare;
  - any other person who has, for the time being, assumed responsibility for the juvenile's welfare.
- must be informed as soon as practicable that the juvenile has been arrested, why they have been arrested and where they are detained. This right is in addition to the juvenile's right in section 5 not to be held incommunicado. See *Note 3C*

3.14 If a juvenile known to be subject to a court order under which a person or organisation is given any degree of statutory responsibility to supervise or otherwise monitor them, reasonable steps must also be taken to notify that person or organisation (the 'responsible officer'). The responsible officer will normally be a member of a Youth Offending Team, except for a curfew order which involves electronic monitoring when the contractor providing the monitoring will normally be the responsible officer.

3.15 If the detainee is a juvenile, mentally disordered or otherwise mentally vulnerable, the custody officer must, as soon as practicable:

- inform the appropriate adult, who in the case of a juvenile may or may not be a person responsible for their welfare, as in *paragraph 3.13*, of:
  - the grounds for their detention;
  - their whereabouts.
- ask the adult to come to the police station to see the detainee.

3.16 It is imperative a mentally disordered or otherwise mentally vulnerable person, detained under the Mental Health Act 1983, section 136, be assessed as soon as possible. If that assessment is to take place at the police station, an approved social worker and a registered medical practitioner shall be called to the station as soon as possible in order to interview and examine the detainee. Once the detainee has been interviewed, examined and suitable arrangements made for their treatment or care, they can no longer be detained under section 136. A detainee must be immediately discharged from detention under section 136 if a registered medical practitioner, having examined them, concludes they are not mentally disordered within the meaning of the Act.

3.17 If the appropriate adult is:

- already at the police station, the provisions of *paragraphs 3.1 to 3.5* must be complied with in the appropriate adult's presence;

- not at the station when these provisions are complied with, they must be complied with again in the presence of the appropriate adult when they arrive.

3.18   The detainee shall be advised that:

- the duties of the appropriate adult include giving advice and assistance;
- they can consult privately with the appropriate adult at any time.

3.19   If the detainee, or appropriate adult on the detainee's behalf, asks for a solicitor to be called to give legal advice, the provisions of *section 6* apply.

3.20   If the detainee is blind, seriously visually impaired or unable to read, the custody officer shall make sure their solicitor, relative, appropriate adult or some other person likely to take an interest in them and not involved in the investigation is available to help check any documentation. When this Code requires written consent or signing the person assisting may be asked to sign instead, if the detainee prefers. This paragraph does not require an appropriate adult to be called solely to assist in checking and signing documentation for a person who is not a juvenile, or mentally disordered or otherwise mentally vulnerable (see *paragraph 3.15*).

(c)   *Persons attending a police station voluntarily*

3.21   Anybody attending a police station voluntarily to assist with an investigation may leave at will unless arrested. If it is decided they shall not be allowed to leave, they must be informed at once that they are under arrest and brought before the custody officer, who is responsible for making sure they are notified of their rights in the same way as other detainees. If they are not arrested but are cautioned as in section 10, the person who gives the caution must, at the same time, inform them they are not under arrest, they are not obliged to remain at the station but if they remain at the station they may obtain free and independent legal advice if they want. They shall be told the right to legal advice includes the right to speak with a solicitor on the telephone and be asked if they want to do so.

3.22   If a person attending the police station voluntarily asks about their entitlement to legal advice, they shall be given a copy of the notice explaining the arrangements for obtaining legal advice. See *paragraph 3.2*

(d)   Documentation

3.23   The grounds for a person's detention shall be recorded, in the person's presence if practicable.

3.24   Action taken under *paragraphs 3.12* to *3.20* shall be recorded.

Notes for guidance

3A   *The notice of entitlements should:*

- *list the entitlements in this Code, including:*
  - *visits and contact with outside parties, including special provisions for Commonwealth citizens and foreign nationals;*
  - *reasonable standards of physical comfort;*
  - *adequate food and drink;*
  - *access to toilets and washing facilities, clothing, medical attention, and exercise when practicable.*
- *mention the:*
  - *provisions relating to the conduct of interviews;*
  - *circumstances in which an appropriate adult should be available to assist the detainee and their statutory rights to make representation whenever the period of their detention is reviewed.*

3B   *In addition to notices in English, translations should be available in Welsh, the main minority ethnic languages and the principal European languages, whenever they are likely to be helpful.*

3C   *If the juvenile is in local authority or voluntary organisation care but living with their parents or other adults responsible for their welfare, although there is no legal obligation to inform them, they should normally be contacted, as well as the authority or organisation unless suspected of involvement in the offence concerned. Even if the juvenile is not living with their parents, consideration should be given to informing them.*

3D   *The right to consult the Codes of Practice does not entitle the person concerned to delay unreasonably any necessary investigative or administrative action whilst they do so. Examples of action which need not be delayed unreasonably include:*

- *procedures requiring the provision of breath, blood or urine specimens under the Road Traffic Act 1988 or the Transport and Works Act 1992*
- *searching detainees at the police station*
- *taking fingerprints or non-intimate samples without consent for evidential purposes.*

3E   *Home Office Circular 32/2000 provides more detailed guidance on risk assessments and identifies key risk areas which should always be considered.*

4   Detainee's property

(a)   Action

4.1   The custody officer is responsible for:

(a)   ascertaining what property a detainee:

(i)   has with them when they come to the police station, whether on:

- arrest or re-detention on answering to bail;
- commitment to prison custody on the order or sentence of a court;
- lodgement at the police station with a view to their production in court from prison custody; transfer from detention at another station or hospital;
- detention under the Mental Health Act 1983, section 135 or 136;

(ii)   might have acquired for an unlawful or harmful purpose while in custody;

(b)   the safekeeping of any property taken from a detainee which remains at the police station.

The custody officer may search the detainee or authorise their being searched to the extent they consider necessary, provided a search of intimate parts of the body or involving the removal of more than outer clothing is only made as in *Annex A*. A search may only be carried out by an officer of the same sex as the detainee. See *Note 4A*

4.2   Detainees may retain clothing and personal effects at their own risk unless the custody officer considers they may use them to cause harm to themselves or others, interfere with evidence, damage property, effect an escape or they are needed as evidence. In this event the custody officer may withhold such articles as they consider necessary and must tell the detainee why.

4.3   Personal effects are those items a detainee may lawfully need, use or refer to while in detention but do not include cash and other items of value.

(b)   Documentation

4.4   The custody officer is responsible for recording all property brought to the police station which a detainee had with them, or had taken from them on arrest. The detainee shall be allowed to check and sign the record of property as correct. Any refusal to sign shall be recorded.

4.5   If a detainee is not allowed to keep any article of clothing or personal effects, the reason must be recorded.

Notes for guidance

4A   *PACE, Section 54(1) and paragraph 4.1 require a detainee to be searched when it is clear the custody officer will have continuing duties in relation to that detainee or when that detainee's behaviour or offence makes an inventory appropriate. They do not require every detainee to be searched, e.g. if it is clear a person will only be detained for a short period and is not to be placed in a cell, the custody officer may decide not to search them. In such a case the custody record will be endorsed 'not searched', paragraph 4.4 will not apply, and the detainee will be invited to sign the entry. If the detainee refuses, the custody officer will be obliged to ascertain what property they have in accordance with paragraph 4.1.*

4B   *Paragraph 4.4 does not require the custody officer to record on the custody record property in the detainee's possession on arrest if, by virtue of its nature, quantity or size, it is not practicable to remove it to the police station.*

4C   *Paragraph 4.4 does not require items of clothing worn by the person be recorded unless withheld by the custody officer as in paragraph 4.2.*

5   Right not to be held incommunicado

(a)   Action

5.1   Any person arrested and held in custody at a police station or other premises may, on request, have one person known to them or likely to take an interest in their welfare informed at public expense of their whereabouts as soon as practicable. If the person cannot be contacted the detainee may choose up to two alternatives. If they cannot be contacted, the person in charge of detention or the investigation has discretion to allow further attempts until the information has been conveyed. See *Notes 5C* and *5D*

5.2   The exercise of the above right in respect of each person nominated may be delayed only in accordance with *Annex B*.

5.3   The above right may be exercised each time a detainee is taken to another police station.

5.4   The detainee may receive visits at the custody officer's discretion. See *Note 5B*

5.5   If a friend, relative or person with an interest in the detainee's welfare enquires about their whereabouts, this information shall be given if the suspect agrees and *Annex B* does not apply. See *Note 5D*

5.6   The detainee shall be given writing materials, on request, and allowed to telephone one person for a reasonable time, see *Notes 5A* and *5E*. Either or both these privileges may be denied or delayed if an officer of inspector rank or above considers sending a letter or making a telephone call may result in any of the consequences in:

(a)   *Annex B paragraphs 1* and *2* and the person is detained in connection with an arrestable or serious arrestable offence; or

(b)   *Annex B paragraphs 8* and *9* and the person is detained under the Terrorism Act 2000, Schedule 7 or section 41

For the purposes of this paragraph, any reference to a serious arrestable offence in *Annex B* includes an arrestable offence. However, nothing in this paragraph permits the restriction or denial of the rights in *paragraphs 5.1* and *6.1*.

5.7   Before any letter or message is sent, or telephone call made, the detainee shall be informed that what they say in any letter, call or message (other than in a communication to a solicitor) may be read or listened to and may be given in evidence. A telephone call may be terminated if it is being abused. The costs can be at public expense at the custody officer's discretion.

(b) *Documentation*

5.8 A record must be kept of any:

(a) request made under this section and the action taken;

(b) letters, messages or telephone calls made or received or visit received;

(c) refusal by the detainee to have information about them given to an outside enquirer. The detainee must be asked to countersign the record accordingly and any refusal recorded.

Notes for guidance

5A *A person may request an interpreter to interpret a telephone call or translate a letter.*

5B *At the custody officer's discretion, visits should be allowed when possible, subject to having sufficient personnel to supervise a visit and any possible hindrance to the investigation.*

5C *If the detainee does not know anyone to contact for advice or support or cannot contact a friend or relative, the custody officer should bear in mind any local voluntary bodies or other organisations who might be able to help. Paragraph 6.1 applies if legal advice is required.*

5D *In some circumstances it may not be appropriate to use the telephone to disclose information under paragraphs 5.1 and 5.5.*

5E *The telephone call at paragraph 5.6 is in addition to any communication under paragraphs 5.1 and 6.1.*

6 Right to legal advice

(a) *Action*

6.1 Unless *Annex B* applies, all detainees must be informed that they may at any time consult and communicate privately with a solicitor, whether in person, in writing or by telephone, and that free independent legal advice is available from the duty solicitor. See *paragraph 3.1, Note 6B* and *Note 6J*

6.2 Not Used

6.3 A poster advertising the right to legal advice must be prominently displayed in the charging area of every police station. See *Note 6H*

6.4 No police officer should, at any time, do or say anything with the intention of dissuading a detainee from obtaining legal advice.

6.5 The exercise of the right of access to legal advice may be delayed only as in *Annex B*. Whenever legal advice is requested, and unless Annex B applies, the custody officer must act without delay to secure the provision of such advice. If, on being informed or reminded of this right, the detainee declines to speak to a solicitor in person, the officer should point out that the right includes the right to speak with a solicitor on the telephone. If the detainee continues to waive this right the officer should ask them why and any reasons should be recorded on the custody record or the interview record as appropriate. Reminders of the right to legal advice must be given as in *paragraphs 3.5, 11.2, 15.4, 16.4* and *16.5* and Code D, *paragraphs 3.17(ii)* and *6.3*. Once it is clear a detainee does not want to speak to a solicitor in person or by telephone they should cease to be asked their reasons. See *Note 6K*

6.6 A detainee who wants legal advice may not be interviewed or continue to be interviewed until they have received such advice unless:

(a)   *Annex B* applies, when the restriction on drawing adverse inferences from silence in *Annex C* will apply because the detainee is not allowed an opportunity to consult a solicitor; or

(b)   an officer of superintendent rank or above has reasonable grounds for believing that:

    (i)   the consequent delay might:

- lead to interference with, or harm to, evidence connected with an offence;
- lead to interference with, or physical harm to, other people;
- lead to serious loss of, or damage to, property;
- lead to alerting other people suspected of having committed an offence but not yet arrested for it;
- hinder the recovery of property obtained in consequence of the commission of an offence.

    (ii)   when a solicitor, including a duty solicitor, has been contacted and has agreed to attend, awaiting their arrival would cause unreasonable delay to the process of investigation.

Note: In these cases the restriction on drawing adverse inferences from silence in *Annex C* will apply because the detainee is not allowed an opportunity to consult a solicitor;

(c)   the solicitor the detainee has nominated or selected from a list:

    (i)   cannot be contacted;

    (ii)   has previously indicated they do not wish to be contacted; or

    (iii)   having been contacted, has declined to attend; and

    the detainee has been advised of the Duty Solicitor Scheme but has declined to ask for the duty solicitor.

    In these circumstances the interview may be started or continued without further delay provided an officer of inspector rank or above has agreed to the interview proceeding.

Note: The restriction on drawing adverse inferences from silence in Annex C will not apply because the detainee is allowed an opportunity to consult the duty solicitor;

(d)   the detainee changes their mind, about wanting legal advice.

    In these circumstances the interview may be started or continued without delay provided that:

    (i)   the detainee agrees to do so, in writing or on tape; and

    (ii)   an officer of inspector rank or above has inquired about the detainee's reasons for their change of mind and gives authority for the interview to proceed.

Confirmation of the detainee's agreement, their change of mind, the reasons for it if given and, subject to *paragraph 2.6A*, the name of the authorising officer shall be recorded in the taped or written interview record. See *Note 6I*. Note: In these circumstances the restriction on drawing adverse inferences from silence in *Annex C* will not apply because the detainee is allowed an opportunity to consult a solicitor if they wish.

6.7   If *paragraph 6.6(b)(i)* applies, once sufficient information has been obtained to avert the risk, questioning must cease until the detainee has received legal advice unless *paragraph 6.6(a), (b)(ii), (c) or (d)* applies.

6.8   A detainee who has been permitted to consult a solicitor shall be entitled on request to have the solicitor present when they are interviewed unless one of the exceptions in *paragraph 6.6* applies.

6.9   The solicitor may only be required to leave the interview if their conduct is such that the interviewer is unable properly to put questions to the suspect. See *Notes 6D* and *6E*

6.10   If the interviewer considers a solicitor is acting in such a way, they will stop the interview and consult an officer not below superintendent rank, if one is readily available, and otherwise an officer not below inspector rank not connected with the investigation. After speaking to the solicitor, the officer consulted will decide if the interview should continue in the presence of that solicitor. If they decide it should not, the suspect will be given the opportunity to consult another solicitor before the interview continues and that solicitor given an opportunity to be present at the interview. See *Note 6E*

6.11   The removal of a solicitor from an interview is a serious step and, if it occurs, the officer of superintendent rank or above who took the decision will consider if the incident should be reported to the Law Society. If the decision to remove the solicitor has been taken by an officer below superintendent rank, the facts must be reported to an officer of superintendent rank or above who will similarly consider whether a report to the Law Society would be appropriate. When the solicitor concerned is a duty solicitor, the report should be both to the Law Society and to the Legal Services Commission.

6.12   'Solicitor' in this Code means:
- a solicitor who holds a current practising certificate
- a trainee solicitor;
- a duty solicitor representative;
- an accredited representative included on the register of representatives maintained by the Legal Services Commission.

6.12A A non-accredited or probationary representative sent to provide advice by, and on behalf of, a solicitor shall be admitted to the police station for this purpose unless an officer of inspector rank or above considers such a visit will hinder the investigation and directs otherwise. Hindering the investigation does not include giving proper legal advice to a detainee as in *Note 6D*. Once admitted to the police station, *paragraphs 6.6* to *6.10* apply.

6.13   In exercising their discretion under paragraph 6.12A, the officer should take into account in particular:
- whether:
  — the identity and status of the non-accredited or probationary representative have been satisfactorily established;
  — they are of suitable character to provide legal advice, e.g. a person with a criminal record is unlikely to be suitable unless the conviction was for a minor offence and not recent.
- any other matters in any written letter of authorisation provided by the solicitor on whose behalf the person is attending the police station. See *Note 6F*

6.14   If the inspector refuses access to a non-accredited or probationary representative or a decision is taken that such a person should not be permitted to remain at an interview, the inspector must notify the solicitor on whose behalf the representative was acting and give them an opportunity to make alternative arrangements. The detainee must be informed and the custody record noted.

6.15   If a solicitor arrives at the station to see a particular person, that person must, unless *Annex B* applies, be so informed whether or not they are being interviewed and asked if they would like to see the solicitor. This applies even if the detainee has declined legal advice or, having requested it, subsequently agreed to be interviewed without receiving advice. The solicitor's attendance and the detainee's decision must be noted in the custody record.

(b)   Documentation

6.16   Any request for legal advice and the action taken shall be recorded.

6.17   A record shall be made in the interview record if a detainee asks for legal advice and an interview is begun either in the absence of a solicitor or their representative, or they have been required to leave an interview.

Notes for guidance

6A   *In considering if paragraph 6.6(b) applies, the officer should, if practicable, ask the solicitor for an estimate of how long it will take to come to the station and relate this to the time detention is permitted, the time of day (i.e. whether the rest period under paragraph 12.2 is imminent) and the requirements of other investigations. If the solicitor is on their way or is to set off immediately, it will not normally be appropriate to begin an interview before they arrive. If it appears necessary to begin an interview before the solicitor's arrival, they should be given an indication of how long the police would be able to wait before 6.6(b) applies so there is an opportunity to make arrangements for someone else to provide legal advice.*

6B   *A detainee who asks for legal advice should be given an opportunity to consult a specific solicitor or another solicitor from that solicitor's firm or the duty solicitor. If advice is not available by these means, or they do not want to consult the duty solicitor, the detainee should be given an opportunity to choose a solicitor from a list of those willing to provide legal advice. If this solicitor is unavailable, they may choose up to two alternatives. If these attempts are unsuccessful, the custody officer has discretion to allow further attempts until a solicitor has been contacted and agrees to provide legal advice. Apart from carrying out these duties, an officer must not advise the suspect about any particular firm of solicitors.*

6C   *Not Used*

6D   *A detainee has a right to free legal advice and to be represented by a solicitor. The solicitor's only role in the police station is to protect and advance the legal rights of their client. On occasions this may require the solicitor to give advice which has the effect of the client avoiding giving evidence which strengthens a prosecution case. The solicitor may intervene in order to seek clarification, challenge an improper question to their client or the manner in which it is put, advise their client not to reply to particular questions, or if they wish to give their client further legal advice. Paragraph 6.9 only applies if the solicitor's approach or conduct prevents or unreasonably obstructs proper questions being put to the suspect or the suspect's response being recorded. Examples of unacceptable conduct include answering questions on a suspect's behalf or providing written replies for the suspect to quote.*

6E   *An officer who takes the decision to exclude a solicitor must be in a position to satisfy the court the decision was properly made. In order to do this they may need to witness what is happening.*

6F   *If an officer of at least inspector rank considers a particular solicitor or firm of solicitors is persistently sending non-accredited or probationary representatives who are unsuited to provide legal advice, they should inform an officer of at least superintendent rank, who may wish to take the matter up with the Law Society.*

6G   *Subject to the constraints of Annex B, a solicitor may advise more than one client in an investigation if they wish. Any question of a conflict of interest is for the solicitor under their professional code of conduct. If, however, waiting for a solicitor to give advice to one client may lead to unreasonable delay to the interview with another, the provisions of paragraph 6.6(b) may apply.*

6H   *In addition to a poster in English, a poster or posters containing translations into Welsh, the main minority ethnic languages and the principal European languages should be displayed wherever they are likely to be helpful and it is practicable to do so.*

6I   *Paragraph 6.6(d) requires the authorisation of an officer of inspector rank or above to the continuation of an interview when a detainee who wanted legal advice changes their mind. It is permissible for such authorisation to be given over the telephone, if the authorising officer is able to satisfy themselves about the reason for the detainee's change of mind and is satisfied it is proper to continue the interview in those circumstances.*

6J   *Whenever a detainee exercises their right to legal advice by consulting or communicating with a solicitor, they must be allowed to do so in private. This right to consult or communicate in private is fundamental. Except as allowed by the Terrorism Act 2000, Schedule 8, paragraph 9, if the requirement for privacy is compromised because what is said or written by the detainee or solicitor for the purpose of giving and receiving legal advice is overheard, listened to, or read by others without the informed consent of the detainee, the right will effectively have been denied. When a detainee chooses to speak to a solicitor on the telephone, they should be allowed to do so in private unless this is impractical because of the design and layout of the custody area or the location of telephones. However, the normal expectation should be that facilities will be available, unless they are being used, at all police stations to enable detainees to speak in private to a solicitor either face to face or over the telephone.*

6K   *A detainee is not obliged to give reasons for declining legal advice and should not be pressed to do so.*

7   Citizens of independent Commonwealth countries or foreign nationals

(a) Action

7.1   Any citizen of an independent Commonwealth country or a national of a foreign country, including the Republic of Ireland, may communicate at any time with the appropriate High Commission, Embassy or Consulate. The detainee must be informed as soon as practicable of:

- this right;
- their right, upon request, to have their High Commission, Embassy or Consulate told of their whereabouts and the grounds for their detention. Such a request should be acted upon as soon as practicable.

7.2   If a detainee is a citizen of a country with which a bilateral consular convention or agreement is in force requiring notification of arrest, the appropriate High Commission, Embassy or Consulate shall be informed as soon as practicable, subject to *paragraph 7.4*. The countries to which this applies as at 1st April 2003 are listed in *Annex F*.

7.3   Consular officers may visit one of their nationals in police detention to talk to them and, if required, to arrange for legal advice. Such visits shall take place out of the hearing of a police officer.

7.4   Notwithstanding the provisions of consular conventions, if the detainee is a political refugee whether for reasons of race, nationality, political opinion or religion, or is seeking political asylum, consular officers shall not be informed of the arrest of one of their nationals or given access or information about them except at the detainee's express request.

(b) Documentation

7.5   A record shall be made when a detainee is informed of their rights under this section and of any communications with a High Commission, Embassy or Consulate.

Note for guidance

7A   *The exercise of the rights in this section may not be interfered with even though Annex B applies.*

8   Conditions of detention

(a) Action

8.1   So far as it is practicable, not more than one detainee should be detained in each cell.

8.2   Cells in use must be adequately heated, cleaned and ventilated. They must be adequately lit, subject to such dimming as is compatible with safety and security to allow people detained overnight to sleep. No additional restraints shall be used within a locked cell unless absolutely necessary and then only restraint equipment, approved for use in that force by the Chief Officer, which is reasonable and necessary in the circumstances having regard to the detainee's demeanour and with a view to ensuring their safety and the safety of others. If a detainee is deaf, mentally disordered or otherwise mentally vulnerable, particular care must be taken when deciding whether to use any form of approved restraints.

8.3   Blankets, mattresses, pillows and other bedding supplied shall be of a reasonable standard and in a clean and sanitary condition. See *Note 8A*

8.4   Access to toilet and washing facilities must be provided.

8.5   If it is necessary to remove a detainee's clothes for the purposes of investigation, for hygiene, health reasons or cleaning, replacement clothing of a reasonable standard of comfort and cleanliness shall be provided. A detainee may not be interviewed unless adequate clothing has been offered.

8.6   At least two light meals and one main meal should be offered in any 24 hour period. See *Note 8B*. Drinks should be provided at meal times and upon reasonable request between meals. Whenever necessary, advice shall be sought from the appropriate health care professional, see *Note 9A*, on medical and dietary matters. As far as practicable, meals provided shall offer a varied diet and meet any specific dietary needs or religious beliefs the detainee may have. The detainee may, at the custody officer's discretion, have meals supplied by their family or friends at their expense. See *Note 8A*

8.7   Brief outdoor exercise shall be offered daily if practicable.

8.8   A juvenile shall not be placed in a police cell unless no other secure accommodation is available and the custody officer considers it is not practicable to supervise them if they are not placed in a cell or that a cell provides more comfortable accommodation than other secure accommodation in the station. A juvenile may not be placed in a cell with a detained adult.

(b) Documentation

8.9   A record must be kept of replacement clothing and meals offered.

8.10   If a juvenile is placed in a cell, the reason must be recorded.

8.11   The use of any restraints on a detainee whilst in a cell, the reasons for it and, if appropriate, the arrangements for enhanced supervision of the detainee whilst so restrained, shall be recorded. See *paragraph 3.9*

Notes for guidance

8A   *The provisions in paragraph 8.3 and 8.6 respectively are of particular importance in the case of a person detained under the Terrorism Act 2000, immigration detainees and others likely to be detained for an extended period. In deciding whether to allow meals to be supplied by family or friends, the custody officer is entitled to take account of the risk of items being concealed in any food or package and the officer's duties and responsibilities under food handling legislation.*

8B   *Meals should, so far as practicable, be offered at recognised meal times, or at other times that take account of when the detainee last had a meal.*

9   Care and treatment of detained persons

(a)   General

9.1   Nothing in this section prevents the police from calling the police surgeon or, if appropriate, some other health care professional, to examine a detainee for the purposes of obtaining evidence relating to any offence in which the detainee is suspected of being involved. See *Note 9A*

9.2   If a complaint is made by, or on behalf of, a detainee about their treatment since their arrest, or it comes to notice that a detainee may have been treated improperly, a report must be made as soon as practicable to an officer of inspector rank or above not connected with the investigation. If the matter concerns a possible assault or the possibility of the unnecessary or unreasonable use of force, an appropriate health care professional must also be called as soon as practicable.

9.3   Detainees should be visited at least every hour. If no reasonably foreseeable risk was identified in a risk assessment, see *paragraphs 3.6–3.10*, there is no need to wake a sleeping detainee. Those suspected of being intoxicated through drink or drugs or whose level of consciousness causes concern must, subject to any clinical directions given by the appropriate health care professional, see *paragraph 9.13*:

   •   be visited and roused at least every half hour

   •   have their condition assessed as in *Annex H*

   •   and clinical treatment arranged if appropriate

   See *Notes 9B, 9C* and *9H*

9.4   When arrangements are made to secure clinical attention for a detainee, the custody officer must make sure all relevant information which might assist in the treatment of the detainee's condition is made available to the responsible health care professional. This applies whether or not the health care professional asks for such information. Any officer or civilian support staff with relevant information must inform the custody officer as soon as practicable.

(b)   Clinical treatment and attention

9.5   The custody officer must make sure a detainee receives appropriate clinical attention as soon as reasonably practicable if the person:

   (a)   appears to be suffering from physical illness; or

   (b)   is injured; or

   (c)   appears to be suffering from a mental disorder; or

   (d)   appears to need clinical attention.

   This applies even if the detainee makes no request for clinical attention and whether or not they have already received clinical attention elsewhere. If the need for attention appears urgent, e.g. when indicated as in *Annex H*, the nearest available health care professional or an ambulance must be called immediately. See *Note 9C*

9.6 *Paragraph 9.5* is not meant to prevent or delay the transfer to a hospital if necessary of a person detained under the Mental Health Act 1983, section 136. See *Note 9D*. When an assessment under that Act takes place at a police station, *see paragraph 3.16*, the custody officer must consider whether an appropriate health care professional should be called to conduct an initial clinical check on the detainee. This applies particularly when there is likely to be any significant delay in the arrival of a suitably qualified medical practitioner.

9.7 If it appears to the custody officer, or they are told, that a person brought to a station under arrest may be suffering from an infectious disease or condition, the custody officer must take reasonable steps to safeguard the health of the detainee and others at the station. In deciding what action to take, advice must be sought from an appropriate health care professional. See *Note 9E*. The custody officer has discretion to isolate the person and their property until clinical directions have been obtained.

9.8 If a detainee requests a clinical examination, an appropriate health care professional must be called as soon as practicable to assess the detainee's clinical needs. If a safe and appropriate care plan cannot be provided, the police surgeon's advice must be sought. The detainee may also be examined by a medical practitioner of their choice at their expense.

9.9 If a detainee is required to take or apply any medication in compliance with clinical directions prescribed before their detention, the custody officer must consult the appropriate health care professional before the use of the medication. Subject to the restrictions in *paragraph 9.10*, the custody officer is responsible for the safekeeping of any medication and for making sure the detainee is given the opportunity to take or apply prescribed or approved medication. Any such consultation and its outcome shall be noted in the custody record.

9.10 No police officer may administer or supervise the self-administration of controlled drugs of the types and forms listed in the Misuse of Drugs Regulations 2001, Schedule 1, 2 or 3. A detainee may only self-administer such drugs under the personal supervision of the registered medical practitioner authorising their use. Drugs listed in Schedule 4 or 5 may be distributed by the custody officer for self-administration if they have consulted the registered medical practitioner authorising their use, this may be done by telephone, and both parties are satisfied self-administration will not expose the detainee, police officers or anyone else to the risk of harm or injury.

9.11 When appropriate health care professionals administer drugs or other medications, or supervise their self-administration, it must be within current medicines legislation and the scope of practice as determined by their relevant professional body.

9.12 If a detainee has in their possession, or claims to need, medication relating to a heart condition, diabetes, epilepsy or a condition of comparable potential seriousness then, even though *paragraph 9.5* may not apply, the advice of the appropriate health care professional must be obtained.

9.13 Whenever the appropriate health care professional is called in accordance with this section to examine or treat a detainee, the custody officer shall ask for their opinion about:

• any risks or problems which police need to take into account when making decisions about the detainee's continued detention;

• when to carry out an interview if applicable; and

• the need for safeguards.

9.14 When clinical directions are given by the appropriate health care professional, whether orally or in writing, and the custody officer has any doubts or is in any way uncertain about any aspect of the directions, the custody officer shall ask for clarification. It is particularly important that directions concerning the frequency of visits are clear, precise and capable of being implemented. See *Note 9F*.

(c) Documentation

9.15   A record must be made in the custody record of:

(a)   the arrangements made for an examination by an appropriate health care professional under *paragraph 9.2* and of any complaint reported under that paragraph together with any relevant remarks by the custody officer;

(b)   any arrangements made in accordance with *paragraph 9.5*;

(c)   any request for a clinical examination under *paragraph 9.8* and any arrangements made in response;

(d)   the injury, ailment, condition or other reason which made it necessary to make the arrangements in (*a*) to (*c*), see *Note 9G*;

(e)   any clinical directions and advice, including any further clarifications, given to police by a health care professional concerning the care and treatment of the detainee in connection with any of the arrangements made in (*a*) to (*c*), see *Note 9F*;

(f)   if applicable, the responses received when attempting to rouse a person using the procedure in *Annex H*, see *Note 9H*.

9.16   If a health care professional does not record their clinical findings in the custody record, the record must show where they are recorded. See *Note 9G*. However, information which is necessary to custody staff to ensure the effective ongoing care and well being of the detainee must be recorded openly in the custody record, see *paragraph 3.8* and *Annex G, paragraph 7*.

9.17   Subject to the requirements of Section 4, the custody record shall include:

•   a record of all medication a detainee has in their possession on arrival at the police station;

•   a note of any such medication they claim to need but do not have with them.

Notes for guidance

9A   *A 'health care professional' means a clinically qualified person working within the scope of practice as determined by their relevant professional body. Whether a health care professional is 'appropriate' depends on the circumstances of the duties they carry out at the time.*

9B   *Whenever possible juveniles and mentally vulnerable detainees should be visited more frequently.*

9C   *A detainee who appears drunk or behaves abnormally may be suffering from illness, the effects of drugs or may have sustained injury, particularly a head injury which is not apparent. A detainee needing or dependent on certain drugs, including alcohol, may experience harmful effects within a short time of being deprived of their supply. In these circumstances, when there is any doubt, police should always act urgently to call an appropriate health care professional or an ambulance. Paragraph 9.5 does not apply to minor ailments or injuries which do not need attention. However, all such ailments or injuries must be recorded in the custody record and any doubt must be resolved in favour of calling the appropriate health care professional.*

9D   *Whenever practicable, arrangements should be made for persons detained for assessment under the Mental Health Act 1983, section 136 to be taken to a hospital. There is no power under that Act to transfer a person detained under section 136 from one place of safety to another place of safety for assessment.*

9E   *It is important to respect a person's right to privacy and information about their health must be kept confidential and only disclosed with their consent or in accordance with clinical advice when it is necessary to protect the detainee's health or that of others who come into contact with them.*

9F   *The custody officer should always seek to clarify directions that the detainee requires constant observation or supervision and should ask the appropriate health care professional to explain precisely what action needs to be taken to implement such directions.*

9G   *Paragraphs 9.15 and 9.16 do not require any information about the cause of any injury, ailment or condition to be recorded on the custody record if it appears capable of providing evidence of an offence.*

9H   *The purpose of recording a person's responses when attempting to rouse them using the procedure in Annex H is to enable any change in the individual's consciousness level to be noted and clinical treatment arranged if appropriate.*

10   Cautions

(a)   *When a caution must be given*

10.1   A person whom there are grounds to suspect of an offence, see *Note 10A*, must be cautioned before any questions about an offence, or further questions if the answers provide the grounds for suspicion, are put to them if either the suspect's answers or silence, (i.e. failure or refusal to answer or answer satisfactorily) may be given in evidence to a court in a prosecution. A person need not be cautioned if questions are for other necessary purposes, e.g.:

(a)   solely to establish their identity or ownership of any vehicle;

(b)   to obtain information in accordance with any relevant statutory requirement, see *paragraph 10.9*;

(c)   in furtherance of the proper and effective conduct of a search, e.g. to determine the need to search in the exercise of powers of stop and search or to seek cooperation while carrying out a search;

(d)   to seek verification of a written record as in *paragraph 11.13*;

(e)   when examining a person in accordance with the Terrorism Act 2000, Schedule 7 and the Code of Practice for Examining Officers issued under that Act, Schedule 14, paragraph 6.

10.2   Whenever a person not under arrest is initially cautioned, or reminded they are under caution, that person must at the same time be told they are not under arrest and are free to leave if they want to. See *Note 10C*

10.3   A person who is arrested, or further arrested, must be informed at the time, or as soon as practicable thereafter, that they are under arrest and the grounds for their arrest, see *Note 10B*.

10.4   A person who is arrested, or further arrested, must also be cautioned unless:

(a)   it is impracticable to do so by reason of their condition or behaviour at the time;

(b)   they have already been cautioned immediately prior to arrest as in *paragraph 10.1*.

(b)   *Terms of the cautions*

10.5   The caution which must be given on:

(a)   arrest;

(b)   all other occasions before a person is charged or informed they may be prosecuted, see *section 16*, should, unless the restriction on drawing adverse inferences from silence applies, see *Annex C*, be in the following terms:

"You do not have to say anything. But it may harm your defence if you do not mention when questioned something which you later rely on in Court. Anything you do say may be given in evidence."

See *Note 10G*

10.6   *Annex C, paragraph 2* sets out the alternative terms of the caution to be used when the restriction on drawing adverse inferences from silence applies.

10.7   Minor deviations from the words of any caution given in accordance with this Code do not constitute a breach of this Code, provided the sense of the relevant caution is preserved. See *Note 10D*

10.8   After any break in questioning under caution, the person being questioned must be made aware they remain under caution. If there is any doubt the relevant caution should be given again in full when the interview resumes. See *Note 10E*

10.9   When, despite being cautioned, a person fails to co-operate or to answer particular questions which may affect their immediate treatment, the person should be informed of any relevant consequences and that those consequences are not affected by the caution. Examples are when a person's refusal to provide:

- their name and address when charged may make them liable to detention;
- particulars and information in accordance with a statutory requirement, e.g. under the Road Traffic Act 1988, may amount to an offence or may make the person liable to a further arrest.

(c)   *Special warnings under the Criminal Justice and Public Order Act 1994, sections 36 and 37*

10.10   When a suspect interviewed at a police station or authorised place of detention after arrest fails or refuses to answer certain questions, or to answer satisfactorily, after due warning, see *Note 10F*, a court or jury may draw such inferences as appear proper under the Criminal Justice and Public Order Act 1994, sections 36 and 37. Such inferences may only be drawn when:

(a)   the restriction on drawing adverse inferences from silence, see *Annex C*, does not apply; and

(b)   the suspect is arrested by a constable and fails or refuses to account for any objects, marks or substances, or marks on such objects found:

- on their person;
- in or on their clothing or footwear;
- otherwise in their possession; or
- in the place they were arrested;

(c)   the arrested suspect was found by a constable at a place at or about the time the offence for which that officer has arrested them is alleged to have been committed, and the suspect fails or refuses to account for their presence there.

When the restriction on drawing adverse inferences from silence applies, the suspect may still be asked to account for any of the matters in (*b*) or (*c*) but the special warning described in *paragraph 10.11* will not apply and must not be given.

10.11   For an inference to be drawn when a suspect fails or refuses to answer a question about one of these matters or to answer it satisfactorily, the suspect must first be told in ordinary language:

(a)   what offence is being investigated;

(b)   what fact they are being asked to account for;

(c)   this fact may be due to them taking part in the commission of the offence;

(d) a court may draw a proper inference if they fail or refuse to account for this fact;

(e) a record is being made of the interview and it may be given in evidence if they are brought to trial.

(d) *Juveniles and persons who are mentally disordered or otherwise mentally vulnerable*

10.12 If a juvenile or a person who is mentally disordered or otherwise mentally vulnerable is cautioned in the absence of the appropriate adult, the caution must be repeated in the adult's presence.

(e) *Documentation*

10.13 A record shall be made when a caution is given under this section, either in the interviewer's pocket book or in the interview record.

Notes for guidance

10A *There must be some reasonable, objective grounds for the suspicion, based on known facts or information which are relevant to the likelihood the offence has been committed and the person to be questioned committed it.*

10B *An arrested person must be given sufficient information to enable them to understand they have been deprived of their liberty and the reason they have been arrested, e.g. when a person is arrested on suspicion of committing an offence they must be informed of the suspected offence's nature, when and where it was committed. If the arrest is made under the general arrest conditions in PACE, section 25, the grounds for arrest must include an explanation of the conditions which make the arrest necessary. Vague or technical language should be avoided.*

10C *The restriction on drawing inferences from silence, see Annex C, paragraph 1, does not apply to a person who has not been detained and who therefore cannot be prevented from seeking legal advice if they want, see paragraph 3.21.*

10D *If it appears a person does not understand the caution, the person giving it should explain it in their own words.*

10E *It may be necessary to show to the court that nothing occurred during an interview break or between interviews which influenced the suspect's recorded evidence. After a break in an interview or at the beginning of a subsequent interview, the interviewing officer should summarise the reason for the break and confirm this with the suspect.*

10F *The Criminal Justice and Public Order Act 1994, sections 36 and 37 apply only to suspects who have been arrested by a constable or Customs and Excise officer and are given the relevant warning by the police or customs officer who made the arrest or who is investigating the offence. They do not apply to any interviews with suspects who have not been arrested.*

10G *Nothing in this Code requires a caution to be given or repeated when informing a person not under arrest they may be prosecuted for an offence. However, a court will not be able to draw any inferences under the Criminal Justice and Public Order Act 1994, section 34, if the person was not cautioned.*

11   Interviews — general

(a) *Action*

11.1A An interview is the questioning of a person regarding their involvement or suspected involvement in a criminal offence or offences which, under *paragraph 10.1*, must be carried out under caution. Whenever a person is interviewed they must be informed of the nature of the offence, or further offence. Procedures under the Road Traffic Act 1988, section 7 or the Transport and Works Act 1992, section 31 do not constitute interviewing for the purpose of this Code.

11.1 Following a decision to arrest a suspect, they must not be interviewed about the relevant offence except at a police station or other authorised place of detention, unless the consequent delay would be likely to:

(a) lead to:

- interference with, or harm to, evidence connected with an offence;
- interference with, or physical harm to, other people; or
- serious loss of, or damage to, property;

(b) lead to alerting other people suspected of committing an offence but not yet arrested for it; or

(c) hinder the recovery of property obtained in consequence of the commission of an offence.

Interviewing in any of these circumstances shall cease once the relevant risk has been averted or the necessary questions have been put in order to attempt to avert that risk.

11.2 Immediately prior to the commencement or re-commencement of any interview at a police station or other authorised place of detention, the interviewer should remind the suspect of their entitlement to free legal advice and that the interview can be delayed for legal advice to be obtained, unless one of the exceptions in *paragraph 6.6* applies. It is the interviewer's responsibility to make sure all reminders are recorded in the interview record.

11.3 Not Used

11.4 At the beginning of an interview the interviewer, after cautioning the suspect, see *section 10*, shall put to them any significant statement or silence which occurred in the presence and hearing of a police officer or civilian interviewer before the start of the interview and which have not been put to the suspect in the course of a previous interview. See *Note 11A*. The interviewer shall ask the suspect whether they confirm or deny that earlier statement or silence and if they want to add anything.

11.4A A significant statement is one which appears capable of being used in evidence against the suspect, in particular a direct admission of guilt. A significant silence is a failure or refusal to answer a question or answer satisfactorily when under caution, which might, allowing for the restriction on drawing adverse inferences from silence, see *Annex C*, give rise to an inference under the Criminal Justice and Public Order Act 1994, Part III.

11.5 No interviewer may try to obtain answers or elicit a statement by the use of oppression. Except as in *paragraph 10.9*, no interviewer shall indicate, except to answer a direct question, what action will be taken by the police if the person being questioned answers questions, makes a statement or refuses to do either. If the person asks directly what action will be taken if they answer questions, make a statement or refuse to do either, the interviewer may inform them what action the police propose to take provided that action is itself proper and warranted.

11.6 The interview or further interview of a person about an offence with which that person has not been charged or for which they have not been informed they may be prosecuted, must cease when the officer in charge of the investigation:

(a) is satisfied all the questions they consider relevant to obtaining accurate and reliable information about the offence have been put to the suspect, this includes allowing the suspect an opportunity to give an innocent explanation and asking questions to test if the explanation is accurate and reliable, e.g. to clear up ambiguities or clarify what the suspect said;

(b) has taken account of any other available evidence; and

    (c)   the officer in charge of the investigation, or in the case of a detained suspect, the custody officer, see *paragraph 16.1*, reasonably believes there is sufficient evidence to provide a realistic prospect of conviction for that offence if the person was prosecuted for it. See *Note 11B*

This paragraph does not prevent officers in revenue cases or acting under the confiscation provisions of the Criminal Justice Act 1988 or the Drug Trafficking Act 1994 from inviting suspects to complete a formal question and answer record after the interview is concluded.

(b) *Interview records*

11.7   (a)   An accurate record must be made of each interview, whether or not the interview takes place at a police station

        (b)   The record must state the place of interview, the time it begins and ends, any interview breaks and, subject to *paragraph 2.6A*, the names of all those present; and must be made on the forms provided for this purpose or in the interviewer's pocket book or in accordance with the Codes of Practice E or F;

        (c)   Any written record must be made and completed during the interview, unless this would not be practicable or would interfere with the conduct of the interview, and must constitute either a verbatim record of what has been said or, failing this, an account of the interview which adequately and accurately summarises it.

11.8   If a written record is not made during the interview it must be made as soon as practicable after its completion.

11.9   Written interview records must be timed and signed by the maker.

11.10   If a written record is not completed during the interview the reason must be recorded in the interview record.

11.11   Unless it is impracticable, the person interviewed shall be given the opportunity to read the interview record and to sign it as correct or to indicate how they consider it inaccurate. If the person interviewed cannot read or refuses to read the record or sign it, the senior interviewer present shall read it to them and ask whether they would like to sign it as correct or make their mark or to indicate how they consider it inaccurate. The interviewer shall certify on the interview record itself what has occurred. See *Note 11E*

11.12   If the appropriate adult or the person's solicitor is present during the interview, they should also be given an opportunity to read and sign the interview record or any written statement taken down during the interview.

11.13   A written record shall be made of any comments made by a suspect, including unsolicited comments, which are outside the context of an interview but which might be relevant to the offence. Any such record must be timed and signed by the maker. When practicable the suspect shall be given the opportunity to read that record and to sign it as correct or to indicate how they consider it inaccurate. See *Note 11E*

11.14   Any refusal by a person to sign an interview record when asked in accordance with this Code must itself be recorded.

(c) *Juveniles and mentally disordered or otherwise mentally vulnerable people*

11.15   A juvenile or person who is mentally disordered or otherwise mentally vulnerable must not be interviewed regarding their involvement or suspected involvement in a criminal offence or offences, or asked to provide or sign a written statement under caution or record of interview, in the absence of the appropriate adult unless *paragraphs 11.1, 11.18 to 11.20* apply. See *Note 11C*

11.16   Juveniles may only be interviewed at their place of education in exceptional circumstances and only when the principal or their nominee agrees. Every effort should be made to notify the parent(s) or other person responsible for the juvenile's welfare and the appropriate adult, if this is a different person, that the police want to interview the juvenile and reasonable time should be allowed to enable the appropriate adult to be present at the interview. If awaiting the appropriate adult would cause unreasonable delay, and unless the juvenile is suspected of an offence against the educational establishment, the principal or their nominee can act as the appropriate adult for the purposes of the interview.

11.17   If an appropriate adult is present at an interview, they shall be informed:

- they are not expected to act simply as an observer; and
- the purpose of their presence is to:
  - — advise the person being interviewed;
  - — observe whether the interview is being conducted properly and fairly;
  - — facilitate communication with the person being interviewed.

(d)   Vulnerable suspects — urgent interviews at police stations

11.18   The following persons may not be interviewed unless an officer of superintendent rank or above considers delay will lead to the consequences in *paragraph 11.1(a)* to *(c)*, and is satisfied the interview would not significantly harm the person's physical or mental state (see Annex G):

(a)   a juvenile or person who is mentally disordered or otherwise mentally vulnerable if at the time of the interview the appropriate adult is not present;

(b)   anyone other than in *(a)* who at the time of the interview appears unable to:

- appreciate the significance of questions and their answers; or
- understand what is happening because of the effects of drink, drugs or any illness, ailment or condition;

(c)   a person who has difficulty understanding English or has a hearing disability, if at the time of the interview an interpreter is not present.

11.19   These interviews may not continue once sufficient information has been obtained to avert the consequences in *paragraph 11.1(a)* to *(c)*.

11.20   A record shall be made of the grounds for any decision to interview a person under *paragraph 11.18*.

Notes for guidance

11A   *Paragraph 11.4 does not prevent the interviewer from putting significant statements and silences to a suspect again at a later stage or a further interview.*

11B   *The Criminal Procedure and Investigations Act 1996 Code of Practice, paragraph 3.4 states 'In conducting an investigation, the investigator should pursue all reasonable lines of enquiry, whether these point towards or away from the suspect. What is reasonable will depend on the particular circumstances.' Interviewers should keep this in mind when deciding what questions to ask in an interview.*

11C   *Although juveniles or people who are mentally disordered or otherwise mentally vulnerable are often capable of providing reliable evidence, they may, without knowing or wishing to do so, be particularly prone in certain circumstances to provide information that may be unreliable, misleading or self-incriminating. Special care should always be taken when questioning such a person, and the appropriate adult should be involved if there is any doubt about a person's age, mental state or capacity. Because of the risk of unreliable evidence it is also important to obtain corroboration of any facts admitted whenever possible.*

11D   Juveniles should not be arrested at their place of education unless this is unavoidable. When a juvenile is arrested at their place of education, the principal or their nominee must be informed.

11E   Significant statements described in paragraph 11.4 will always be relevant to the offence and must be recorded. When a suspect agrees to read records of interviews and other comments and sign them as correct, they should be asked to endorse the record with, e.g. 'I agree that this is a correct record of what was said' and add their signature. If the suspect does not agree with the record, the interviewer should record the details of any disagreement and ask the suspect to read these details and sign them to the effect that they accurately reflect their disagreement. Any refusal to sign should be recorded.

12   Interviews in police stations

(a)   Action

12.1   If a police officer wants to interview or conduct enquiries which require the presence of a detainee, the custody officer is responsible for deciding whether to deliver the detainee into the officer's custody.

12.2   Except as below, in any period of 24 hours a detainee must be allowed a continuous period of at least 8 hours for rest, free from questioning, travel or any interruption in connection with the investigation concerned. This period should normally be at night or other appropriate time which takes account of when the detainee last slept or rested. If a detainee is arrested at a police station after going there voluntarily, the period of 24 hours runs from the time of their arrest and not the time of arrival at the police station. The period may not be interrupted or delayed, except:

(a)   when there are reasonable grounds for believing not delaying or interrupting the period would:

(i)   involve a risk of harm to people or serious loss of, or damage to, property;

(ii)   delay unnecessarily the person's release from custody;

(iii)   otherwise prejudice the outcome of the investigation;

(b)   at the request of the detainee, their appropriate adult or legal representative;

(c)   when a delay or interruption is necessary in order to:

(i)   comply with the legal obligations and duties arising under *section 15*;

(ii)   to take action required under section 9 or in accordance with medical advice.

If the period is interrupted in accordance with *(a)*, a fresh period must be allowed. Interruptions under *(b)* and *(c)*, do not require a fresh period to be allowed.

12.3   Before a detainee is interviewed the custody officer, in consultation with the officer in charge of the investigation and appropriate health care professionals as necessary, shall assess whether the detainee is fit enough to be interviewed. This means determining and considering the risks to the detainee's physical and mental state if the interview took place and determining what safeguards are needed to allow the interview to take place. See *Annex G*. The custody officer shall not allow a detainee to be interviewed if the custody officer considers it would cause significant harm to the detainee's physical or mental state.Vulnerable suspects listed at *paragraph 11.18* shall be treated as always being at some risk during an interview and these persons may not be interviewed except in accordance with *paragraphs 11.18 to 11.20*.

12.4   As far as practicable interviews shall take place in interview rooms which are adequately heated, lit and ventilated.

12.5 A suspect whose detention without charge has been authorised under PACE, because the detention is necessary for an interview to obtain evidence of the offence for which they have been arrested, may choose not to answer questions but police do not require the suspect's consent or agreement to interview them for this purpose. If a suspect takes steps to prevent themselves being questioned or further questioned, e.g. by refusing to leave their cell to go to a suitable interview room or by trying to leave the interview room, they shall be advised their consent or agreement to interview is not required. The suspect shall be cautioned as in *section 10*, and informed if they fail or refuse to co-operate, the interview may take place in the cell and that their failure or refusal to co-operate may be given in evidence. The suspect shall then be invited to co-operate and go into the interview room.

12.6 People being questioned or making statements shall not be required to stand.

12.7 Before the interview commences each interviewer shall, subject to *paragraph 2.6A*, identify themselves and any other persons present to the interviewee.

12.8 Breaks from interviewing should be made at recognised meal times or at other times that take account of when an interviewee last had a meal. Short refreshment breaks shall be provided at approximately two hour intervals, subject to the interviewer's discretion to delay a break if there are reasonable grounds for believing it would:

   (i)   involve a:
       •   risk of harm to people;
       •   serious loss of, or damage to, property;
   (ii)   unnecessarily delay the detainee's release;
   (iii) otherwise prejudice the outcome of the investigation.

   See *Note 12B*

12.9 If during the interview a complaint is made by or on behalf of the interviewee concerning the provisions of this Code, the interviewer should:

   (i)   record it in the interview record;
   (ii)   inform the custody officer, who is then responsible for dealing with it as in *section 9*.

(b   *Documentation*

12.10 A record must be made of the:
   •   time a detainee is not in the custody of the custody officer, and why
   •   reason for any refusal to deliver the detainee out of that custody

12.11 A record shall be made of:
   (a)   the reasons it was not practicable to use an interview room; and
   (b)   any action taken as in *paragraph 12.5*.

   The record shall be made on the custody record or in the interview record for action taken whilst an interview record is being kept, with a brief reference to this effect in the custody record.

12.12 Any decision to delay a break in an interview must be recorded, with reasons, in the interview record.

12.13 All written statements made at police stations under caution shall be written on forms provided for the purpose.

12.14 All written statements made under caution shall be taken in accordance with *Annex D*. Before a person makes a written statement under caution at a police station they shall be reminded about the right to legal advice. See *Note 12A*

Notes for guidance

12A   It is not normally necessary to ask for a written statement if the interview was recorded or taped at the time and the record signed by the interviewee in accordance with paragraph 11.11. Statements under caution should normally be taken in these circumstances only at the person's express wish. A person may however be asked if they want to make such a statement.

12B   Meal breaks should normally last at least 45 minutes and shorter breaks after two hours should last at least 15 minutes. If the interviewer delays a break in accordance with paragraph 12.8 and prolongs the interview, a longer break should be provided. If there is a short interview, and another short interview is contemplated, the length of the break may be reduced if there are reasonable grounds to believe this is necessary to avoid any of the consequences in paragraph 12.8(i) to (iii).

13   Interpreters

(a)   General

13.1   Chief officers are responsible for making sure appropriate arrangements are in place for provision of suitably qualified interpreters for people who:

- are deaf;
- do not understand English.

(b)   Foreign languages

13.2   Unless *paragraphs 11.1, 11.18 to 11.20* apply, a person must not be interviewed in the absence of a person capable of interpreting if:

(a)   they have difficulty understanding English;

(b)   the interviewer cannot speak the person's own language;

(c)   the person wants an interpreter present.

13.3   The interviewer shall make sure the interpreter makes a note of the interview at the time in the person's language for use in the event of the interpreter being called to give evidence, and certifies its accuracy. The interviewer should allow sufficient time for the interpreter to note each question and answer after each is put, given and interpreted. The person should be allowed to read the record or have it read to them and sign it as correct or indicate the respects in which they consider it inaccurate. If the interview is tape-recorded or visually recorded, the arrangements in Code E or F apply.

13.4   In the case of a person making a statement other than in English:

(a)   the interpreter shall record the statement in the language it is made;

(b)   the person shall be invited to sign it;

(c)   an official English translation shall be made in due course.

(c)   Deaf people and people with speech difficulties

13.5   If a person appears to be deaf or there is doubt about their hearing or speaking ability, they must not be interviewed in the absence of an interpreter unless they agree in writing to being interviewed without one or *paragraphs 11.1, 11.18 to 11.20* apply.

13.6   An interpreter should also be called if a juvenile is interviewed and the parent or guardian present as the appropriate adult appears to be deaf or there is doubt about their hearing or speaking ability, unless they agree in writing to the interview proceeding without one or *paragraphs 11.1, 11.18 to 11.20* apply.

13.7   The interviewer shall make sure the interpreter is allowed to read the interview record and certify its accuracy in the event of the interpreter being called to give evidence. If the interview is tape-recorded or visually recorded, the arrangements in Code E or F apply.

(d) Additional rules for detained persons

13.8   All reasonable attempts should be made to make the detainee understand that interpreters will be provided at public expense.

13.9   If *paragraph 6.1* applies and the detainee cannot communicate with the solicitor because of language, hearing or speech difficulties, an interpreter must be called. The interpreter may not be a police officer or civilian support staff when interpretation is needed for the purposes of obtaining legal advice. In all other cases a police officer or civilian support staff may only interpret if the detainee and the appropriate adult, if applicable, give their agreement in writing or if the interview is tape-recorded or visually recorded as in Code E or F.

13.10 When the custody officer cannot establish effective communication with a person charged with an offence who appears deaf or there is doubt about their ability to hear, speak or to understand English, arrangements must be made as soon as practicable for an interpreter to explain the offence and any other information given by the custody officer.

(e) Documentation

13.11 Action taken to call an interpreter under this section and any agreement to be interviewed in the absence of an interpreter must be recorded.

14   Questioning — special restrictions

14.1   If a person is arrested by one police force on behalf of another and the lawful period of detention in respect of that offence has not yet commenced in accordance with PACE, section 41 no questions may be put to them about the offence while they are in transit between the forces except to clarify any voluntary statement they make.

14.2   If a person is in police detention at a hospital they may not be questioned without the agreement of a responsible doctor. See *Note 14A*

Note for guidance

14A   *If questioning takes place at a hospital under paragraph 14.2, or on the way to or from a hospital, the period of questioning concerned counts towards the total period of detention permitted.*

15   Reviews and extensions of detention

(a) Persons detained under PACE

15.1   The review officer is responsible under PACE, section 40 for periodically determining if a person's detention, before or after charge, continues to be necessary. This requirement continues throughout the detention period and except as in *paragraph 15.10*, the review officer must be present at the police station holding the detainee. See *Notes 15A* and *15B*

15.2   Under PACE, section 42, an officer of superintendent rank or above who is responsible for the station holding the detainee may give authority any time after the second review to extend the maximum period the person may be detained without charge by up to 12 hours. Further detention without charge may be authorised only by a magistrates' court in accordance with PACE, sections 43 and 44. See *Notes 15C, 15D* and *15E*

15.3   Before deciding whether to authorise continued detention the officer responsible under *paragraphs 15.1* or *15.2* shall give an opportunity to make representations about the detention to:

(a)   the detainee, unless in the case of a review as in *paragraph 15.1*, the detainee is asleep;

(b)   the detainee's solicitor if available at the time; and

(c)   the appropriate adult if available at the time.

15.3A   Other people having an interest in the detainee's welfare may also make representations at the authorising officer's discretion.

15.3B   Subject to paragraph 15.10, the representations may be made orally in person or by telephone or in writing. The authorising officer may, however, refuse to hear oral representations from the detainee if the officer considers them unfit to make representations because of their condition or behaviour. See *Note 15C*

15.4   Before conducting a review or determining whether to extend the maximum period of detention without charge, the officer responsible must make sure the detainee is reminded of their entitlement to free legal advice, see *paragraph 6.5*, unless in the case of a review the person is asleep.

15.5   If, after considering any representations, the officer decides to keep the detainee in detention or extend the maximum period they may be detained without charge, any comment made by the detainee shall be recorded. If applicable, the officer responsible under *paragraph 15.1* or *15.2* shall be informed of the comment as soon as practicable. See also *paragraphs 11.4* and *11.13*

15.6   No officer shall put specific questions to the detainee:

- regarding their involvement in any offence; or
- in respect of any comments they may make;
    - when given the opportunity to make representations; or
    - in response to a decision to keep them in detention or extend the maximum period of detention.

Such an exchange could constitute an interview as in *paragraph 11.1A* and would be subject to the associated safeguards in *section 11* and, in respect of a person who has been charged, *paragraph 16.5*. See also *paragraph 11.13*

15.7   A detainee who is asleep at a review, see *paragraph 15.1*, and whose continued detention is authorised must be informed about the decision and reason as soon as practicable after waking.

(b)   Persons detained under the Terrorism Act 2000

15.8   In terrorism cases:

(a)   the powers and duties of the review officer are in the Terrorism Act 2000, Schedule 8, Part II;

(b)   a police officer of at least superintendent rank may apply to a judicial authority for a warrant of further detention under the Terrorism Act 2000, Schedule 8, Part III.

(c)   Telephone review of detention

15.9   PACE, section 40A provides that the officer responsible under section 40 for reviewing the detention of a person who has not been charged, need not attend the police station holding the detainee and may carry out the review by telephone if:

(a)   it is not reasonably practicable for the officer to be present;

(b)   PACE, section 45A, in respect of the use of video conferencing facilities, does not apply or it is not reasonably practicable to use such facilities.

See *Note 15F*

15.10   When a telephone review is carried out, an officer at the station holding the detainee shall be required by the review officer to fulfil that officer's obligations under PACE section 40 or this Code by:

(a)   making any record connected with the review in the detainee's custody record;

(b)   if applicable, making a record in (*a*) in the presence of the detainee; and

(c)   giving the detainee information about the review.

15.11   When a telephone review is carried out, the requirement in *paragraph 15.3* will be satisfied:

(a)   if facilities exist for the immediate transmission of written representations to the review officer, e.g. fax or email message, by giving the detainee an opportunity to make representations:

(i)   orally by telephone; or

(ii)   in writing using those facilities; and

(b)   in all other cases, by giving the detainee an opportunity to make their representations orally by telephone.

(d)   Documentation

15.12   It is the officer's responsibility to make sure all reminders given under *paragraph 15.4* are noted in the custody record.

15.13   The grounds for, and extent of, any delay in conducting a review shall be recorded.

15.14   When a telephone review is carried out, a record shall be made of:

(a)   the reason the review officer did not attend the station holding the detainee;

(b)   the place the review officer was;

(c)   the method representations, oral or written, were made to the review officer, see *paragraph 15.11*.

15.15   Any written representations shall be retained.

15.16   A record shall be made as soon as practicable about the outcome of each review or determination whether to extend the maximum detention period without charge or an application for a warrant of further detention or its extension. If *paragraph 15.7* applies, a record shall also be made of when the person was informed and by whom. If an authorisation is given under PACE, section 42, the record shall state the number of hours and minutes by which the detention period is extended or further extended. If a warrant for further detention, or extension, is granted under section 43 or 44, the record shall state the detention period authorised by the warrant and the date and time it was granted.

Notes for guidance

15A   *Review officer for the purposes of:*

- *PACE, sections 40 and 40A means, in the case of a person arrested but not charged, an officer of at least inspector rank not directly involved in the investigation and, if a person has been arrested and charged, the custody officer;*

- *the Terrorism Act 2000, means an officer not directly involved in the investigation connected with the detention and of at least inspector rank, for reviews within 24 hours of the detainee's arrest or superintendent for all other reviews.*

15B   *The detention of persons in police custody not subject to the statutory review requirement in paragraph 15.1 should still be reviewed periodically as a matter of good practice. The purpose of such reviews is to check the particular power under which a detainee is held continues to apply, any associated conditions are complied with and to make sure appropriate action is taken to deal with any changes. This includes the detainee's prompt release when the power no longer applies, or their transfer if the power requires the detainee be taken elsewhere as soon as the necessary arrangements are made. Examples include persons:*

(a)   *arrested on warrant because they failed to answer bail to appear at court;*

(b)   *arrested under the Bail Act 1976, section 7(3) for breaching a condition of bail granted after charge;*

(c)   *in police custody for specific purposes and periods under the Crime (Sentences) Act 1997, Schedule 1;*

(d)   *convicted, or remand prisoners, held in police stations on behalf of the Prison Service under the Imprisonment (Temporary Provisions) Act 1980, section 6;*

(e)   *being detained to prevent them causing a breach of the peace;*

(f)   *detained at police stations on behalf of the Immigration Service.*

The detention of persons remanded into police detention by order of a court under the Magistrates' Courts Act 1980, section 128 is subject to a statutory requirement to review that detention. This is to make sure the detainee is taken back to court no later than the end of the period authorised by the court or when the need for their detention by police ceases, whichever is the sooner.

15C   *In the case of a review of detention, but not an extension, the detainee need not be woken for the review. However, if the detainee is likely to be asleep, e.g. during a period of rest allowed as in paragraph 12.2, at the latest time a review or authorisation to extend detention may take place, the officer should, if the legal obligations and time constraints permit, bring forward the procedure to allow the detainee to make representations. A detainee not asleep during the review must be present when the grounds for their continued detention are recorded and must at the same time be informed of those grounds unless the review officer considers the person is incapable of understanding what is said, violent or likely to become violent or in urgent need of medical attention.*

15D   *An application to a Magistrates' Court under PACE, sections 43 or 44 for a warrant of further detention or its extension should be made between 10am and 9pm, and if possible during normal court hours. It will not usually be practicable to arrange for a court to sit specially outside the hours of 10am to 9pm. If it appears a special sitting may be needed outside normal court hours but between 10am and 9pm, the clerk to the justices should be given notice and informed of this possibility, while the court is sitting if possible.*

15E   *In paragraph 15.2, the officer responsible for the station holding the detainee includes a superintendent or above who, in accordance with their force operational policy or police regulations, is given that responsibility on a temporary basis whilst the appointed long-term holder is off duty or otherwise unavailable.*

15F   *The provisions of PACE, section 40A allowing telephone reviews do not apply to reviews of detention after charge by the custody officer or to reviews under the Terrorism Act 2000, Schedule 8, Part II in terrorism cases. When video conferencing is not required, they allow the use of a telephone to carry out a review of detention before charge if it is not reasonably practicable for the review officer to attend the station holding the detainee, e.g. when severe weather conditions or an unforeseen operational emergency prevent the review officer from attending. The procedure under PACE, section 42 must be done in person.*

16   Charging detained persons

(a)   Action

16.1   When the officer in charge of the investigation reasonably believes there is sufficient evidence to provide a realistic prospect of the detainee's conviction, see *paragraph 11.6*, they shall without delay, and subject to the following qualification, inform the custody officer who will be responsible for considering whether the detainee should be charged. See *Notes 11B* and *16A*. When a person is detained in respect of more than one offence it is permissible to delay informing the custody officer until the above conditions are satisfied in respect of all the offences, but see *paragraph 11.6*. If the detainee is a juvenile, mentally disordered or otherwise mentally vulnerable, any resulting action shall be taken in the presence of the appropriate adult if they are present at the time. See *Note 16B* and *16C*

16.2 When a detainee is charged with or informed they may be prosecuted for an offence, see *Note 16B*, they shall, unless the restriction on drawing adverse inferences from silence applies, see *Annex C*, be cautioned as follows:

'You do not have to say anything. But it may harm your defence if you do not mention now something which you later rely on in court. Anything you do say may be given in evidence.'

Annex C, paragraph 2 sets out the alternative terms of the caution to be used when the restriction on drawing adverse inferences from silence applies.

16.3 When a detainee is charged they shall be given a written notice showing particulars of the offence and, subject to *paragraph 2.6A*, the officer's name and the case reference number. As far as possible the particulars of the charge shall be stated in simple terms, but they shall also show the precise offence in law with which the detainee is charged. The notice shall begin:

' You are charged with the offence(s) shown below.' Followed by the caution.

If the detainee is a juvenile, mentally disordered or otherwise mentally vulnerable, the notice should be given to the appropriate adult.

16.4 If, after a detainee has been charged with or informed they may be prosecuted for an offence, an officer wants to tell them about any written statement or interview with another person relating to such an offence, the detainee shall either be handed a true copy of the written statement or the content of the interview record brought to their attention. Nothing shall be done to invite any reply or comment except to:

(a) caution the detainee, *'You do not have to say anything, but anything you do say may be given in evidence.'*; and

(b) remind the detainee about their right to legal advice.

16.4A If the detainee:

- cannot read, the document may be read to them

- is a juvenile, mentally disordered or otherwise mentally vulnerable, the appropriate adult shall also be given a copy, or the interview record shall be brought to their attention

16.5 A detainee may not be interviewed about an offence after they have been charged with, or informed they may be prosecuted for it, unless the interview is necessary:

- to prevent or minimise harm or loss to some other person, or the public

- to clear up an ambiguity in a previous answer or statement

- in the interests of justice for the detainee to have put to them, and have an opportunity to comment on, information concerning the offence which has come to light since they were charged or informed they might be prosecuted

Before any such interview, the interviewer shall:

(a) caution the detainee, *'You do not have to say anything, but anything you do say may be given in evidence.'*;

(b) remind the detainee about their right to legal advice.

See *Note 16B*

16.6 The provisions of *paragraphs 16.2* to *16.5* must be complied with in the appropriate adult's presence if they are already at the police station. If they are not at the police station then these provisions must be complied with again in their presence when they arrive unless the detainee has been released.

See *Note 16C*

16.7 When a juvenile is charged with an offence and the custody officer authorises their continued detention after charge, the custody officer must try to make arrangements for the juvenile to be taken into the care of a local authority to be detained pending appearance in court unless the custody officer certifies it is impracticable to do so or, in the case of a juvenile of at least 12 years old, no secure accommodation is available and there is a risk to the public of serious harm from that juvenile, in accordance with PACE, section 38(6). See *Note 16D*

(b) Documentation

16.8   A record shall be made of anything a detainee says when charged.

16.9   Any questions put in an interview after charge and answers given relating to the offence shall be recorded in full during the interview on forms for that purpose and the record signed by the detainee or, if they refuse, by the interviewer and any third parties present. If the questions are tape recorded or visually recorded the arrangements in Code E or F apply.

16.10   If it is not practicable to make arrangements for a juvenile's transfer into local authority care as in *paragraph 16.7*, the custody officer must record the reasons and complete a certificate to be produced before the court with the juvenile. See *Note 16D*

Notes for guidance

16A   *The custody officer must take into account alternatives to prosecution under the Crime and Disorder Act 1998, reprimands and warning applicable to persons under 18, and in national guidance on the cautioning of offenders, for persons aged 18 and over.*

16B   *The giving of a warning or the service of the Notice of Intended Prosecution required by the Road Traffic Offenders Act 1988, section 1 does not amount to informing a detainee they may be prosecuted for an offence and so does not preclude further questioning in relation to that offence.*

16C   *There is no power under PACE to detain a person and delay action under paragraphs 16.2 to 16.5 solely to await the arrival of the appropriate adult. After charge, bail cannot be refused, or release on bail delayed, simply because an appropriate adult is not available, unless the absence of that adult provides the custody officer with the necessary grounds to authorise detention after charge under PACE, section 38.*

16D   *Except as in paragraph 16.7, neither a juvenile's behaviour nor the nature of the offence provides grounds for the custody officer to decide it is impracticable to arrange the juvenile's transfer to local authority care. Similarly, the lack of secure local authority accommodation does not make it impracticable to transfer the juvenile. The availability of secure accommodation is only a factor in relation to a juvenile aged 12 or over when the local authority accommodation would not be adequate to protect the public from serious harm from them. The obligation to transfer a juvenile to local authority accommodation applies as much to a juvenile charged during the daytime as to a juvenile to be held overnight, subject to a requirement to bring the juvenile before a court under PACE, section 46.*

ANNEX A — INTIMATE AND STRIP SEARCHES

A   Intimate search

1.   An intimate search consists of the physical examination of a person's body orifices other than the mouth. The intrusive nature of such searches means the actual and potential risks associated with intimate searches must never be underestimated.

(a) Action

2.   Body orifices other than the mouth may be searched only if authorised by an officer of inspector rank or above who has reasonable grounds for believing that:

(a)   the person may have concealed on themselves

(i)   anything which they could and might use to cause physical injury to themself or others at the station; or

(ii)   a Class A drug which they intended to supply to another or to export; and

(b)   an intimate search is the only means of removing those items.

2A.   The reasons an intimate search is considered necessary shall be explained to the person before the search begins.

3.   An intimate search may only be carried out by a registered medical practitioner or registered nurse, unless an officer of at least inspector rank considers this is not practicable and the search is to take place under *paragraph 2(a)(i)*, in which case a police officer may carry out the search. See *Notes A1 to A5*

3A.   Any proposal for a search under *paragraph 2(a)(i)* to be carried out by someone other than a registered medical practitioner or registered nurse must only be considered as a last resort and when the authorising officer is satisfied the risks associated with allowing the item to remain with the detainee outweigh the risks associated with removing it. See *Notes A1 to A5*

4.   An intimate search under:

• *paragraph 2(a)(i)* may take place only at a hospital, surgery, other medical premises or police station

• *paragraph 2(a)(ii)* may take place only at a hospital, surgery or other medical premises and must be carried out by a registered medical practitioner or a registered nurse

5.   An intimate search at a police station of a juvenile or mentally disordered or otherwise mentally vulnerable person may take place only in the presence of an appropriate adult of the same sex, unless the detainee specifically requests a particular adult of the opposite sex who is readily available. In the case of a juvenile the search may take place in the absence of the appropriate adult only if the juvenile signifies in the presence of the appropriate adult they do not want the adult present during the search and the adult agrees. A record shall be made of the juvenile's decision and signed by the appropriate adult.

6.   When an intimate search under *paragraph 2(a)(i)* is carried out by a police officer, the officer must be of the same sex as the detainee. A minimum of two people, other than the detainee, must be present during the search. Subject to *paragraph 5*, no person of the opposite sex who is not a medical practitioner or nurse shall be present, nor shall anyone whose presence is unnecessary. The search shall be conducted with proper regard to the sensitivity and vulnerability of the detainee.

(b) Documentation

7.   In the case of an intimate search the custody officer shall as soon as practicable, record:

• which parts of the detainee's body were searched

• who carried out the search

• who was present

• the reasons for the search including the reasons to believe the article could not otherwise be removed

• the result.

8.   If an intimate search is carried out by a police officer, the reason why it was impracticable for a registered medical practitioner or registered nurse to conduct it must be recorded.

B   Strip search

9. A strip search is a search involving the removal of more than outer clothing. In this Code, outer clothing includes shoes and socks.

(a)   Action

10. A strip search may take place only if it is considered necessary to remove an article which a detainee would not be allowed to keep, and the officer reasonably considers the detainee might have concealed such an article. Strip searches shall not be routinely carried out if there is no reason to consider that articles are concealed.

The conduct of strip searches

11. When strip searches are conducted:

(a)   a police officer carrying out a strip search must be the same sex as the detainee;

(b)   the search shall take place in an area where the detainee cannot be seen by anyone who does not need to be present, nor by a member of the opposite sex except an appropriate adult who has been specifically requested by the detainee;

(c)   except in cases of urgency, where there is risk of serious harm to the detainee or to others, whenever a strip search involves exposure of intimate body parts, there must be at least two people present other than the detainee, and if the search is of a juvenile or mentally disordered or otherwise mentally vulnerable person, one of the people must be the appropriate adult. Except in urgent cases as above, a search of a juvenile may take place in the absence of the appropriate adult only if the juvenile signifies in the presence of the appropriate adult that they do not want the adult to be present during the search and the adult agrees. A record shall be made of the juvenile's decision and signed by the appropriate adult. The presence of more than two people, other than an appropriate adult, shall be permitted only in the most exceptional circumstances;

(d)   the search shall be conducted with proper regard to the sensitivity and vulnerability of the detainee in these circumstances and every reasonable effort shall be made to secure the detainee's co-operation and minimise embarrassment. Detainees who are searched shall not normally be required to remove all their clothes at the same time, e.g. a person should be allowed to remove clothing above the waist and redress before removing further clothing;

(e)   if necessary to assist the search, the detainee may be required to hold their arms in the air or to stand with their legs apart and bend forward so a visual examination may be made of the genital and anal areas provided no physical contact is made with any body orifice;

(f)   if articles are found, the detainee shall be asked to hand them over. If articles are found within any body orifice other than the mouth, and the detainee refuses to hand them over, their removal would constitute an intimate search, which must be carried out as in *Part A*;

(g)   a strip search shall be conducted as quickly as possible, and the detainee allowed to dress as soon as the procedure is complete.

(b)   Documentation

12. A record shall be made on the custody record of a strip search including the reason it was considered necessary, those present and any result.

Notes for guidance

A1 *Before authorising any intimate search, the authorising officer must make every reasonable effort to persuade the detainee to hand the article over without a search. If the detainee agrees, a registered medical practitioner or registered nurse should whenever possible be asked to assess the risks involved and, if necessary, attend to assist the detainee.*

A2 *If the detainee does not agree to hand the article over without a search, the authorising officer must carefully review all the relevant factors before authorising an intimate search. In particular, the officer must consider whether the grounds for believing an article may be concealed are reasonable.*

A3 *If authority is given for a search under paragraph 2(a)(i), a registered medical practitioner or registered nurse shall be consulted whenever possible. The presumption should be that the search will be conducted by the registered medical practitioner or registered nurse and the authorising officer must make every reasonable effort to persuade the detainee to allow the medical practitioner or nurse to conduct the search.*

A4 *A constable should only be authorised to carry out a search as a last resort and when all other approaches have failed. In these circumstances, the authorising officer must be satisfied the detainee might use the article for one or more of the purposes in paragraph 2(a)(i) and the physical injury likely to be caused is sufficiently severe to justify authorising a constable to carry out the search.*

A5 *If an officer has any doubts whether to authorise an intimate search by a constable, the officer should seek advice from an officer of superintendent rank or above.*

ANNEX B — DELAY IN NOTIFYING ARREST OR ALLOWING ACCESS TO LEGAL ADVICE

A Persons detained under PACE

1. The exercise of the rights in *Section 5* or *Section 6*, or both, may be delayed if the person is in police detention, as in PACE, section 118(2), in connection with a serious arrestable offence, has not yet been charged with an offence and an officer of superintendent rank or above, or inspector rank or above only for the rights in *Section 5*, has reasonable grounds for believing their exercise will:
    (i)   lead to:
          *   interference with, or harm to, evidence connected with a serious arrestable offence; or
          *   interference with, or physical harm to, other people; or
    (ii) lead to alerting other people suspected of having committed a serious arrestable offence but not yet arrested for it; or
    (iii) hinder the recovery of property obtained in consequence of the commission of such an offence.

2. These rights may also be delayed if the serious arrestable offence is:
    (i)   a drug trafficking offence and the officer has reasonable grounds for believing the detainee has benefited from drug trafficking, and the recovery of the value of the detainee's proceeds from drug trafficking will be hindered by the exercise of either right;
    (ii) an offence to which the Criminal Justice Act 1988, Part VI (confiscation orders) applies and the officer has reasonable grounds for believing the detainee has benefited from the offence, and the exercise of either right will hinder the recovery of the value of the:
          *   property obtained by the detainee from or in connection with the offence

- pecuniary advantage derived by the detainee from or in connection with it.

3. Authority to delay a detainee's right to consult privately with a solicitor may be given only if the authorising officer has reasonable grounds to believe the solicitor the detainee wants to consult will, inadvertently or otherwise, pass on a message from the detainee or act in some other way which will have any of the consequences specified under *paragraphs 1* or *2*. In these circumstances the detainee must be allowed to choose another solicitor. See *Note B3*

4. If the detainee wishes to see a solicitor, access to that solicitor may not be delayed on the grounds they might advise the detainee not to answer questions or the solicitor was initially asked to attend the police station by someone else. In the latter case the detainee must be told the solicitor has come to the police station at another person's request, and must be asked to sign the custody record to signify whether they want to see the solicitor.

5. The fact the grounds for delaying notification of arrest may be satisfied does not automatically mean the grounds for delaying access to legal advice will also be satisfied.

6. These rights may be delayed only for as long as grounds exist and in no case beyond 36 hours after the relevant time as in PACE, section 41. If the grounds cease to apply within this time, the detainee must, as soon as practicable, be asked if they want to exercise either right, the custody record must be noted accordingly, and action taken in accordance with the relevant section of the Code.

7. A detained person must be permitted to consult a solicitor for a reasonable time before any court hearing.

B   Persons detained under the Terrorism Act 2000

8. The rights as in *sections 5* or *6*, may be delayed if the person is detained under the Terrorism Act 2000, section 41 or Schedule 7, has not yet been charged with an offence and an officer of superintendent rank or above has reasonable grounds for believing the exercise of either right will:

    (i)   lead to:

    - interference with, or harm to, evidence connected with a serious arrestable offence;
    - interference with, or physical harm to, other people; or

    (ii)   lead to the alerting of other people suspected of having committed a serious arrestable offence but not yet arrested for it; or

    (iii) hinder the recovery of property:

    - obtained in consequence of the commission of such an offence; or
    - in respect of which a forfeiture order could be made under that Act, section 23;

    (iv)   lead to interference with the gathering of information about the commission, preparation or instigation of acts of terrorism; or

    (v)   by alerting any person, make it more difficult to prevent an act of terrorism or secure the apprehension, prosecution or conviction of any person in connection with the commission, preparation or instigation of an act of terrorism.

9. These rights may also be delayed if the officer has reasonable grounds for believing:

    (a)   the detainee:

    (i)   has committed an offence to which the Criminal Justice Act 1988, Part VI (confiscation orders) applies;

(ii)   has benefited from the offence; and

(b)   the exercise of either right will hinder the recovery of the value of that benefit.

10.   In these cases *paragraphs 3 (with regards to the consequences specified at paragraphs 8 and 9), 4* and *5* apply.

11.   These rights may be delayed only for as long as is necessary but not beyond 48 hours from the time of arrest if arrested under section 41, or if detained under the Terrorism Act 2000, Schedule 7 when arrested under section 41, from the beginning of their examination. If the above grounds cease to apply within this time the detainee must as soon as practicable be asked if they wish to exercise either right, the custody record noted accordingly, and action taken in accordance with the relevant section of this Code.

12.   In this case *paragraph 7* applies.

C   Documentation

13.   The grounds for action under this Annex shall be recorded and the detainee informed of them as soon as practicable.

14.   Any reply given by a detainee under *paragraphs 6* or *11* must be recorded and the detainee asked to endorse the record in relation to whether they want to receive legal advice at this point.

D   Cautions and special warnings

When a suspect detained at a police station is interviewed during any period for which access to legal advice has been delayed under this Annex, the court or jury may not draw adverse inferences from their silence.

Notes for guidance

B1   *Even if Annex B applies in the case of a juvenile, or a person who is mentally disordered or otherwise mentally vulnerable, action to inform the appropriate adult and the person responsible for a juvenile's welfare if that is a different person, must nevertheless be taken as in paragraph 3.13 and 3.15.*

B2   *In the case of Commonwealth citizens and foreign nationals, see Note 7A.*

B3   *A decision to delay access to a specific solicitor is likely to be a rare occurrence and only when it can be shown the suspect is capable of misleading that particular solicitor and there is more than a substantial risk that the suspect will succeed in causing information to be conveyed which will lead to one or more of the specified consequences.*

ANNEX C — RESTRICTION ON DRAWING ADVERSE INFERENCES FROM SILENCE AND TERMS OF THE CAUTION WHEN THE RESTRICTION APPLIES

(a)   *The restriction on drawing adverse inferences from silence*

1.   The Criminal Justice and Public Order Act 1994, sections 34, 36 and 37 as amended by the Youth Justice and Criminal Evidence Act 1999, section 58 describe the conditions under which adverse inferences may be drawn from a person's failure or refusal to say anything about their involvement in the offence when interviewed, after being charged or informed they may be prosecuted. These provisions are subject to an overriding restriction on the ability of a court or jury to draw adverse inferences from a person's silence. This restriction applies:

(a)   to any detainee at a police station, see *Note 10C* who, before being interviewed, see *section 11* or being charged or informed they may be prosecuted, see *section 16*, has:

(i)   asked for legal advice, see *section 6, paragraph 6.1*;

       (ii)   not been allowed an opportunity to consult a solicitor, including the duty solicitor, as in this Code: and

       (iii)   not changed their mind about wanting legal advice, see *section 6, paragraph 6.6(d)*

      Note the condition in (ii) will

        —   apply when a detainee who has asked for legal advice is interviewed before speaking to a solicitor as in *section 6, paragraph 6.6(a)* or *(b)*.

        —   not apply if the detained person declines to ask for the duty solicitor, see *section 6, paragraphs 6.6(c)* and *(d)*;

(b)   to any person charged with, or informed they may be prosecuted for, an offence who:

      (i)   has had brought to their notice a written statement made by another person or the content of an interview with another person which relates to that offence, see *section 16, paragraph 16.4*;

      (ii)   is interviewed about that offence, see *section 16, paragraph 16.5*; or

      (iii)   makes a written statement about that offence, see *Annex D paragraphs 4* and *9*.

(b)   Terms of the caution when the restriction applies

2.   When a requirement to caution arises at a time when the restriction on drawing adverse inferences from silence applies, the caution shall be:

    'You do not have to say anything, but anything you do say may be given in evidence.'

3.   Whenever the restriction either begins to apply or ceases to apply after a caution has already been given, the person shall be re-cautioned in the appropriate terms. The changed position on drawing inferences and that the previous caution no longer applies shall also be explained to the detainee in ordinary language. See *Note C2*

Notes for guidance

C1   *The restriction on drawing inferences from silence does not apply to a person who has not been detained and who therefore cannot be prevented from seeking legal advice if they want to, see paragraphs 10.2 and 3.15.*

C2   *The following is suggested as a framework to help explain changes in the position on drawing adverse inferences if the restriction on drawing adverse inferences from silence:*

    (a)   begins to apply:

       'The caution you were previously given no longer applies. This is because after that caution:

       (i)   you asked to speak to a solicitor but have not yet been allowed an opportunity to speak to a solicitor.' See paragraph 1(a); or

       (ii)   you have been charged with/informed you may be prosecuted.' See paragraph 1(b).

       'This means that from now on, adverse inferences cannot be drawn at court and your defence will not be harmed just because you choose to say nothing. Please listen carefully to the caution I am about to give you because it will apply from now on. You will see that it does not say anything about your defence being harmed.'

    (b)   ceases to apply before or at the time the person is charged or informed they may be prosecuted, see paragraph 1(a);

'The caution you were previously given no longer applies. This is because after that caution you have been allowed an opportunity to speak to a solicitor. Please listen carefully to the caution I am about to give you because it will apply from now on. It explains how your defence at court may be affected if you choose to say nothing.'

ANNEX D — WRITTEN STATEMENTS UNDER CAUTION

(a) Written by a person under caution

1. A person shall always be invited to write down what they want to say.

2. A person who has not been charged with, or informed they may be prosecuted for, any offence to which the statement they want to write relates, shall:

    (a) unless the statement is made at a time when the restriction on drawing adverse inferences from silence applies, see Annex C, be asked to write out and sign the following before writing what they want to say:

      'I make this statement of my own free will. I understand that I do not have to say anything but that it may harm my defence if I do not mention when questioned something which I later rely on in court. This statement may be given in evidence.';

    (b) if the statement is made at a time when the restriction on drawing adverse inferences from silence applies, be asked to write out and sign the following before writing what they want to say;

      'I make this statement of my own free will. I understand that I do not have to say anything. This statement may be given in evidence.'

3. When a person, on the occasion of being charged with or informed they may be prosecuted for any offence, asks to make a statement which relates to any such offence and wants to write it they shall:

    (a) unless the restriction on drawing adverse inferences from silence, see *Annex C*, applied when they were so charged or informed they may be prosecuted, be asked to write out and sign the following before writing what they want to say:

      'I make this statement of my own free will. I understand that I do not have to say anything but that it may harm my defence if I do not mention when questioned something which I later rely on in court. This statement may be given in evidence.';

    (b) if the restriction on drawing adverse inferences from silence applied when they were so charged or informed they may be prosecuted, be asked to write out and sign the following before writing what they want to say:

      'I make this statement of my own free will. I understand that I do not have to say anything. This statement may be given in evidence.'

4. When a person, who has already been charged with or informed they may be prosecuted for any offence, asks to make a statement which relates to any such offence and wants to write it they shall be asked to write out and sign the following before writing what they want to say:

    'I make this statement of my own free will. I understand that I do not have to say anything. This statement may be given in evidence.';

5. Any person writing their own statement shall be allowed to do so without any prompting except a police officer or civilian interviewer may indicate to them which matters are material or question any ambiguity in the statement.

(b) Written by a police officer or civilian interviewer

6. If a person says they would like someone to write the statement for them, a police officer, or civilian interviewer shall write the statement.

7. If the person has not been charged with, or informed they may be prosecuted for, any offence to which the statement they want to make relates they shall, before starting, be asked to sign, or make their mark, to the following:

(a)   unless the statement is made at a time when the restriction on drawing adverse inferences from silence applies, see *Annex C*:

'I, ..., wish to make a statement. I want someone to write down what I say. I understand that I do not have to say anything but that it may harm my defence if I do not mention when questioned something which I later rely on in court. This statement may be given in evidence.';

(b)   if the statement is made at a time when the restriction on drawing adverse inferences from silence applies:

'I, ..., wish to make a statement. I want someone to write down what I say. This statement may be given in evidence.'

8.   If, on the occasion of being charged with or informed they may be prosecuted for any offence, the person asks to make a statement which relates to any such offence they shall before starting be asked to sign, or make their mark to, the following:

(a)   unless the restriction on drawing adverse inferences from silence applied, see *Annex C*,when they were so charged or informed they may be prosecuted:

'I, ..., wish to make a statement. I want someone to write down what I say. I understand that I do not have to say anything but that it may harm my defence if I do not mention when questioned something which I later rely on in court. This statement may be given in evidence.';

(b)   if the restriction on drawing adverse inferences from silence applied when they were so charged or informed they may be prosecuted:

'I, ..., wish to make a statement. I want someone to write down what I say. This statement may be given in evidence.'

9.   If, having already been charged with or informed they may be prosecuted for any offence, a person asks to make a statement which relates to any such offence they shall before starting, be asked to sign, or make their mark to:

'I, ..., wish to make a statement. I want someone to write down what I say. This statement may be given in evidence.'

10.   The person writing the statement must take down the exact words spoken by the person making it and must not edit or paraphrase it. Any questions that are necessary, e.g. to make it more intelligible, and the answers given must be recorded at the same time on the statement form.

11.   When the writing of a statement is finished the person making it shall be asked to read it and to make any corrections, alterations or additions they want. When they have finished reading they shall be asked to write and sign or make their mark on the following certificate at the end of the statement:

'I have read the above statement, and I have been able to correct, alter or add anything I wish. This statement is true. I have made it of my own free will.'

12.   If the person making the statement cannot read, or refuses to read it, or to write the above mentioned certificate at the end of it or to sign it, the person taking the statement shall read it to them and ask them if they would like to correct, alter or add anything and to put their signature or make their mark at the end. The person taking the statement shall certify on the statement itself what has occurred.

ANNEX E — SUMMARY OF PROVISIONS RELATING TO MENTALLY DISORDERED AND OTHERWISE MENTALLY VULNERABLE PEOPLE

1.   If an officer has any suspicion, or is told in good faith, that a person of any age may be mentally disordered or otherwise mentally vulnerable, or mentally incapable of understanding the significance of questions or their replies that

person shall be treated as mentally disordered or otherwise mentally vulnerable for the purposes of this Code. See *paragraph 1.4*

2.   In the case of a person who is mentally disordered or otherwise mentally vulnerable, 'the appropriate adult' means:

  (a)   a relative, guardian or other person responsible for their care or custody;

  (b)   someone experienced in dealing with mentally disordered or mentally vulnerable people but who is not a police officer or employed by the police;

  (c)   failing these, some other responsible adult aged 18 or over who is not a police officer or employed by the police.

See *paragraph 1.7(b)* and *Note 1D*

3.   If the custody officer authorises the detention of a person who is mentally vulnerable or appears to be suffering from a mental disorder, the custody officer must as soon as practicable inform the appropriate adult of the grounds for detention and the person's whereabouts, and ask the adult to come to the police station to see them. If the appropriate adult:

  •   is already at the station when information is given as in *paragraphs 3.1* to *3.5* the information must be given in their presence

  •   is not at the station when the provisions of paragraph 3.1 to 3.5 are complied with these provisions must be complied with again in their presence once they arrive. See *paragraphs 3.15* to *3.17*

4.   If the appropriate adult, having been informed of the right to legal advice, considers legal advice should be taken, the provisions of *section 6* apply as if the mentally disordered or otherwise mentally vulnerable person had requested access to legal advice. See *paragraph 3.19* and *Note E1*

5.   The custody officer must make sure a person receives appropriate clinical attention as soon as reasonably practicable if the person appears to be suffering from a mental disorder or in urgent cases immediately call the nearest health care professional or an ambulance. It is not intended these provisions delay the transfer of a detainee to a place of safety under the Mental Health Act 1983, section 136 if that is applicable. If an assessment under that Act is to take place at a police station, the custody officer must consider whether an appropriate health care professional should be called to conduct an initial clinical check on the detainee. See *paragraph 9.5* and *9.6*

6.   It is imperative a mentally disordered or otherwise mentally vulnerable person detained under the Mental Health Act 1983, section 136 be assessed as soon as possible. If that assessment is to take place at the police station, an approved social worker and registered medical practitioner shall be called to the station as soon as possible in order to interview and examine the detainee. Once the detainee has been interviewed, examined and suitable arrangements been made for their treatment or care, they can no longer be detained under section 136. A detainee should be immediately discharged from detention if a registered medical practitioner having examined them, concludes they are not mentally disordered within the meaning of the Act. See *paragraph 3.16*

7.   If a mentally disordered or otherwise mentally vulnerable person is cautioned in the absence of the appropriate adult, the caution must be repeated in the appropriate adult's presence. See *paragraph 10.12*

8.   A mentally disordered or otherwise mentally vulnerable person must not be interviewed or asked to provide or sign a written statement in the absence of the appropriate adult unless the provisions of *paragraphs 11.1* or *11.18* to *11.20* apply. Questioning in these circumstances may not continue in the absence of the appropriate adult once sufficient information to avert the risk has been obtained.

A record shall be made of the grounds for any decision to begin an interview in these circumstances. See *paragraphs 11.1, 11.15* and *11.18* to *11.20*

9. If the appropriate adult is present at an interview, they shall be informed they are not expected to act simply as an observer and the purposes of their presence are to:

    •   advise the interviewee

    •   observe whether or not the interview is being conducted properly and fairly

    •   facilitate communication with the interviewee

    See *paragraph 11.17*

10. If the detention of a mentally disordered or otherwise mentally vulnerable person is reviewed by a review officer or a superintendent, the appropriate adult must, if available at the time, be given an opportunity to make representations to the officer about the need for continuing detention. See *paragraph 15.3*

11. If the custody officer charges a mentally disordered or otherwise mentally vulnerable person with an offence or takes such other action as is appropriate when there is sufficient evidence for a prosecution this must be done in the presence of the appropriate adult. The written notice embodying any charge must be given to the appropriate adult. See *paragraphs 16.1* to *16.4A*

12. An intimate or strip search of a mentally disordered or otherwise mentally vulnerable person may take place only in the presence of the appropriate adult of the same sex, unless the detainee specifically requests the presence of a particular adult of the opposite sex. A strip search may take place in the absence of an appropriate adult only in cases of urgency when there is a risk of serious harm to the detainee or others. See Annex A, *paragraphs 5* and *11(c)*

13. Particular care must be taken when deciding whether to use any form of approved restraints on a mentally disordered or otherwise mentally vulnerable person in a locked cell. See *paragraph 8.2*

Notes for guidance

E1 *The purpose of the provision at paragraph 3.19 is to protect the rights of a mentally disordered or otherwise mentally vulnerable detained person who does not understand the significance of what is said to them. If the detained person wants to exercise the right to legal advice, the appropriate action should be taken and not delayed until the appropriate adult arrives. A mentally disordered or otherwise mentally vulnerable detained person should always be given an opportunity, when an appropriate adult is called to the police station, to consult privately with a solicitor in the absence of the appropriate adult if they want.*

E2 *Although people who are mentally disordered or otherwise mentally vulnerable are often capable of providing reliable evidence, they may, without knowing or wanting to do so, be particularly prone in certain circumstances to provide information that may be unreliable, misleading or self-incriminating. Special care should always be taken when questioning such a person, and the appropriate adult should be involved if there is any doubt about a person's mental state or capacity. Because of the risk of unreliable evidence, it is important to obtain corroboration of any facts admitted whenever possible.*

E3 *Because of the risks referred to in Note E2, which the presence of the appropriate adult is intended to minimise, officers of superintendent rank or above should exercise their discretion to authorise the commencement of an interview in the appropriate adult's absence only in exceptional cases, if it is necessary to avert an immediate risk of serious harm. See paragraphs 11.1, 11.18 to 11.20*

ANNEX F — COUNTRIES WITH WHICH BILATERAL CONSULAR CONVENTIONS OR AGREEMENTS REQUIRING NOTIFICATION OF THE ARREST AND DETENTION OF THEIR NATIONALS ARE IN FORCE AS AT 1 APRIL 2003

Armenia	Kazakhstan
Austria	Macedonia
Azerbaijan	Mexico
Belarus	Moldova
Belgium	Mongolia
Bosnia-Herzegovina	Norway
Bulgaria	Poland
China*	Romania
Croatia	Russia
Cuba	Slovak Republic
Czech Republic	Slovenia
Denmark	Spain
Egypt	Sweden
France	Tajikistan
Georgia	Turkmenistan
German Federal Republic	Ukraine
Greece	USA
Hungary	Uzbekistan
Italy	Yugoslavia
Japan	

* Police are required to inform Chinese officials of arrest/detention in the Manchester consular district only. This comprises Derbyshire, Durham, Greater Manchester, Lancashire, Merseyside, North South and West Yorkshire, and Tyne and Wear.

ANNEX G — FITNESS TO BE INTERVIEWED

1. This Annex contains general guidance to help police officers and health care professionals assess whether a detainee might be at risk in an interview.

2. A detainee may be at risk in an interview if it is considered that:
   (a) conducting the interview could significantly harm the detainee's physical or mental state;
   (b) anything the detainee says in the interview about their involvement or suspected involvement in the offence about which they are being interviewed **might** be considered unreliable in subsequent court proceedings because of their physical or mental state.

3. In assessing whether the detainee should be interviewed, the following must be considered:
   (a) how the detainee's physical or mental state might affect their ability to understand the nature and purpose of the interview, to comprehend what is being asked and to appreciate the significance of any answers given and make rational decisions about whether they want to say anything;
   (b) the extent to which the detainee's replies may be affected by their physical or mental condition rather than representing a rational and accurate explanation of their involvement in the offence;
   (c) how the nature of the interview, which could include particularly probing questions, might affect the detainee.

4. It is essential health care professionals who are consulted consider the functional ability of the detainee rather than simply relying on a medical diagnosis, e.g. it is

possible for a person with severe mental illness to be fit for interview.

5.   Health care professionals should advise on the need for an appropriate adult to be present, whether reassessment of the person's fitness for interview may be necessary if the interview lasts beyond a specified time, and whether a further specialist opinion may be required.

6.   When health care professionals identify risks they should be asked to quantify the risks. They should inform the custody officer:

- whether the person's condition:
  — is likely to improve
  — will require or be amenable to treatment; and
- indicate how long it may take for such improvement to take effect

7.   The role of the health care professional is to consider the risks and advise the custody officer of the outcome of that consideration. The health care professional's determination and any advice or recommendations should be made in writing and form part of the custody record.

8.   Once the health care professional has provided that information, it is a matter for the custody officer to decide whether or not to allow the interview to go ahead and if the interview is to proceed, to determine what safeguards are needed. Nothing prevents safeguards being provided in addition to those required under the Code. An example might be to have an appropriate health care professional present during the interview, in addition to an appropriate adult, in order constantly to monitor the person's condition and how it is being affected by the interview.

ANNEX H — DETAINED PERSON: OBSERVATION LIST

1.   If any detainee fails to meet any of the following criteria, an appropriate health care professional or an ambulance must be called.

2.   When assessing the level of rousability, consider:

Rousability – can they be woken?

- go into the cell
- call their name
- shake gently

Response to questions – can they give appropriate answers to questions such as:

- What's your name?
- Where do you live?
- Where do you think you are?

Response to commands – can they respond appropriately to commands such as:

- Open your eyes!
- Lift one arm, now the other arm!

3.   Remember to take into account the possibility or presence of other illnesses, injury, or mental condition, a person who is drowsy and smells of alcohol may also have the following:

- Diabetes
- Epilepsy
- Head injury
- Drug intoxication or overdose
- Stroke

Police and Criminal Evidence Act 1984

Code D

Code of Practice for the Identification of Persons by Police Officers

Commencement — Transitional Arrangements

This code has effect in relation to any identification procedure carried out after midnight on 31st March 2003.

1   Introduction

1.1   This Code of Practice concerns the principal methods used by police to identify people in connection with the investigation of offences and the keeping of accurate and reliable criminal records.

1.2   Identification by witnesses arises, e.g., if the offender is seen committing the crime and a witness is given an opportunity to identify the suspect in a video identification, identification parade or similar procedure. The procedures are designed to:

•   test the witness' ability to identify the person they saw on a previous occasion

•   provide safeguards against mistaken identification.

While this Code concentrates on visual identification procedures, it does not preclude the police making use of aural identification procedures such as a "voice identification parade", where they judge that appropriate.

1.3   Identification by fingerprints applies when a person's fingerprints are taken to:

•   compare with fingerprints found at the scene of a crime

•   check and prove convictions

•   help to ascertain a person's identity.

1.4   Identification by body samples and impressions includes taking samples such as blood or hair to generate a DNA profile for comparison with material obtained from the scene of a crime, or a victim.

1.5   Taking photographs of arrested people applies to recording and checking identity and locating and tracing persons who:

•   are wanted for offences

•   fail to answer their bail.

1.6   Another method of identification involves searching and examining detained suspects to find, e.g., marks such as tattoos or scars which may help establish their identity or whether they have been involved in committing an offence.

1.7   The provisions of the Police and Criminal Evidence Act 1984 (PACE) and this Code are designed to make sure fingerprints, samples, impressions and photographs are taken, used and retained, and identification procedures carried out, only when justified and necessary for preventing, detecting or investigating crime. If these provisions are not observed, the application of the relevant procedures in particular cases may be open to question.

2   General

2.1   This Code must be readily available at all police stations for consultation by:

•   police officers

•   detained persons

•   members of the public

2.2 The provisions of this Code:
- include the *Annexes*
- do not include the *Notes for guidance*.

2.3 Code C, paragraph 1.4, regarding a person who may be mentally disordered or otherwise mentally vulnerable and the *Notes for guidance* applicable to those provisions apply to this Code.

2.4 Code C, paragraph 1.5, regarding a person who appears to be under the age of 17 applies to this Code.

2.5 Code C, paragraph 1.6, regarding a person who appears blind, seriously visually impaired, deaf, unable to read or speak or has difficulty orally because of a speech impediment applies to this Code.

2.6 In this Code:
- 'appropriate adult' means the same as in Code C, paragraph 1.7,
- 'solicitor' means the same as in Code C, paragraph 6.12

and the *Notes for guidance* applicable to those provisions apply to this Code.

2.7 References to custody officers include those performing the functions of custody officer.

2.8 When a record of any action requiring the authority of an officer of a specified rank is made under this Code, subject to *paragraph 2.18*, the officer's name and rank must be recorded.

2.9 When this Code requires the prior authority or agreement of an officer of at least inspector or superintendent rank, that authority may be given by a sergeant or chief inspector who has been authorised to perform the functions of the higher rank under PACE, section 107.

2.10 Subject to *paragraph 2.18*, all records must be timed and signed by the maker.

2.11 Records must be made in the custody record, unless otherwise specified. References to 'pocket book' include any official report book issued to police officers or civilian support staff.

2.12 If any procedure in this Code requires a person's consent, the consent of a:
- mentally disordered or otherwise mentally vulnerable person is only valid if given in the presence of the appropriate adult
- juvenile, is only valid if their parent's or guardian's consent is also obtained unless the juvenile is under 14, when their parent's or guardian's consent is sufficient in its own right. If the only obstacle to an identification procedure in *section 3* is that a juvenile's parent or guardian refuses consent or reasonable efforts to obtain it have failed, the identification officer may apply the provisions of *paragraph 3.21*. See *Note 2A*.

2.13 If a person is blind, seriously visually impaired or unable to read, the custody officer or identification officer shall make sure their solicitor, relative, appropriate adult or some other person likely to take an interest in them and not involved in the investigation is available to help check any documentation. When this Code requires written consent or signing, the person assisting may be asked to sign instead, if the detainee prefers. This paragraph does not require an appropriate adult to be called solely to assist in checking and signing documentation for a person who is not a juvenile, or mentally disordered or otherwise mentally vulnerable (see Note 2B and Code C *paragraph 3.15*).

2.14 If any procedure in this Code requires information to be given to or sought from a suspect, it must be given or sought in the appropriate adult's presence if the suspect is mentally disordered, otherwise mentally vulnerable or a juvenile. If the appropriate adult is not present when the information is first given or sought, the procedure must be repeated in the presence of the appropriate adult when they arrive. If the suspect appears deaf or there is doubt about their hearing or speaking ability or ability to understand English, and effective communication cannot be established, the information must be given or sought through an interpreter.

2.15 Any procedure in this Code involving the participation of a person (whether as a suspect or a witness) who is mentally disordered, otherwise mentally vulnerable or a juvenile, must take place in the presence of the appropriate adult. However, the adult must not be allowed to prompt any identification of a suspect by a witness.

2.16 References to:
- 'taking a photograph', include the use of any process to produce a single, still, visual image
- 'photographing a person', should be construed accordingly
- 'photographs', 'films', 'negatives' and 'copies' include relevant visual images recorded, stored, or reproduced through any medium
- 'destruction' includes the deletion of computer data relating to such images or making access to that data impossible.

2.17 Except as described, nothing in this Code affects the powers and procedures:
   (i) for requiring and taking samples of breath, blood and urine in relation to driving offences, etc, when under the influence of drink, drugs or excess alcohol under the:
   - Road Traffic Act 1988, sections 4 to 11
   - Road Traffic Offenders Act 1988, sections 15 and 16
   - Transport and Works Act 1992, sections 26 to 38;
   (ii) under the Immigration Act 1971, Schedule 2, paragraph 18, for taking photographs and fingerprints from persons detained under that Act, Schedule 2, paragraph 16 (Administrative Controls as to Control on Entry etc.); for taking fingerprints in accordance with the Immigration and Asylum Act 1999; sections 141 and 142(3), or other methods for collecting information about a person's external physical characteristics provided for by regulations made under that Act, section 144;
   (iii) under the Terrorism Act 2000, Schedule 8, for taking photographs, fingerprints, skin impressions, body samples or impressions from people:
   - arrested under that Act, section 41,
   - detained for the purposes of examination under that Act, Schedule 7, and to whom the Code of Practice issued under that Act, Schedule 14, paragraph 6, applies ('the terrorism provisions')
   See *Note 2C*;
   (iv) for taking photographs, fingerprints, skin impressions, body samples or impressions from people who have been:
   - arrested on warrants issued in Scotland, by officers exercising powers under the Criminal Justice and Public Order Act 1994, section 136(2)
   - arrested or detained without warrant by officers from a police force in Scotland exercising their powers of arrest or detention under the Criminal Justice and Public Order Act 1994, section 137(2), (Cross Border powers of arrest etc.).
   Note: In these cases, police powers and duties and the person's rights and entitlements whilst at a police station in England and Wales are the same as if the person had been arrested in Scotland by a Scottish police officer.

2.18   Nothing in this Code requires the identity of officers or civilian support staff to be recorded or disclosed:

(a)   in the case of enquiries linked to the investigation of terrorism;

(b)   if the officers or civilian support staff reasonably believe recording or disclosing their names might put them in danger.

In these cases, they shall use warrant or other identification numbers and the name of their police station. See *Note 2D*

2.19   In this Code:

(a)   'designated person' means a person other than a police officer, designated under the Police Reform Act 2002, Part 4, who has specified powers and duties of police officers conferred or imposed on them;

(b)   any reference to a police officer includes a designated person acting in the exercise or performance of the powers and duties conferred or imposed on them by their designation.

2.20   If a power conferred on a designated person:

(a)   allows reasonable force to be used when exercised by a police officer, a designated person exercising that power has the same entitlement to use force;

(b)   includes power to use force to enter any premises, that power is not exercisable by that designated person except:

(i)   in the company, and under the supervision, of a police officer; or

(ii)   for the purpose of:

•   saving life or limb; or

•   preventing serious damage to property.

2.21   Nothing in this Code prevents the custody officer, or other officer given custody of the detainee, from allowing civilian support staff who are not designated persons to carry out individual procedures or tasks at the police station if the law allows. However, the officer remains responsible for making sure the procedures and tasks are carried out correctly in accordance with the Codes of Practice. Any such civilian must be:

(a)   a person employed by a police authority maintaining a police force and under the control and direction of the Chief Officer of that force;

(b)   employed by a person with whom a police authority has a contract for the provision of services relating to persons arrested or otherwise in custody.

2.22   Designated persons and other civilian support staff must have regard to any relevant provisions of the Codes of Practice.

Notes for guidance

2A   *For the purposes of paragraph 2.12, the consent required from a parent or guardian may, for a juvenile in the care of a local authority or voluntary organisation, be given by that authority or organisation. In the case of a juvenile, nothing in paragraph 2.12 requires the parent, guardian or representative of a local authority or voluntary organisation to be present to give their consent, unless they are acting as the appropriate adult under paragraphs 2.14 or 2.15. However, it is important that a parent or guardian not present is fully informed before being asked to consent. They must be given the same information about the procedure and the juvenile's suspected involvement in the offence as the juvenile and appropriate adult. The parent or guardian must also be allowed to speak to the juvenile and the appropriate adult if they wish. Provided the consent is fully informed and is not withdrawn, it may be obtained at any time before the procedure takes place.*

2B *People who are seriously visually impaired or unable to read may be unwilling to sign police documents. The alternative, i.e. their representative signing on their behalf, seeks to protect the interests of both police and suspects.*

2C *Photographs, fingerprints, samples and impressions may be taken from a person detained under the terrorism provisions to help determine whether they are, or have been, involved in terrorism, as well as when there are reasonable grounds for suspecting their involvement in a particular offence.*

2D *The purpose of paragraph 2.18(b) is to protect those involved in serious organised crime investigations or arrests of particularly violent suspects when there is reliable information that those arrested or their associates may threaten or cause harm to the officers. In cases of doubt, an officer of inspector rank or above should be consulted.*

3 Identification by witnesses

3.1 A record shall be made of the suspect's description as first given by a potential witness. This record must:

(a) be made and kept in a form which enables details of that description to be accurately produced from it, in a visible and legible form, which can be given to the suspect or the suspect's solicitor in accordance with this Code; and

(b) unless otherwise specified, be made before the witness takes part in any identification procedures under *paragraphs 3.5 to 3.10, 3.21 or 3.23*.

A copy of the record shall where practicable, be given to the suspect or their solicitor before any procedures under *paragraphs 3.5 to 3.10, 3.21 or 3.23* are carried out. See *Note 3E*

(a) Cases when the suspect's identity is not known

3.2 In cases when the suspect's identity is not known, a witness may be taken to a particular neighbourhood or place to see whether they can identify the person they saw. Although the number, age, sex, race, general description and style of clothing of other people present at the location and the way in which any identification is made cannot be controlled, the principles applicable to the formal procedures under *paragraphs 3.5 to 3.10* shall be followed as far as practicable. For example:

(a) where it is practicable to do so, a record should be made of the witness' description of the suspect, as in paragraph 3.1(a), before asking the witness to make an identification;

(b) care must be taken not to direct the witness' attention to any individual unless, taking into account all the circumstances, this cannot be avoided. However, this does not prevent a witness being asked to look carefully at the people around at the time or to look towards a group or in a particular direction, if this appears necessary to make sure that the witness does not overlook a possible suspect simply because the witness is looking in the opposite direction and also to enable the witness to make comparisons between any suspect and others who are in the area; See *Note 3F*

(c) where there is more than one witness, every effort should be made to keep them separate and witnesses should be taken to see whether they can identify a person independently;

(d) once there is sufficient information to justify the arrest of a particular individual for suspected involvement in the offence, e.g., after a witness makes a positive identification, the provisions set out from paragraph 3.4 onwards shall apply for any other witnesses in relation to that individual. Subject to *paragraphs 3.12* and *3.13*, it is not necessary for the witness who makes such a positive identification to take part in a further procedure;

(e)   the officer or civilian support staff accompanying the witness must record, in their pocket book, the action taken as soon as, and in as much detail, as possible. The record should include: the date, time and place of the relevant occasion the witness claims to have previously seen the suspect; where any identification was made; how it was made and the conditions at the time (e.g., the distance the witness was from the suspect, the weather and light); if the witness's attention was drawn to the suspect; the reason for this; and anything said by the witness or the suspect about the identification or the conduct of the procedure.

3.3   A witness must not be shown photographs, computerised or artist's composite likenesses or similar likenesses or pictures (including 'E-fit' images) if the identity of the suspect is known to the police and the suspect is available to take part in a video identification, an identification parade or a group identification. If the suspect's identity is not known, the showing of such images to a witness to obtain identification evidence must be done in accordance with *Annex E*.

(b)   Cases when the suspect is known and available

3.4   If the suspect's identity is known to the police and they are available, the identification procedures set out in paragraphs 3.5 to 3.10 may be used. References in this section to a suspect being 'known' mean there is sufficient information known to the police to justify the arrest of a particular person for suspected involvement in the offence. A suspect being 'available' means they are immediately available or will be within a reasonably short time and willing to take an effective part in at least one of the following which it is practicable to arrange;

- video identification;
- identification parade; or
- group identification.

Video identification

3.5   A 'video identification' is when the witness is shown moving images of a known suspect, together with similar images of others who resemble the suspect. See paragraph 3.21 for circumstances in which still images may be used.

3.6   Video identifications must be carried out in accordance with *Annex A*.

Identification parade

3.7   An 'identification parade' is when the witness sees the suspect in a line of others who resemble the suspect.

3.8   Identification parades must be carried out in accordance with *Annex B*.

Group identification

3.9   A 'group identification' is when the witness sees the suspect in an informal group of people.

3.10   Group identifications must be carried out in accordance with *Annex C*.

Arranging identification procedures

3.11   Except for the provisions in *paragraph 3.19*, the arrangements for, and conduct of, the identification procedures in paragraphs 3.5 to 3.10 and circumstances in which an identification procedure must be held shall be the responsibility of an officer not below inspector rank who is not involved with the investigation, 'the identification officer'. Unless otherwise specified, the identification officer may allow another officer or civilian support staff, see *paragraph 2.21*, to make arrangements for, and conduct, any of these identification procedures. In delegating these procedures, the identification officer must be able to supervise effectively and either intervene or be contacted for advice. No officer or any other person involved with the investigation of the case against the suspect, beyond the extent required by these procedures, may take any part in these procedures or act as the identification officer. This does not prevent the identification officer from consulting the officer in charge of the investigation to determine which procedure to use. When an identification procedure is required, in the interest of fairness to suspects and witnesses, it must be held as soon as practicable.

Circumstances in which an identification procedure must be held

3.12   Whenever:

(i)   a witness has identified a suspect or purported to have identified them prior to any identification procedure set out in paragraphs 3.5 to 3.10 having been held; or

(ii)   there is a witness available, who expresses an ability to identify the suspect, or where there is a reasonable chance of the witness being able to do so, and they have not been given an opportunity to identify the suspect in any of the procedures set out in paragraphs 3.5 to 3.10,

and the suspect disputes being the person the witness claims to have seen, an identification procedure shall be held unless it is not practicable or it would serve no useful purpose in proving or disproving whether the suspect was involved in committing the offence. For example, when it is not disputed that the suspect is already well known to the witness who claims to have seen them commit the crime.

3.13   Such a procedure may also be held if the officer in charge of the investigation considers it would be useful.

Selecting an identification procedure

3.14   If, because of paragraph 3.12, an identification procedure is to be held, the suspect shall initially be offered either a video identification or identification unless:

(a)   a video identification is not practicable; or

(b)   an identification parade is both practicable and more suitable than a video identification; or

(c)   paragraph 3.16 applies.

The identification officer and the officer in charge of the investigation shall consult each other to determine which option is to be offered. An identification parade may not be practicable because of factors relating to the witnesses, such as their number, state of health, availability and travelling requirements. A video identification would normally be more suitable if it could be arranged and completed sooner than an identification parade.

3.15   A suspect who refuses the identification procedure first offered shall be asked to state their reason for refusing and may get advice from their solicitor and/or if present, their appropriate adult. The suspect, solicitor and/or appropriate adult shall be allowed to make representations about why another procedure should be used. A record should be made of the reasons for refusal and any representations made. After considering any reasons given, and representations made, the identification officer shall, if appropriate, arrange for the suspect to be offered an alternative which the officer considers suitable and practicable. If the officer decides it is not suitable and practicable to offer an alternative identification procedure, the reasons for that decision shall be recorded.

3.16   A group identification may initially be offered if the officer in charge of the investigation considers it is more satisfactory than a video identification or an identification parade and the identification officer considers it practicable to arrange.

Notice to suspect

3.17   Unless *paragraph 3.20* applies, before a video identification, an identification parade or group identification is arranged, the following shall be explained to the suspect:

(i)   the purposes of the video identification, identification parade or group identification;

(ii)   their entitlement to free legal advice; see Code C, paragraph 6.5;

(iii)   the procedures for holding it, including their right to have a solicitor or friend present;

(iv)   that they do not have to consent to or co-operate in a video identification, identification parade or group identification;

(v)   that if they do not consent to, and co-operate in, a video identification, identification parade or group identification, their refusal may be given in evidence in any subsequent trial and police may proceed covertly without their consent or make other arrangements to test whether a witness can identify them, see *paragraph 3.21*

(vi)   whether, for the purposes of the video identification procedure, images of them have previously been obtained, see *paragraph 3.20*, and if so, that they may co-operate in providing further, suitable images to be used instead;

(vii)   if appropriate, the special arrangements for juveniles;

(viii) if appropriate, the special arrangements for mentally disordered or otherwise mentally vulnerable people;

(ix)   that if they significantly alter their appearance between being offered an identification procedure and any attempt to hold an identification procedure, this may be given in evidence if the case comes to trial, and the identification officer may then consider other forms of identification, see *paragraph 3.21* and *Note 3C*;

(x)   that a moving image or photograph may be taken of them when they attend for any identification procedure;

(xi)   whether, before their identity became known, the witness was shown photographs, a computerised or artist's composite likeness or similar likeness or image by the police; see *Note 3B*

(xii)   that if they change their appearance before an identification parade, it may not be practicable to arrange one on the day or subsequently and, because of the appearance change, the identification officer may consider alternative methods of identification; see *Note 3C*

(xiii) that they or their solicitor will be provided with details of the description of them as first given by any witnesses who are to attend the video identification, identification parade, group identification or confrontation, see *paragraph 3.1*.

3.18   This information must also be recorded in a written notice handed to the suspect. The suspect must be given a reasonable opportunity to read the notice, after which, they should be asked to sign a second copy to indicate if they are willing to co-operate with the making of a video or take part in the identification parade or group identification. The signed copy shall be retained by the identification officer.

3.19   The duties of the identification officer under *paragraphs 3.17* and *3.18* may be performed by the custody officer or other officer not involved in the investigation if:

(a)   it is proposed to hold an identification procedure at a later date, e.g., if the suspect is to be bailed to attend an identification parade; and

(b)   an inspector is not available to act as the identification officer, see *paragraph 3.11*, before the suspect leaves the station.

The officer concerned shall inform the identification officer of the action taken and give them the signed copy of the notice. See *Note 3C*

3.20   If the identification officer and officer in charge of the investigation suspect, on reasonable grounds that if the suspect was given the information and notice as in *paragraphs 3.17* and *3.18*, they would then take steps to avoid being seen by a witness in any identification procedure, the identification officer may arrange for images of the suspect suitable for use in a video identification procedure to be obtained before giving the information and notice. If suspect's images are obtained in these circumstances, the suspect may, for the purposes of a video identification procedure, co-operate in providing suitable new images to be used instead, see *paragraph 3.17(vi)*.

(c)   Cases when the suspect is known but not available

3.21   When a known suspect is not available or has ceased to be available, see *paragraph 3.4*, the identification officer may make arrangements for a video identification (see Annex A). If necessary, the identification officer may follow the video identification procedures but using **still** images. Any suitable moving or still images may be used and these may be obtained covertly if necessary. Alternatively, the identification officer may make arrangements for a group identification. See *Note 3D*. These provisions may also be applied to juveniles where the consent of their parent or guardian is either refused or reasonable efforts to obtain that consent have failed (see *paragraph 2.12*).

3.22   Any covert activity should be strictly limited to that necessary to test the ability of the witness to identify the suspect.

3.23   The identification officer may arrange for the suspect to be confronted by the witness if none of the options referred to in paragraphs 3.5 to 3.10 or 3.21 are practicable. A "confrontation" is when the suspect is directly confronted by the witness. A confrontation does not require the suspect's consent. Confrontations must be carried out in accordance with Annex D.

3.24   Requirements for information to be given to, or sought from, a suspect or for the suspect to be given an opportunity to view images before they are shown to a witness, do not apply if the suspect's lack of co-operation prevents the necessary action.

(d)   Documentation

3.25   A record shall be made of the video identification, identification parade, group identification or confrontation on forms provided for the purpose.

3.26   If the identification officer considers it is not practicable to hold a video identification or identification parade requested by the suspect, the reasons shall be recorded and explained to the suspect.

3.27   A record shall be made of a person's failure or refusal to co-operate in a video identification, identification parade or group identification and, if applicable, of the grounds for obtaining images in accordance with *paragraph 3.20*.

(e)   Showing films and photographs of incidents and information released to the media

3.28   Nothing in this Code inhibits showing films or photographs to the public through the national or local media, or to police officers for the purposes of recognition and tracing suspects. However, when such material is shown to potential witnesses, including police officers, see *Note 3A*, to obtain identification evidence, it shall be shown on an individual basis to avoid any possibility of collusion, and, as far as possible, the showing shall follow the principles for video identification if the suspect is known, see *Annex A*, or identification by photographs if the suspect is not known, see *Annex E*.

3.29   When a broadcast or publication is made, see *paragraph 3.28*, a copy of the relevant material released to the media for the purposes of recognising or tracing the suspect, shall be kept. The suspect or their solicitor shall be allowed to view such material before any procedures under *paragraphs 3.5* to *3.10, 3.21* or *3.23* are carried out, provided it is practicable and would not unreasonably delay the investigation. Each witness involved in the procedure shall be asked, after they have taken part, whether they have seen any broadcast or published films or photographs relating to the offence or any description of the suspect and their replies shall be recorded. This paragraph does not affect any separate requirement under the Criminal Procedure and Investigations Act 1996 to retain material in connection with criminal investigations.

(f)   Destruction and retention of photographs and images taken or used in identification procedures

3.30   PACE, section 64A, provides powers to take photographs of suspects detained at police stations and allows these photographs to be used or disclosed only for purposes related to the prevention or detection of crime, the investigation of offences or the conduct of prosecutions by, or on behalf of, police or other law enforcement and prosecuting authorities inside and outside the United Kingdom. After being so used or disclosed, they may be retained but can only be used or disclosed for the same purposes.

3.31   Subject to *paragraph 3.33*, the photographs (and all negatives and copies), of suspects not detained and any moving images, (and copies), of suspects whether or not they have been detained which are taken for the purposes of, or in connection with, the identification procedures in *paragraphs 3.5* to *3.10, 3.21* or *3.23* must be destroyed unless the suspect:

(a)   is charged with, or informed they may be prosecuted for, a recordable offence;

(b)   is prosecuted for a recordable offence;

(c)   is cautioned for a recordable offence or given a warning or reprimand in accordance with the Crime and Disorder Act 1998 for a recordable offence; or

(d)   gives informed consent, in writing, for the photograph or images to be retained for purposes described in *paragraph 3.30*.

3.32   When *paragraph 3.31* requires the destruction of any photograph or images, the person must be given an opportunity to witness the destruction or to have a certificate confirming the destruction if they request one within five days of being informed that the destruction is required.

3.33   Nothing in *paragraph 3.31* affects any separate requirement under the Criminal Procedure and Investigations Act 1996 to retain material in connection with criminal investigations.

Notes for guidance

3A   *Except for the provisions of Annex E, paragraph 1, a police officer who is a witness for the purposes of this part of the Code is subject to the same principles and procedures as a civilian witness.*

3B   *When a witness attending an identification procedure has previously been shown photographs, or been shown or provided with computerised or artist's composite likenesses, or similar likenesses or pictures, it is the officer in charge of the investigation's responsibility to make the identification officer aware of this.*

3C *The purpose of paragraph 3.19 is to avoid or reduce delay in arranging identification procedures by enabling the required information and warnings, see sub-paragraphs 3.17(ix) and 3.17(xii), to be given at the earliest opportunity.*

3D *Paragraph 3.21 would apply when a known suspect deliberately makes themself 'unavailable' in order to delay or frustrate arrangements for obtaining identification evidence. It also applies when a suspect refuses or fails to take part in a video identification, an identification parade or a group identification, or refuses or fails to take part in the only practicable options from that list. It enables any suitable images of the suspect, moving or still, which are available or can be obtained, to be used in an identification procedure.*

3E *When it is proposed to show photographs to a witness in accordance with Annex E, it is the responsibility of the officer in charge of the investigation to confirm to the officer responsible for supervising and directing the showing, that the first description of the suspect given by that witness has been recorded. If this description has not been recorded, the procedure under Annex E must be postponed. See Annex E paragraph 2*

3F *The admissibility and value of identification evidence obtained when carrying out the procedure under paragraph 3.2 may be compromised if:*

(a) *before a person is identified, the witness' attention is specifically drawn to that person; or*

(b) *the suspect's identity becomes known before the procedure.*

4 Identification by fingerprints

(A) *Taking fingerprints in connection with a criminal investigation*

(a) *General*

4.1 References to 'fingerprints' means any record, produced by any method, of the skin pattern and other physical characteristics or features of a person's:

(i) fingers; or

(ii) palms.

(b) *Action*

4.2 A person's fingerprints may be taken in connection with the investigation of an offence only with their consent or if *paragraph 4.3* applies. If the person is at a police station consent must be in writing.

4.3 PACE, section 61, provides powers to take fingerprints without consent from any person over the age of ten years:

(a) under section 61(3)(a), from a detainee at a police station if authorised by an officer of at least inspector rank who has reasonable grounds for suspecting that person is involved in a criminal offence and for believing their fingerprints will tend to confirm or disprove involvement, or assist in establishing their identity (including showing that they are not a particular person), or both. However, authority may not be given solely to establish the person's identity unless they have refused to identify themselves or the authorising officer has reasonable grounds to suspect the person is not who they claim to be.

(b) under section 61(3)(b), from a detainee at a police station who has been charged with a recordable offence, see *Note 4A*, or informed they will be reported for such an offence if, in the course of the investigation of that offence:

(i) they have not had their fingerprints taken; or

(ii)   the fingerprints taken do not constitute a complete set of their fingerprints or some, or all, of the fingerprints are not of sufficient quality to allow satisfactory analysis, comparison or matching;

(c)   under section 61(4A), from a person who has been bailed to appear at a court or police station if the person:

(i)   has answered to bail for a person whose fingerprints were taken previously and there are reasonable grounds for believing they are not the same person; or

(ii)   who has answered to bail claims to be a different person from a person whose fingerprints were previously taken;

and in either case, the court or an officer of inspector rank or above, authorises the fingerprints to be taken at the court or police station;

(d)   under section 61(6), from a person who has been:

(i)   convicted of a recordable offence;

(ii)   given a caution in respect of a recordable offence which, at the time of the caution, the person admitted; or

(iii)   warned or reprimanded under the Crime and Disorder Act 1998, section 65, for a recordable offence.

4.4   PACE, section 27, provides power to:

(a)   require the person as in *paragraph 4.3(d)* to attend a police station to have their fingerprints taken if the:

(i)   person has not been in police detention for the offence and has not had their fingerprints taken in the course of the investigation of that offence; or

(ii)   fingerprints that were taken from the person in the course of the investigation of that offence, do not constitute a complete set or some, or all, of the fingerprints are not of sufficient quality to allow satisfactory analysis, comparison or matching; and

(b)   arrest, without warrant, a person who fails to comply with the requirement.

Note: The requirement must be made within one month of the date the person is convicted, cautioned, warned or reprimanded and the person must be given a period of at least 7 days within which to attend. This 7 day period need not fall during the month allowed for making the requirement.

4.5   A person's fingerprints may be taken, as above, electronically.

4.6   Reasonable force may be used, if necessary, to take a person's fingerprints without their consent under the powers as in *paragraphs 4.3* and *4.4*.

4.7   Before any fingerprints are taken with, or without, consent as above, the person must be informed:

(a)   of the reason their fingerprints are to be taken;

(b)   of the grounds on which the relevant authority has been given if the powers mentioned in *paragraph 4.3(a)* or *(c)* apply;

(c)   that their fingerprints may be retained and may be subject of a speculative search against other fingerprints, see *Note 4B*, unless destruction of the fingerprints is required in accordance with *Annex F, Part (a)*; and

(d)   that if their fingerprints are required to be destroyed, they may witness their destruction as provided for in *Annex F, Part (a)*.

(c) Documentation

4.8 A record must be made as soon as possible, of the reason for taking a person's fingerprints without consent. If force is used, a record shall be made of the circumstances and those present.

4.9 A record shall be made when a person has been informed under the terms of *paragraph 4.7(c)*, of the possibility that their fingerprints may be subject of a speculative search.

(B) Taking fingerprints in connection with immigration enquiries

Action

4.10 A person's fingerprints may be taken for the purposes of Immigration Service enquiries in accordance with powers and procedures other than under PACE and for which the Immigration Service (not the police) are responsible, only with the person's consent in writing or if *paragraph 4.11* applies.

4.11 Powers to take fingerprints for these purposes without consent are given to police and immigration officers under the:

(a) Immigration Act 1971, Schedule 2, paragraph 18(2), when it is reasonably necessary for the purposes of identifying a person detained under the Immigration Act 1971, Schedule 2, paragraph 16 (Detention of person liable to examination or removal);

(b) Immigration and Asylum Act 1999, section 141(7)(a), from a person who fails to produce, on arrival, a valid passport with a photograph or some other document satisfactorily establishing their identity and nationality if an immigration officer does not consider the person has a reasonable excuse for the failure;

(c) Immigration and Asylum Act 1999, section 141(7)(b), from a person who has been refused entry to the UK but has been temporarily admitted if an immigration officer reasonably suspects the person might break a condition imposed on them relating to residence or reporting to a police or immigration officer, and their decision is confirmed by a chief immigration officer;

(d) Immigration and Asylum Act 1999, section 141(7)(c), when directions are given to remove a person:

• as an illegal entrant,

• liable to removal under the Immigration and Asylum Act 1999, section 10,

• who is the subject of a deportation order from the UK;

(e) Immigration and Asylum Act 1999, section 141(7)(d), from a person arrested under UK immigration laws under the Immigration Act 1971, Schedule 2, paragraph 17;

(f) Immigration and Asylum Act 1999, section 141(7)(e), from a person who has made a claim:

• for asylum

• under Article 3 of the European Convention on Human Rights; or

(g) Immigration and Asylum Act 1999, section 141(7)(f), from a person who is a dependant of someone who falls into (b) to (f) above.

4.12 The Immigration and Asylum Act 1999, section 142(3), gives a police and immigration officer power to arrest, without warrant, a person who fails to comply with a requirement imposed by the Secretary of State to attend a specified place for fingerprinting.

4.13   Before any fingerprints are taken, with or without consent, the person must be informed:

(a)   of the reason their fingerprints are to taken;

(b)   the fingerprints, and all copies of them, will be destroyed in accordance with *Annex F, Part B.*

4.14   Reasonable force may be used, if necessary, to take a person's fingerprints without their consent under powers as in *paragraph 4.11.*

4.15   *Paragraphs 4.1* and *4.8* apply.

Notes for guidance

4A   *References to 'recordable offences' in this Code relate to those offences for which convictions, cautions, reprimands and warnings may be recorded in national police records. See PACE, section 27(4). The recordable offences current at the time when this Code was prepared, are any offences which carry a sentence of imprisonment on conviction (irrespective of the period, or the age of the offender or actual sentence passed) as well as the non-imprisonable offences under the Street Offences Act 1959, section 1 (loitering or soliciting for purposes of prostitution), the Telecommunications Act 1984, section 43 (improper use of public telecommunications systems), the Road Traffic Act 1988, section 25 (tampering with motor vehicles), the Malicious Communications Act 1988, section 1 (sending letters, etc. with intent to cause distress or anxiety) and others listed in the National Police Records (Recordable Offences) Regulations 2000.*

4B   *Fingerprints or a DNA sample (and the information derived from it) taken from a person arrested on suspicion of being involved in a recordable offence, or charged with such an offence, or informed they will be reported for such an offence, may be subject of a speculative search. This means the fingerprints or DNA sample may be checked against other fingerprints and DNA records held by, or on behalf of, the police and other law enforcement authorities in, or outside, the UK, or held in connection with, or as a result of, an investigation of an offence inside or outside the UK. Fingerprints and samples taken from a person suspected of committing a recordable offence but not arrested, charged or informed they will be reported for it, may be subject to a speculative search only if the person consents in writing. The following is an example of a basic form of words:*

> *"I consent to my fingerprints and DNA sample and information derived from it being retained and used only for purposes related to the prevention and detection of a crime, the investigation of an offence or the conduct of a prosecution either nationally or internationally.*
>
> *I understand that my fingerprints or this sample may be checked against other fingerprint and DNA records held by or on behalf of relevant law enforcement authorities, either nationally or internationally.*
>
> *I understand that once I have given my consent for the sample to be retained and used I cannot withdraw this consent."*

See Annex F regarding the retention and use of fingerprints taken with consent for elimination purposes.

5   Examinations to establish identity and the taking of photographs

(A)   *Detainees at police stations*

(a)   *Searching or examination of detainees at police stations*

5.1   PACE, section 54A (1), allows a detainee at a police station to be searched or examined or both, to establish:

(a)   whether they have any marks, features or injuries that would tend to identify them as a person involved in the commission of an offence and to photograph any identifying marks, see *paragraph 5.5*; or

(b)   their identity, see *Note 5A.*

A person detained at a police station to be searched under a stop and search power, see Code A, is not a detainee for the purposes of these powers.

5.2   A search and/or examination to find marks under section 54A(1)(a) may be carried out without the detainee's consent, see *paragraph 2.12*, only if authorised by an officer of at least inspector rank when consent has been withheld or it is not practicable to obtain consent, see *Note 5D*.

5.3   A search or examination to establish a suspect's identity under section 54A(1)(b) may be carried out without the detainee's consent, see *paragraph 2.12*, only if authorised by an officer of at least inspector rank when the detainee has refused to identify themselves or the authorising officer has reasonable grounds for suspecting the person is not who they claim to be.

5.4   Any marks that assist in establishing the detainee's identity, or their identification as a person involved in the commission of an offence, are identifying marks. Such marks may be photographed with the detainee's consent, see *paragraph 2.12*; or without their consent if it is withheld or it is not practicable to obtain it, see *Note 5D*.

5.5   A detainee may only be searched, examined and photographed under section 54A, by a police officer of the same sex.

5.6   Any photographs of identifying marks, taken under section 54A, may be used or disclosed only for purposes related to the prevention or detection of crime, the investigation of offences or the conduct of prosecutions by, or on behalf of, police or other law enforcement and prosecuting authorities inside, and outside, the UK. After being so used or disclosed, the photograph may be retained but must not be used or disclosed except for these purposes, see *Note 5B*.

5.7   The powers, as in *paragraph 5.1*, do not affect any separate requirement under the Criminal Procedure and Investigations Act 1996 to retain material in connection with criminal investigations.

5.8   Authority for the search and/or examination for the purposes of *paragraphs 5.2* and *5.3* may be given orally or in writing. If given orally, the authorising officer must confirm it in writing as soon as practicable. A separate authority is required for each purpose which applies.

5.9   If it is established a person is unwilling to co-operate sufficiently to enable a search and/or examination to take place or a suitable photograph to be taken, an officer may use reasonable force to:

(a)   search and/or examine a detainee without their consent; and

(b)   photograph any identifying marks without their consent.

5.10 The thoroughness and extent of any search or examination carried out in accordance with the powers in section 54A must be no more than the officer considers necessary to achieve the required purpose. Any search or examination which involves the removal of more than the person's outer clothing shall be conducted in accordance with Code C, Annex A, paragraph 11.

5.11 An intimate search may not be carried out under the powers in section 54A.

(b)   Photographing detainees at police stations

5.12 Under PACE, section 64A, an officer may photograph a detainee at a police station:

(a)   with their consent; or

(b)   without their consent if it is:

(i)   withheld; or

(ii)   not practicable to obtain their consent.

See *Note 5E*

and *paragraph 5.6* applies to the retention and use of photographs taken under this section as it applies to the retention and use of photographs taken under section 54A, see *Note 5B*.

5.13   The officer proposing to take a detainee's photograph may, for this purpose, require the person to remove any item or substance worn on, or over, all, or any part of, their head or face. If they do not comply with such a requirement, the officer may remove the item or substance.

5.14   If it is established the detainee is unwilling to co-operate sufficiently to enable a suitable photograph to be taken and it is not reasonably practicable to take the photograph covertly, an officer may use reasonable force:

(a)   to take their photograph without their consent; and

(b)   for the purpose of taking the photograph, remove any item or substance worn on, or over, all, or any part of, the person's head or face which they have failed to remove when asked.

5.15   For the purposes of this Code, a photograph may be obtained without the person's consent by making a copy of an image of them taken at any time on a camera system installed anywhere in the police station.

(c)   Information to be given

5.16   When a person is searched, examined or photographed under the provisions as in *paragraph 5.1* and *5.12*, or their photograph obtained as in *paragraph 5.15*, they must be informed of the:

(a)   purpose of the search, examination or photograph;

(b)   grounds on which the relevant authority, if applicable, has been given; and

(c)   purposes for which the photograph may be used, disclosed or retained.

This information must be given before the search or examination commences or the photograph is taken, except if the photograph is:

(i)   to be taken covertly;

(ii)   obtained as in *paragraph 5.15*, in which case the person must be informed as soon as practicable after the photograph is taken or obtained.

(d)   Documentation

5.17   A record must be made when a detainee is searched, examined, or a photograph of the person, or any identifying marks found on them, are taken. The record must include the:

(a)   identity, subject to paragraph 2.18, of the officer carrying out the search, examination or taking the photograph;

(b)   purpose of the search, examination or photograph and the outcome;

(c)   detainee's consent to the search, examination or photograph, or the reason the person was searched, examined or photographed without consent;

(d)   giving of any authority as in *paragraphs 5.2* and *5.3*, the grounds for giving it and the authorising officer.

5.18   If force is used when searching, examining or taking a photograph in accordance with this section, a record shall be made of the circumstances and those present.

(B)   Persons at police stations not detained

5.19   When there are reasonable grounds for suspecting the involvement of a person in a criminal offence, but that person is at a police station **voluntarily** and not detained, the provisions of *paragraphs 5.1* to *5.18* should apply, subject to the modifications in the following paragraphs.

5.20   References to the 'person being detained' and to the powers mentioned in *paragraph 5.1* which apply only to detainees at police stations shall be omitted.

5.21 Force may not be used to:

(a) search and/or examine the person to:

(i) discover whether they have any marks that would tend to identify them as a person involved in the commission of an offence; or

(ii) establish their identity, see *Note 5A*;

(b) take photographs of any identifying marks, see *paragraph 5.4*; or

(c) take a photograph of the person.

5.22 Subject to *paragraph 5.24*, the photographs or images, of persons not detained, or of their identifying marks, must be destroyed (together with any negatives and copies) unless the person:

(a) is charged with, or informed they may be prosecuted for, a recordable offence;

(b) is prosecuted for a recordable offence;

(c) is cautioned for a recordable offence or given a warning or reprimand in accordance with the Crime and Disorder Act 1998 for a recordable offence; or

(d) gives informed consent, in writing, for the photograph or image to be retained as in *paragraph 5.6*.

5.23 When *paragraph 5.22* requires the destruction of any photograph or image, the person must be given an opportunity to witness the destruction or to have a certificate confirming the destruction provided they so request the certificate within five days of being informed the destruction is required.

5.24 Nothing in *paragraph 5.22* affects any separate requirement under the Criminal Procedure and Investigations Act 1996 to retain material in connection with criminal investigations.

Notes for guidance

5A *The conditions under which fingerprints may be taken to assist in establishing a person's identity, are described in Section 4.*

5B *Examples of purposes related to the prevention or detection of crime, the investigation of offences or the conduct of prosecutions include:*

(a) *checking the photograph against other photographs held in records or in connection with, or as a result of, an investigation of an offence to establish whether the person is liable to arrest for other offences;*

(b) *when the person is arrested at the same time as other people, or at a time when it is likely that other people will be arrested, using the photograph to help establish who was arrested, at what time and where;*

(c) *when the real identity of the person is not known and cannot be readily ascertained or there are reasonable grounds for doubting a name and other personal details given by the person, are their real name and personal details. In these circumstances, using or disclosing the photograph to help to establish or verify their real identity or determine whether they are liable to arrest for some other offence, e.g. by checking it against other photographs held in records or in connection with, or as a result of, an investigation of an offence;*

(d) *when it appears any identification procedure in section 3 may need to be arranged for which the person's photograph would assist;*

(e) *when the person's release without charge may be required, and if the release is:*

(i) *on bail to appear at a police station, using the photograph to help verify the person's identity when they answer their bail and if the person does not answer their bail, to assist in arresting them; or*

  (ii) *without bail, using the photograph to help verify their identity or assist in locating them for the purposes of serving them with a summons to appear at court in criminal proceedings;*

 (f) *when the person has answered to bail at a police station and there are reasonable grounds for doubting they are the person who was previously granted bail, using the photograph to help establish or verify their identity;*

 (g) *when the person arrested on a warrant claims to be a different person from the person named on the warrant and a photograph would help to confirm or disprove their claim;*

 (h) *when the person has been charged with, reported for, or convicted of, a recordable offence and their photograph is not already on record as a result of (a) to (f) or their photograph is on record but their appearance has changed since it was taken and the person has not yet been released or brought before a court.*

5C *There is no power to arrest a person convicted of a recordable offence solely to take their photograph. The power to take photographs in this section applies only where the person is in custody as a result of the exercise of another power, e.g. arrest for fingerprinting under PACE, section 27.*

5D *Examples of when it would not be practicable to obtain a detainee's consent, see paragraph 2.12, to a search, examination or the taking of a photograph of an identifying mark include:*

 (a) *when the person is drunk or otherwise unfit to give consent;*

 (b) *when there are reasonable grounds to suspect that if the person became aware a search or examination was to take place or an identifying mark was to be photographed, they would take steps to prevent this happening, e.g. by violently resisting, covering or concealing the mark etc and it would not otherwise be possible to carry out the search or examination or to photograph any identifying mark;*

 (c) *in the case of a juvenile, if the parent or guardian cannot be contacted in sufficient time to allow the search or examination to be carried out or the photograph to be taken.*

5E *Examples of when it would not be practicable to obtain the person's consent, see paragraph 2.12, to a photograph being taken include:*

 (a) *when the person is drunk or otherwise unfit to give consent;*

 (b) *when there are reasonable grounds to suspect that if the person became aware a photograph, suitable to be used or disclosed for the use and disclosure described in paragraph 5.6, was to be taken, they would take steps to prevent it being taken, e.g. by violently resisting, covering or distorting their face etc, and it would not otherwise be possible to take a suitable photograph;*

 (c) *when, in order to obtain a suitable photograph, it is necessary to take it covertly; and*

 (d) *in the case of a juvenile, if the parent or guardian cannot be contacted in sufficient time to allow the photograph to be taken.*

6 Identification by body samples and impressions

(A) General

6.1 References to:

 (a) an 'intimate sample' mean a dental impression or sample of blood, semen or any other tissue fluid, urine, or pubic hair, or a swab taken from a person's body orifice other than the mouth;

 (b) a 'non-intimate sample' means:

  (i) a sample of hair, other than pubic hair, which includes hair plucked with the root, see *Note 6A*;

(ii)   a sample taken from a nail or from under a nail;

(iii)   a swab taken from any part of a person's body including the mouth but not any other body orifice;

(iv)   saliva;

(v)   a skin impression which means any record, other than a fingerprint, which is a record, in any form and produced by any method, of the skin pattern and other physical characteristics or features of the whole, or any part of, a person's foot or of any other part of their body.

(B)   Action

(a)   *Intimate samples*

6.2   PACE, section 62, provides that intimate samples may be taken under:

(a)   section 62(1), from a person in police detention only:

(i)   if a police officer of inspector rank or above has reasonable grounds to believe such an impression or sample will tend to confirm or disprove the suspect's involvement in a recordable offence, see Note 4A, and gives authorisation for a sample to be taken; and

(ii)   with the suspect's written consent;

(b)   section 62(1A), from a person not in police detention but from whom two or more non-intimate samples have been taken in the course of an investigation of an offence and the samples, though suitable, have proved insufficient if:

(i)   a police officer of inspector rank or above authorises it to be taken; and

(ii)   the person concerned gives their written consent. See *Notes 6B* and *6C*

6.3   Before a suspect is asked to provide an intimate sample, they must be warned that if they refuse without good cause, their refusal may harm their case if it comes to trial, see *Note 6D*. If the suspect is in police detention and not legally represented, they must also be reminded of their entitlement to have free legal advice, see Code C, *paragraph 6.5*, and the reminder noted in the custody record. If *paragraph 6.2(b)* applies and the person is attending a station voluntarily, their entitlement to free legal advice as in Code C, *paragraph 3.21* shall be explained to them.

6.4   Dental impressions may only be taken by a registered dentist. Other intimate samples, except for samples of urine, may only be taken by a registered medical practitioner or registered health care professional.

(b)   *Non-intimate samples*

6.5   A non-intimate sample may be taken from a detainee only with their written consent or if *paragraph 6.6* applies.

6.6   A non-intimate sample may be taken from a person without consent in accordance with PACE. The principal circumstances provided for are as follows:

(a)   under section 63(3), from a person in police detention, or police custody on the authority of a court, if a police officer of inspector rank or above has reasonable grounds to believe the sample will tend to confirm or disprove the suspect's involvement in a recordable offence, see *Note 4A*, and gives authorisation for a sample to be taken. However, the officer may not give authorisation to take a non-intimate sample consisting of a skin impression if a skin impression of the same part of the body has already been taken from that person in the course of the investigation of the offence and the impression previously taken is not one that has proved insufficient;

(b)   under section 63(3A), from a person charged with a recordable offence or informed they will be reported for such an offence: and

> (i)   that person has not had a non-intimate sample taken from them in the course of the investigation; or
>
> (ii)   if they have had a sample taken, it proved unsuitable or insufficient for the same form of analysis, see *Note 6B*; or

(c)   under section 63(3B), from a person convicted of a recordable offence after the date on which that provision came into effect. PACE, section 63A, describes the circumstances in which a police officer may require a person convicted of a recordable offence to attend a police station for a non-intimate sample to be taken.

6.7   Reasonable force may be used, if necessary, to take a non-intimate sample from a person without their consent under the powers mentioned in *paragraph 6.6*.

6.8   Before any intimate sample is taken with consent or non-intimate sample is taken with, or without, consent, the person must be informed:

(a)   of the reason for taking the sample;

(b)   of the grounds on which the relevant authority has been given, including, if appropriate, the nature of the suspected offence;

(c)   that the sample or information derived from the sample may be retained and subject of a speculative search, see *Note 6E*, unless their destruction is required as in *Annex F*, Part A.

6.9   When clothing needs to be removed in circumstances likely to cause embarrassment to the person, no person of the opposite sex who is not a registered medical practitioner or registered health care professional shall be present, (unless in the case of a juvenile, mentally disordered or mentally vulnerable person, that person specifically requests the presence of an appropriate adult of the opposite sex who is readily available) nor shall anyone whose presence is unnecessary. However, in the case of a juvenile, this is subject to the overriding proviso that such a removal of clothing may take place in the absence of the appropriate adult only if the juvenile signifies, in their presence, that they prefer the adult's absence and they agree.

(c)   Documentation

6.10   A record of the reasons for taking a sample or impression and, if applicable, of its destruction must be made as soon as practicable. If force is used, a record shall be made of the circumstances and those present. If written consent is given to the taking of a sample or impression, the fact must be recorded in writing.

6.11   A record must be made of a warning given as required by *paragraph 6.3*.

6.12   A record shall be made of the fact that a person has been informed as in *paragraph 6.8(c)* that samples may be subject of a speculative search.

Notes for guidance

6A   *When hair samples are taken for the purpose of DNA analysis (rather than for other purposes such as making a visual match), the suspect should be permitted a reasonable choice as to what part of the body the hairs are taken from. When hairs are plucked, they should be plucked individually, unless the suspect prefers otherwise and no more should be plucked than the person taking them reasonably considers necessary for a sufficient sample.*

6B   (a)   *An insufficient sample is one which is not sufficient either in quantity or quality to provide information for a particular form of analysis, such as DNA analysis. A sample may also be insufficient if enough information cannot be obtained from it by analysis because of loss, destruction, damage or contamination of the sample or as a result of an earlier, unsuccessful attempt at analysis.*

(b)   An unsuitable sample is one which, by its nature, is not suitable for a particular form of analysis.

6C   Nothing in paragraph 6.2 prevents intimate samples being taken for elimination purposes with the consent of the person concerned but the provisions of paragraph 2.12 relating to the role of the appropriate adult, should be applied. Paragraph 6.2(b) does not, however, apply where the non-intimate samples were previously taken under the Terrorism Act 2000, Schedule 8, paragraph 10.

6D   In warning a person who is asked to provide an intimate sample as in paragraph 6.3, the following form of words may be used:

"You do not have to provide this sample/allow this swab or impression to be taken, but I must warn you that if you refuse without good cause, your refusal may harm your case if it comes to trial."

6E   Fingerprints or a DNA sample and the information derived from it taken from a person arrested on suspicion of being involved in a recordable offence, or charged with such an offence, or informed they will be reported for such an offence, may be subject of a speculative search. This means they may be checked against other fingerprints and DNA records held by, or on behalf of, the police and other law enforcement authorities in or outside the UK or held in connection with, or as a result of, an investigation of an offence inside or outside the UK. Fingerprints and samples taken from any other person, e.g. a person suspected of committing a recordable offence but who has not been arrested, charged or informed they will be reported for it, may be subject to a speculative search only if the person consents in writing to their fingerprints being subject of such a search. The following is an example of a basic form of words:

"I consent to my fingerprints/DNA sample and information derived from it being retained and used only for purposes related to the prevention and detection of a crime, the investigation of an offence or the conduct of a prosecution either nationally or internationally.

I understand that this sample may be checked against other fingerprint/DNA records held by or on behalf of relevant law enforcement authorities, either nationally or internationally.

I understand that once I have given my consent for the sample to be retained and used I cannot withdraw this consent."

See Annex F regarding the retention and use of fingerprints and samples taken with consent for elimination purposes.

ANNEX A — VIDEO IDENTIFICATION

(a)   General

1.   The arrangements for obtaining and ensuring the availability of a suitable set of images to be used in a video identification must be the responsibility of an identification officer, who has no direct involvement with the case.

2.   The set of images must include the suspect and at least eight other people who, so far as possible, resemble the suspect in age, height, general appearance and position in life. Only one suspect shall appear in any set unless there are two suspects of roughly similar appearance, in which case they may be shown together with at least twelve other people.

3.   The images used to conduct a video identification shall, as far as possible, show the suspect and other people in the same positions or carrying out the same sequence of movements. They shall also show the suspect and other people under identical conditions unless the identification officer reasonably believes:

(a)   because of the suspect's failure or refusal to co-operate or other reasons, it is not practicable for the conditions to be identical; and

      (b)   any difference in the conditions would not direct a witness' attention to any individual image.

4. The reasons identical conditions are not practicable shall be recorded on forms provided for the purpose.

5. Provision must be made for each person shown to be identified by number.

6. If police officers are shown, any numerals or other identifying badges must be concealed. If a prison inmate is shown, either as a suspect or not, then either all, or none of, the people shown should be in prison clothing.

7. The suspect or their solicitor, friend, or appropriate adult must be given a reasonable opportunity to see the complete set of images before it is shown to any witness. If the suspect has a reasonable objection to the set of images or any of the participants, the suspect shall be asked to state the reasons for the objection. Steps shall, if practicable, be taken to remove the grounds for objection. If this is not practicable, the suspect and/or their representative shall be told why their objections cannot be met and the objection, the reason given for it and why it cannot be met shall be recorded on forms provided for the purpose.

8. Before the images are shown in accordance with *paragraph 7*, the suspect or their solicitor shall be provided with details of the first description of the suspect by any witnesses who are to attend the video identification. When a broadcast or publication is made, as in *paragraph 3.28*, the suspect or their solicitor must also be allowed to view any material released to the media by the police for the purpose of recognising or tracing the suspect, provided it is practicable and would not unreasonably delay the investigation.

9. The suspect's solicitor, if practicable, shall be given reasonable notification of the time and place the video identification is to be conducted so a representative may attend on behalf of the suspect. If a solicitor has not been instructed, this information shall be given to the suspect. The suspect may not be present when the images are shown to the witness(es). In the absence of the suspect's representative, the viewing itself shall be recorded on video. No unauthorised people may be present.

(b) Conducting the video identification

10. The identification officer is responsible for making the appropriate arrangements to make sure, before they see the set of images, witnesses are not able to communicate with each other about the case or overhear a witness who has already seen the material. There must be no discussion with the witness about the composition of the set of images and they must not be told whether a previous witness has made any identification.

11. Only one witness may see the set of images at a time. Immediately before the images are shown, the witness shall be told that the person they saw on a specified earlier occasion may, or may not, appear in the images they are shown and that if they cannot make a positive identification, they should say so. The witness shall be advised that at any point, they may ask to see a particular part of the set of images or to have a particular image frozen for them to study. Furthermore, it should be pointed out to the witness that there is no limit on how many times they can view the whole set of images or any part of them. However, they should be asked not to make any decision as to whether the person they saw is on the set of images until they have seen the whole set at least twice.

12. Once the witness has seen the whole set of images at least twice and has indicated that they do not want to view the images, or any part of them, again, the witness shall be asked to say whether the individual they saw in person on a specified earlier occasion has been shown and, if so, to identify them by number of the

image. The witness will then be shown that image to confirm the identification, see *paragraph 17*.

13. Care must be taken not to direct the witness' attention to any one individual image or give any indication of the suspect's identity. Where a witness has previously made an identification by photographs, or a computerised or artist's composite or similar likeness, the witness must not be reminded of such a photograph or composite likeness once a suspect is available for identification by other means in accordance with this Code. Nor must the witness be reminded of any description of the suspect.

14. After the procedure, each witness shall be asked whether they have seen any broadcast or published films or photographs, or any descriptions of suspects relating to the offence and their reply shall be recorded.

(c) Image security and destruction

15. Arrangements shall be made for all relevant material containing sets of images used for specific identification procedures to be kept securely and their movements accounted for. In particular, no-one involved in the investigation shall be permitted to view the material prior to it being shown to any witness.

16. As appropriate, *paragraph 33* or *31* applies to the destruction or retention of relevant sets of images.

(d) Documentation

17. A record must be made of all those participating in, or seeing, the set of images whose names are known to the police.

18. A record of the conduct of the video identification must be made on forms provided for the purpose. This shall include anything said by the witness about any identifications or the conduct of the procedure and any reasons it was not practicable to comply with any of the provisions of this Code governing the conduct of video identifications.

ANNEX B — IDENTIFICATION PARADES

(a) General

1. A suspect must be given a reasonable opportunity to have a solicitor or friend present, and the suspect shall be asked to indicate on a second copy of the notice whether or not they wish to do so.

2. An identification parade may take place either in a normal room or one equipped with a screen permitting witnesses to see members of the identification parade without being seen. The procedures for the composition and conduct of the identification parade are the same in both cases, subject to *paragraph 8* (except that an identification parade involving a screen may take place only when the suspect's solicitor, friend or appropriate adult is present or the identification parade is recorded on video).

3. Before the identification parade takes place, the suspect or their solicitor shall be provided with details of the first description of the suspect by any witnesses who are attending the identification parade. When a broadcast or publication is made as in *paragraph 3.28*, the suspect or their solicitor should also be allowed to view any material released to the media by the police for the purpose of recognising or tracing the suspect, provided it is practicable to do so and would not unreasonably delay the investigation.

(b) Identification parades involving prison inmates

4. If a prison inmate is required for identification, and there are no security problems about the person leaving the establishment, they may be asked to participate in an identification parade or video identification.

5. An identification parade may be held in a Prison Department establishment but shall be conducted, as far as practicable under normal identification parade rules. Members of the public shall make up the identification parade unless there are serious security, or control, objections to their admission to the establishment. In such cases, or if a group or video identification is arranged within the establishment, other inmates may participate. If an inmate is the suspect, they are not required to wear prison clothing for the identification parade unless the other people taking part are other inmates in similar clothing, or are members of the public who are prepared to wear prison clothing for the occasion.

(c) Conduct of the identification parade

6. Immediately before the identification parade, the suspect must be reminded of the procedures governing its conduct and cautioned in the terms of Code C, paragraphs 10.5 or 10.6, as appropriate.

7. All unauthorised people must be excluded from the place where the identification parade is held.

8. Once the identification parade has been formed, everything afterwards, in respect of it, shall take place in the presence and hearing of the suspect and any interpreter, solicitor, friend or appropriate adult who is present (unless the identification parade involves a screen, in which case everything said to, or by, any witness at the place where the identification parade is held, must be said in the hearing and presence of the suspect's solicitor, friend or appropriate adult or be recorded on video).

9. The identification parade shall consist of at least eight people (in addition to the suspect) who, so far as possible, resemble the suspect in age, height, general appearance and position in life. Only one suspect shall be included in an identification parade unless there are two suspects of roughly similar appearance, in which case they may be paraded together with at least twelve other people. In no circumstances shall more than two suspects be included in one identification parade and where there are separate identification parades, they shall be made up of different people.

10. If the suspect has an unusual physical feature, e.g., a facial scar, tattoo or distinctive hairstyle or hair colour which cannot be replicated on other members of the identification parade, steps may be taken to conceal the location of that feature on the suspect and the other members of the identification parade if the suspect and their solicitor, or appropriate adult, agree. For example, by use of a plaster or a hat, so that all members of the identification parade resemble each other in general appearance.

11. When all members of a similar group are possible suspects, separate identification parades shall be held for each unless there are two suspects of similar appearance when they may appear on the same identification parade with at least twelve other members of the group who are not suspects. When police officers in uniform form an identification parade any numerals or other identifying badges shall be concealed.

12. When the suspect is brought to the place where the identification parade is to be held, they shall be asked if they have any objection to the arrangements for the identification parade or to any of the other participants in it and to state the reasons for the objection. The suspect may obtain advice from their solicitor or friend, if present, before the identification parade proceeds. If the suspect has a reasonable objection to the arrangements or any of the participants, steps shall, if practicable, be taken to remove the grounds for objection. When it is not practicable to do so, the suspect shall be told why their objections cannot be met

and the objection, the reason given for it and why it cannot be met, shall be recorded on forms provided for the purpose.

13. The suspect may select their own position in the line, but may not otherwise interfere with the order of the people forming the line. When there is more than one witness, the suspect must be told, after each witness has left the room, that they can, if they wish, change position in the line. Each position in the line must be clearly numbered, whether by means of a number laid on the floor in front of each identification parade member or by other means.

14. Appropriate arrangements must be made to make sure, before witnesses attend the identification parade, they are not able to:
    (i)   communicate with each other about the case or overhear a witness who has already seen the identification parade;
    (ii) see any member of the identification parade;
    (iii) see, or be reminded of, any photograph or description of the suspect or be given any other indication as to the suspect's identity; or
    (iv) see the suspect before or after the identification parade.

15. The person conducting a witness to an identification parade must not discuss with them the composition of the identification parade and, in particular, must not disclose whether a previous witness has made any identification.

16. Witnesses shall be brought in one at a time. Immediately before the witness inspects the identification parade, they shall be told the person they saw on a specified earlier occasion may, or may not, be present and if they cannot make a positive identification, they should say so. The witness must also be told they should not make any decision about whether the person they saw is on the identification parade until they have looked at each member at least twice.

17. When the officer or civilian support staff (see paragraph 3.11) conducting the identification procedure is satisfied the witness has properly looked at each member of the identification parade, they shall ask the witness whether the person they saw on a specified earlier occasion is on the identification parade and, if so, to indicate the number of the person concerned, see *paragraph 28*.

18. If the witness wishes to hear any identification parade member speak, adopt any specified posture or move, they shall first be asked whether they can identify any person(s) on the identification parade on the basis of appearance only. When the request is to hear members of the identification parade speak, the witness shall be reminded that the participants in the identification parade have been chosen on the basis of physical appearance only. Members of the identification parade may then be asked to comply with the witness' request to hear them speak, see them move or adopt any specified posture.

19. If the witness requests that the person they have indicated remove anything used for the purposes of *paragraph 10* to conceal the location of an unusual physical feature, that person may be asked to remove it.

20. If the witness makes an identification after the identification parade has ended, the suspect and, if present, their solicitor, interpreter or friend shall be informed. When this occurs, consideration should be given to allowing the witness a second opportunity to identify the suspect.

21. After the procedure, each witness shall be asked whether they have seen any broadcast or published films or photographs or any descriptions of suspects relating to the offence and their reply shall be recorded.

22. When the last witness has left, the suspect shall be asked whether they wish to make any comments on the conduct of the identification parade.

(d) Documentation

23. A video recording must normally be taken of the identification parade. If that is impracticable, a colour photograph must be taken. A copy of the video recording or photograph shall be supplied, on request, to the suspect or their solicitor within a reasonable time.

24. As appropriate, *paragraph 3.30* or *3.31*, should apply to any photograph or video taken as in *paragraph 23*.

25. If any person is asked to leave an identification parade because they are interfering with its conduct, the circumstances shall be recorded.

26. A record must be made of all those present at an identification parade whose names are known to the police.

27. If prison inmates make up an identification parade, the circumstances must be recorded.

28. A record of the conduct of any identification parade must be made on forms provided for the purpose. This shall include anything said by the witness or the suspect about any identifications or the conduct of the procedure, and any reasons it was not practicable to comply with any of this Code's provisions.

ANNEX C — GROUP IDENTIFICATION

(a) General

1. The purpose of this Annex is to make sure, as far as possible, group identifications follow the principles and procedures for identification parades so the conditions are fair to the suspect in the way they test the witness' ability to make an identification.

2. Group identifications may take place either with the suspect's consent and cooperation or covertly without their consent.

3. The location of the group identification is a matter for the identification officer, although the officer may take into account any representations made by the suspect, appropriate adult, their solicitor or friend.

4. The place where the group identification is held should be one where other people are either passing by or waiting around informally, in groups such that the suspect is able to join them and be capable of being seen by the witness at the same time as others in the group. For example people leaving an escalator, pedestrians walking through a shopping centre, passengers on railway and bus stations, waiting in queues or groups or where people are standing or sitting in groups in other public places.

5. If the group identification is to be held covertly, the choice of locations will be limited by the places where the suspect can be found and the number of other people present at that time. In these cases, suitable locations might be along regular routes travelled by the suspect, including buses or trains or public places frequented by the suspect.

6. Although the number, age, sex, race and general description and style of clothing of other people present at the location cannot be controlled by the identification officer, in selecting the location the officer must consider the general appearance and numbers of people likely to be present. In particular, the officer must reasonably expect that over the period the witness observes the group, they will be able to see, from time to time, a number of others whose appearance is broadly similar to that of the suspect.

7. A group identification need not be held if the identification officer believes, because of the unusual appearance of the suspect, none of the locations it would

be practicable to use satisfy the requirements of paragraph 6 necessary to make the identification fair.

8. Immediately after a group identification procedure has taken place (with or without the suspect's consent), a colour photograph or video should be taken of the general scene, if practicable, to give a general impression of the scene and the number of people present. Alternatively, if it is practicable, the group identification may be video recorded.

9. If it is not practicable to take the photograph or video in accordance with *paragraph 8*, a photograph or film of the scene should be taken later at a time determined by the identification officer if the officer considers it practicable to do so.

10. An identification carried out in accordance with this Code remains a group identification even though, at the time of being seen by the witness, the suspect was on their own rather than in a group.

11. Before the group identification takes place, the suspect or their solicitor shall be provided with details of the first description of the suspect by any witnesses who are to attend the identification. When a broadcast or publication is made, as in *paragraph 3.28*, the suspect or their solicitor should also be allowed to view any material released by the police to the media for the purposes of recognising or tracing the suspect, provided that it is practicable and would not unreasonably delay the investigation.

12. After the procedure, each witness shall be asked whether they have seen any broadcast or published films or photographs or any descriptions of suspects relating to the offence and their reply recorded.

(b) Identification with the consent of the suspect

13. A suspect must be given a reasonable opportunity to have a solicitor or friend present. They shall be asked to indicate on a second copy of the notice whether or not they wish to do so.

14. The witness, the person carrying out the procedure and the suspect's solicitor, appropriate adult, friend or any interpreter for the witness, may be concealed from the sight of the individuals in the group they are observing, if the person carrying out the procedure considers this assists the conduct of the identification.

15. The person conducting a witness to a group identification must not discuss with them the forthcoming group identification and, in particular, must not disclose whether a previous witness has made any identification.

16. Anything said to, or by, the witness during the procedure about the identification should be said in the presence and hearing of those present at the procedure.

17. Appropriate arrangements must be made to make sure, before witnesses attend the group identification, they are not able to:
    (i)   communicate with each other about the case or overhear a witness who has already been given an opportunity to see the suspect in the group;
    (ii) see the suspect; or
    (iii) see, or be reminded of, any photographs or description of the suspect or be given any other indication of the suspect's identity.

18. Witnesses shall be brought one at a time to the place where they are to observe the group. Immediately before the witness is asked to look at the group, the person conducting the procedure shall tell them that the person they saw may, or may not, be in the group and that if they cannot make a positive identification, they should say so. The witness shall be asked to observe the group in which the suspect is to appear. The way in which the witness should do this will depend on whether the group is moving or stationary.

Moving group

19.   When the group in which the suspect is to appear is moving, e.g. leaving an escalator, the provisions of *paragraphs 20 to 24* should be followed.

20.   If two or more suspects consent to a group identification, each should be the subject of separate identification procedures. These may be conducted consecutively on the same occasion.

21.   The person conducting the procedure shall tell the witness to observe the group and ask them to point out any person they think they saw on the specified earlier occasion.

22.   Once the witness has been informed as in *paragraph 21* the suspect should be allowed to take whatever position in the group they wish.

23.   When the witness points out a person as in *paragraph 21* they shall, if practicable, be asked to take a closer look at the person to confirm the identification. If this is not practicable, or they cannot confirm the identification, they shall be asked how sure they are that the person they have indicated is the relevant person.

24.   The witness should continue to observe the group for the period which the person conducting the procedure reasonably believes is necessary in the circumstances for them to be able to make comparisons between the suspect and other individuals of broadly similar appearance to the suspect as in *paragraph 6*.

Stationary groups

25.   When the group in which the suspect is to appear is stationary, e.g. people waiting in a queue, the provisions of *paragraphs 26 to 29* should be followed.

26.   If two or more suspects consent to a group identification, each should be subject to separate identification procedures unless they are of broadly similar appearance when they may appear in the same group. When separate group identifications are held, the groups must be made up of different people.

27.   The suspect may take whatever position in the group they wish. If there is more than one witness, the suspect must be told, out of the sight and hearing of any witness, that they can, if they wish, change their position in the group.

28.   The witness shall be asked to pass along, or amongst, the group and to look at each person in the group at least twice, taking as much care and time as possible according to the circumstances, before making an identification. Once the witness has done this, they shall be asked whether the person they saw on the specified earlier occasion is in the group and to indicate any such person by whatever means the person conducting the procedure considers appropriate in the circumstances. If this is not practicable, the witness shall be asked to point out any person they think they saw on the earlier occasion.

29.   When the witness makes an indication as in *paragraph 28*, arrangements shall be made, if practicable, for the witness to take a closer look at the person to confirm the identification. If this is not practicable, or the witness is unable to confirm the identification, they shall be asked how sure they are that the person they have indicated is the relevant person.

All cases

30.   If the suspect unreasonably delays joining the group, or having joined the group, deliberately conceals themselves from the sight of the witness, this may be treated as a refusal to co-operate in a group identification.

31.   If the witness identifies a person other than the suspect, that person should be informed what has happened and asked if they are prepared to give their name and address. There is no obligation upon any member of the public to give these

details. There shall be no duty to record any details of any other member of the public present in the group or at the place where the procedure is conducted.

32. When the group identification has been completed, the suspect shall be asked whether they wish to make any comments on the conduct of the procedure.

33. If the suspect has not been previously informed, they shall be told of any identifications made by the witnesses.

(c) Identification without the suspect's consent

34. Group identifications held covertly without the suspect's consent should, as far as practicable, follow the rules for conduct of group identification by consent.

35. A suspect has no right to have a solicitor, appropriate adult or friend present as the identification will take place without the knowledge of the suspect.

36. Any number of suspects may be identified at the same time.

(d) Identifications in police stations

37. Group identifications should take place in police stations only for reasons of safety, security or because it is not practicable to hold them elsewhere.

38. The group identification may take place either in a room equipped with a screen permitting witnesses to see members of the group without being seen, or anywhere else in the police station that the identification officer considers appropriate.

39. Any of the additional safeguards applicable to identification parades should be followed if the identification officer considers it is practicable to do so in the circumstances.

(e) Identifications involving prison inmates

40. A group identification involving a prison inmate may only be arranged in the prison or at a police station.

41. When a group identification takes place involving a prison inmate, whether in a prison or in a police station, the arrangements should follow those in *paragraphs 37* to *39*. If a group identification takes place within a prison, other inmates may participate. If an inmate is the suspect, they do not have to wear prison clothing for the group identification unless the other participants are wearing the same clothing.

(f) Documentation

42. When a photograph or video is taken as in *paragraph 8* or *9*, a copy of the photograph or video shall be supplied on request to the suspect or their solicitor within a reasonable time.

43. *Paragraph 3.30* or *3.31*, as appropriate, shall apply when the photograph or film taken in accordance with *paragraph 8* or *9* includes the suspect.

44. A record of the conduct of any group identification must be made on forms provided for the purpose. This shall include anything said by the witness or suspect about any identifications or the conduct of the procedure and any reasons why it was not practicable to comply with any of the provisions of this Code governing the conduct of group identifications.

ANNEX D — CONFRONTATION BY A WITNESS

1. Before the confrontation takes place, the witness must be told that the person they saw may, or may not, be the person they are to confront and that if they are not that person, then the witness should say so.

2. Before the confrontation takes place the suspect or their solicitor shall be provided with details of the first description of the suspect given by any witness who is to attend. When a broadcast or publication is made, as in *paragraph 3.28*, the suspect

or their solicitor should also be allowed to view any material released to the media for the purposes of recognising or tracing the suspect, provided it is practicable to do so and would not unreasonably delay the investigation.

3. Force may not be used to make the suspect's face visible to the witness.

4. Confrontation must take place in the presence of the suspect's solicitor, interpreter or friend unless this would cause unreasonable delay.

5. The suspect shall be confronted independently by each witness, who shall be asked "Is this the person?". If the witness identifies the person but is unable to confirm the identification, they shall be asked how sure they are that the person is the one they saw on the earlier occasion.

6. The confrontation should normally take place in the police station, either in a normal room or one equipped with a screen permitting a witness to see the suspect without being seen. In both cases, the procedures are the same except that a room equipped with a screen may be used only when the suspect's solicitor, friend or appropriate adult is present or the confrontation is recorded on video.

7. After the procedure, each witness shall be asked whether they have seen any broadcast or published films or photographs or any descriptions of suspects relating to the offence and their reply shall be recorded.

ANNEX E — SHOWING PHOTOGRAPHS

(a) Action

1. An officer of sergeant rank or above shall be responsible for supervising and directing the showing of photographs. The actual showing may be done by another officer or civilian support staff, see *paragraph 3.11*.

2. The supervising officer must confirm the first description of the suspect given by the witness has been recorded before they are shown the photographs. If the supervising officer is unable to confirm the description has been recorded they shall postpone showing the photographs.

3. Only one witness shall be shown photographs at any one time. Each witness shall be given as much privacy as practicable and shall not be allowed to communicate with any other witness in the case.

4. The witness shall be shown not less than twelve photographs at a time, which shall, as far as possible, all be of a similar type.

5. When the witness is shown the photographs, they shall be told the photograph of the person they saw may, or may not, be amongst them and if they cannot make a positive identification, they should say so. The witness shall also be told they should not make a decision until they have viewed at least twelve photographs. The witness shall not be prompted or guided in any way but shall be left to make any selection without help.

6. If a witness makes a positive identification from photographs, unless the person identified is otherwise eliminated from enquiries or is not available, other witnesses shall not be shown photographs. But both they, and the witness who has made the identification, shall be asked to attend a video identification, an identification parade or group identification unless there is no dispute about the suspect's identification.

7. If the witness makes a selection but is unable to confirm the identification, the person showing the photographs shall ask them how sure they are that the photograph they have indicated is the person they saw on the specified earlier occasion.

8. When the use of a computerised or artist's composite or similar likeness has led to there being a known suspect who can be asked to participate in a video

identification, appear on an identification parade or participate in a group identification, that likeness shall not be shown to other potential witnesses.

9.   When a witness attending a video identification, an identification parade or group identification has previously been shown photographs or computerised or artist's composite or similar likeness (and it is the responsibility of the officer in charge of the investigation to make the identification officer aware that this is the case), the suspect and their solicitor must be informed of this fact before the identification procedure takes place.

10.   None of the photographs shown shall be destroyed, whether or not an identification is made, since they may be required for production in court. The photographs shall be numbered and a separate photograph taken of the frame or part of the album from which the witness made an identification as an aid to reconstituting it.

(b) Documentation

11.   Whether or not an identification is made, a record shall be kept of the showing of photographs on forms provided for the purpose. This shall include anything said by the witness about any identification or the conduct of the procedure, any reasons it was not practicable to comply with any of the provisions of this Code governing the showing of photographs and the name and rank of the supervising officer.

12.   The supervising officer shall inspect and sign the record as soon as practicable.

ANNEX F — FINGERPRINTS AND SAMPLES — DESTRUCTION AND SPECULATIVE SEARCHES

(a) Fingerprints and samples taken in connection with a criminal investigation

1.   When fingerprints or DNA samples are taken from a person in connection with an investigation and the person is not suspected of having committed the offence, see *Note F1*, they must be destroyed as soon as they have fulfilled the purpose for which they were taken unless:

(a)   they were taken for the purposes of an investigation of an offence for which a person has been convicted; and

(b)   fingerprints or samples were also taken from the convicted person for the purposes of that investigation.

However, subject to *paragraph 2*, the fingerprints and samples, and the information derived from samples, may not be used in the investigation of any offence or in evidence against the person who is, or would be, entitled to the destruction of the fingerprints and samples, see *Note F2*.

2.   The requirement to destroy fingerprints and DNA samples, and information derived from samples, and restrictions on their retention and use in *paragraph 1* do not apply if the person gives their written consent for their fingerprints or sample to be retained and used after they have fulfilled the purpose for which they were taken, see *Note F1*.

3.   When a person's fingerprints or sample are to be destroyed:

(a)   any copies of the fingerprints must also be destroyed;

(b)   the person may witness the destruction of their fingerprints or copies if they ask to do so within five days of being informed destruction is required;

(c)   access to relevant computer fingerprint data shall be made impossible as soon as it is practicable to do so and the person shall be given a certificate to this effect within three months of asking; and

(d)   neither the fingerprints, the sample, or any information derived from the sample, may be used in the investigation of any offence or in evidence against the person who is, or would be, entitled to its destruction.

4.   Fingerprints or samples, and the information derived from samples, taken in connection with the investigation of an offence which are not required to be destroyed, may be retained after they have fulfilled the purposes for which they were taken but may be used only for purposes related to the prevention or detection of crime, the investigation of an offence or the conduct of a prosecution in, as well as outside, the UK and may also be subject to a speculative search. This includes checking them against other fingerprints and DNA records held by, or on behalf of, the police and other law enforcement authorities in, as well as outside, the UK.

(b)   Fingerprints taken in connection with Immigration Service enquiries

5.   Fingerprints taken for Immigration Service enquiries in accordance with powers and procedures other than under PACE and for which the Immigration Service, not the police, are responsible, must be destroyed as follows:

(a)   fingerprints and all copies must be destroyed as soon as practicable if the person from whom they were taken proves they are a British or Commonwealth citizen who has the right of abode in the UK under the Immigration Act 1971, section 2(1)(b);

(b)   fingerprints taken under the power as in *paragraph 4.11(g)* from a dependant of a person in *4.11(b)* to *(f)* must be destroyed when that person's fingerprints are to be destroyed;

(c)   fingerprints taken from a person under any power as in *paragraph 4.11* or with the person's consent which have not already been destroyed as above, must be destroyed within ten years of being taken or within such period specified by the Secretary of State under the Immigration and Asylum Act 1999, section 143(5).

Notes for guidance

F1   *Fingerprints and samples given voluntarily for the purposes of elimination play an important part in many police investigations. It is, therefore, important to make sure innocent volunteers are not deterred from participating and their consent to their fingerprints and DNA being used for the purposes of a specific investigation is fully informed and voluntary. If the police or volunteer seek to have the sample or fingerprints retained for use after the specific investigation ends, it is important the volunteer's consent to this is also fully informed and voluntary.*

Examples of consent for:

*   *DNA/fingerprints – to be used only for the purposes of a specific investigation;*

*   *DNA/fingerprints – to be used in the specific investigation **and** retained by the police for future use.*

*To minimise the risk of confusion, each consent should be physically separate and the volunteer should be asked to sign one or the other, **not both**.*

(a)   *DNA:*

(i)   *DNA sample taken for the purposes of elimination or as part of an intelligence-led screen and to be used only for the purposes of that investigation and destroyed afterwards:*

"I consent to my DNA/mouth swab being taken for forensic analysis. I understand that the sample will be destroyed at the end of the case and that my profile will only be compared to the crime stain profile from this enquiry. I have been advised that

the person taking the sample may be required to give evidence and/or provide a written statement to the police in relation to the taking of it".

(ii)   *DNA sample to be retained on the National DNA database and used in the future:*

"I consent to my DNA sample and information derived from it being retained and used only for purposes related to the prevention and detection of a crime, the investigation of an offence or the conduct of a prosecution either nationally or internationally."

"I understand that this sample may be checked against other DNA records held by, or on behalf of, relevant law enforcement authorities, either nationally or internationally".

"I understand that once I have given my consent for the sample to be retained and used I cannot withdraw this consent."

(b)   *Fingerprints:*

(i)   *Fingerprints taken for the purposes of elimination or as part of an intelligence-led screen and to be used only for the purposes of that investigation and destroyed afterwards:*

"I consent to my fingerprints being taken for elimination purposes. I understand that the fingerprints will be destroyed at the end of the case and that my fingerprints will only be compared to the fingerprints from this enquiry. I have been advised that the person taking the fingerprints may be required to give evidence and/or provide a written statement to the police in relation to the taking of it."

(ii)   *Fingerprints to be retained for future use:*

"I consent to my fingerprints being retained and used only for purposes related to the prevention and detection of a crime, the investigation of an offence or the conduct of a prosecution either nationally or internationally".

"I understand that my fingerprints may be checked against other records held by, or on behalf of, relevant law enforcement authorities, either nationally or internationally."

"I understand that once I have given my consent for my fingerprints to be retained and used I cannot withdraw this consent."

F2   *The provisions for the retention of fingerprints and samples in paragraph 1 allow for all fingerprints and samples in a case to be available for any subsequent miscarriage of justice investigation.*

Index

abetting 11
absconding 54
absolute discharge 145
access to legal advice 21-2, 25
accomplices 11
  joinder of offences and offenders 100
  as witnesses against each other 134
accused person *see* defendant; suspect in police station
action plan orders 168
actual bodily harm 10-11, 65
adjournments 52
admissibility of evidence 67, 119-23
  challenge to 105-6, 120
  confessions 125-8
  opinion evidence 121-2
  privilege 122-3
  self-made evidence 120-1
admissions
  formal 108-9
advice
  access to 21-2, 25
advice and assistance
  public funding 47-8
affirmation
  witnesses 112
age as mitigating factor 163
aggravation 144, 150, 163
aiding 11
ancillary orders 156-7
answering questions 33-4
appeals 1, 6, 171-2, 194, 195
  courts 3
  from preparatory hearings 95
  notice of 260
appropriate adults 26-7
arrest
  interview following 22
  persons under 18-19, 21
  serious arrestable offences 17-18
assault
  common 10
  occasioning actual bodily harm 10-11, 65
associated offences 143-4
associations
  bail decision and 57
attendance centre orders 148, 168

bail 1, 20-1, 54-62
  challenging grants of 61-2
  committal proceedings 80
  committal to Crown Court for sentencing and 159-60
  conditions 58-9
    variation and breach of conditions 59-60
  factors taken into account 56-7
  further applications when bail refused 60-1

bail – *continued*
  human rights issues 62
  Law Commission Guidance 307-11
  limitations on 54-5
  nature of 54
  preliminary hearings 88
  procedure 60, 182
  prosecution request for reconsideration of 62
  record of decision 237
  right to 55
    exceptions 55-6, 57-8
barristers 1
  briefing counsel 95, 256-7
battery 10
behaviour
  similar fact evidence 137-8
bill of indictment 87
body samples 41
briefing counsel 95, 256-7
burglary 6-7, 65
business documents 129-30

careless driving 45
case stated
  appeal by 171-2
cautions 25-6
  conditional 42
  formal 41-2
  informal 42
chambers
  preliminary hearings in 89
character evidence 136-7
charging 3, 5, 46-7
  charge sheet 226-7
  decision to charge 20
  detention without charge 19
  interview after charge 23
children and young people
  interviewing 26
  related either way offences 91
  sentencing 167-9
    community sentences 147, 148, 168
    custodial sentences 148, 167
  youth courts 2, 167-9
clerk to the justices 2
closing speeches 106-7
  defence side 102
committal proceedings 77-82, 196
  bail 80
  conduct of 77
  with consideration of evidence 80-1, 189
    deciding on 81-2
  evidence admissible at 78-9
  offer of committal 79
  procedure 80, 81
  reporting restrictions 78
  types of 77

committal proceedings – *continued*
    deciding on 81-2
  without consideration of evidence 79-80, 188
    deciding on 82
common assault 10
community punishment orders 146, 168
**community punishment and rehabilitation
  orders** 146-7, 168
community rehabilitation orders 146, 168
community sentences 143, 145-8
  breach of 148
  children and young people 147, 148, 168
  refusal of 150
community ties
  bail decision and 57
compellability of witnesses 112
  defendant 134-6
compensation
  compensation orders 156
  voluntary compensation as mitigating factor 164
competence of witnesses 111-12
  defendant 134-6
conditional cautions 42
conditional discharge 145
confessions 35, 40, 124-8
confiscation orders 156
conflicts of interest 13
confrontation 37, 38, 39
conspiracy 10
continuance
  doctrine of 109
conviction
  appeal against 171
  remands before and after 53
corroboration evidence 116-17
costs
  defence costs 156-7
  prosecution costs 156
  public funding for *see* **public funding**
  summary trial 102-3
counsel
  briefing 95, 256-7
counselling 11
Court of Appeal 3, 172
courts 2-3
  duty not to mislead 12
  duty solicitors 52
credit
  cross-examination as to 115
criminal contempt 54
Criminal Defence Service 4, 47-52
  advice and assistance 47-8
  court duty solicitors 52
  representation orders 1, 48-52, 61, 80, 83, 236
criminal law 6-11
criminal offences 6-11
  classification of 1
  see also ***individual offences***
criminal proceedings
  alternatives to 41-2
  commencement 45-62, 181
  overview 5-6, 177
  time limits 45

criminal proceedings – *continued*
  see also ***individual topics***
cross-examination 4, 48-9, 50, 114-15
  defendant 138-41
Crown Court 2
  appeals from 172
  appeals to 171
  committal for sentencing to 158-60
  further application when bail refused 60-1
  plea and directions hearing 88, 93-4
    judge's questionnaire 252-5
  pre-trial hearings 94
  preparation for trial 87-96
    briefing council 95
    cases committed for trial 87-8
    cases sent for trial 88-92
    disclosure 92
    notices of further evidence 92
    plea and directions hearing 88, 93-4, 252-5
    pre-trial hearings 94
    preparatory hearings 94-5
  preparatory hearings 94-5
  representation orders in 52
  statement of means for 83-4, 244-51
  trial 95-6
Crown Prosecution Service (CPS) 3, 20
curfew
  as condition of bail 59
  curfew orders 147, 168
custodial sentences 143, 148-50
  aggravating and mitigating factors 150
  children and young people 148, 167
  criteria for deciding length of 150
  qualification for 149-50
  seriousness test 149
  suspended 150-1
  violent and sexual offences 149-50
custody officers 18-19, 20, 27
custody record 201-4
  inspection of 19, 27

dangerous driving 45
deception
  obtaining property by 7
defect in process 100
defence side 4
  application for dismissal 89-90
  costs 156-7
  defence statement 261, 262
  disclosure by 12, 72-3
    consequences of failure to disclose 74-5
  evidence 102, 106
    burden of proof 108
  final speech 102
  no case to answer submission 101-2, 106, 107-8
  objections to written evidence 79
  opening speech 102
  professional ethics 12-13
  representations by 66
  writing to prosecution 98
defendant
  character evidence 136-7
  cross-examination 138-41

defendant – *continued*
  previous convictions *see* **previous convictions**
  restrictions on right to cross-examine 114-15
  rights and duties of 240-2, 243
  similar fact evidence 137-8
  as witness 111, 134-41
    competence and compellability 134-6
delaying access to legal advice 21-2, 25
depositions
  at committal proceedings 78
  from reluctant witnesses 89
  right to object to 243
  use at trial 87-8
detention
  conditions 26
  police powers 18-21
  see also **suspect in police station**
detention and training orders 167
discharge 145, 169
disclosure of evidence
  defence 12, 72-3
    consequences of failure to disclose 74-5
  prosecution 5-6, 63, 69-75, 185, 190
    advance information 69-70, 92, 97
    application to court for 74
    committal proceedings 79
    consequences of failure to disclose 74
    continuing duty 74
    primary 70-2
  public interest immunity 74
  secondary 73
  unused material 70, 79, 92, 97-8
dismissal
  application for 89-90
disqualification from driving 152-4
  avoidance of 154-6
district judges 2
documentary evidence 116
  business documents 129-30
  hearsay 128-34, 183, 184
driving offences *see* **road traffic offences**
drugs
  drug treatment and testing orders 147, 168
  possession 7-9, 66
    with intent to supply 9-10, 66
  production or supply 9, 66
duty solicitors 52

early administrative hearing (EAH) 46
early first hearing (EFH) 46
either way offences 1, 5, 46-7
  disclosure of prosecution evidence 5-6, 63, 70
  prosecution of 63-8
  related 90-1
electronic tagging 147
endorsement of driving licences 152
  avoidance of 154-5
equivocal plea 101
ethics 12-13
European Convention on Human Rights 13-16
evidence 40, 105-42
  admissibility 67, 119-23
    challenge to 105-6, 120, 125-8

evidence – *continued*
  opinion evidence 121-2
  privilege 122-3
  relevance 120
  self-made evidence 120-1
  bail and strength of evidence considerations 57
  burden and standards of proof 107-8
  character evidence 136-7
  committal proceedings
    admissible evidence 78-9
    with consideration of evidence 80-1, 189
  corroboration evidence 116-17
  court's discretion to exclude 110-11
  defence 102, 106
    burden of proof 108
  defendant 134-41
  disclosure of *see* **disclosure of evidence**
  documentary 116
    business documents 129-30
    hearsay 128-34, 183, 184
  evidential burden 107-8
  expert 99, 122
  hearsay 123-34
    confessions 124-8
    documentary 128-34, 183, 184
    res gestae 124
    rule against 123-4
  identification evidence 37-40, 111
    disputed 117-19
  improperly obtained 109
  methods of proof 111-16
  notices of further evidence 92
  oral evidence 112-15
  presentation of 105-7
  professional ethics and 12
  proof by 108-9
  prosecution 101, 102, 105-6
    burden of proof 107-8
  real 116
  relevance 120
  similar fact evidence 137-8
  unsworn 112
examination-in-chief 113-14
exculpatory statements 121
expert evidence 99, 122

facts
  formal admissions 108-9
  inferences 109
  judicial notice 109
  similar fact evidence 137-8
fair trial right 15-16
false names 13
finding a suspect 37
fines 143, 145, 169
forfeiture orders 156
formal admissions 108-9
formal cautions 41-2
fraud 66

grievous bodily harm 11, 65
group identification 37, 39

guilt
  admission of 12
  guilty plea 93
    as mitigating factor 164

health
  as mitigating factor 163
hearsay 123-34
  confessions 124-8
  documentary 128-34, 183, 184
  res gestae 124
  rule against 123-4
High Court (Queen's Bench Division) 3
  appeals to 171-2
hostile witnesses 114
House of Lords 3
human rights issues 13-16
  bail and 62
  right to silence and 29

identification 37-40, 111
  disputed evidence 117-19
  PACE Code of Practice 359-91
  parades 37, 38, 217-25
improperly obtained evidence 109
inconsistent instructions 12
indictable only offences 1, 5, 47
  disclosure of prosecution evidence 70
indictment 87
  briefing council 95
  cases committed to Crown Court for trial 87-8
  cases sent to Crown Court for trial 88-92
  disclosure 92
  notices of further evidence 92
  plea and directions hearing 88, 93-4, 252-5
  pre-trial hearings 94
  preparation for trial on 87-96
  preparatory hearings 94-5
  trial on 95-6
    appeals 195
inferences 108
  drawn from departure from case disclosed 95
  drawn from silence 28-9, 135, 297-9
    challenging 40
  of fact 109
informal cautions 42
interview of client 98
interview of suspects 22-3
  cautions 25-6
  comments outside interview 24
  confessions 35, 40
  methods of 23-4
  preparation for 35
  presence of solicitor 25
    tactical considerations 27-37
  right to silence 28-33
    inferences drawn from 28-9, 40
  solicitor's role 35-7
interview of witnesses 13, 50, 98
intimate samples 41

joinder of offences and offenders 100

judges
  Court of Appeal 3
  Crown Court 2
  district judges 2
  High Court (Queen's Bench Division) 3
  House of Lords 3
  pre-trial hearings 94
  preparatory hearings 94-5
  questionnaire for plea and directions hearing 252-5
judicial notice 109
juveniles *see* **children and young people**

law
  points of law in summary trial 102
  substantial questions of 48, 50
  substantive criminal law 6-11
Law Commission Guidance on bail 307-11
leading questions 113
Legal Services Commission 4, 47, 52
legislation
  human rights issues and 14
liberty
  deprivation of 48, 49
  right to 15
linked summary offences 84-5
livelihood
  loss of 48, 49
location visit 98

magistrates 2
Magistrates' Association Sentencing Guidelines 166, 263-96
magistrates' courts
  adjournments 52
  appeals from 171-2
  bail 54
    further application when bail refused 60-1
  committal proceedings 77-82, 196
  committal to Crown Court for sentencing 158-60
  criminal proceedings 5
  either way offences 63-8
  mode of trial procedure 64-6, 187
  personnel 2
  plea before venue procedure 63, 187
  preliminary hearing 83
  representation orders in 51
  role 2
  sending for trial procedure 82-4, 197
  sentencing procedure 160-1, 193
  summary trial 97-103, 198
    appeals 194
    disclosure 97-8
    not guilty plea 100-3, 186
    preparation of case 98-100
    procedure 100-3
  youth courts 2, 167-9
    appeals from 171-2
marks
  failure to account for 29-30
means
  means enquiry form 161
  statement of 83-4, 244-51

memory refreshing 113-14
mental handicap and illness
    interviewing of suspects 26-7
mitigation 150, 162-5
mode of trial procedure 64-6, 187
motoring offences *see* road traffic offences

Newton hearing 161
no case to answer submission 101-2, 106, 107-8
non-intimate samples 41
not guilty plea 93
    trial procedure after 100-3, 186, 191

oaths
    witnesses 112
objects
    failure to account for 29-30
obtaining property by deception 7
offences taken into consideration (TICs) 161,
    258-9
opening speeches
    defence side 102
    prosecution side 101
opinion evidence 121-2
oppression
    confessions and 125
oral warnings 42

PACE Codes of Practice 313-91
parades
    identification 37, 38, 217-25
plea
    equivocal plea 101
    guilty plea 93
    summary trial 101
    see also **not guilty plea**
plea before venue procedure 63, 187
plea and directions hearing 88, 93-4
    judge's questionnaire 252-5
police
    bail 20-1
    charging by 3, 5
    co-operation with police as mitigating factor 163
    custody officers 18-19, 20, 27
    detention of suspects *see* **suspect in police station**
    exculpatory statements made to 121
    interview of suspects *see* **interview of suspects**
    investigations 5
    ranks 178
    reporting to police station as condition of bail 59
pre-sentence reports 160, 161
pre-trial hearings 94
pre-trial review 101
preliminary hearings 83, 88-9
preparation for trial 87-96
    briefing council 95
    cases committed to Crown Court for trial 87-8
    cases sent to Crown Court for trial 88-92
    disclosure 92
    notices of further evidence 92
    plea and directions hearing 88, 93-4, 252-5
    pre-trial hearings 94
    preparatory hearings 94-5

preparatory hearings 94-5
presence
    failure to account for presence at place 30-1
previous convictions 13
    bail decision and 56
    sentencing and 144
    spent convictions 141
prison *see* **custodial sentences**
privilege
    legal professional privilege 33, 123
    public policy 122
    self-incrimination privilege 123
probation service
    pre-sentence reports 160
process
    defect in 100
procuring 11
professional ethics 12-13
proof
    burden of 107-8
    by evidence 108-9
    methods of 111-16
    standards of 107
prosecution side 3
    costs 156
    deciding on committal proceedings 81-2
    disclosure by 5-6, 63, 69-75, 185, 190
        advance information 69-70, 92, 97
        application to court for 74
        committal proceedings 79
        consequences of failure to disclose 74
        continuing duty 74
        primary 70-2
        public interest immunity 74
        secondary 73
        unused material 70, 79, 92, 97-8
    evidence 101, 102, 105-6
        burden of proof 107-8
    interviewing of prosecution witnesses 13
    offer of committal 79
    opening speech 101
    professional ethics 12
    request for reconsideration of bail 62
    service of case 89
    writing to 98
public funding 4, 47-52
    advice and assistance 47-8
    application for right to representation 230-5
    court duty solicitors 52
    representation orders 1, 48-52, 61, 80, 83,
        236
public interest immunity 74
public policy privilege 122

questions
    answering 33-4
    inferences drawn from failure to answer 28-9, 135,
        297-9
    leading 113
    written statements 34-5, 211

racial aggravation 144
real evidence 116

recent possession
  doctrine of 109
recovery of defence costs order (RDCO) 156-7
related either way offences 90-1
related summary offences 91-2
relevance of evidence 120
religious aggravation 144
remands 52-4
  duration 53-4
remorse as mitigating factor 164
reparation orders 169
reporting restrictions
  committal proceedings 78
reports
  pre-sentence 160, 161
representation orders 1, 48-52, 236
  bail applications 61
  committal proceedings 80
  guidelines 49-50
  how to apply 50
  interests of justice test 48-9
  payment of fees under 51-2
  refusal of representation 51
  scope 51
  through orders 50, 83
  where to apply 50
representations by defence 66
reputation
  damage to 48, 49
res gestae 121, 124
residence as condition of bail 59
retrospective offences 16
road traffic offences 45
  penalties 152-6
robbery 7

samples 41
secondary participation 11
security
  for bail 59
  right to 15
selective silence 33
self-incrimination privilege 123
self-made evidence 120-1
sending for trial procedure 82-4, 197
sentencing 67, 143-66, 192, 193
  ancillary orders 156-7
  appeal against sentence 171
  children and young people 167-9
    community sentences 147, 148, 168
    custodial sentences 148, 167
  committal to Crown Court for 158-60
  community sentences see community sentences
  custodial see custodial sentences
  deferment of sentence 157-8
  discharge 145, 169
  fines 143, 145, 169
  guidelines 165-6, 263-96
  plea in mitigation 162-5
  powers of court 143-60
  pre-sentence reports 160, 161
  procedure 160-1
  road traffic offences 152-6

sentencing – continued
  suspended sentences 150-1
serious offences
  bail decision and 56
  serious arrestable offences 17-18
sexual offences 149-50
silence
  advising client on 32-3, 297-305
  inferences drawn from 28-9, 135, 297-9
    challenging 40
  right to 28-33
  selective 33
similar fact evidence 137-8
social workers
  pre-sentence reports 160
solicitors
  advising on choice of court in either way offences
    66
  advising on silence of client 32-3, 297-305
  inspection of custody records 19, 27
  legal professional privilege 33, 123
  plea in mitigation 162-5
  presence at interview 25
  professional ethics 12-13
  public funding 4, 47-52
    advice and assistance 47-8
    court duty solicitors 52
    representation orders 1, 48-52, 61, 80, 83
  record of attendance at police station 212-16
  right to advice from 21-2, 25
  rights of audience 4
  role of 1
spent convictions 141
spouses as witnesses 136
statements
  defence statement 261, 262
  exculpatory statements made to police 121
  statement of means 83-4, 244-51
stipendiary magistrates 2
substances
  failure to account for 29-30
substantive criminal law 6-11
summary offences 1, 5, 46-7
  disclosure of prosecution evidence 5, 69-70
  linked 84-5
  related 91-2
summary trial 97-103, 198
  appeals 194
  disclosure 97-8
  not guilty plea 100-3, 186
  preparation of case 98-100
  procedure 100-3
summonses 5, 47, 228-9
supervision orders 168
sureties for bail 58-9
suspect in police station 1, 17-43, 179, 180
  alternatives to prosecution 41-2
  cautions 25-6
  evidential considerations 40
  identification 37-40
  interview of 22-3
    confessions 35, 40
    methods of 23-4

suspect in police station – *continued*
  preparation for 35
  presence of solicitor 25, 27-37
  right to silence 28-33, 40
  solicitor's role 35-7
  tactical considerations 27-37
  notice of entitlements 207-8
  notice to detained persons 206
  PACE Codes of Practice 313-91
  persons at risk 26-7
  powers of detention 18-21
  right to legal advice 21-2, 25
  safeguards for 25-7
  solicitors record of attendance at police station 212-16
  taking samples 41
  voluntary attendance 18, 21, 205
suspended sentences 150-1

tagging 147
taken into consideration (TICs) 161, 258-9
tape recording interviews 23, 209-10
theft 6, 66
through representation orders 50, 83
time limits
  criminal proceedings 45
  disclosure of evidence
    defence disclosure 73
    primary prosecution disclosure 71
    secondary prosecution disclosure 73
  remands 53-4
torture
  prohibition of 15
trial 95-6
  fair trial right 15-16
  preparation for 87-96
    briefing council 95
    cases committed to Crown Court for trial 87-8
    cases committed for trial 87-8
    cases sent to Crown Court for trial 88-92
    disclosure 92
    notices of further evidence 92
    plea and directions hearing 88, 93-4, 252-5
    pre-trial hearings 94
    preparatory hearings 94-5
  summary trial 97-103, 198
    appeals 194
    disclosure 97-8
    not guilty plea 100-3, 186
    preparation of case 98-100
    procedure 100-3

unfavourable witnesses 114
unsworn evidence 112

unused material
  disclosure of 70, 79, 92, 97-8

verdict 107
  summary trial 102
victim impact statement 160
video identification 37, 38
violent offences 149-50
voluntary attendance at police station 18, 21, 205

warnings
  oral 42
witnesses
  compellability 112
    defendant 134-6
  competence 111-12
    defendant 134-6
  cross-examination 4, 48-9, 50, 114-15
    defendant 138-41
  defendant as 111, 134-41
    competence and compellability 134-6
  depositions *see* **depositions**
  dispensing with attendance 99-100
  examination-in-chief 113-14
  exclusion from court before giving evidence 101
  expert evidence 99, 122
  hostile 114
  interviewing of 13, 50, 98
  non-communication with witnesses as condition of bail 59
  opinion evidence 121-2
  oral evidence 112-15
  reluctant 89
  securing attendance of 99
  special measures 112-13
  spouses as 136
  swearing 112
  tracing 50
  unfavourable 114
wounding 11, 65
writing to prosecution 98
written *see* **written statements**
written statements 115-16, 238-9
  as answer to police questions 34-5, 211
  at committal proceedings 78, 79
  right to object to 243
  use at trial 87-8

young people *see* **children and young people**
youth courts 2, 167-9
  appeals from 171-2
youth offender panels 169